Where Have the Old Words Got Me?

Where Have the Old Words Got Me?

Explications of Dylan Thomas's
Collected Poems

RALPH MAUD

UNIVERSITY OF WALES PRESS
CARDIFF
2003

British Library Cataloguing in Publication Data
A catalogue record for this book is available from the British Library.

ISBN   0–7083–1779–0 paperback
      0–7083–1780–4 hardback

The right of Ralph Maud to be identified as author of this work has been asserted by him in accordance with the Copyright, Designs and Patents Act 1988.

Typeset by Bryan Turnbull
Printed in Great Britain by The Cromwell Press Ltd, Trowbridge, Wiltshire

Contents

Acknowledgements

The author and publishers gratefully acknowledge the permission granted by the following:

Extracts from Dylan Thomas, *Early Prose Writings*, ed. Walford Davies (J. M. Dent, 1971); *The Poems*, ed. Daniel Jones, revised edn (J. M. Dent, 1982); *Collected Stories*, ed. Walford Davies (1983; J. M. Dent/Everyman, 1995); *The Collected Letters*, ed. Paul Ferris (J. M. Dent, 1985; new edition, 2000); *Collected Poems, 1934–1953*, ed. Walford Davies and Ralph Maud (J. M. Dent, 1988); *The Notebook Poems, 1930–34*, ed. Ralph Maud (J. M. Dent, 1989); *The Broadcasts*, ed. Ralph Maud (J. M. Dent, 1991); *The Filmscripts*, ed. John Ackerman (J. M. Dent, 1995); *Under Milk Wood*, ed. Walford Davies and Ralph Maud (J. M. Dent, 1995), reproduced by permission of the estate of Dylan Thomas and J. M. Dent, London.

US rights:
'excerpts' by Dylan Thomas, edited by Ralph Maud, from *On the Air with Dylan Thomas* copyright © 1953 by the Trustees for the Copyrights of Dylan Thomas. Reprinted by permission of New Directions Publishing Corp.

'excerpts' by Dylan Thomas, from *Collected Stories of Dylan Thomas*, copyright © 1984 by the Trustees for the Copyrights of Dylan Thomas, Reprinted by permission of New Directions Publishing Corp.

'excerpts' by Dylan Thomas from *Under Milk Wood*, copyright © 1952 by Dylan Thomas. Reprinted by Permission of New Directions Publishing Corp.

'excerpts' by Dylan Thomas, from *Portrait of the Artist as a Young Dog*, copyright © 1940 by New Directions Publishing Corp. Reprinted by Permission of New Directions Publishing Corp.

'excerpts' by Dylan Thomas, from *The Poems of Dylan Thomas*,

Abbreviations of works cited

Adam	*Adam International Review*, 238 (1953).
Brinnin	John Malcolm Brinnin, *Dylan Thomas in America* (Boston: Little, Brown and Co., 1955).
Broadcasts	Dylan Thomas, *The Broadcasts*, ed. Ralph Maud (London: J. M. Dent, 1991).
Caitlin	Caitlin Thomas with George Tremlett, *Caitlin: A Warring Absence* (London: Secker & Warburg, 1986).
Caitlin (Ferris)	Paul Ferris, *Caitlin: The Life of Caitlin Thomas* (London: Hutchinson, 1993).
Casebook	*A Casebook on Dylan Thomas*, ed. John Malcolm Brinnin (New York: Thomas Y. Crowell Co., 1960).
Collected Poems	Dylan Thomas, *Collected Poems 1934-1953*, ed. Walford Davies and Ralph Maud (London: J. M. Dent, 1988).
Collected Stories	Dylan Thomas, *The Collected Stories*, ed. Walford Davies (London: J. M. Dent, 1983).
Companion	John Ackerman, *A Dylan Thomas Companion* (London: Macmillan, 1991).
Concordance	Robert Coleman Williams, *A Concordance of the Collected Poems of Dylan Thomas* (Lincoln, NE: University of Nebraska Press, 1967).
Davies	Walford Davies, *Dylan Thomas* (Milton Keynes: Open University Press, 1986).
Days of Dylan Thomas	Bill Read, *The Days of Dylan Thomas* (New York: McGraw-Hill Book Co., 1964).
DE	Dylan Thomas, *Deaths and Entrances* (London: J. M. Dent, 1946).
Druid	Aneirin Talfan Davies, *Dylan: Druid of the Broken Body* (London: J. M. Dent, 1964).
Early Prose	Dylan Thomas, *Early Prose Writings*, ed. Walford Davies (London: J. M. Dent, 1971).
18 Poems	Dylan Thomas, *18 Poems* (London: The Sunday Referee and the Parton Bookshop, 1934).
Emery	Clark Emery, *The World of Dylan Thomas* (Coral Gables, FL: University of Miami Press, 1962).
Entrances	Ralph Maud, *Entrances to Dylan Thomas' Poetry* (Pittsburgh: University of Pittsburgh Press, 1963).
Ferris	Paul Ferris, *Dylan Thomas* (Harmondsworth: Penguin Books, 1978).
Filmscripts	Dylan Thomas, *The Filmscripts*, ed. John Ackerman (London: J. M. Dent, 1995).

FitzGibbon	Constantine FitzGibbon, *The Life of Dylan Thomas* (London: J. M. Dent, 1965).
Kleinman	H. H. Kleinman, *The Religious Sonnets of Dylan Thomas* (Berkeley: University of California Press, 1963).
Korg	Jacob Korg, *Dylan Thomas* (New York: Twayne Publishers, 1965).
Letters	*The Collected Letters of Dylan Thomas*, ed. Paul Ferris (London: J. M. Dent, 1985; new edition from the same publisher, 2000).
Lindsay	Jack Lindsay, *Meetings with Poets* (London: Frederick Muller, 1968).
LVW	Dylan Thomas, *Letters to Vernon Watkins*, ed. Vernon Watkins (London: J. M. Dent and Faber & Faber, 1957).
Moynihan	William T. Moynihan, *The Craft and Art of Dylan Thomas* (Ithaca, NY: Cornell University Press, 1966).
My Friend Dylan Thomas	Daniel Jones, *My Friend Dylan Thomas* (London: J. M. Dent, 1977).
Notebook Poems	Dylan Thomas, *The Notebook Poems 1930–1934*, ed. Ralph Maud (London: J. M. Dent, 1989).
Olson	Elder Olson, *The Poetry of Dylan Thomas* (Chicago: University of Chicago Press, 1954).
Padberg	Inglinde Padberg, *A Crocodile before the Chrysalis*, typescript translation of the German text published by Peter Lang, 1994.
Places	James A. Davies, *Dylan Thomas's Places* (Swansea: Christopher Davies, 1987).
Portrait of a Friend	Gwen Watkins, *Portrait of a Friend* (Llandysul: Gomer Press, 1983); reprint *Dylan Thomas and Vernon Watkins: Portrait of a Friendship* (Seattle: University of Washington Press, 1983).
Portrait of the Artist	Dylan Thomas, *Portrait of the Artist as a Young Dog* (London: J. M. Dent, 1940).
Selected Poems	Dylan Thomas, *Selected Poems*, ed. Walford Davies (London: J. M. Dent, 1974).
Tedlock	E. W. Tedlock, *Dylan Thomas: The Legend and the Poet* (London: Heinemann, 1960).
The Poems	Dylan Thomas, *The Poems*, ed. Daniel Jones (London: J. M. Dent, 1971).
Tindall	William York Tindall, *A Reader's Guide to Dylan Thomas* (New York: The Noonday Press, 1962).
Twenty-five Poems	Dylan Thomas, *Twenty-five Poems* (London: J. M. Dent, 1936).
UMW	Dylan Thomas, *Under Milk Wood* (London: J. M. Dent, 1995).

Introduction

From a very early age Dylan Thomas (1914–53) was remembered for his precocity, mischievousness and poetic talent. He was a 'character' in school, performed in dramatic roles, and edited the school magazine. He wrote and published poems every year of his life from the age of eleven to his death at thirty-nine. His first book of poems was accepted for publication when he was nineteen, and caused a sensation in literary London. He became the image of Poet for his time. He became a celebrity in broadcasting for the BBC. He drew crowds in every pub he entered. His American poetry tours were the stuff of legend. He wrote a funny and moving radio play, *Under Milk Wood*, which will be performed forever, just as Christmases into the future will always include his 'A Child's Christmas in Wales'.

We are dealing, then, with a conspicuous literary figure about whom there is much biographical information. John Malcolm Brinnin's *Dylan Thomas in America* came first, in 1955. Then, *Letters to Vernon Watkins* (1957), the biographical element now amplified after Watkins's death by Gwen Watkins in *Portrait of a Friend* (1983). The first commissioned biography, *The Life of Dylan Thomas*, was by Constantine FitzGibbon (1965), with his editing of a *Selected Letters* published the following year. Paul Ferris did a full-scale biography (1977), out in Penguin Books in 1978. Daniel Jones published *My Friend Dylan Thomas* in 1977. Caitlin Thomas had expressed the full flow of her emotions in *Leftover Life to Kill* in 1957. That book has been reprinted, but much more biographical information was collected on tape from her by George Tremlett and presented in book form in 1986 as *Caitlin: A Warring Absence*. She also supplied information for Paul Ferris's *Caitlin: The Life of Caitlin Thomas* (1983). Other books written by persons close to the poet include Aneirin Talfan Davies's *Dylan: Druid of the Broken Body* (1964), Bill Read's *The Days of Dylan Thomas* (1964) and Glyn Jones's *The Dragon has Two Tongues* (1968). Reminiscences published in periodical form are too numerous to mention, but they have all been rewardingly consulted during the course of the explications of Thomas's poems that constitute the present volume.

Since my working principle has been that the poems, even the more obscure poems, will open up their meaning when we can discover what Thomas's preoccupations were at the time of writing each of them, it has always been biography that has taken me into the doorway of a poem; and what I brought with me when I left was a sense of the poem's place in the poet's life of need and desire.

Unaided by all these resources, I tried to write this book in 1954. Weekend by weekend for an intense year, and with very devoted partners in the enterprise, Beryl and Peggy Jones of Utley, Keighley, Yorkshire,[1] I went through all the poems, image by image. It was a trial by metaphor, an initiation that stood me in good stead through a Ph.D. dissertation, later rewritten and published as *Entrances to Dylan Thomas' Poetry* (1963). But this was merely the announcement of a methodology, a prolegomenon to the volume of explications that might some day be possible. One could say something useful about how Thomas's poems might be handled, while at the same time being embarrassingly uncertain about what the poet is getting at in all but a handful of anthology pieces.

The enabling event that turned things around was Paul Ferris's publication in 1985 of *The Collected Letters of Dylan Thomas*.[2] People tended to keep Dylan's letters, and so we are given a fairly comprehensive view of the life at any moment. Other definitive volumes have been coming on apace. First *The Collected Stories* (1983); then *Collected Poems 1934–1953* (1988) in tandem with *The Notebook Poems 1930–1934* (1989); followed by *The Broadcasts* (1991), *The Filmscripts* (1995) and *Under Milk Wood* (1995). Though there were no great surprises in these volumes, all the texts had the devoted attention of scholars concerned that the history of the individual pieces be clear in all possible detail.

The re-editing of the *Collected Poems* is especially pertinent to the present volume, which explicates those texts included there and no others.[3] The editors of *Collected Poems 1934–1953*, Walford Davies and myself, were at great pains to retain the integrity of the *Collected*

---

[1] Beryl had done a fine review article on *Deaths and Entrances* when it came out in 1946 for Gwyn Jones's *Welsh Review*, 1, 2 (June 1946), 145–50.

[2] The 2nd edn of the *Collected Letters* published by J. M. Dent in 2000 has also been consulted. I thank editor Paul Ferris for an advance copy. Page number references in the explications are to both editions.

[3] There are thus a total of 93 poems, or 102 if the sonnets are counted separately. The text and editorial notes of *Collected Poems 1934–1953* constitute an essential companion to the explications in the present work.

Poems 1934–1952 as presented to the world by the poet himself before he died. The actual emendations were few, mainly made in deference to the texts of the five original volumes, *18 Poems* (1934), *Twenty-five Poems* (1936), *The Map of Love* (1939), *Deaths and Entrances* (1946), and *In Country Sleep* (1952), which had simply been amalgamated by Thomas to form the *Collected Poems*. 'In Country Heaven' and 'Elegy' were added, those lines completed during the time before his death. I have judged this the proper canon for explication at this time.

What may be considered curious is the fact that I have not here followed the order of the *Collected Poems*. Thomas arranged the constituent five volumes of poems with some care at the time he published them; but the poet's ordering offers no guidance as far as explication is concerned. Even an attempt at a strict chronological order would be only minimally helpful; for, from the time it was discovered that Thomas went back to his notebooks and revised early poems for later publication, the whole notion of chronology of composition has been blurred.[4] For my purposes here, I have avoided being distracted by the question of the poet's 'development', which I take to be less a property of the poet than a construct by critics. 'I am not interested in poetry', Thomas once told Constantine FitzGibbon. 'I am only interested in poems' (FitzGibbon, p. 260). Taking my cue from that, I have emphasized the individuality of the poems by presenting the explications in a purely arbitrary way, in alphabetical order by title.

After all, Thomas wrote the poems one at a time, out of whatever creative momentum had been built up by the particular situation he was in. I have found that it is only seldom that one poem can help in explicating another,[5] and that it is misplaced effort to try to smooth out what appear to be inconsistencies in Thomas's corpus. There definitely are inconsistencies; they are a result of giving full rein to whatever he was moved to do at any one time. The endeavour of the moment: we should apply our attention to that. At any rate, in this volume I do.

Obviously all the poems do not require the same amount or kind of attention from the explicator. In the case of poems easy to read at first try, I have made general comments without labouring things. The more

---

[4] See 'Chronology of composition' in the appendix to *Entrances to Dylan Thomas' Poetry*. The consequence is that the only way a student might gain a proper sense of Thomas's poetic output would be to read *The Notebook Poems 1930–1934* in its entirety before embarking on the *Collected Poems 1934–1953*.

[5] One should be wary also of relying on early versions of a poem in explicating the final version. Thomas sometimes used the same image differently later, and changed the whole direction of the poem.

thorough explications have proceeded by means of the poem's text interspersed with explanatory words or phrases in square brackets at the point most needed. I have called this device 'rephrasement': it is a way of talking the reader *through* the difficult terrain rather than talking *about* it. Only once, in the case of 'I, in my intricate image', have I abnegated my duty to go through a difficult poem painstakingly. But I would claim that this, too, is the appropriate way to treat that particular poem.

It would go quite against the principles operating in this book to proceed here to summarize Thomas's poetic techniques. The effects achieved in every line are unique and can only be examined in context. In any case, I am not interested in technique so much as the resultant meaning. Nor am I drawn to 'problems'; I try to say what I think there is in the poem after all the problems have been mulled over and the basic meaning discerned.

The 'basic' meaning! Aye, there's the rub. There may be a myriad of remotely possible meanings hovering around an image in Thomas. How does one get to the basic meaning? I believe there is always, or almost always, one meaning given by the context that rings true. How does one find it? One grits one's teeth as though on a roundabout, holding on as meanings of lesser purchase are thrown off by centrifugal force. The thing that one is holding on to is a strong central idea in the poem, what Thomas once referred to, in a conversation with John Malcolm Brinnin, as the poem's 'hypothesis' (Brinnin, p. 126):

He had picked up somewhere a notion that he liked: poems are hypothetical and theorematic. In this view the hypothesis of a poem would be the emotional experience, the instant of vision or insight, the source of radiance, the minute focal point of impulse and impression. While these make up what is commonly called inspiration, poetic logic should prove the validity of the ephemeral moments they describe.

The poem demonstrates its 'hypothesis' well when all the elements contribute meaningfully to it. Looking at it the other way round, the 'basic' meaning of any element is the one which the logic of the poem would need in order to 'prove the validity of the ephemeral moments' of inspiration.

The problem of multiple meanings is everywhere in Thomas's poetry, so that one could almost pick an illustration at random. The opening lines of 'A Winter's Tale' come to mind.

It is a winter's tale
That the snow blind twilight ferries over the lakes
And floating fields from the farm in the cup of the vales,
Gliding windless through the hand folded flakes,
The pale breath of cattle at the stealthy sail,

And the stars falling cold,
And the smell of hay in the snow, and the far owl
Warning among the folds, and the frozen hold
Flocked with the sheep white smoke of the farm house cowl
In the river wended vales where the tale was told.

There is a tale to be told. It is imagined as coming to the poet from a farmhouse across a snow-filled valley as though ferried by the twilight itself. An atmosphere of leisurely care is being created by common words such as 'warning', 'stealthy' and 'wended', while the apt and accurate 'cowl', the hood-shaped protector over a chimney, furthers the sense of rural husbandry. The farm is in the 'cup' of the vales, as though held in cupped hands by the landscape. This is a poet who delights in diction and makes words work.

What I am coming to is the fourth line where the tale is described as gliding windless 'through the hand folded flakes'. I can think of two meanings for the adjective 'hand folded': (1) that the flakes are coming down so peacefully they are like people sitting contented with their hands folded, or (2) the flakes have each been made by hand by folding paper in the way we all know how to from our childhood. I like the second one better here. It elongates the occasion, the diligence of the individual attention to each flake, the folding and cutting producing a million cared-for uniquenesses. It seems to be well within Thomas's poetic idiom to have an image thus thought out. I believe he would say, Yes, let's have meaning number two here, and I'll give you meaning number one later – as he does in stanza 8: 'no sound flowed down the hand folded air'. In this case the air is quiet; it has its hands folded.

There are many enormously more complicated cruxes than this example. To argue them all thoroughly would be a worthy ambition, though fraught with frustration. Thomas is often hard to pin down. There is an abundance of alternative meanings sometimes. One has to be positively *Puritan* – was that Christopher Ricks's term? – to refrain from such diversified investments. There is a tendency to let the hard work go by and say an image means this *or* this *or* this. The cold Puritan in us will not allow such self-indulgence, and I think Thomas would approve of the shearing down. There is only one right word, he would say, and it is the right word because of the prosodic elements involved, but also because of the consideration of meaning. Whether or not Thomas always gives enough clues in the context for a reader to find the right meaning is debatable. It is a debate that will probably go on for ever.[6] Consensus is a hard-won thing. A volume three times the size of this, by examining hundreds of points that have actually been disputed, might show that the task of forging agreement would be endless. My general practice in this book has been to ignore what I do not think is present in a poem.

As to what I think is present in a poem, I offer it with varying degrees of hesitancy and bravado, much of which tentativeness, like a seasoned debater, I may not always show. In the mulling over that preceded the typing out of the explications, I found doors opening to meanings I had never thought of before; even at this late stage the weather turned around for me in many of these poems. It makes me wonder what would happen if I came back to them a year from now. Further illumination? Almost certainly. But a line has to be drawn, and the baton passed on to the next explicator in the relay.

I look forward to ensuing discussions, especially the reports I know I shall receive from those devotees of Thomas with whom I have had rewarding colloquies in recent years, Robert Williams (Bruree, Ireland), Inglinde Padberg (Marl, Germany), Walford Davies (Aberystwyth, Wales) and John Ackerman (Chelsea, London). I also wish to thank John Harris, my summer neighbour at St David's Quay, for holding himself as the reader of choice for these efforts; and Ned Thomas as the indispensable specific audience that a long work needs to have in mind to get itself written.

T. S. Eliot wrote the following tribute to Dylan Thomas for inclusion in Constantine FitzGibbon's biography (FitzGibbon, pp. 92–3). These words deserve requoting.

> I remember being shown a number of his poems before his work was taken on by Richard Church for Dents and I remember discussing the poems with Sir Herbert Read. I think he agreed with me but I will not swear to this,

---

[6] For instance, I cannot quite shake off an allied meaning for 'hand folded flakes', say (2a), where each flake is folded by hand like white laundry. Is it possible to think of the snowflakes folded in this way and as folded cut-outs *at the same time*? Logic resists it; yet if Thomas does not pin the meaning down for us, what else can we – in the extreme cases – do? (I am indebted to Mary Maillard, who, in keying my typescript into a computer, raised this and other questions.)

when I came to the conclusion that I wished all the poems were as good as the best. I regret having been so fussy because Dylan Thomas's work was always hit or miss. It was a peculiarity of his type of genius that he either wrote a great poem or something approaching nonsense and one ought to have accepted the inferior with the first-rate. I certainly regarded him always as a poet of considerable importance.

Eliot's amiable discrimination set me my task. Thomas's 'great poem' can largely take care of itself; it is the 'something approaching nonsense' that I have particularly relished taking on, to prove if possible that there is a lot more sense there than was previously thought. I know it is the noble function of literary criticism to argue for only the best and to propose we avert our attention from the rest. This seems to me too much like claiming to improve a brush by pulling out most of its bristles. Rather, it is the totality of the poet's output which is intrinsically interesting because it is only by means of the whole that we can get to the poet's soul, where the meaning we are seeking ultimately lies. It is the expressed life that we are after, no matter that the artistry is also moving. The present volume aims to be a full inventory of the ingredients that Thomas's *Collected Poems* supply towards knowing what this poet's life can mean to us.

I have taken the book's title from a manuscript at Texas which lists five projects Thomas was intending to work on at the time of his death, only the first of which do we have any evidence of:

> In Country Heaven
> Where Have the Old Words Got Me
> Poem to Caitlin
> Poem to Colm
> Continuation of White Giant.

The most intriguing of these is 'Where Have the Old Words Got Me'. Under this title Thomas might have made an assessment of what he thought he had achieved with his poems. With respect, I have appropriated it for my own attempts to do the same.

After the funeral

(please turn to *Collected Poems*, p. 73)

This poem about Thomas's aunt of Fernhill farm, subtitled 'In memory of Ann Jones', was written in stages, a circumstance that affects the way we finally must see it, not as an elegy but as a struggle of the poet with his own feelings. This struggle is immediately presented to us in the contortions of the first few lines. If 'After the funeral' is one of Thomas's more popular poems it is so in spite of the compressed syntax of its opening. Theodore Roethke recalled that Thomas thought the poem 'creaked a bit at the beginning: that he had not worked hard enough on it' (Tedlock, p. 51).

> After the funeral, mule praises, brays,
> Windshake of sailshaped ears, muffle-toed tap
> Tap happily of one peg in the thick
> Grave's foot, blinds down the lids, the teeth in black,
> The spittled eyes, the salt ponds in the sleeves . . .

We have not yet reached a main verb, and will not for another seven lines, but I interrupt the poem here because these five lines represent the first stage in the writing, derived as they are from what Thomas wrote into his notebook on 10 February 1933, the day of the funeral itself[1] (*Notebook Poems* pp. 129–30):

> After the funeral, mule praises, brays,
> Shaking of mule heads betoken
> Grief at the going to the earth of man
> Or woman, at yet another long woe broken,
> Another theme to play on and surprise
> Fresh faults and till then hidden flaws
> Faded beyond ears and eyes,
> At him or her, loved or else hated well,
> So far from love or hate in a deep hole.

---

[1] Or soon thereafter. The tombstone at Llanybri chapel (illustrated in *Collected Poems*, p. 224) indicates that Ann died on 7 February 1933 (at age seventy).

> The mourners in their Sabbath black
> Drop tears unheeded or choke back a sob,
> Join in the hymns, and mark with dry bright looks
> The other heads, bent, spying, on black books.

This is so much a general satire of the hypocrisy of mourners that Thomas talks of a 'him or her', not about Ann Jones personally. The nineteen-year-old poet was keeping an ironic distance from the event. It is this cold notebook poem that Thomas had in front of him as he began a revision in March 1938. We can make a rephrasement of the first five lines as follows:

> After the funeral, [after] mule [braying] praises, [after] brays [mourning hymns], [after] windshake of sailshaped [mule-like] ears [mourners nodding in agreement], [after] muffle-toed tap tap happily of one peg in the thick grave's foot,[2] [after] blinds [veils] down [covering] the [eye-] lids, [after] teeth in black [exaggerated mourning], [after] the spittled eyes [tears made with saliva], [after] the salt ponds [pretended abundance of tears not quite hidden] in the sleeves . . .

Thomas's first act in expanding the poem beyond the range of the notebook version was to add himself to the list as an arch-hypocritical mourner.

> Morning smack of the spade that wakes up sleep,
> Shakes a desolate boy who slits his throat
> In the dark of the coffin and sheds dry leaves . . .

'Desolate' is an emotive word, but it is, I think, part of the outward show; slitting his throat in the coffin is hopelessly exaggerated; and in the end he has only dry leaves instead of blood and tears. We know how callous Thomas was at the time through a letter he wrote to Trevor Hughes in London. The letter is undated, but in the midst of it a telegram arrives at 5 Cwmdonkin Drive, Swansea, calling his

---

[2] Is this a tap dance by a one-legged sexton digging a grave, as has been proposed? Rather than this improbable circumstance, we should understand these words as saying the same thing as the surrounding lines: the people at the graveside are merely pretending to mourn. They may have muffled their toes as mules or horses drawing a funeral cart traditionally had their hooves padded, but they betray themselves through their happy tap tap. They may themselves have one peg in the grave, but they are too self-satisfied to know it.

mother to his aunt's bedside in Carmarthen Infirmary. The poet is blasé (*Letters*, p. 13/30):

> The old aunt will be dead by the time she arrives. This is a well-worn incident in fiction, & one that has happened time after time in real life. The odour of death stinks through a thousand books & in a thousand homes. I have rarely encountered it (apart from journalistic enquiries), & find it rather pleasant. It lends a little welcome melodrama to the drawing-room tragi-comedy of my most uneventful life. After Mother's departure I am left alone in the house, feeling slightly theatrical.

Thomas goes on to explain why he should, because of their closeness, be moved by his aunt's illness:

> Many summer weeks I spent happily with the cancered aunt on her insanitary farm. She loved me quite inordinately, gave me sweets & money, though she could little afford it, petted, patted, & spoiled me. She writes – is it, I wonder, a past tense yet – regularly. Her postscripts are endearing. She still loves – or loved – me, though I don't know why. And now she is dying . . .

We can confirm this endearing picture of his aunt from the later short story 'The Peaches', which describes one of those summer visits to Fernhill farm: 'I ran into the kitchen and into Annie's arms. There was welcome then. The clock struck twelve as she kissed me, and I stood among the shining and striking like a prince' (*Collected Stories*, p. 130). And so on. At the time of her death, we learn from the letter to Hughes, Thomas's mood was very different (*Letters*, p. 13/31):

> She is dying. She is dead. She is alive. It is all the same thing. I shall miss her bi-annual postal orders. That's all. And yet I like – liked – her. She loves – loved – me. Am I, he said, with the diarist's unctuous, egotistic preoccupation with his own blasted psychological reactions to his own trivial affairs, callous & nasty? Should I weep? Should I pity the old thing? For a moment, I feel I should. There must be something lacking in me.

It is this disparity between how he should feel and his total unfeelingness that Thomas remembered when he came to include his young self in the revised 'After the funeral', attributing to him the hyperbolic act of slitting his throat 'in the dark of the coffin', something even more florid than Laertes leaping into his sister's grave (*Hamlet*, 5.1). Self-immolation for a near kin is not part of south Wales Presbyterianism. It is true

that the 'morning smack of the spade' (line 6) has woken him up from a
sleep of apathy. But the spade has broken only 'one bone to light with a
judgment clout' (line 9). One bone does not a Judgment Day make. I
cannot take this line as being in any way devotional. On the contrary, it
sums up scornfully the ridiculous aspects of the funeral and the 'desolate' boy's place in it. If he's the one bone that's broken to light, with a
smack like a doctor gives a newborn, it is to *self*-awareness that he has
been roused. It is important to the ultimate movement of the poem that
the boy's egotistical desolation is not at all a tribute to Ann Jones.

The memorial to Ann does not begin until later, full five years after
the funeral. The 'I' who stands finally alone with purpose in the
presence of his loss is no longer the callous boy but the man writing
in 1938, ready now to try a funeral oration (lines 10–13):

> After the feast of tear-stuffed time and thistles
> In a room with a stuffed fox and a stale fern,
> I stand, for this memorial's sake, alone
> In the snivelling hours with dead, humped Ann . . .

He imagines himself enduring a lonely all-night vigil. This is not the
boy; this is the grown man, the bard, the praise-poet, whose job is to
eulogize dead Ann's life. She was one (lines 14–15)

> Whose hooded, fountain heart once fell in puddles
> Round the parched worlds of Wales and drowned each sun.

Wales is a dry desert of a place, but the milk of human kindness
flowed like water in abundance from Ann's heart and drowned the
suns that were parching it. With this magnificent – or at least
'magnified' (line 17) – image, the poet seems to be making a claim to
have wiped out the guilt of his previous unfeelingness.

At one point he did feel satisfied with the attempt, for he sent these
fifteen lines to Vernon Watkins as a finished poem.[3] But almost

---

[3] If Watkins saw the poem in three stages, as he states in *Letters to Vernon Watkins*
(*LVW*, p. 57), then the fifteen-line first version would have been sent with the
letter of 7 February 1938. One version was sent to Watkins on 21 March 1938
(*Letters*, p. 279/326). Thomas refers to it in the next letter, 1 April 1938 (*Letters*, p.
287/336): 'The poem in memory of Anne Jones I am completely rewriting . . . I'm
making it longer and, I hope, better than any of my recent simple poems.' This
was a 20-line version, as Thomas makes quite clear when sending the finished 40-
line poem as we now have it, in an undated letter of later in April 1938 (*Letters*, p.
288/337). Unfortunately none of these drafts were preserved.

immediately Thomas realized that the image praising Ann contained too much hype. He added the next five lines, saying that Ann would not have wanted to be remembered in that way. The 'hooded, fountain heart' (I suppose a fountain can have the general shape of a hood, but it is also here to be thought of as covering in a protective flow the whole of Wales) was a 'monstrous' image, too many puddles everywhere. He does not want to sink in this holy flood; he now simply wants to say that 'her death was a still drop' (line 17). She would be embarrassed to have him say more. This addition turned the elegiac flow around; Ann is now praised for her modesty, her desired anonymity: she does not stand in need of a bard or 'druid of her broken body' (line 20).

But Thomas was not content with this either. He told Watkins (*Letters*, p. 288/337) that he considered it 'feeble as it stood', and the lines he had just added, those he ultimately placed in parentheses, were 'too facile and, almost, grandiosely sentimental'. Something more was needed. He wrote the further twenty lines 'in a rush' (*LVW*, p. 57).

The completed poem certainly maintains a grandiose pitch, but we must consider what it is that Thomas injected to ensure that it would not suffer the criticism of being too sentimental. What he did was to acknowledge that he was carving this monument to Ann Jones *for his own purposes*. The 'raised hearth' where the psychic action of the poem is taking place is at New Inn house, Caitlin's mother's home, in Blashford in the south of England. From there, on 21 March 1938, the same day he sent a draft of the poem to Vernon Watkins, Thomas also wrote to an editor (*Letters*, pp. 277/324–5):

> I really am in a very bad, distressing position now, living on charity, unable to buy for myself even the smallest necessary luxuries, and having little peace of mind from those most small and nagging worries to work as well and carefully as I should like. I may have to stop writing altogether very soon – for writing is obviously full-time or not at all – and try to obtain some little, sure work. I'm sorry to write as meanly and wretchedly as this, but the way in which I'm forced to live has begun to colour everything.

Two days later he is writing to Henry Treece (*Letters*, p. 280/327):

> Do you, I wonder and hope not, know what it is to live outlegally on the extreme fringe of society, to bear all the responsibilities of possession-lessness – which are more and heavier than is thought, for great demands

are made of the parasite, and charity, though soon enough you can learn to slip it on with a pathetic feeling of comfort, is a mountain to take – and to live from your neighbour's hand to your mouth? I have achieved poverty with distinction, but never poverty with dignity; the best I can manage is dignity with poverty, and I would sooner smarm like a fart-licking spaniel than starve in a world of fat bones. A poem, obviously, cannot be begun with the strength and singlemindedness it demands and deserves unless there is enough money behind it to assure its completion: by the second verse the writer, old-fashioned fool, may need food and drink.

This (not the year of Ann Jones's death) is the 'crooked year' he is speaking of in line 30 of 'After the funeral'. In the room whose windows are wet with his tears of chagrin he is 'fiercely mourning' the passing of his carefree life, now a married man utterly without income or prospects of same. So what is he going to do? His instincts tell him that if he has nothing he had better set to work to build something out of nothing.

In these matters Dylan is a fighter. Something he told Lawrence Durrell the previous Christmas is pertinent. Durrell had been trying to get Thomas to return with him to the sunshine of Greece. Though cold and penniless, Thomas was still up to retorting (*Letters*, p. 266/309): 'England is the very place for a fluent and fiery writer. The highest hymns of the sun are written in the dark.' In 'After the funeral', one of the highest hymns he attempted, Thomas is proving this contention true. From a broken body (line 20) he is creating a 'skyward statue' (line 27). This is his job. He is a fluent and fiery writer. He is a bard. He can do no other than 'call all / The seas to service' (lines 21–2). He will have Ann's 'wood-tongued virtue / Babble like a bellbouy over the hymning heads' (lines 22–3). He will raise her far above the mulish mourners. Why not? It is not the real Ann; it's a glorification, a hymn of the sun. That is what poets can sometimes do, in the darkest night. They can make something glorious out of nothing. In sculpting this statue, then, Thomas is against all odds – and there is an undeniable strain – exerting his boldest creative powers.

Ann Jones was, at that moment, the subject which called forth these powers, for Thomas had unfinished business with his aunt and her funeral. He had been unable to mourn at the time of her death this perfectly kind, amiable, generous aunt. 'There must be something lacking in me', he suggested in the letter to Trevor Hughes (*Letters*, p. 13/31). This deficiency is still nagging at him. Even now, as he goes back through 'tear-stuffed' time to Fernhill's front parlour with 'stuffed fox' and 'stale fern' (lines 10–11), he cannot mourn properly; calling the vigil at the coffin 'the snivelling hours' (line 13) does not seem quite right. He is still ironic. The poem as it proceeds is trying to find the means to get out of the ironic mode without falling into sentimentality. It is the poet's need to tell the precise truth of his feelings that pushes this poem.

In order to accomplish this aim Thomas is going to take two tacks. While he is telling the raw truth about his aunt, he will at the same time build a magnified mirror image. Ann's flesh 'meek as milk' is the actuality; the 'wild breast and blessed and giant skull' is what he persists in making of it (line 28). He knows Ann's work-worn hands and brain ('her wits drilled hollow' – line 33) were crippled by religion and its 'damp word'; he knows her pain-tightened face revealed a very painful death from which God did not spare his hand-maiden (line 34). As against this reality, he is sculpturing an Ann who is 'seventy years of stone'. It is as though every year of her un-rewarded virtue added a cubit to the statue till it reached the clouds. It becomes an awesome power to effect a change in the poet. He calls it an 'argument' and it looks as though it will be overwhelming:

> These cloud-sopped, marble hands, this monumental
> Argument of the hewn voice, gesture and psalm
> Storm me forever over her grave until
> The stuffed lung of the fox twitch and cry Love
> And the strutting fern lay seeds on the black sill.

He cannot say that it has happened yet, but he is asking for the image he has created to force his dry-leaved heart to love and be fruitful. The humble life of his 'ancient peasant aunt' (*Letters*, p. 288/337) has been written so big that its message cannot be ignored. What is the message? That one lives on in humility and generosity no matter how little the world appreciates it. Endurance, true to oneself: this is the message that Thomas needed, for his own sanity, to hear in the depressing early months of 1938. During this dire lack of progress in his chosen life, he turned to the best model he knew of good-natured patience. He had a notebook poem in which he scorned the world of hypocritical mourners; he added himself as a callous youth; and then began to prepare, in the logic of the poem, an image that he could not ignore, that would 'storm' him, as though he were held in a tornado over Ann's grave, harried by the voice, the gesture and the

psalm which constituted the monumental argument. He is asking to
be coerced into love so that he can cancel the theatrical self-centred
boy he was at the funeral and now bless the spirit of his beloved aunt
as he has already asked the natural world of the countryside to do.
To stop with this blessing, however, would be to place 'After the
funeral' entirely within the Wordsworthian tradition of elevating
common folk by means of heightened expression. The poem would
not escape the accusation of sentimentality. Line 20 has already
convincingly stated that Ann has no need of such a blessing. After
that point in the poem, when 'Ann's bard' persists in raising up a
monument it is not for sentimental reasons but because someone is
really in need of a blessing, the poet himself, a blessing that he knows
will only come to those who can, through whatever sufficiently
powerful intermediary is theirs to invent, bless.

Note on 'After the funeral'

John Ackerman's *Companion* has a long section on this poem (pp.
100–5). An ingenious reading is offered for line 15 ('Round the
parched worlds of Wales'), according to which 'parched' has a second
meaning derived from the Welsh word *parchedig*, 'reverend'; that is,
Wales is not only thirsty but also full of preachers. In *Under Milk
Wood* there is a reference to 'a beer tent black with parchs' (*UMW*, p.
17), so I would not put it past Thomas to have flashed on the
bilingual pun, where a preachered Wales is dry as dust, parched. But I
would maintain that the pun does not operate within 'After the
funeral'. Perhaps it exists as a nod and a wink between author and an
in-group of readers, but essentially outside the poem. My approach is
to try to determine what a poem meant to the poet, but we do not
have to say that everything that may have crossed his mind while
writing it has a permanent place in the finished poem, only those
things that make the poem work.

A grief ago

(please turn to *Collected Poems*, p. 47)

A typescript of this love poem (now at Texas) is dated January 1935. It was a time of romantic crisis. Pamela Hansford Johnson was beginning to realize that Dylan resident in London was an entirely different proposition from the eager, solicitous, amusing correspondent and occasional visitor he had been. On 16 November 1934, only five days after Thomas made the move to rooms near Earls Court, she wrote in her diary (now at Buffalo): 'puzzled to death by the vagaries of Dylan'. On 21 November: 'D still awful as ever'. The next day she records that Dylan proposed marriage, but the day after she decided 'to do nothing of the sort'. On 4 December she wrote to Dylan for the return of her letters, but he came over to Battersea 'conciliatory'. Thomas went home to Swansea for Christmas 1935 (and probably began 'A grief ago' there – it being a rather better place to concentrate than 5 Redcliffe Street). On his return to London, Pamela wrote in her diary: 'Says he loves me but can't resist Comrade Bottle. Am just watching and praying.' On 8 January she wrote: 'I told him I was kissing him goodbye for good, but I dunno.' She finally did so a few months later (when Caitlin came along), but during the time of 'A grief ago' the two of them were, as new photographs from the estate of Pamela Hansford Johnson reveal,[1] an affectionate and sexy couple. The question that this poem raises is, 'Did they or didn't they?' The later Lady Snow said they did not. In that case, the 'she who was who I hold' was someone else, and *she* did. For 'A grief ago' is a poem of coitus.

We are all experts in the word-play that finds many ways to say the same thing, this one thing. Taking the first two stanzas of this poem, we could have a sexual innuendo quiz. 'A stem cementing' – yes; 'wrestled up the tower' – yes; 'masted venus' – yes; 'the paddler's bowl' – yes; 'the leaden bud shot through the leaf' – yes; 'the rod the aaron rose cast to plague' – oh, yes. In this poem, there is nothing one cannot say 'yes' to. The Rose of Sharon (of the Song of Solomon) rhymes with Aaron (of Exodus), who 'cast down his rod before Pharaoh and his servants, and it became a serpent' (Exodus 7:10). The rod also caused the rivers of Egypt to become blood, frogs to

[1] See *Companion*, after p. 145.

infest the land, and gnats to produce plague (8:17). Because of these deeds, it was called 'the finger of God'. Yes, to all of that.

Despite all the yeses, these stanzas are far from erotic, partly because of the extremely far-fetched quality of the 'metaphysical' leaps, but also because of an inherent nobility of rhythm and a syntax that paces the flow. The total earnestness of the sexual punning raises it above anything that might have happened in Battersea. 'Wrenched by my fingerman': amazing that these words, in context, achieve such a lofty tone when, if one had to, one would have to say that the phrase simply meant 'screwed'.[2]

In the first line the word 'grief' could be translated as 'sexual encounter' and in the second stanza as 'sexual partner'. The word sums up all the *tristitia* of sex: the young people have come to grief. This sad tone governs the remaining three stanzas of the poem, which are about the result not so much desired as suffered: conception. It is certainly the life force at work here. The girl is viewed as a representative of her ancestors and the male seems only the means whereby her history is transmitted to the future. The poem is not about sex, it is about DNA.

> And she who lies, like exodus [withdrawn] a chapter [away] from the garden [of paradise, la gloire], [now a] brand [as from a branding iron] of the lily's[3] anger on her ring [genitals], TUGGED[4] through the days [up to this moment] her ropes of heritage [attaching her to her forbears], [which have involved tugs-of-wars, feuds] the wars of pardon [for the sin in the Garden], [with] the twelve triangles of the cherub wind [as on ancient maps] engraving [her] going on field and sand [with the passing of time].

The past is being dragged into the present by the sexual act and conception, whereby hereditary characteristics are acquired by the zygote. The impregnated woman is defined only by her 'people' at that moment. And the man is nowhere.

---

[2] I doubt that the reader needs or desires any further decoding of the images of these first two stanzas. I was misguided enough to offer such in *Entrances*, pp. 91–2.

[3] It was a lily that Gabriel is portrayed as bringing to Mary at the Annunciation. Thomas might also have known of the 'lily-iron' harpoon used in swordfishing. Adam and Eve were driven out of the Garden to populate the earth, threatened with a burning sword.

[4] Here and in the other rephrasements of Thomas's poems in this volume, SMALL CAPITAL LETTERS have been used to identify the main verbs.

Who then is she, she holding me? The people's sea DRIVES on her, DRIVES out the father from the caesared [conquered] camp [womb]; the dens of shape [where the genes have been waiting] SHAPE all her whelps [biological offspring] with the long voice of water [in the womb], [in order] that [the] she [whom] I have, [whom] the country-handed grave boxed into love, rise [pregnant] before dark [death].

This last image is one of the things mentioned by Edith Sitwell in her review of *Twenty-Five Poems* in the *Sunday Times* of 15 November 1936. Thomas wrote to Henry Treece the following rebuttal (*Letters*, pp. 300–1/348):

> She makes a few interesting misreadings, or, rather, half-readings. She says the 'country-handed grave' in my poem A Grief Ago is 'that simple nurse of grief, that countryman growing flowers and corn'. My image, principally, did not make the grave a gentle cultivator but a tough possessor, a warring and complicated raper rather than a simple nurse or an innocent gardener. I meant that the grave had a country for each hand, that it raised those hands up and 'boxed' the hero of my poem into love. 'Boxed' has the coffin and the pug-glove in it.

We are being asked to take the image very literally indeed. The grave here is certainly heavy-handed: it has a 'country' for each hand, the domains of the two sets of ancestors that come together at conception. The grave is depicted as the force which brings this fusion about, as though it were a boxer coercing the lovers into bed. It is effective in this because it threatens them with that other 'boxing', being boxed into their coffin. Future death is what forces lovers to make of themselves the conduit whereby ancestors become progeny. This is a most unromantic love poem.

> The night [death] is near, a nitric [corrosive acid] shape that leaps [rapes] her, [it being] time and [mortician's] acid; I TELL her this: before the suncock [proclaiming the Day of Judgment] cast her bone to fire, LET her inhale her dead [ancestors], draw in their seas [history] through [by means of] seed and solid [coition], so [let her] cross her hand [to gain her future] with their grave gipsy eyes, and [let her] close her fist [to hold the egg firm until birthpangs].

No, it was not Pamela Hansford Johnson. She was no gypsy. Or maybe Dylan knew something we don't.

✧

All all and all

(please turn to *Collected Poems*, p. 29)

Thomas enclosed this poem in a letter to Pamela Hansford Johnson of 20 July 1934. The same letter included a long 'Political Corner' in which the young poet, with his intellectual hat on, wrote out the results of his conversations with his passionately left-wing friend Bert Trick. Thomas strikes a very serious tone in making his Marxist predictions (*Letters*, pp. 158–9/185):

> Convince people that a thing is bad, and they are ready to listen to a reasonable plan for its overthrow. There is and always must be a stream of revolutionary energy generated when society is composed, at top and bottom, of financial careerists and a proletarian army of dispossessed. Out of the negation of the negation must rise the new synthesis. The new synthesis must be a classless society.

There is much more in the same vein. It is nothing less than the advocacy of communist revolution (*Letters*, p. 159/185):

> If constitutional government cannot, in the space of a year after the next General Election, fulfil their policies, then a united front must be made, the army and the police force must be subdued, and property be taken by force.

Is it not possible that Thomas wrote at least one poem in this mood, within the context of revolutionary thought? We should look at the poem he included in the same letter, where we find a line like 'Flower, flower the people's fusion' (part III, line 6). Could this not refer to the 'united front' Thomas was calling for in the letter, where he also refers, in an adjacent passage, to 'a fine revolutionary flower' (*Letters*, p. 158/185)? 'If it can be forced home on the consciousness of people that the present economic system is ethically bad, the seed has been planted that may in time grow into a fine revolutionary flower.'

In the above sentence, to make his political point graspable, Thomas is using a familiar botanical image. What if this botanical image were the key to the obscurities of 'All all and all'? It makes sense that it might be. Thomas would then be using the unifying theme of seed growing into a fine revolutionary flower. The 'dry worlds' would be the opposing forces with their 'levers', 'synthetic blood' and 'screws'. Fear would be the inhibiting factor to be overcome before the flowering. What would be at stake is all, all, and all. Thomas once told someone that his obscurity is based on 'a preconceived symbolism derived from the cosmic significance of the human anatomy' (*Letters*, p. 98/122). Why should this not be so in disguised political utterance as well as anything else?

We have to put it in question form, because there is nothing to go on except the obscure poem itself.[1] And the first thing we come up against is the first stanza with its volcanic image, nothing botanical about it at all. We will then have to say that this must be the arid world of present society before any seed has caught hold. The dry worlds rule.

> The dry worlds LEVER [mechanically move] all all and all, [including] the solid ocean, [and] the stage of the ice [they lever or extract] all from the oil, [which results in] the pound of lava.

But the dry worlds cannot help but produce their opposite. The capitalist system, by creating a deprived class, produces its opposite, the socialist movement. The volcano builds up:

> City of spring [the new future], [which will be] the [well-] governed flower, TURNS [at present buried] in the earth that turns the ashen [potentially destroyed in revolution] towns around on a wheel of fire [the revoluting volcano].

The city of spring is waiting trapped underground, turning as an 'ashen' town, post-volcanic ahead of time, ready to be fired out as a revolutionary flowering.

The second stanza is all anatomy, with only the word 'morrow' to connect it to the theme I am proposing is there: the society of the future. The flesh's present condition ('skinny as sin') is to be decoded as the current society of want. The dry worlds lever all of the flesh: we have a corpse for a lover, our marrow is foaming at the mouth.

Part II is hortatory. If it were a political speech it would be asking the worker audience not to be downhearted about the state of the world. Our lives are vulnerable to metal; we are as close to it daily as

---

[1] In sending the poem to Pamela Hansford Johnson, Thomas said only one thing: ' "Flower," by the way, in my "All all and all" (Bradawl, Nuttall, and Bugger-all) is a two-syllabled word' (*Letters*, p. 158/184). This is a complete red herring; the three names lead nowhere.

a lover might be; but we are not to fear it. Know the cage you are in and, it is implied, the knowledge will set you free. This is, I believe, a series of images with the same intent as a political harangue.

'Out of the negation of the negation', said Thomas in the above-quoted letter, 'must rise the new synthesis.' Part III of the poem expresses this. The synthesis is inevitable; the dry worlds have to couple, and square the circle. Part of the charm of Marxism is the proposal that history cannot but move in its preordained dialectical way, where contradictory elements magically lead to a third force. The flowering of the 'people's fusion' is a destined miracle. I take it that 'the people' here means the same as we ordinarily mean when we talk of states and democracy. If that is true, it is a fixed point by reference to which we can interpret the rest of the poem.

The poem had special importance to Thomas in that he chose it as the final poem for his first volume, *18 Poems*. He intended a strong ending, we can be sure. A truly political poem, though covert in great degree, would fit the bill. 'All, all, and all': not a bad rallying cry for a new society.

Altarwise by owl-light

(please turn to *Collected Poems*, p. 58)

What strategy have we for reading this famous (or, from an explicator's point of view, nefarious) sonnet sequence? Should we treat the ten sonnets as separate poems or as one whole? Thomas gives us the option. In sending a selection of typescript poems to Denys Kilham Roberts for consideration for *The Year's Poetry* (1935 edition), Thomas included the first seven sonnets, suggesting that the editor could use any of them alone: 'though they are linked together by a certain obscure narrative, they're entirely self-contained' (*Letters*, p. 921/264). Again, in offering them to Robert Herring for publication in *Life and Letters Today* as 'the first passages of what's going to be a very long poem indeed', Thomas stressed that 'each section is a more-or-less self-contained short poem' and that he could use 'one, or two, or all, or whatever you like of them' (*Letters*, p. 204/231). His advice to Richard Church of Dent's was to print them in *Twenty-five Poems* each on a separate page, 'for, although the poem as a whole is to be a poem in, and by, itself, the separate parts can be regarded as individual poems' (*Letters*, p. 202/229). Taking these hints, then, we might postpone our curiosity as to what the linkage might be – if Thomas calls it an 'obscure narrative' we had better believe him! – and treat the sonnets one by one.

Yet, identifying the first sonnet as having a Christian theme, we are reinforced by the rather obvious Christian references later on: 'the Lord's Prayer' (sonnet VII), 'the crucifixion' (sonnet VIII), 'Christian voyage' (sonnet X), etc. We need such supportive evidence that the 'obscure narrative' has Christian characteristics, for the Christian story is given unusual slants. Probably, the overriding narrative is not the New Testament story at all, but something more personal to the poet, a Thomas journey overlaid with Christian signposts.

Sonnet I

Altarwise [in the shape of a cross] by owl-light [dusk at time of Christ's death] in the half-way house [between living and dying] the gentleman [Christ] LAY graveward with his furies [mortal combatants]; Abaddon [devil in Revelation 9:11] in the hangnail [flesh] CRACKED [off] from Adam [or mankind], and, from his fork [the gentleman's crotch], a dog among the fairies, [who is] an atlas-eater with a jaw for news, BIT OUT the mandrake[1] with tomorrow's scream.

The crucifixion scene has here been intensified by a macabre unfamiliarity: it is a castration, performed by an 'atlas-eater' because of his fear of the enormous progeny of the seed of sinful humankind.

We are on firmer ground here than anywhere else in the sonnets because Thomas himself supplied a gloss of sorts in a letter to Henry Treece of 1 June 1938 (*Letters*, p. 302/348):

---

[1] Traditionally a dog was supposed to be used to uproot the mandrake whose scream could kill a human and often killed the dog. H. H. Kleinman's book devoted to these poems, *The Religious Sonnets of Dylan Thomas* (1963), reveals a possibly specific source. A work called *The Mystic Mandrake* by C. J. S. Thompson had been published in London in 1934, just before the sonnets were started. The following might have intrigued Thomas: 'In some parts of Wales . . . its leaves and fruit were called 'charnel food' and it was believed only to grow beside the gallows tree . . . In other districts of Wales there was a belief in the legend that the mandrake grew from the tears of an innocent man who had been hanged on the gallows' – quoted in Kleinman, pp. 19–20.

Edith Sitwell's analysis, in a letter to the Times, of the lines 'The atlas-eater with a jaw for news / Bit out the mandrake with tomorrow's scream,' seems to me very vague and Sunday-journalish. She says the lines refer to 'the violent speed and the sensation-loving, horror-loving craze of modern life.' She doesn't take the literal meaning: that a world-devouring ghost creature bit out the horror of tomorrow from a gentleman's loins. A 'jaw for news' is an obvious variation of a 'nose for news', & means that the mouth of the creature can taste already the horror that has not yet come or can sense it coming, can thrust its tongue into news that has not yet been made, can savour the enormity of the progeny before the seed stirs, can realise the crumbling of dead flesh before the opening of the womb that delivers that flesh to tomorrow. What is this creature? It's the dog among the fairies, the rip and cur among the myths, the snapper at demons, the scarer of ghosts, the wizard's heel-chaser. This poem is a particular incident in a particular adventure, not a general, elliptical deprecation of this 'horrible, crazy, speed-life'.

This glimpse into the way the poet's mind works as he writes is helpful. Without his gloss we wouldn't guess the half of it. We can only have a despairing admiration for how much Thomas put into his lines. If *he* were doing explications, it would take volumes. Much of his commentary involves riding an image into new areas of mystery. So our job is increased rather than eased.

'Abaddon in the hangnail cracked from Adam': this should be straightforward. Mortal sin came into the world with Adam; the crucifixion is a redemption of sin by a moment of deliberate self-sacrifice. The cracking off from Adam of the devil in the flesh is a way of stating that moment. What follows in the rest of the sentence should be something similar. In biting out the mandrake, the dog is self-sacrificing; this must be Christ as a traditional sin-eater taking from Adam his sin and conquering death on behalf of us all.

Yet Christ as a 'dog among the fairies, the rip and cur among the myths, the snapper at demons, the scarer of ghosts, the wizard's heel-chaser' – this does not seem right. If Christ is the 'gentleman' ('gentle Jesus' of our childhood hymns) then, according to Thomas's gloss, it is *his* loins that the 'ghost creature' is biting the 'horror of tomorrow' from. Can we sort out who is doing what to whom here? In an earlier try at explicating this poem I suggested we take Thomas up on that word 'ghost' and postulate the Holy Ghost as the agent.[2] If we want

---

[2] *Entrances to Dylan Thomas' Poetry*, p. 99: 'After all, it is none other than Christ himself who gave himself up to torture and death. This is a one-man drama,

to preserve Christ's dignity as the 'gentleman', this still seems the best way out. The Holy Ghost is a 'cur among the myths' in the sense brought out in Milton's 'Nativity Ode', one of Thomas's favourite poems, where the pagan gods flee before him, or it. It is perhaps better not to stick to the conventional Trinity. The spiritual part of Christ could be working (violently, in this instance) the miracle of redemption on the physical Christ/Adam.

In any case, whatever the precise events on what Thomas calls his 'literal' level, the Christian story is thrust at us by the cumulation of indirect allusion and, unmistakably, by the phrase 'Christward shelter' later in the poem. 'That night of time' (line 12) will surely have to be Christ's death on the cross. I cannot help but see the 'one leg' of line 10 as the two legs reduced to one by being nailed to the one upright of the cross. This may strike some as far-fetched; I wonder what Thomas would say of it if he were glossing it. We will never know; we are on our own.

> Then, penny-eyed [dead, with pennies to keep his eyelids closed], that gentleman of wounds [Christ], old cock ['gentleman' in British slang] from nowheres [American slang] and the heaven's egg [divine insemination], with bones unbuttoned to the halfway winds [of mortality like King Lear], HATCHED from the windy salvage [what is saved, i.e. the world] on one leg, SCRAPED at my cradle [Swansea 27 October 1914] in a walking word [for the future poet] that night of time [black moment] under the Christward [ward of Christ] shelter, [']I am the long world's gentleman,['] he said, [']And share my bed with Capricorn and Cancer.[']

The 'gentleman', like the sun, is confined between the two antipodes; but Goat and Crab do not good bedpartners make. Cancer has never been a pleasant word. Thomas is having Christ reveal unsavoury aspects by the company he keeps. Later, Thomas referred to the Long Gentleman 'who shared his bed with grapefruit and windscreens and everything' (*Letters*, p. 224/251). Thomas often referred irreverently to serious poems, so one does not have to take this ridicule of the gentleman as a final judgement. Nevertheless, it adds to the irreverence that the sonnet already contains. If what this poem is saying is that Thomas considers himself to have been touched by the crucified

which Thomas splits into multiple roles.' This early treatment of the first sonnet has received welcome endorsement from Damian Walford Davies's article 'In the path of Blake: Dylan Thomas's "Altarwise by Owl-Light", Sonnet I', *Romanticism* 3/1 (1997), 93.

Christ at his birth, we cannot, given the tone, assume that the touch was entirely wholesome. 'Scraped' only adds to our discomfort.

The old cock from nowheres, unbuttoned, eyeing pennies, this 'gentleman' is a limping tramp! One can conclude one of two things: either this harsh way of talking is tough-minded devotion or it is really scathing. If I prefer to explore the latter possibility, it is because I do not believe that devotion would need to be hidden in such a drastic way. These poems are hermetically sealed. I think Thomas had something to hide.

The phrase 'castrated Saviour' appeared in a letter to Pamela Hansford Johnson written on Armistice Day 1933. The poet, born at the beginning of the 1914–18 war, considered that his generation 'were children born out of blood into blood'. The Saviour must be a neuter not to have stopped that bloodbath (*Letters*, pp. 54/71–2): 'We, with the cross of a castrated Saviour cut on our brows, sink deeper and deeper with the days into the pit of the West. The head of Christ is to be inspected in the museum, dry as a mole's hand in its glass case.' Is it a mole that scraped at Thomas's cradle?

Sonnet II

Not only the last four lines but the whole of sonnet II might best be taken as a speech by 'the hollow agent' – who again seems to be to be the Holy Ghost, defamed as empty, hollow not holy, and the agent-spokesman of death. The history of any one of us, all the developmental shapes we go through, are aspects of death. Death is a final end – like Socrates' hemlock, and it is tinctured into all the hemlock hairs of our heads. Whatever metaphor a poet might want to make, perhaps trying to dodge death with something like 'life is a Christian pilgrimage', is stymied: for death is there whatever the metaphor. There is only one history allowed us: death's.

> [']Death is all metaphors, [is all] shape in one history; the child that sucketh long is shooting up [like a shooting star], the planet-ducted [having cosmic orbits of the milk ducts in the breast] pelican[3] of circles [breasts] weans[4] on an artery the gender's strip [engendered stripling]; child of the short spark [coition] in a shapeless country [the womb before conception]

---

[3] The traditional emblem of Christ the nurturer, the pelican is supposed to pierce its breast to provide blood as food for its young.

[4] The sense here surely is feeding on an artery, not being weaned off it. Perhaps Thomas meant 'feeds until weaned'.

soon SETS ALIGHT a long stick [like a sparkler having the duration of his lifespan] from the cradle; the horizontal cross-bones [symbols of piracy and death] of Abaddon, you [being] by the cavern over the black stairs [to hell and death], RUNG bone and blade, the verticals of Adam, and, manned [made into a man] by midnight [blackness], [rung] Jacob to the stars [in the same way the youth is shooting up]; . . . [']

This Jacob's ladder image draws on Genesis 28: 12, where Jacob's dream of angels ascending and descending a ladder up to heaven is a reiteration of God's covenant with his chosen people. It is perverted by Thomas to become part of the general curse of mortality. The ladder of Adam's skeleton (perhaps the rib-cage in particular, but also the shoulder blades) has rungs made of devil's bones. It is the 'cross-bones of Abaddon' that rung the ladder with the horizontal steps that denote the stages of manhood. It is not auspicious that this *runging* takes place at midnight by a cavern over black stairs, which, in this game of snakes and ladders, seem to be omnipresent for backsliders as they dream with Jacob of the stars.

When it comes to the skull part of the skeletal ladder of the growing youth, we see in the four final lines of the sonnet that the hairs of our heads are deadly.

> Hairs of your head, then said the hollow agent,
> Are but the roots of nettles and of feathers
> Over these groundworks thrusting through a pavement
> And hemlock-headed in the wood of weathers.

We should take these feathers as death's feathers (as Thomas does in several other poems), and the 'groundworks' as the earth which is our bodies, the 'pavement' the head through which our poisonous hair thrusts. The best gloss on this passage is in a letter to Pamela Hansford Johnson of 5 November 1933 (*Letters*, p. 39/57):

> The body, its appearance, death, and diseases, is a fact, sure as the fact of a tree. It has its roots in the same earth as the tree. The greatest description I know of our own 'earthiness' is to be found in John Donne's Devotions, where he describes man as earth of the earth, his body earth, his hair a wild shrub growing out of the land.

If we are only earth, and shrubs are growing out of us, we have not risen above our mortality, despite some mention of the stars. Any ladder we are has been runged by the forces of darkness.

Sonnet III

Thomas was leafing through his notebook of early 1933 and read poem numbered 'Twenty Eight' (*Notebook Poems*, pp. 155–6):

> First there was the lamb on knocking knees,
> The ousel and the maniac greens of spring;
> I caught on yard of canvas inch of wing,
> Kingfisher's, gull's swooping feather and bone,
> Goodnight and goodmorning of moon and sun;
> First there was the lamb which grew a sheep.
> . . .
> First there was the young man who grew old.
>
> Summer spent spring's hoard, fell spent on winter;
> Brown in the clouds rose autumn's rumour,
> A season's fancy formed into a tumour;
> The lamb grown sheep had lambs around its belly,
> And teats like turnips for the lambs to bully;
> First there was a body which grew cold.
> . . .
> The seasons parturate; spring begets summer,
> And summer autumn; autumn begets another,
> The black sheep, shuffling of the fold, old winter;
> And love's first litter begets more.
> First there was innocence and then desire,
> A maggot in the veins; there's nothing now.
>
> There's nothing but the lamb on knocking knees . . .

This is a poem of loss of youth, without relief or compensation. Thomas picked up lines for use in his sonnet sequence, which is now pushing forward with chronological leaps like Rip Van Winkle's (in Washington Irving's story). This is sudden aging, indeed.

The first question that might come to mind is whether or not the lamb is Christ. Perhaps, but it was not in the notebook anything but a symbol of youth, the spring season of life; and such, it seems to me, it remains in sonnet III, where the end of innocence comes quickly with the second line: 'And three dead seasons on a climbing grave.'

First there WAS the lamb [the young boy] on knocking knees [about to fall] and three dead seasons [summer, autumn, winter] on a climbing grave [growing, but already as good as dead] that Adam's wether [castrated ram] in the flock of horns, [the ram being] butt [thick part] of the tree-tailed worm [Satan in the Tree] that mounted Eve, horned down [engendered by thumping the earth] with skullfoot [or clubfoot] and the skull of toes on thunderous [pounded] pavements [groundwork] in the garden [of Eden] time; . . .

'Skullfoot' as a battering ram will be the male member of generation, and 'skull of toes' should be the same, though how it works as a metaphor is not self-evident. (Even Kleinman, who can usually be counted on to provide an overabundance of possible references to choose from comes up empty-handed on this one.) Anyway, we are all 'climbing graves' as we clamber through our lives. We are victims of Original Death. The next four lines of the poem are a statement of the intimacy of birth and death.

Rip of the vaults [having been ripped from a sarcophagus womb], I TOOK my marrow-ladle [for ladling his marrow into his bones] out of the wrinkled undertaker's van [thus at the same time an embalming implement], and, Rip Van Winkle [suddenly old] from a timeless [lacking time] cradle, [I] DIPPED me breast-deep [immersed in his own body] in the descended [fallen] bones; . . .

I do not think the phrase 'timeless cradle' is enough to bring Christ into this sonnet. It is old Rip Van Wink (or forty winks), not having experienced a life, who is 'timeless'. The poem's 'I' is feeling ancient before he even starts, as Rip also felt. The black ram of winter is all that is left for him.

The black ram, shuffling [the lame part] of the year, old winter, [now being] alone alive among his mutton [dead sheep] fold, [']We rung our weathering [mortal] changes on the ladder [the skeleton of sonnet II],['] SAID the antipodes, [']and twice spring chimed.[']

That fateful pair, Capricorn and Cancer, are *runging* – and this time also ringing – the changes happening to our hero, old before his time. This is positively Hutchinson-Gilford syndrome, and Thomas is being sarcastic about spring chiming twice. According to all the evidence of the poem, it didn't even strike once.

Sonnet IV

This sonnet proceeds from hopeless questioning to hopeless love (which is, after all, the big question of adolescence) and back again to despair. I doubt that the questions posed in the first few lines are remotely capable of an answer. If they were, they would not be 'nagging' questions; a 'wounded whisper' would be able to answer them. They are like 'What colour is glory?' of 'My world is pyramid', samples of the enigmatic stumblings of existence. They are 'hunchbacks', crippling to the boy who would be otherwise as straight as a poker. He wants to be straightened out on these matters, but his marrow bones need the support of corsetting. The questions are 'a hump of splinters' on which he urges himself to button a bodice, that the world might not seem so fragmentary. If he can do this, his camel's eye (the questioning eye that is saddled with a camel's hump of splinters) will 'needle through' to a solution. But since the needle of his inquisitiveness is going through a shroud it will find, perforce, only a corpse. Death, then, is all answers. It is futile to probe into all these pseudo-specific questions when the overall and ultimate answer is Death.

The last four lines do provide an answer to the question, 'What is love?' But it is not very encouraging.

> Love's a[5] reflection of the mushroom [growing at night] features [faces], [which are] stills [photographs] snapped by night [before birth into daylight] in the bread-sided field [the womb feeding and enclosing the foetus], once [then] close-up smiling [like movie stars] in the [womb's] wall of pictures [faces of those who will be loved], [subsequently] ark-lamped thrown back upon the cutting flood.

'Ark-lamped' of the periodical printing was changed to 'arc-lamped' in *Twenty-five Poems*. I suspect this was done by someone at Dent's who was unsettled by the puns. The primary image is the one that continues the womb scene. The faces of the ones to be loved, pictured on the screen of the womb, are now arc-lamped, projected at birth like an ark on the waters that burst in a flood from the sac in the birth process, which also involves the cutting of the umbilical cord. But the images are thrown back, discarded like film on a cutting-room floor that descends in waves of celluloid.

---

[5] The 1988 edited *Collected Poems* restores the 'a' found in the first printing of this poem in *Life and Letters Today*. It was dropped (unintentionally, I believe) in *Twenty-five Poems*, which version was followed for the 1952 *Collected Poems*, resulting in unnecessary and misleading ambiguity.

For anyone who thinks that the idea of future loved ones pictured on the wall of the womb is an impossibly far-fetched interpretation of these lines, I have news. In Edith Sitwell's copy of *Twenty-five Poems* now deposited in the Texas library Thomas wrote a marginal note.

> Love is a reflection of the features (the features of
> those you will know and love *after* the womb) which are
> photographed before birth on the wall of the womb
>   the womb being surrounded by food; a field being its
> own field, and the womb being its own food.

To have one's future loves as pin-ups in the womb is a striking way of saying that we are fated in our loving by a genetic disposition. We love because we had an image given to us before we were born. It is something we can do nothing about, any more than we can answer all the other questions that plague our existence in adolescence and beyond. Love, like doubt, comes as an overwhelming flood, and when this becomes a 'cutting' flood, as it does in the last line of the poem, everything is thrown back; we are cut off from the promised happiness.

Sonnet V

Three things are happening in this sonnet: (1) the 'fake gentleman' is telling about a Christ who is cheating at cards, (2) the poet's alter ego 'Byzantine Adam' experiences extremes of hardship, and (3) as 'salt Adam' he swims to an angel who is frozen. The synapses between these three mythemes are too large for us to leap across with much confidence, but I think the best way to look at this triptych is as the representation of a crisis in faith. The questioning youth experiences false religion, suffers a dark night of pain, and finds no relief.

> [']And from the windy [wild] West CAME two-gunned [cowboy angel hero] Gabriel [of the Last Trump], from Jesu's sleeve [where aces would be hidden] TRUMPED UP [fabricated trump cards] the king of spots [blemished], the sheath-decked [prophylactic-wearing] jacks, queen with a shuffled [transvestite] heart['];[6] SAID the fake gentleman [Anti-Christ] in suit of spades [sexton's black], . . .

[6] The punctuation does not help. If the first three lines are what the 'fake gentleman' said, we would not expect a semi-colon, rather a comma. The copy-editor at Dent's changed the *Twenty-five Poems* comma at the end of l. 5 and the semi-colon at the end of l. 6 to periods in desperation (also the semi-colon at the end of l. 10 to a comma). The former punctuation was restored for the *Collected Poems* (1988), but former problems remain.

Just prior to writing the sonnets Thomas had gone through a period of revulsion against the Christianity being preached around him. On 6 July 1934 the *Swansea and West Wales Guardian* under the headline 'The Real Christ – and the False' printed a piece by Thomas written after listening to 'a Christian orator promising his audience a celestial mansion on the condition they give themselves to Christ': 'The orator's Christ is a pussyfoot and a vegetarian, and what is more, a Deity superbly indifferent to the crimes of His children against His children, to the blasphemous blackening of the air as an English Bishop buys foreign controlled armament shares' (*Letters*, p. 150/177). To put it succinctly with a colloquialism: Thomas does not like the way Christ has been dealt a bad hand by these cardsharps, these 'Christ-denying Christians' (*Letters*, p. 142/169).

The next lines, 'Black-tongued and tipsy from salvation's bottle, / Rose my Byzantine Adam in the night', denote the effect of false religion on the protagonist Thomas. They lead on to the dark night of the soul, which begins with a biblical wilderness image that Thomas, in this case, lifted out of a notebook poem of 25 September 1933: 'For loss of blood I fell where stony hills / Had milk and honey flowing from their cracks' (*Notebook Poems*, p. 195), and adding Ishmael, the outcast of Genesis 21: 14–20. The sea of Asia casts the 'I' down and Jonah's and Melville's Moby Dick snatches him by the hair, which reminds one of another lost son, Absalom. All these images may be read as metaphors for internal upheaval. We do not have to treat this as allegory where 'loss of blood', 'milky mush-rooms', 'climbing sea' and 'Jonah's Moby' have to be translated into a sequential progression of events in the life of the poet. The verbs sum up a single condition: 'I fell', 'had me down', 'slew', 'snatched me'. The poet is overwhelmed. The details remain in the images, which amalgamate into a generalized concept and emotion.

We cannot help but be curious about the significance of certain references, 'Byzantine' in particular, which remains a conundrum. But even if we had a reliable clue, it might still leave us strangely suspended in a surreal landscape.

> Cross-stroked salt Adam to the frozen angel
> Pin-legged on pole-hills with a black medusa
> By waste seas where the white bear quoted Virgil
> And sirens singing from our lady's sea-straw.

The 'white bear quoted Virgil' of the next to last line of the sonnet was shown by R. Bickerstaff in *John O'London's Weekly* (10 March 1960) to be a reference to Anatole France's *Penguin Island*, where someone had a vision of 'a white bear . . . murmuring in a low voice this verse of Virgil: *Incipe parve puer*'. Since there seems to be nothing from that context to help us make sense of the line in the sonnet, we are not much better off. The quotation from Virgil has been taken by some to be a prophecy of the birth of Christ. Since it obviously was no such thing, it is difficult to know which way Thomas would want us to take it, supposing that he expected us to know of it at all. As it stands, it adds a surrealist detail to the image of an arctic crucifixion scene: a frozen angel is pin-legged on pole-hills. The angel is either stung by the poison of a jellyfish or petrified by the apparition of the Gorgon Medusa. It perhaps does not matter precisely how one gets to be frozen. Frozen the angel is when the 'salt' (long experienced) Adam swims 'cross-stroke'[7] for succour across the waste seas. Nor will he get much help from the traditionally deceptive and wreck-inducing sirens, who have usurped the role of the comforting Virgin Mary.[8] The poet is frozen out.

Sonnet VI

By the end of the fourth line it seems clear that, in the seven ages of man, we have reached the poet with his eye in fine frenzy.

> [Producing what amounts to a] cartoon of slashes on the tide-traced [marked by the tides] [volcanic] crater, he in a book of water [as large as the seven seas] tallow-eyed [like candlelight] by lava's light SPLIT THROUGH [shucked] the oyster [tight closed] vowels and BURNED sea silence on a [candle] wick of words; . . .

We then get cartoon characters from previous sonnets acting out the violence that seems to be involved for the poet in ending his silence. 'Old cock from nowheres' we thought of as a jocular description of

---

[7] Kleinman (p. 68) quotes John Donne's poem 'The crosse': 'Swimme, and at every stroake, thou art thy Crosse.' This is very attractive as a source for Thomas's image. Each breast-stroke with which he has fronted life has been a personal crucifixion. And 'salt' Adam has salt in his wounds. Perhaps, as another literary allusion, 'byzantine' is meant to invoke the weariness of Yeats's 'Sailing to Byzantium': 'I have sailed the seas and come'.

[8] Thomas may have known the plant 'Our Lady's bedstraw', which folk belief says was in the manger at Bethlehem (Kleinman, p. 73). Kleinman (p. 40) refers to a weed called 'Sussex sea-straw' as something Thomas would not have been likely to know.

the divine progenitor in sonnet I. Is God here cutting off the poet's tongue? But wait, this was supposedly requested by the 'pin-hilled nettle' (or stinging jellyfish). The obscurity intensifies. The romantic-sounding word 'minstrel' is especially distressing to the explicator. It does not seem that it can possibly be good to 'lop off' a minstrel's tongue. Yet this act seems to release 'the fats of midnight' so that 'the salt is singing', and presumably the poet also. The poem seems to get us to the poet's singing without any rational means. The details remain a surrealist puzzle.

In his reflective moments Thomas acknowledged that these poems would inevitably be puzzling in this way, and he was ready to accept it as his own failure. 'I think I do know', he said, writing to his editor Richard Church on 9 December 1935, 'what some of the main faults of my writing are: immature violence, rhythmic monotony, frequent muddleheadedness, and a very much overweighted imagery that leads too often to incoherence' (*Letters*, p. 205/232). There we are. It is not our fault. We have the poet's permission to blame him if we find these lines incoherent. But not quite; for he continues the letter: 'the reader *is* meant to understand every poem by thinking and feeling about it, not by sucking it in through his pores, or whatever he is meant to do with surrealist writing' (*Letters*, p. 205/232). He is resisting Richard Church's accusation of surrealism. I have used the word 'surrealist' above in bewildered self-defence, left on the outside by the poem because its images are too opaque to allow one in. Thomas in the letter is saying that from the inside the intention and the logic of the images, no matter how weird the narrative may be, are clear. (Witness the brilliance of the poet's own explications whenever he does give them.) He is right, therefore, that they do not have the deliberate obtuseness of the surrealist poetry in vogue contemporaneously with Thomas's early poetry. But, if they end by giving the same impression as surrealistic poetry, where are we, as an audience, except at what seems the same sort of sideshow? The answer, of course, is to swallow one's pride and come back repeatedly to the poems and work with all the explicatory skill one can muster and hope for entry.

One does have a foot in the door with 'burned sea silence on a wick of words' (line 4), which is clear enough as the beginning of speech. Then there are definite signals that sex comes into this time of creativity, and maybe is coincident with poetry writing. I think I know, as an image, what is happening when the 'fats of midnight' are being blown from 'the wax's tower' when the 'wick of words' is showing.

When the same candle of 'manwax' (line 14) makes a wound, I think I know, as an image, what the 'blood gauze' is that the 'bagpipe-breasted ladies' with their awful noise are blowing out. But I find these interpretations too disagreeable to declare myself on them when there is no certainty, when they are so 'overweighted' as to allow only hunches.

What does seem fairly certain, however, is that poetry has come to the poet in a most unsavoury context. The phrase (line 12) 'evil index' gives us our foot in the door on that one.

Sonnet VII

Thomas once said mockingly that the task of the poet was simple: just write 'God is Love' and go out and play golf. In sonnet VII he is seriously asking himself as poet to get down to essentials. He does; but the answer is not 'God is Love'. 'Now stamp the Lord's Prayer on a grain of rice' is not, I believe, an act of religious devotion; it is simply an image for getting a lot into a little space. Another different, vernal image for the same idea of stripping down to the primal truth follows, again in the hortative voice:

> A Bible-leaved [wood of myriad pages and high significance] of all the written woods [words] STRIP [reduce] to this [one] tree: [which will be] a rocking alphabet [cradle ABC], Genesis in the root [first born growth of deep meaning], the scarecrow [elemental] word, and one light's language [a concentrated single thought] in the book of trees; . . .

The poet has given himself quite a job, to express the alpha and omega in a sentence. But, with some foreboding, he knows that it is all too easy. He has done it already many times. How many 'wind-turned statements' does *18 Poems* contain? Hundreds. All Thomas's early poems are buffeted by the winds of mortality. Every time the weathercock turns it says to him, 'Death'. And so it is here.

> Time's tune [death knell] my ladies with the [bagpipe] teats of music, [who are] the [music] scaled sea-sawers [sirens], FIX [like a repetitive recording] in a naked [truth] sponge who sucks the bell-voiced [buoyant] Adam [poet] out of magic.

The truth of time's effect depletes the poet of the magic powers that came with the mother's milk of innocence.

Time [or Mutability] ɪꜱ the [theme] tune my ladies [of sea-change] lend [bring to] their heartbreak [bad news], [and] from bald pavilions and the house of bread[9] Time [personified] tracks [like a slug] the sound [track] of shape [mortality] on man and cloud, [and] the ringing [death-knelling and also wringing] handprint [leaving its mark] on rose [sick] and icicle [melting].

'God is Death' would perhaps be the succinct statement to which Thomas is leading. No golf follows; more likely the 'oven' that he keeps threatening himself with (for example, *Letters*, p. 127/153). 'Doom' was one of his favourite words. It is not reserved only for 'deniers' (line 6) – though in this context that could mean everybody. *A Doom on the Sun* was the abortive novel Thomas was writing about this time (*Letters*, p. 134/160). That title about sums it up.

Sonnet VIII

The text for this sonnet could be St Paul in Galatians 2:20: 'I am crucified with Christ; nevertheless I live.' 'This portrait of the developing artist continues with the poet's crucifixion' (Tindall, p. 138). Or we can give Thomas a simile: this period was *like* a crucifixion. It is entirely possible that this sonnet was written in Donegal, Ireland, in one of the most remote cottages imaginable. Thomas went there with Geoffrey Grigson around 21 July 1935. Grigson left after two weeks, and Thomas was attacked by the silence and loneliness. 'There's a hill with a huge echo', he wrote to Bert Trick in an undated letter of August; 'you shout, and the dead Irish answer from behind the hill. I've forced them into confessing that they are sad, grey, lost, forgotten, dead and damned forever' (*Letters*, pp. 190–1/218). This is Dylan shouting into the Irish night, 'Why hast thou forsaken me?'

Another aspect of the Irish sojourn that may be pertinent is the fact that Thomas's neighbour and provider was a deaf farmer who, as he put it in the same letter, 'burns a red lamp under a religious magazine reproduction of somebody's hideous head of Christ; even his calendars are Christian: I always expect to find a cross in my

---

[9] I do not think learning that 'house of bread' is a literal translation of the place name Bethlehem can in itself manage to drag this poem for us into the Bible story. Still it is better than nothing, better than 'bald pavilions', an allusion which remains entirely shorn of plausible referent.

soup, or find a chicken crucified by skewers to a fatty plate' (*Letters*, p. 192/219). Thomas does not need Crashaw here; lurid pictorial Christianity is thrust at him at every meal: vinegar, blood, thorns, God's Mary, nails, thieves, sun.

> This [experience just gone through] WAS the [poet's] crucifixion on the mountain, [this was] Time's nerve [painfully preserved] in vinegar, [this was] the gallow[10] grave as tarred [by lynching] with blood as [were] the bright [piercing with light] thorns [sharp tears] I wept; . . .

The narrative then changes from past to present tense, a continuing present, the poet contemplating the immediate past.

> The world's [the cause of] my wound, God's Mary in her grief, bent like three trees [or crosses] and bird-papped [like the blood-giving pelican] through her shift, with pins [like thorns] for teardrops IS the long wound's woman [her pain equal to his own].

> This [thing experienced] WAS the sky, [and was] Jack [everyman] Christ, [and] each minstrel angle [or ministering angel] DROVE IN [hammered] the heaven-driven of the nails till . . .

At this moment in the poem there enters an epiphanic tone. The nails of the poet's crucifixion are as though driven in by the powers of heaven, and the effect is to produce a rainbow from his breast that encloses the world from pole to pole in its promise. The rainbow is 'three-coloured' as in Milton's *Paradise Lost* (Kleinman, p. 99). The world, which is the wound, is 'snail-waked' – pain is turning into its opposite with an immediate rush and then a slower realization.

> I [being] by the tree of thieves [Eden/Calvary], all glory's sawbones[11] UNSEX [as in sonnet I] the [my] skeleton [to utter nullity] this mountain [peak experience] minute, and by this blowclock [time/death destroying] witness [observing presence] of the sun [awakening power] SUFFER the heaven's [blessed] children [to come unto me] through my heartbeat [of love].

---

[10] As an adjective made from 'gallows' this would be a neologism. Thomas may have wanted the word to work to include bitter 'gall' and the archaic 'fearful'.

[11] These are bones that saw away the sex (and later suffer the children). This interpretation is required by the syntax when there is no comma at the end of the line, which was the case in the periodical printing and in *Twenty-five Poems*. The 1952 *Collected Poems* added a comma and thereby gave us 'sawbones' as colloquial doctor in apposition with the 'I'. This was a great justification for seeing the narrator 'I' as Christ, an interpretation hardly possible with the *Collected Poems* (1988), which deletes the comma.

'I am crucified with Christ: nevertheless I live.' Is this, then, a Christian conversion? Has Thomas come this far on the road to Tarsus? I think not. 'I care not a damn for Christ,' he wrote in a New Year letter for 1934, 'but only for his symbol, the symbol of death' (*Letters*, p. 82/99). He uses Christ to express what is happening to himself and others: 'All around us, now and forever, a spirit is bearing and killing and resurrecting a body.' Resurrection, yes; not The Resurrection. Just because he says 'suffer the heaven's children' in the last line of this poem does not mean he is a Mother Teresa. He is, I am convinced, using a New Testament phrase as a correlative for an incipient feeling of warmth and security after loneliness and fear.

In fact, the one thing we have on record from the weeks in Ireland is that Thomas was feeling a permanent homelessness. In his letter to Bert Trick in Swansea he talks about the Uplands and Cwmdonkin park, but says, 'I wouldn't be at home if I were at home' (*Letters*, p. 191/218):

> Everywhere I find myself seems to be nothing but a resting place between places that become resting places themselves. This is an essential state of being, an abstraction as concrete as a horsefly that's always worrying the back of your neck, plaguing and bothering before it draws blood. I'm at home when the blood's spilt, but only until the pricked vein heals up again, and my water and sugar turn red again, and the body and the brain, all the centres of movement, must shift or die. It may be a primary loneliness that makes me out-of-home.

When his blood is spilt – even if only by a horsefly – that's when he feels right with the world. This places Thomas smack in the middle of the Romantic poets and others who fall upon the thorns of life and recognize it as their proper existence. In Ireland he is 'further away than ever from the permanent world, the one real world in a house or a room' (*Letters*, p. 19/2247). He is writing this to his closest boyhood friend, Daniel Jones, with whom during his school years he created a sort of cocoon of irresponsible creativity (*Letters*, pp. 197–8/225):

> Here in this terribly out-of-the-way and lonely place, I feel the need for that world, the necessity for its going on, and the fear that it might be dying to you, that I'm trying to resurrect my bit of it, and make you realise again what you realise already; the importance of that world because it's the only one, the importance of us, too, and the fact that our

poems and music won't and can't be anything without it. Soon I'm going
out for a walk in the dark by myself; that'll make me happy as hell . . .

This may seem a long way from 'God's Mary in her grief' (line 4), but
it is the evidence we have, outside the poem, for the painful upheaval
that took place for Thomas during six lonely weeks on the west coast
of Ireland. Thomas's loneliness was always present to him, but he
intensified it by choice this once in his life, knowing the consequences. Knowing too what poems might result, he could not let
that cup pass from him.

Sonnet IX

This 'resurrection in the desert' (line 7) has none of the triumph and
ecstasy associated with the Christian story. Thomas seems too tired
for that. He just wants to put his sorrows to bed: 'With priest and
pharaoh bed my gentle wound' (line 11). He has chosen the imagery
of Egyptian mummification as more in keeping with his mood after
the struggle is over. Immortality lies in the materials and methods of
preparing the tomb and in the inscribing of passages from the Book
of the Dead on the mummy wrappings.

Kleinman proposed that Thomas took the first six lines of this
sonnet from E. A. Wallis Budge's *The Mummy* (Cambridge University Press, 1925), a likely enough source, given that the poet must
have got the allusions from somewhere. Speaking of a pyramid tomb
in upper Egypt, Budge says that

> on the back of the parchment sheath is a design, stamped in black ink . . .
> contained in a pad of vegetable fibre or linen . . . made of lamp black . . .
> It was customary to inscribe texts upon the mummy cloths . . . The nails
> of the hands are tinted with *hinna* . . . The king is shown wearing . . .
> royal head-dress, with a uraeus [serpent] over the forehead.

And so on. On the basis of many more such passages (Kleinman, pp.
108–10) we have the confidence to see what the poet is about,
without having to untangle the 'literal' narrative in which he has
combined, juggled and overweighted the elements of mummification,
the treatment of the corpse with chemistry and literary adornment.
Perhaps it is sufficient to say of these opening lines that the poet
seems ready to prepare himself and his work for cold storage.

It is more crucial to the kinetic of the poem to see what the scholars are doing: from the oracular archives (line 1) the mask of scholars rants (line 8). Actually the syntax gives us the mask of scholars ranting *gold* on 'such features', one of Thomas's stranger constructions. Maybe it is Wallis Budge who bestows the only immortality. The 'linen spirit' or embalming fluid only weds his 'long gentleman' to dusts and furies. He[12] is lying 'graveward' again, as in sonnet I, but with none of the cosmic disturbances. There is a great deal of resignation in the last four lines of the poem, and also quiet expectation:

> With priest [ritual] and pharaoh [royalty] BED my gentle wound [lessened pain], [cover my] world in the sand [of healing time], on the triangle [pyramid] landscape, with stones [amulets] of odyssey [long journey] for ash [wand] and garland [victory wreath] and rivers of the dead [Egyptian name for the Milky Way] around my neck [as penates].

He does not seem too uncomfortable. Perhaps these are, after all, images of home.

Sonnet X

This final sonnet reveals that we have been listening to a tale told by a 'sailor from a Christian voyage' (line 1) – a 'Rime of the Adolescent Mariner', perhaps. His crisis of faith of course has to do with Christianity in part, but we cannot be at all sure that the solution has been found within Christianity. I suspect the opposite. We have to bear in mind that Thomas was also writing at this time a 'new story' to be called 'Daniel Dom', based on *Pilgrim's Progress* but telling 'the adventures of Anti-Christian in his travels from the City of Zion to the City of Destruction' (*Letters*, p. 193/220), that is, the epitome of irreverence. Even though in Ireland he said, 'I'm lonely as Christ sometimes and can't even speak to my Father on an ethereal wave-

---

12   The context of sonnet I gave us 'the long gentleman' as Christ, or perhaps the Christ in the person, the Christian soul. It is probably safer to assume, as other sonnets have forced us to, that Christian imagery is just that: imagery, imagery for the poet's own stages of the cross. So the 'gentleman' figure will serve Thomas in various ways. Here it is in parallel with 'my gentle wound' and probably should be thought of as the poet's inner being.

length' (*Letters*, p. 190/127), he was not feeling Christian, just being flippant.

> LET the tale's sailor from a Christian voyage [ending faith] atlaswise [worldliwise] HOLD halfway off [agnostically] the dummy bay [unsubstantiated final conviction] Time's ship-racked [tortured] gospel [Christianity] on the globe I balance [undecided]: . . .

He is suspended, and suffering, and turning, and, in some part of him, yearning for the Day (he does capitalize it in line 12), but receiving no satisfaction.

The best evidence outside the sonnets for Thomas's dialectical struggle between faith and doubt can be found in letters, such as the New Year's Resolution letter for 1934 (*Letters*, p. 81/98):

> I so passionately believed and so passionately *want* to believe, in the magic of this burning and bewildering universe, in the meaning and the power of symbols, in the miracle of myself & of all mortals, in the divinity that is so near us and so longing to be nearer.

In sonnet X the 'word' is still blown hither and yon, and, on the seas that he is imaging and feeling, December's holly is still despairingly screwed into a crucified brow of thorns (line 6). He is balancing in a state of numb neutrality a world of troubles, like Atlas. Time's ship with its 'racked' gospel (literally: 'swaying from side to side' – not able to make up its mind) had better just stay where it is, halfway off the bay, which is still not ready for it, not yet a real home. Then we will all, us birds in a winged, bird-filled harbour (line 4), see Thomas's situation as it is: not belief, but a wish to believe.

> LET the first [fisherman] Peter [fishing] from a rainbow's quayrail [hope's harbour] ASK the tall fish [the potential mate] swept from the bible east [the source of the old religion], [']What rhubarb man [male member] peeled [skin rubbed off] in her foam-blue [Aphrodite-Mary] channel HAS SOWN a flying [ejaculated] garden [seeded] round that sea-ghost [the returned opportunity]?[']

This is the sort of question that could only be asked if the answer was the poet himself. It is a way of putting himself at the centre of the poem, and repeating the question about faith in a sustained sexual image. Seed is sown; is it the seed of doubt or of faith?

'When I was refugeeing across China (in 1937–9),' William
Empson remarked in a review of the *Collected Poems* in 1954, 'it was
worth carrying the poems of Dylan Thomas because they were
equally [like mathematics] inexhaustible' (*Casebook*, p. 112). He was
thinking mainly of the 'Altarwise by owl-light' sonnet series, which
he considered mannered, 'but when it is good it is ragingly good'
(*Casebook*, p. 114). He quotes the last four lines of sonnet X, and
comments on them:

> Green as beginning, let the garden diving
> Soar, with its two bark towers, to that Day
> When the worm builds with the gold straws of venom
> My nest of mercies in the rude, red tree.

> I hope I do not annoy anyone by explaining that the Cross of Jesus is also
> the male sexual organ; Dylan would only have thought that tiresomely
> obvious a basis for his remark. But when you get to the worms instead of
> the birds able to build something valuable in this tree, and the
> extraordinary shock of the voice of the poet in his reverence and release
> (at the end of the whole poem) when he gets to his nest, you do begin to
> wonder whether he meant something wiser than he knew.

What moves me is Empson's taking for granted that 'the rude, red
tree' is a conscious phallic symbol. Who can disagree? The aural pun
'rude/rood' gives us Christ's cross ('rood') and something 'rude' –
what else than what Empson suggests? The 'rhubarb man' sounds
equally rude. And 'the worm' (not 'worms', Mr Empson) will build
itself up as the venue of the Day of Judgement – or let us just say
Thomas's own red-letter day.

This phallic imagery has certainly desanctified the tale the sailor
from a Christian voyage had to tell. Have we here reached the
real subject of the sonnets? The 'long stick from the cradle'
(sonnet II); Abaddon as a bad one; and even the 'long gentleman'
himself? It would be wrong to go that far. Like the Christian
imagery, the phallic imagery is merely helping to do the work of
the poem, which is to provide metaphors for life, specifically
life as felt by the poet at the time of writing. So I think there are
just two penises present in sonnet X: the tree in the last line – why
else would it be rude and red? And the second would be the
'rhubarb man', who 'peeled' in a female's 'foam-blue channel', sows
seed into the air. They both represent, I believe, the agency of

regeneration, the thing that Thomas is asking for as the sonnet sequence ends.[13]

So Thomas has made a beginning at finding a position. He has made a garden in air; it is green with potentiality. Maybe it will fly. It could be a new Eden; it is an aeroplane powered by two trees, the two in Eden, here not only associated with 'fall' but also with 'soar'. The last two lines of the poem represent that state of mediation Thomas often wants to come to in a situation he has set up as a dichotomy between the forces of good and evil. The 'worm', 'venom', and 'the rude, red tree' (in one of its senses) would form the chord of evil, and the 'gold straws' and 'nest of mercies' would be the balance. The fusion of the two, in the hortatory voice, holds out a possible synthesis. It is as William Empson put it in his previously quoted review: Thomas's 'chief power as a stylist is to convey a sickened loathing which somehow at once (within the phrase) enforces a welcome for the eternal necessities of the world' (*Casebook*, p. 113). The 'eternal necessities' provide simple root meanings for these poems. The poet's dual reaction to these necessities, expressed *within the phrase*, is what buffets us. Thomas once spoke of 'the conscious rapidity with which I changed the angles of the images' (*Letters*, p. 77/94). These shifting angles are what we experience in dreams, when the dream process works on everyday events. Dreams seem to be trying out dramatic narrative permutations on life situations using unlikely settings and characters. The sleeping mind seems to yearn to expand in strange ways the range of human trials and feelings. When we see Thomas's poetry doing something similar, moving us through a wondrous landscape where images change their angle with dream-like but conscious rapidity, when we also know that the necessities of the world are being addressed by means of these myriad details, we might feel, with Empson, that Thomas's poem means 'something wiser than he knew' or, if we have an inclination to give the poet the benefit of the doubt, something which is the wisest that, at that time,

---

[13] The 'tall fish' would fit into this exhortation as Jesus Christ, widely represented as a fish in early symbology, except that the fish here does seem to have to be female, as there is no other referent for the 'her' of 'her foam-blue channel'. Thomas does not mind mixing his metaphors. Peter is there because of the fish metaphor; the rhubarb man is there because of the garden metaphor. I believe this would be Thomas's way of thinking about it. He would feel that the two metaphors would justify the presence of these two improbable characters. Most characteristics of the two need not operate, only that quality which the metaphor can use.

he knew. Who are we to say that the young poet could not see in his poem all that we can, or more?

Among those Killed in the Dawn Raid was a Man Aged a Hundred

(please turn to *Collected Poems*, p. 112)

When reading this poem on the BBC Overseas Service on 25 May 1942, Thomas commented that the title came from a headline in a newspaper. This is confirmed by the account of Charles Lautour: he and Thomas were working for Strand Films on location in Bradford 'about 1940–41' and saw the report of the air-raid death of a centenarian in another town, Hull. 'I remember we were both very taken up with this story of the old man, and talked wildly about it.'[1]

The poem begins flatly enough. Perhaps the only thing to look out for in the first five lines is the canal locks image, for when the locks yawn loose they are also jaws. Then the image of the old man begins to be magnified, somewhat along the lines of Ann Jones in 'After the funeral':

> TELL his street [knocked out] on its back [that] he stopped a sun [bomb] and the craters [the explosion made] of his eyes grew springshoots [exploding flowers] and fire when all the keys [of the houses] shot from the locks, and rang [in the explosion].

This description of the event already puts it on a cosmic plane. The final sextet of this fairly regular sonnet is a sort of refusal to mourn: no mundane funeral can match the glory of his passing into the elements of air.

---

[1] 'After a while Dylan turned over the script and on the back of the page wrote down words, changed them, crossed out and re-wrote. In a very short time he took a clean sheet and, using the incredible short stub of pencil he always wrote with whenever at least I saw him writing or he was working with me, wrote out complete the enclosed poem and gave it to me.' This note accompanies the manuscript of the poem at Texas.

DIG no more [in the bomb rubble] for the chains [or locks or bindings] of his [old] grey-haired heart. The heavenly ambulance [to rush him to heaven] drawn [attracted] by a wound assembling[2] [gathering up the remains] WAITS for the spade's ring on the [rib] cage. O KEEP his bones away from that common cart [the usual way to heaven], [for already] the morning is flying [with new power] on the wings of his age [in celebration of a hundred years] and a hundred storks [to replenish the population] perch [in honour] on the sun's right hand.

As Jacob Korg aptly summarizes it: 'Having thus passed into the fabric of nature in a pagan apotheosis, he has no need of the "common cart" of the passage into a formalized Christian heaven' (Korg, p. 116).

On the whole, Thomas has managed to avoid the dangers of sentimentality inherent in the news story. Except for the number of storks, this elegy could have been written for any victim of the air raids that so haunted Thomas's imagination.

---

[2] 'Assembling' was apparently supplied by Vernon Watkins. Line 11 of the draft sent to Watkins on 15 July 1941 began differently: 'I am a bit dubious about 'Through ruin' in the third line of the sextet. Originally I had "All day"' (*Letters*, p. 491/554). Since Watkins's reply to Thomas does not exist, we cannot know on what grounds the word 'Assembling' was recommended, but Thomas thanks him for it in the next letter: 'Thank you for "Assembling". Of course' (*Letters*, p. 492/554). This borrowed word exists in all published versions, from the first printing in *Life and Letters Today* of August 1941.

And death shall have no dominion

(please turn to *Collected Poems*, p. 56)

In conversation, A. E. Trick has said that this poem originated when he and Thomas had a friendly competition to see who could write the best poem on the subject of 'Immortality'.[1] The deliberateness of

---

[1] Trick's attempt was printed in a local paper and appears in *Collected Poems* (notes, p. 209). Thomas's was written as an early draft in a notebook in April 1933 (see *Notebook Poems*, p. 146).

this assignment does not absolutely preclude this poem's being evidence of a deeply rooted faith on the part of the young poet of nineteen, but it might make us wary.

The line which provides the title and begins and ends each stanza implies a Christian orthodoxy. Thomas took it from Romans 6: 9: 'Christ being raised from the dead dieth no more; death hath no dominion over him.' Lines 7–8 of the first stanza could fall into the Christian frame of resurrection: 'Though they go mad they shall be sane, / Though they sink through the sea they shall rise again.' But already in line 2 the 'dead men naked' have been given an entirely secular immortality in becoming one with the wind, moon and stars. Then there is a different tack before we end the stanza: 'though lovers be lost love shall not' – as though it is only important that the Platonic Idea of love be eternal, not individuals.

Stanza 2 seems to be saying that 'they' will not really die at all. Even in extreme situations like torture, they will not crack. Most of stanza 3 is a beautiful lament for dear departed, with no hint of immortality until lines 6–7 with its Donne image: 'Though they be mad and dead as nails / Heads of the characters hammer through the daisies.'[2] With their heads as hard as nails, the dead can, from underground, hammer daisies up through the surface of the earth into blossom. They are, in common parlance, 'pushing up daisies'. Which, no matter how you say it, is hardly what we think of as immortality. Nor is the penultimate line of the poem likely to be very satisfying in this regard. It exhorts us to 'break in the sun till the sun breaks down'. That is not very long as light years go, certainly not eternity.

The poem has a very powerful sense of defiance of death, but it is puzzling how this is accomplished. It is more in the reiteration of a strong rhythmical biblical phrase rather than any of the arguments sandwiched in between, which offer no religious consolation.

---

[2] Thomas knew of Donne's *The Devotions*, where man is described as earth, 'his hair a wild shrub growing out of the land' (*Letters*, p. 39/57).

A process in the weather of the heart

(please turn to *Collected Poems*, p. 10)

This is the quintessential 'process' poem, a term which has been used to categorize the majority of the poems in Thomas's first volume, *18 Poems* (see *Entrances*, pp. 57–80). It stands as an ideological signpost, announcing the theme of the parallel between the physical forces operating in the body and in the poet's state of mind. This is the point Thomas had thrust at Pamela Hansford Johnson in one of his earliest letters (5 November 1933 – *Letters*, p. 39/57):

> All thoughts and actions emanate from the body. Therefore the description of a thought or action – however abstruse it may be – can be beaten home by bringing it onto a physical level. Every idea, intuitive or intellectual, can be imaged and translated in terms of the body, its flesh, skin, blood, sinews, veins, glands, organs, cells, or senses.
>
> Through my small, bone-bound island I have learnt all I know, experienced all, and sensed all. All I write is inseparable from the island. As much as possible, therefore, I employ the scenery of the island to describe the scenery of my thoughts, the earthquakes of the body to describe the earthquakes of the heart.

Thomas was describing the kind of poetry he had already embarked upon, notably with 'The force that through the green fuse' of 12 October 1933. He had done at least eight such poems before 'A process in the weather of the heart', so he knew what he was about. This is the one 'process poem' that actually uses the word 'process'; it has the air of a formal demonstration.

Ambiguity, deliberate specific duality, is the essence of the method in the verse as in the metabolism of the body and the polar moods of the mental weather. For instance, in the first sentence of the poem, 'damp' and 'dry' are both in themselves ambiguous: dampness in most situations is felt to be unpleasant and dryness an improvement, but water is essential to life and a dry heart would be a dead one. In explicating the poem one takes what seems to be the dominant mood of the line, with full knowledge that a contrary may be imbedded in a wording which contains opposites as equivalences (see table).

Everything seems to contain its opposite as a hidden half. While a positive thing is happening, a negative is waiting, or is, within the

Lines	Wording	Equivalences
2–3:	'golden shot'	seed from the sun's shotgun and/or lightning flash
	'storms in the freezing tomb'	fertilizes the womb and/or blasts it
5–6:	'blood in the suns'	source of power and/or wounds bleeding
	'lights up the living worm'	engorging the penis and/or revealing mortality
11–12:	'the fathomed sea'	having depth and/or plumbed, ruled
	'breaks on unangled land'	brings water to previously unfishable land and/or destroying itself on an alien shore
13–15:	'the seed that makes a forest of the loin'	pubic hair and/or feral sexuality
	'forks half its fruit and half drops down slow in a sleeping wind'	sexual intercourse and conception with the alternative: wet dreams

same image, happening at the same time. The poem asserts that both forces, positive and negative, are together the process.

Lines 7–9 emphasize the downside of duality, which is inherent in mortality: the living eye foresees blindness, the fertilized womb ends with miscarriage as 'life leaks out'. And it all ends on a rather negative note:

> A process blows the moon into the sun,
> Pulls down the shabby curtains of the skin;
> And the heart gives up its dead.

The week before writing 'A process in the weather of the heart' Thomas had sent a letter to Pamela Hansford Johnson, which is described in her diary as 'rather depressing and acrid in tone' (MS at Buffalo). Unfortunately the letter is missing, but the poem well represents that mood. There is an overwhelming sense of mortality. The interchangeability of 'womb' and 'tomb' – which might be a cliché in a context less solemn than Thomas's early poems – here makes the dire point about universal process.[1]

---

[1] There was a literal interchange in the notebook. The original phrasing of ll. 8–9 was 'the tomb / Drives in a death'. The poet crosses out the 't' of 'tomb' and interlined a 'w', and so we have 'womb' in the final version, which only serves to make the assertion more fearful (*Notebook Poems*, p. 276).

Yet the positive side is there as a balance – the 'living worm', after all, 'forks half its fruit' (a harvesting image); and, though the 'shabby curtains of the skin' are pulled down by death, the stage hand, there is in the last line of the poem, where the heart gives up its dead as in a plague, an echo of Revelation 20: 13, 'And the sea gave up the dead in it.' If one can hear this resurrection theme here, then Thomas has managed once again to sneak in a positive ending to an otherwise fairly depressing poem.

A Refusal to Mourn the Death, by Fire, of a Child in London

(please turn to *Collected Poems*, p. 85)

Thomas's great funeral Mass, 'Ceremony After a Fire Raid', was published in May 1944, with its final organ 'voluntary', as he called it (*Letters*, p. 518/580):

> The masses of the sea
> The masses of the sea under
> The masses of the infant-bearing sea
> Erupt, fountain, and enter to utter for ever
> Glory glory glory
> The sundering ultimate kingdom of genesis' thunder.

After pulling out all the stops in this poem, Thomas could not contemplate any further elegy. But, a year later, the horror of the burnt children of London air raids had not gone away. He had to take it up again. It was a duty, as though he had been appointed the poet laureate of the Blitz. An alternate title for part II of 'Ceremony after a Fire Raid' is written on the Texas manuscript of that poem: 'Among Those Burned To Death Was a Child Aged A Few Hours.' Thomas was haunted by this nightmare and could only give himself rest by finding the proper form for expressing the pity and horror. The technique of reportage as used in the 1941 poem 'Among those Killed in the Dawn Raid was a Man Aged a Hundred' was obviously in his mind, but he could only, in the end, proceed when he finally found the deeply ironic title, 'A Refusal to Mourn' (which seems as though it should have a precedent in classic English literature, but apparently does not). The shocking title released him to write a masterpiece of controlled form and contained emotion, which amounts to a brilliant way of *not* refusing. In addition, there is the sense that if one can find and offer resignation in the face of such a death, or all our deaths, mourning perhaps *should* be refused. A different sort of attitude is called for.

> Never until the mankind-making[,] bird-beast-and-flower-fathering[,] and all-humbling darkness [the void that both creates and destroys] tells with silence the last light breaking [the end of the world] and the still hour is come of the sea tumbling in harness [the moon's control] and I must enter again the round zion [completed circle of life ending in the promised land] and the synagogue [holy place] of the ear of corn [i.e. entering nature], SHALL I LET PRAY [even] the shadow of a sound or sow [weep] my salt seed in the least valley of sackcloth [wailing raiment] to mourn the majesty and burning of the child's death.

Never will he say a word or shed a tear of mourning for this dead child until he dies. Then he will have joined her in the water and the wheat. As for now, he should say very little.

> I SHALL NOT MURDER [with overkill of words] the mankind [universal significance] of her going with a grave truth [oversolemn funereal triteness] nor BLASPHEME [by gross impropriety] down the stations of breath [the throat as stations of the Cross] with any further [more than he has already done] elegy of innocence and youth.

> Deep with the first dead [all who have gone before] LIES London's daughter [the one standing for many], robed in the long friends [the eternal elements of the earth], the grains beyond age [molecular particles], the dark veins [of ore] of her mother [earth], secret [unconspicuous] by the unmourning water of the riding [forever boat-bobbing] Thames.

The child is secure now with mother earth. She will not have to face another death. She is possessed of what we all must expect: the comfort of undisturbed oblivion.

There have been many suggestions for the meaning of that final evocative line, 'After the first death, there is no other.' I have gravitated to a minimalist interpretation. I hope I am not in violation of the poet's intention. The sense of haven could have been expressed in Christian terms, but I see no evidence of this is in the poem, whose emotive imagery comes rather from the Old Testament. If the first dead were to be specified, it would be Adam and Eve. But we do not, in the poem, go to Abraham's bosom; we are absorbed in the grain and veins of earth. After that, we are no more, and cannot die again. That the dignified pacing and lilt of the lines can convince us that this fate is a consolation is, to my mind, one of the great achievements in the poetry of our age.

A saint about to fall

(please turn to *Collected Poems*, p. 78)

The crucial lines to consider, in order to grasp the 'plot' of this poem, are lines 8–9 of the middle stanza. At exactly halfway into the poem, there is a blatant change of viewpoint. 'Heaven fell with his fall': and that is the end of heaven. In the next line, the fallen 'saint' is addressed directly: 'O wake in me in my house in the mud'.

Let us settle first what we definitely know about this. The 'house in the mud' is the cottage in Gosport Street, Laugharne, which Dylan and Caitlin rented on 1 May 1938. A letter written during their first week there said 'the sea is mostly mud' (*Letters*, p. 294/340), and another described the cottage as 'four rooms like stained boxes in a workman's and a fisherman's row, with a garden leading down to mud and sea' (*Letters*, p. 304/352). This is where Llewelyn was conceived – possibly on the first night in the place (he was born 30 January 1939).

The poem, I believe, takes us back to that first night: 'the double-bed is a swing band with coffin, oompah, slush-pump, gob-stick, and almost wakes the deaf, syphilitic neighbours' (*Letters*, p. 296/343, 16 May 1938). Of course the poem was not begun until they knew of the pregnancy, which was about the middle of July 1938 ('a very nice mistake, and neither of us worries at all' – *Letters*, p. 312/361, 13 July 1938). The poem was percolating in Thomas's mind by 24 August 1938 when he referred to the unborn Llewelyn as 'our saint or monster' (*Letters*, p. 318/367). The finished poem was sent to Vernon

Watkins on 14 October 1938 and was to be titled 'In September', indicating the month of its main composition. It is important to get the chronology right because the poem appeared in a periodical printing as 'Poem in the Ninth Month'. This title was suggested by Watkins, and Thomas promised to use it (*Letters*, p. 344/393), but it is quite misleading. As we have seen, the poem was written months before the birth.

I conclude that the saint falling from heaven is not being born: the setting is really conception. When the mother says 'O wake in me', that is the beginning of gestation not the end of it, the 'in me' means literally in her womb.

Once we are clear about the 'fall' as conception, we can also see that the poet takes that act as committing the child to this world. 'All the heavenly business I use', Thomas told Desmond Hawkins (*Letters*, p. 398/450), 'because it makes a famous and noble landscape from which to plunge this figure on to the bloody, war-barbed, etc earth.' What the child will face is, in the second part of the poem, phrased as a series of exhortations to the foetus, while yet in a newly conceived state, to wake and look at the world, and see what it will be born into.

O WAKE [become aware] in me [in the womb] in my house in the mud [fallen heaven] of the crotch of the squawking shores, [having been] flicked [moved quickly] from the carbolic[1] city [disinfected heaven] PUZZLE [contemplate with bewilderment like Job] in a bed of sores the scudding [driven by mortal winds] base of the familiar [previously seen from heaven] sky, [and] the lofty roots [the lowest part as seen from above] of the clouds. From an odd [strange] room in a split [off from heaven] house STARE, milk [of heaven] in your mouth, at the sour floods [of mortal existence] that bury [overcome] the sweet street [of heaven] slowly, [and] SEE [that] the skull of the earth is barbed [like Christ's crown of thorns] with a war of burning brains and hair.

The poem is telling the unborn child 'what a world it will see, what horrors and hells' (*Letters*, p. 328/377). Thomas told Watkins that the war scare of the Munich crisis of September 1938, 'a terrible war

---

[1] 'I agree that "carbolic" and "strike" cd be bettered, but, at the moment, I'll just leave them' (*Letters*, pp. 333/381–2). Thomas is here making a rejoinder to a letter from Vernon Watkins now not extant, so that we do not know what issues he was considering in relation to these two words. I take 'carbolic' to indicate the extreme cleanliness of heaven versus the mud of the saint's new home. The word 'strike' has many meanings – the one most appropriate to the womb is the movement of the fists of the foetus.

month' (*Letters*, p. 328/376), provided the violent visionary imagery of the poem, such as the last phrase quoted above. It 'might appear', he told Watkins, 'just a long jumble of my old anatomical clichés, but if, in the past, I've used "burning brains and hair" etc too loosely, this time I used them – as the only words – in dead earnest' (*Letters*, pp. 328/376–7).

STRIKE [thrust] in the time-bomb [set for nine months] town, RAISE [with shouting] the live rafters of the eardrum, THROW your fear [as though it were a Cronus, a cannibal] a parcel of stone [instead of yourself the foetus] through [across] the dark asylum [womb], lapped [held on the lap] among [child-slaying] herods WAIL as their [sword] blade marches in [to kill you] that the eyes are already murdered [i.e. the evil work has already been done and does not have to be done again], [that] the stocked heart [in stocks] is [already] forced [violated], and agony [already] has another mouth to feed.

In other words, the mother is telling the child how to be safe in the womb from all who might want to kill it. The safety lies in being already (being mortal) as good as dead and, on that ground, able to persuade the threatening ones to desist. The agony is, as it were, inherent in having been conceived, and cannot really be added to.

The foetus is then asked to witness its own birth-to-be:

O WAKE to see, after a noble [from heaven] fall, the old [primeval] mud hatch [give birth] again, [see] the horrid [causing fear] woe drip [in sweat during labour] from the dishrag hands [of the housewife, now exhausted mother] and the pressed sponge of the [perspiring] forehead, [and see] the breath draw back [in birth pangs] like a bolt through white oil [to open a white hot door] and [from the womb] a stranger [previously unknown] enter [from the womb] like iron [hurting].

Since this anticipation of the birth is present in the poem, Thomas was strictly correct in saying in a letter of 14 August 1939, 'It's a poem written on the birth of my son' (*Letters*, p. 398/450), but birth is not the whole, nor the main, story. The poet is even more misleading when he says in the same letter to Desmond Hawkins that 'about to fall' means 'to be born' – or let us say that Thomas was not at that point bothering to make a distinction between conception and birth. To be more precise he could have said that the 'fall' was the beginning of the whole birth process.

'Glory cracked like a flea' (stanza 2) is not an image of birth but of orgasm and its abrupt end. The 'saint' is not a Wordsworthian innocent trailing clouds of glory. The 'glory' here is 'la gloire' of sexual climax, and he is a saint only in terms of that moment of heaven in his parents' bedroom. The first lines of the poem do not actually say 'the earth moved' but image after image is saying heaven moved. The 'saint' in the seed is about to spill over the edge of heaven. The 'saint' is canonized by that moment of ecstasy, which is also an eruption leading to downfall – notably on the father's part.

I suggest that the first half of this poem is so charged with sexual innuendo that the only practical way of handling explication is to propose that readers give free rein to whatever skills they have with double entendres, with the assurance that they are unlikely to go far wrong. The hints in the rephrasement below point in the general direction.

A saint [sanctified in the act of love] [being] about to fall [with conception], the stained [with love juices] flats[2] of heaven [having been] hit [by earthquake] and razed [and raised] to [the level of] the kissed [in prayer] kite [hawk high] hems of his [prayer] shawl, on the last street wave [of the climactic earthquake] PRAISED the unwinding [ejaculating], song [flowing melody] by rock [seed after seed], of the woven [veined] wall [erection] of his father's house [tower] in the sands [sinking like a sandcastle], [praised] the vanishing [detumescence] of the musical [rhythmical] ship-work [bobbing on the sea] and the chucked [tossed out] bells [with their clappers], [and praised] the wound-down [expired] cough [expulsion of breath] of the blood counting [beating time with blood pulses] clock behind a [clock] face of hands [pointing out time],

HYMNED his shrivelling [getting smaller] flock on the angelic etna[3] of the last whirring featherlands [ultimate flailing of wings of the two-backed

---

[2] Thomas wrote about these lines to Desmond Hawkins (*Letters*, p. 398/450):

the stained flats, the lowlying lands, that is, *and* the apartment houses all discoloured by the grief of his going, ruined for ever by his departure (for heaven must fall with every falling saint): on the last wave of a flowing street before the cities flow to the edge of heaven where he stands about to fall, praising his making and unmaking & the dissolution of his father's house etc.

He offers Hawkins a double meaning of 'flats' to chew on without giving much away, except he adds that the 'father's house' is 'his father-on-the-earth's veins', which I take to be a way of talking about the phallus.

[3] Thomas managed perversely to explain these lines to Desmond Hawkins without

angel], [the father's] wind-heeled [fast-running] foot [or whatever] [stuck running] in the hole of a fireball [female ball of fire],

SANG on the last [hay] rick's tip [protuberance] [near] by spilled [exhausted] wine-wells until heaven [bliss] was hungry [famished] and the quick [alive] cut [stopped] Christbread [the wheat and wine of the love act] [became] spitting vinegar [sour sperm][;]

and all the mazes [intricate windings] of his praise and envious [of the father] tongue WERE WORKED [as on a tapestry] in flames and shells [of the sexual explosion].

It is as though the 'saint's' praising of the father's sexual efforts filled the mazes of the veins of the organ doing the work. The word 'envious' is interesting; it is not backed up by much in the context, but it is very striking, and must mean that the 'saint' is envious of the father. When you think of it (in the way I think Thomas might think of it), there is not too much incentive for the 'saint' to become incarnate except for an envy of the heaven that, in the moment of conception, gave him his sainthood.

If it is the orgasm he is envious of, then he is doomed to almost immediate disappointment.

Glory [the moment of bliss] CRACKED like a flea [squashed]. The sun-leaved [blazing] holy candlewoods [resinous trees easily ignited] DRIVELLED DOWN [in detumescence] to one singeing [not flaming] tree with a stub [remaining part of a cut tree] of black [burnt out] buds,

the [formerly] sweet, fish-gilled [at home in the sea] boats bringing blood [for the erection] LURCHED [now] through a scuttled [boat-sunken] sea with a hold of leeches [sucking away the blood] and straws [without tensile strength],

heaven [the moment of orgasm] FELL [coincident] with his fall [into incarnation] and one crocked [broken] bell BEAT [ineffectually] the left air [abandoned by heaven at the end of coition].

revealing the sexual subtext (*Letters*, p. 398/450): 'Standing on an angelic (belonging to heaven's angels & heavenly itself) volcanic hill (everything is in disruption, eruption) on the last feathers of his fatherlands (and whirring is a noise of wings).' Again Thomas's insistence that we take the narrative of the images 'literally' means he leaves to us the task of saying what this literal narrative is getting at. The heavenly earthquake is not just a piece of fancifulness (as the poet's limited explanation would leave it) but part of a narrative expressing what it means to be mortal.

So in the first part of the poem Thomas has rigorously trans-
mogrified the euphemistic cliché of orgasm as heavenly into a series
of visceral images getting closer to actuality by this literalization of
heaven's 'landscape'.

The last four lines of 'A saint about to fall' take us back to this
moment of conception.

> CRY joy that this witchlike midwife second [the moment of conception that
> makes a changeling of the saint] bullies [willy nilly] into rough seas [in
> which the foetus suffers much chopping and changing] you so gentle and
> makes with a flick of the thumb [penis] and sun [heat of love] a
> thundering bullring [struggle where death is inevitable] of your [formerly]
> silent [because empty] and girl-circled island [the womb].

Even the word 'midwife' does not get us to the actual birth. We have
still the shock of conception, which the poet wants to record as the
contrast between the heaven of love/sex and the violent physicality of
the growth of the womb, a premonition of birth into a murderous
world. The essence is captured in the line, 'Glory cracked like a flea'
(at the beginning of the second stanza). Thomas wrote to Watkins,
wondering if the line shocked him: 'I think you'll see it *must* come
there, or some equally grotesque contrast' (*Letters*, p. 328/376). The
production of a child is the end of the honeymoon: this is the
contrast Thomas must have felt as a fall. With a sinewy metaphysical
conceit he expressed this 'downer' through the situation of a seed
fertilized first in sainthood and immediately after in mud.

But Thomas, as often, wanted to end on a positive note, relying
here very much on the two words, 'Cry joy'. As he wrote to Vernon
Watkins (*Letters*, p. 328/377):

> The last four lines of the poem, especially the last but two, may seem
> ragged, but I've altered the rhythm purposely; 'you so gentle' must be very
> soft & gentle, & the last line must roar. It's an optimistic, taking-
> everything, poem. The two most important words are 'Cry Joy'.

We are asked to hear it as a cry of joy that glory cracks and the
womb then contains no saint but a mere mortal.

A Winter's Tale

(please turn to *Collected Poems*, p. 99)

The tale proper is a symbolic story of a man brought to death's door by love of a she-bird who eludes him but in the end saves him from despair, carrying him off to wedded paradise. It is a tale heard by the narrator as coming through the snowy evening from the distant past, perhaps medieval times; but his attention to it and the verve of the retelling makes us feel that it is his own story too. The narrator and the man of the story seem to fuse, but actually the poem is consistent in *talking about* the story in the present tense and *telling it* in the past tense. Walford Davies has clearly presented the way the poem's stanzas are apportioned (*Selected Poems*, p. 126): the present tense frame is contained in stanzas 1–2, 12–13, 15–16, 23–4, leaving for the story itself stanza 3–11, 14, 17–22, 25–6. With this reassurance as to the poem's methodology, readers should have no difficulty enjoying 'A Winter's Tale'. Thomas himself feared that it had not 'come off': 'It isn't really one piece, though, God I tried to make it one' (*Letters*, p. 548/611). I do not think there is any need to share the author's apprehension. A long ago mystical story experienced by someone in the present as his own: it comes off.

The ultimate meaning of an allegory like this resides in what it is saying about the poet's life. Thomas did not sit down one day and decide to write about a man and a she-bird, judging there would be a market for a medieval visionary love poem perhaps. He did not have to imagine a man who knelt and wept and prayed, whose 'naked need struck him howling and bowed' (stanza 8). He was that man, and had to write the poem because he could do no other. At least it is my instinct to go on that assumption. To me it brings more grandeur to the poem, not less. The she-bird would not be so interesting if it were not Caitlin Thomas.

When Thomas sent 'A Winter's Tale' to Vernon Watkins on 28 March 1945 he said he had been 'working on it for months' (*Letters*, p. 548/611). I believe the poem came to him when he took his family down from New Quay in mid-Wales to Caitlin's mother's house at Blashford, Ringwood, Hampshire, for Christmas 1944.[1] For this is a

---

[1] There is not at present any hard and fast proof of this Christmas 1944 visit, but they were in London at least by 14 December 1944 when Thomas recorded 'Quite Early One Morning' at the BBC. There is a letter sent from Gryphon Films in London on 19 December and another on 31 December 1944. These two dates would bracket a Christmas trip somewhere, and where else than Blashford?

Blashford poem; the lakes and the river-wended vale are what one finds in the Avon Valley there, not – unfortunately for some interpretations – at Fern Hill or any other location Thomas might have been in Wales. Bill Read went to see the place and presents a description with a photograph in his *The Days of Dylan Thomas* (pp. 86–7):

> Mrs Macnamara's house, the New Inn House, a charming old place at a fork in the road called Blashford, lies just outside the market town of Ringwood, Hampshire. Once it was a farm. Fields around the house are rambling flower gardens. Before its days as a farmhouse, more than a hundred years ago, it was a pub – The New Inn – and the public room, with its bay window, now serves as the family dining room. At the rear there is a modern addition – a woodshed converted into a one-story large rectangular room, the Big Room, with a writing table in front of a large window looking onto one section of the garden. It was in this studio room that Dylan worked and reworked many poems.

Read is speaking of an earlier period, soon after their marriage, when Dylan and Caitlin were at Blashford from October 1937 to April 1938. Paul Ferris in his biography gives us this picture of their honeymoon (quoting *Letters*, pp. 261/301–2):

> 'This is a very lovely place,' he wrote to Watkins late in October 1937. 'Caitlin & I ride into the New Forest every day, into Bluebell Wood or onto Cuckoo Hill. There's no one else about; Caitlin's mother is away; we are quiet and small and cigarette-stained and very young.' He liked to see them as two terrible children, said Caitlin; she remembered the start of their marriage as 'our first, know-nothing, lamb-sappy days'. When her sister Nicolette stayed there she would see them going off on the bus for a lunchtime beer in Ringwood and returning an hour later with paper bags of dolly mixtures and liquorice allsorts, and bottles of fizzy children's drinks, all of them things that Thomas loved. In the afternoon they disappeared to bed with the sweets and pop; their voices could be heard reading to one another. Some days they went to the coast and collected shells to use as counters in card games. Caitlin, by all accounts, was good for him sexually. Below the surface he was uneasy with women; probably she could comfort him as mother and mistress in ways he found agreeable or even essential. She was buxom then, and he was still skinny; she claimed to have carried him across streams under one arm. (Ferris, p. 162)

Dylan was twenty-three, Caitlin approximately the same age – actually ten months older, and, as she once put it, 'I think I was a bit stronger than him' (Ferris, p. 162). Yes, she could rise with him, 'flowering in her melting snow', as the last line of the poem has it.

> In those early days she could be quiet in company, sipping a beer or lemonade, lost in a dream; marriage, wrote Nicolette, 'quelled Caitlin's early wildness and soothed her scratchy grudge against the world'. But she never ceased to catch the eye, with her bright-coloured skirts and the high colour in her cheeks. Sometimes she looked bird-like – a bird of prey or paradise, depending on her mood. Nigel Henderson met her in London and found her 'like the figurehead of a ship, a fantastic poet's girl, a sort of corn-goddess'. (Ferris, p. 162)

These are the views from the outside; 'A Winter's Tale' is the inner story, an allegory of some seriously felt rejection followed by total abjection; and then surrender, in which the man is saved by the she-bird. One can quite easily imagine that some time during that outwardly idyllic honeymoon Caitlin asserted her great female power by withdrawing herself, that she went off somewhere, if only briefly, maybe just into herself or into her dancing, and left Dylan on his knees. We have the poem 'I make this in a warring absence' (finished about November 1937, only four months after their marriage) as testimony to rivalries and estrangements. 'A Winter's Tale' should be taken as a sequel to 'I make this in warring absence'. It is the love poem that Thomas had been waiting to write. Seven years after that time in the New Forest, with its sweets and also its presumed anxieties, the return winter visit to Blashford for Christmas 1944 made it possible for the poet to recall the first moment when he really felt accepted by his wife, when he 'unrolled / The scrolls of fire that burned in his heart and head'. Out of the 'sheep white smoke' from a neighbouring farm house he created the mystical she-bird that brought him to 'the home of prayers and fires', his own death, or a desolation like death, which corresponded to the worst of the winter of 1937–8: 'at that point of love' he felt a 'nameless need', he felt 'forsaken and afraid', stumbled through the snow 'all night lost and long wading in the wake of' the phantom of perfect bliss. In the poem he began to write during Christmas 1944 this was a 'she-bird' that danced ahead of him, torturing him, before the miracle of acceptance occurred.

The 'tale ended', according to the poem, at stanza 22. Of the four remaining stanzas, the first two represent the mood he has come to in writing the poem in January–March 1945. The visionary winter's tale, with its magics and emotions, has been fully told. The poet is depleted.

> The dancing [the tale] PERISHES on the white, no longer growing [village] green, and, [the] minstrel [now] dead, the singing BREAKS [off] in the snow shoed [for dancing] villages of wishes that once cut [carved in the snow] the figures of birds on the deep bread [snow] and over the glazed [with ice] lakes skated [figured] the shapes of fishes flying [amazingly]. The [love] rite IS SHORN [finished] of nightingale [beauty] and centaur dead horse [mythic marvel]. The springs [of feeling] WITHER back. Lines of age [poetry grown old] SLEEP on the stones [pages] till trumpeting dawn [Judgment Day]. Exultation LIES DOWN [tired]. Time BURIES [in memory] the spring weather that belled and bounded with the dew reborn.

'Spring weather' – yes, the tale really does end, in the final two stanzas of the poem, with spring and rebirth, with a new life of love for the couple, though expressed mystically. The word 'For' begins an explanation of how the dew has been 'reborn':

> For the bird lay bedded
> In a choir of wings, as though she slept or died,
> And the wings glided wide and he was hymned and wedded,
> And through the thighs of the engulfing bride,
> The woman breasted and the heaven headed
>
> Bird, he was brought low,
> Burning in the bride bed of love, in the whirl-
> Pool at the wanting centre, in the folds
> Of paradise, in the spun bud of the world.
> And she rose with him flowering in her melting snow.

Poets' failures have shown us how difficult it is to express ecstasy in a convincing manner. I am convinced by Thomas in the last two stanzas of 'A Winter's Tale'. The relief that a woman can bring, with her strong, nest-making presence, to a man's agonies: this is marvellously written down, lines on ice.

Ballad of the Long-legged Bait

(please turn to *Collected Poems*, p. 126)

This is far from a conventional ballad. Vernon Watkins had, at the time, been doing some quasi-ballads, such as 'Ballad of the Rough Sea'. Thomas may have been trying to top him. A 'rough sea' would suggest to Thomas, if not to Watkins, the whole buffeting mishmash of sex.

Thomas told John Davenport in a letter of 8 January 1941: 'I've been sitting down trying to write a poem about a man who fished with a woman for bait and caught a horrible collection' (*Letters*, p. 472/533). Do not expect anything seductive here. The sea-fishing narrative imbues the poem with imagery of the most metaphysical sort – nothing warm or pruriently physical. According to John Malcolm Brinnin in *Dylan Thomas in America* (p. 16), Thomas's three-word summary of 'Ballad of the Long-legged Bait' was 'so lewd and searing as to stop conversation altogether'. The poem has a similar jaw-dropping effect on the reader for its audacity. Paul Ferris found out what the three words were and quoted them in his biography (Penguin edition, p. 251). The first two words were 'A gigantic'. The third, a four-letter word, tells the whole story – except that as the overriding factor, and the final product, we have another four-letter word, the p-o-e-m.

I believe the poem is as described above. Within the prowess and decline of the single sex act, however, Thomas seems to be packing half a lifetime's sexual history. Sitting at the bar one afternoon at Cavanagh's on West 23rd Street, New York, Thomas told William York Tindall what the poem was about: A young man goes fishing for sexual experience and 'catches the church and the village green' (p. 248). Tindall interpreted this as 'the wantoning that leads to the sobrieties and responsibilities of marriage. A happy boy becomes an adult with mixed feelings. The catcher is caught' (p. 248). There are the unforgettable lines towards the end of the poem where the town leads 'her prodigal home to his terror, / The furious ox-killing house of love' (stanza 50) and it seems that the fisherman is to be a violent martyr to domesticity. But we see nothing further along these lines, and the final scene has him standing alone at the door of his home 'with his long-legged heart in his hand'. He is subdued, certainly; but is there also an air of expectancy of return to the sea? In the archetypal sex act, the man every time begins as a happy boy going fishing and ends with mixed feelings, back on land, stranded.

If, then, our ballad presents an archetypal act under which all premarital sex is subsumed, we will probably have to forgo the normal expectations of narrative where one event causes another succeeding event. To avoid the frustration of attempting to find normally motivated dramatic action, we will be better off if we take these narrated experiences as a series of tableaux, dioramas that constitute a thesaurus of sexual intercourse.

The first diorama is the embarkation. The bows glide down the launching ramp to begin the rampage. The anchor is already free, mast high (stanza 2), a phallic erection, indeed. Pretty soon (stanza 10) the anchor will be miles high, in a storm which is ready to bellow and fall, ready to blow the rain from its throat, ready to aim and fire at the starlit sky and rake with its bullets the firmament where Christ's blood streams. And immediately (not to say prematurely) we have 'oil and bubbles' on the water (stanzas 11–12). End of first scene.

We turn now to the long-legged girl (stanza 6) thrown into the sea 'with his hooks through her lips'. Tindall (p. 251) refers to a local Carmarthen story of a man hooking through the lips a mermaid in the river Towy: a good enough source, though it has not been proved that Thomas knew of it, never mind needed it. The fisherman's hearing the bait 'buck in the wake and tussle in a shoal of loves' (stanza 8) can be thought of as producing the extraordinary erection of the anchor into the clouds and the 'oil and bubble', the consequent rainfall from the storm's 'fuming bows and ram of ice'.

The poem could have ended right here. There isn't much else a man can do. But the poem goes on. The girl takes over. The 'bushed bait'[1] on his rod ('lips' as labia?) is dodging the whales, 'those humpbacked tons' (stanza 13). She nips and dives (stanza 15) 'Till every beast blared down in a swerve / Till every turtle crushed from his shell / Till every bone in the rushing grave / Rose and crowed and fell!' Listening to the force of this imagery we must conclude that there has been another wave of orgasm, continuing through stanzas 16–20: 'My mast is a bell-spire . . . my decks are drums.' Someone called Samson Jack, as the fisherman was in some of the worksheets of the 'Ballad'

---

[1] 'Bushed' means 'pushed and butted' in a now obsolete sense, but one completely appropriate here. The modern 'bushed' as referring to pubic hair or a state of tiredness is gratuitous.

in the Buffalo library, should have stamina enough. Male sensuality is only part of the story, however. Interwoven is a sense of threat from the woman (Samson's problem too, one might recall). Thomas told Tindall that 'whales mean rivals' (p. 254). So, when the 'bulls of Biscay and their calves' are making under the sea 'the long-legged beautiful bait their wives', this is 'bad news' (stanza 18). Caitlin's thinking about other men during sex is apparently something that Dylan knew about. We have it in 'Into her lying down head' too. She no doubt knew how to wound her prodigal with such taunting during fights.[2]

Stanzas 16–21, then, will be the diorama of the female's ignoring, or using, poor Samson Jack and making out in her own voyage. To his dismay, he has to work the rod, while sea creatures are lured to bring the bait to climax, until 'the seal has kissed her dead' and she lies, finished, on the 'cruel bed' of the sea (stanza 21). Apropos this image, Vernon Watkins, who 'saw this poem grow from its first fifteen lines through all stages of its composition', reported (*Portrait of a Friend*, p. 91):

> It was so much a visual poem that he made a coloured picture for it which he pinned on the wall of his room, a picture of a woman lying at the bottom of the sea. She was a new Loreley revealing the pitfalls of destruction awaiting those who attempted to put off the flesh.

Watkins's idea that the bait has 'attempted to put off the flesh' seems wide of the mark. There is no sign of frigidity or self-denial here, only completion of desire. She is the 'wanting flesh' (stanza 23) not in the sense of lacking flesh but in being lustful – first, as a measure of the man's lust and the threat that that is to him, and, second, as lusting in her own right – the man's 'enemy' in both aspects.

At this juncture, when there is quietude 'old as water and plain as an eel' (stanza 24), we might pause and say something about the degree of obscurity in these images. For instance, why water should be linked with 'old' and an eel be called 'plain' is the kind of puzzle that Thomas continually throws out to the enquiring mind. But, when you come to think of it, water *is* old and an eel *is* quite plain. I suppose the thing we resist more is that this can be proposed as an appropriate description of the calm post coitus. But, again, old water

---

[2] We have a right to speak biographically: the names 'Dylan and Caitlin' appear on p. 32 of the 'Ballad' worksheets at Buffalo.

and a plain eel are not radically inappropriate representations for what is left after sex. What is perhaps more strange is why these words should be sung and howled, respectively, by a nightingale and hyena, 'rejoicing for that drifting death' (stanza 22). Much of the 'Ballad' from the beginning has been put into the mouths of entities who only by great poetic licence would speak such lines: 'the looking land' (stanza 3), 'the dwindling ships' (stanza 6), 'the cathedral chimes' (stanza 9), 'the whirled boat' (stanza 17). All these narrate the action and comment on it. We have here another of Thomas's devices for moving a poem forward unstraightforwardly. It certainly adds to the dream-like quality of the poem if 'She longs among [sea-]horses and angels [angel-fish]' are words that that the 'rocked buoys' float out in their chimes across the water (stanza 7). To puzzle over how Thomas assigns these speeches is probably not wise. In a sense, it does not matter who says what so long as it gets said and the poet achieves his purpose of filling the poem with qualities and happenings that add up to a total effect. In the case of the nightingale (romantic love) and hyena (love as carrion) the poet expresses in a compressed way the whole spectrum of love's condition, as we say goodbye to sex in two images: (1) as bread scattered on the water and eaten by gulls (stanza 24); and (2) as a corpse on the sea-bed (stanza 25). Again, appropriateness is pushed to its limits. But that is Thomas's way, his unique achievement: to dare us to see disparate things as appropriate. Who says that metaphors should not be mixed? The mind is stretched to subsume mixed metaphors, if not logically then intuitively, under a single notion that sustains the poem.

The poem proceeds with other things that have disappeared along with 'his flame of brides' (stanza 27). The first to go is 'The tempter under the eyelid / Who shows to the selves asleep / Mast-high moon-white women naked / Walking in wishes and lovely for shame.' This reference to sexually arousing night thoughts is a nice glimpse into what we can assume was the source of the 'long-legged bait' herself: she is the work of the nocturnal tempter. Caitlin enters the poem as the proverbial succubus.

Then follow several biblical references (stanzas 27–9). The first is to the Apocrypha story of the bearded elders spying on the beautiful Susanna while she is bathing; hence, to denote the end of sexual desire, she is imaged as drowned in a stream of beards. The second reference is to Sheba, King Solomon's partner in the Song of Songs; now she also is drowned, and only king crabs make advances. A third reference, 'Sin who had a woman's shape', is Milton's Eve, no doubt; but one might prefer to think of Delilah, to give Samson's nemesis a proper place in the poem. Finally, Mr Sin himself, 'that bird's dropping' (stanza 29) 'melted away' when the bait's breath was 'vaulted' (that is, put into a vault or coffin). And for good measure, Venus, the goddess of amatory affairs, is 'star-struck' in the wound of love, and the 'ruins' of sensuality make 'seasons' over the 'liquid world' (stanza 30).

But Thomas's sense of reality always requires the di-polar, and we might think here of 'the boys of summer in their ruin'. These arch-bifurcators 'split up the brawned womb's weathers', summoning death 'from a summer woman' but also a 'muscling life from lovers in their cramp' (*Collected Poems*, pp. 7–9). Death is never unopposed: 'O see the pulse of summer in the ice'. Death here, in 'Ballad of the Long-legged Bait', is the dying in love's climax, and the 'sensual ruins' of stanza 30 initiate a new pulse. I think 'making seasons over the liquid world' is code for gestation, and the line 'White springs in the dark' is pivotal to the poem. Out of the dark something white springs. Seasons are made. The poet has not prepared us for anything so positive at this moment, but that never seems to stop him from expecting his words to pull off these sudden shifts from pole to pole, here from negative to positive, from black to white.

The reversal of sexual death is conception. The fisherman has 'no more desire than a ghost' (stanza 31), but the lightning flash of stanza 32 indicates that something other than passion has been ignited: 'Oh miracle of fishes! The long dead bite!' (stanza 35). The catch that comes up with the bait in stanzas 34–8 is a 'heavy haul' that he must 'strike' (that is, lower as cargo into the hold). 'His fathers cling to the hand of the girl' (stanza 37): the genetic role of the ancestors in conception is a notion we find elsewhere in Thomas, in 'A grief ago', for instance ('Let her inhale her dead, through seed and solid / Draw in their seas'). The fact is flatly stated in stanza 39: 'Time is bearing another son.'

That Thomas associates this new development with the boat's swimming into 'the six-year weather' (stanza 33) is something that cannot be ignored, though its specificity is a problem. Perhaps it should be taken as something as general as the 'seven-year itch', six years being long enough for the sexual passions to freeze up and at the same time produce the miraculous conception. This would, then, be one of those moments in the poem where the diorama widens to take in a long view, which is then miniaturized as a mood or stage within the single sex act.[3]

If the phrase 'the six-year weather' seems to burst the seams of the poem-as-single-sex-act container, we can only surmise that the poet was not concerned on this score. Inconsistencies of certain kinds did not bother him. He had his eye on something else, a poem of its unique shape and parts, and a unity which makes nothing mentioned inconsistent. It is our job to make the best of it, to make the very best we can out of the poet's apparent arbitrariness and establish a meaning from the aggregation of disparities. The point then? 'Time is bearing another son.'

But in this stanza 39, a stanza given prominence by its italicization, there is a violent intervention in the birth process.

> *Time is bearing another son.*
> *Kill Time! She turns in her pain!*
> *The oak is felled in the acorn*
> *And the hawk in the egg kills the wren.*

Again, I am going to assume it is too unproductive to try to settle why the people who have been assigned these lines should want to say them. The words demand to be spoken, and that is all that matters in this drama of fluid characters where the poet hands out parts to whomever is around. Be that as it may, 'Kill Time!' is an exhortation to murder. Time is giving birth, and the birth must be stopped. The mother 'turns in her pain' as the birth is ruthlessly aborted. The oak that could have been is killed in the seed; the wren that could have been is killed by a hawk, the twin in the egg. In short: one dies in sex and produces life, which new life is then killed.

There is no record in the biographies of an abortion at this time or,

---

[3] If sex is to be thought of as going on for six years before conception, this is not true of the poet's actual marriage. Llewelyn was conceived within the first year after the wedding in July 1937. There may have been another unannounced conception in January 1941 at the time the 'Ballad' was begun, which would be the beginning of the sixth year from the time the couple first met in April 1936. But this would be such private knowledge that there must be a more public meaning. In a letter Thomas once railed against the delay between onset of puberty and marriage: 'Sex must be caged up for six or more years' (*Letters*, p. 59/76). So that 'six-year weather' could be his shorthand way of referring to the years of youthful sexual desire, or the culmination of them in marriage.

outside of this stanza, thoughts of abortion.[4] But here it is certainly given emphasis. It is the most horrible of the 'horrible collection' dragged from the sea of sex. It is so horrible that the next stanzas (40 and 41) portray god (who started the fiery universe and died, as it were, at the stake) as also coming up with the bait, and weeping. It is a tableau of extreme unction.

At this extremity the voyage out ends, and the return home is begun. Stanzas 42–52 are a sustained image of the sea being overlaid piecemeal with things pertaining to the land ('the surge is sown with barley', etc.). These stanzas flow with a certain ease as we are rehabilitated into the familiar. The 'Time' of stanza 44, for instance, is a much more mundane thing than 'Time' of stanza 39. The surreal horses of the sea become – well, not quite ordinary yet, as their manes still have thunderbolts in them (stanza 48). Jack is slowly getting back to the town from which he started. The poet gives us cities in the superlative degree: Rome, London, and 'Sodom Tomorrow'. In this last one, Thomas clearly cannot resist playing with words even at his most serious. 'Sodom Tomorrow' rhymes with Sodom and Gomorrah. Those wretched towns are restored by the benediction of pun. There *is* a future after cursed debauchery.

What is the diorama of the future? Tindall's memory of Thomas's summary was that the profligate 'catches the church and village green' (p. 248). It sounds as though the hero has, through his voyage, turned finally to religion and a settled family life. I do not believe that the poem bears out this conclusion. 'Steeples' are mentioned as part of the approaching town (stanza 49) but, unless one is to interpret the 'furious ox-killing house of love' (stanza 50) as a church (which I do not), the church as such only appears in the penultimate stanza: 'The anchor dives through the floors of a church'. I take this to be an image of detumescence to match the hyperbole of the anchor at mast-high erection at the beginning of the voyage. The church is used in this image because it has tombs for the anchor to dive into, where there is still the lingering sound of the sea. That 'the pacing, famous sea' still has its speech (stanza 53) is, I think, a strong hint about the future. The bait may be 'drowned among hayricks', but the sea is still 'talkative' (stanza 53). There is an air of finality about the 'ox-killing house of love' (stanza 50) – and I do believe that Thomas wanted at that moment to assert that binding love can be the outcome of sex – but the

---

[4] As Robert Williams has been at pains to demonstrate in his unpublished work, Thomas may have been emotionally damaged by learning in his teens of the fact that his parents' first child was stillborn.

final lines present a much more tentative picture. The fisherman is lost on the land – but can that be other than temporary?

> He stands alone at the door of his home,
> With his long-legged heart in his hand.

Is he standing facing the door and therefore a petitioner? Or is he at his door in a moment of stasis, alone, forlorn but looking outward, ready to move with his heart after an interval? Thomas's acumen – it does not call for a great deal and Thomas had plenty – would see that cyclical sexuality is what is true to life, and he would not be inclined to run counter to that. The poem does not require a dead end.

Note on 'Ballad of the Long-legged Bait'

Rimbaud's *Bateau ivre* has been proposed as a source for this poem. Thomas knew Norman Cameron's translation in *New Verse* (June– July 1936). However, he disowned this influence, and I see no similarity to speak of.

Thomas's prose piece, 'An Adventure from a Work in Progress' has a boat voyage and shares much of its vocabulary with the 'Ballad'; but, since it is more stubbornly obscure than the poem, it offers no opportunity for elucidation.

Because the pleasure-bird whistles

(please turn to *Collected Poems*, p. 67)

Writing to Henry Treece on 31 December 1938 – the date is significant – Thomas said he would 'have a poem, not a very long one, completed by the middle of January' (*Letters*, p. 348/398). He was writing a poem about looking back on the old year just ending. By the time it was sent out for publication early in February (*Letters*, p. 355/406) he had shifted it a little. It was entitled 'January 1939', and was a prayer that 1939 would not be as bad as 'the past table', 1938. Being a 'present grace', as it were at the beginning of a meal, Thomas saw it as a kind of preface, and placed it first in *The Map of Love*, the collection published that year.

A desolate year's end produced a rather disconsolate poem. Thomas was confined at Blashford with Caitlin and her mother. He told Charles Fisher on about 16 January 1939 (*Letters*, p. 352/403):

> I sit and hate my mother-in-law, glowering at her from corners and grumbling about her in the sad, sticky quiet of the lavatory, I take little walks over the Bad Earth. Our baby should be born at the end of next week, we wait and it kicks. Lack of money still pours in.

And in a letter of 26 January 1939, when 'half a poem', that is, 'Because the pleasure-bird whistles', was on his table, he is blatant to Henry Treece about his mood (*Letters*, p. 353/404). 'I'm not feeling better. I'm worried and lazy and morose, I've got a hundred headaches and a barbed mouth, I hate every living person with the exception of a Mrs MacCarthy who lives in Chelsea.'

The poem grows out of this despondent mood, and, such is the depth of the gloom, we wonder if it can transcend it. At first it seems unlikely.

> Because the pleasure-bird whistles after the hot wires,
> Shall the blind horse sing sweeter?

Just because it is thought that suffering has helped some linnet-poets to write, shall *this* suffering horse be expected to sing sweeter? The answer implied is that the poet could not be expected to do so.

Yet there is more in these lines than special pleading. We can be confident of this because Thomas himself commented on them. In a letter of 14 August 1939 to Desmond Hawkins he said (*Letters*, p. 396/448): 'The poem begins with a queer question about a bird and a horse: because one thing is made sweeter (qualify this word) through suffering what it doesn't understand, does that mean everything is sweeter through incomprehensible, or blind, suffering?' The poet is reminding us of what the logic of the poem requires us to see in this rhetorical question. It is not the bird's suffering as such, but its blindness, that makes it sing sweeter.[1] That does not, however, mean

---

[1] This is a folk tradition without factual basis, as reference to Thomas's possible source, Arthur Mee's *Children's Encyclopedia*, would attest. (I am indebted to Robert Williams for giving me the specific page number for this item, p. 2057.) The horse of Thomas's image does not come out of tradition, but from a dream. As Gwen Watkins tells it in *Portrait of a Friend* (p. 68), Thomas related a dream

that a poet will write better poetry with his head in the sand. Thomas, by using a sort of Aesop fable, is in an unexpected way raising the question of social awareness in poetry.

The next two lines of the poem indicate parenthetically how aware the poet is of his practice of utilizing symbols – here animal symbols – to make his points:

> Convenient bird and beast lie lodged to suffer
> The supper and knives of a mood.

Thomas explains to Hawkins (*Letters*, pp. 396/448–9):

> Then I, the putter of the question, turn momentarily aside from the question and, in a sort of burst of technical confidence, say that the bird and beast are merely convenient symbols that just *have* to suffer what my mood dictates, just *have* to be the objects my mood (wit or temper? but here 'mood' alone) has decided to make a meal upon and also the symbolic implements with which I cut the meal and objects up.

This is the poet commenting self-reflectively on his own methodology. The slight tinge of apology in these lines adds to the melancholy of the poem. It is as though, given the sorry state of things, the poetry can only splutter into explanation.

In lines 5–12 we have a picture of a man who is, in Thomas's words (*Letters*, p. 396/448), 'standing suffering on the tip of the new year and refusing, blindly, to look back at, if you like, the *lessons* of the past year to help him'. This is the poet's alter ego, the drugged part of himself:

> In the sniffed [like cocaine] and poured [like absinthe] snow on the tip of the tongue [the can't quite remember part] of the year that clouts [or clots[2]] the spittle [of the mouth that should speak] like bubbles [bursting] with broken rooms,
>   an enamoured [narcissus] man alone by the twigs [campfire] of his eyes, two fires, and camped [unsettled] in the drug-white [snow] shower of [bad] nerves and food [insubstantial], SAVOURS [merely] the lick [of the tongue] of the times [events] through a deadly [cold] wood of hair [in front of his eyes] in a wind that plucked a goose [making snow], nor ever,

'in which a horse stood in a cage made of wires which gradually became red-hot, on which a man standing by said, "He sings better now." ' The red-hot wires make the connection to the blinding of the bird.

[2] Thomas wrote a parallel phrase in a letter to Watkins of 8 January 1939, that the truth must be made effective or the result may well be a 'clot' of truths (*Letters*, p. 351/401).

as the wild [prophetic] tongue [of the new year] breaks its tomb [like Christ to speak], ROUNDS [turns round] to look at the red, wagged [used for talking] root [of the tongue].

This 'enamoured' man, who cannot see beyond himself, who cannot look to the root causes of things, this is no man for these times. Why will he not look back? Does he fear the same fate as Lot's wife, the figure in Genesis who was turned to a pillar of salt for looking back at Sodom? When the poet speaks in the first person in the next lines (lines 13–19) he says *he* is not afraid to look back.

Because there stands, [being] one story [exemplum] out of the bum city [Sodom], that frozen [immobile] [Lot's] wife whose juices drift like a fixed [Dead] sea secretly [hidden] in statuary [a pillar], SHALL I, struck [in epiphany] on the hot [unfrozen] and rocked [unfixed] street, not SPIN to stare at an old year toppling and burning [like Sodom] in the muddle of towers and galleries like the mauled [much handled] pictures of boys [cigarette cards swapped by boys]?

London would be Dylan's Sodom. He had made a recent trip to the capital and was rather jaded. He told Vernon Watkins on 20 December 1938 (*Letters*, pp. 343/392–3):

I've just come back from three dark days in London, city of the restless dead. It really is an insane city, & filled me with terror. Every pavement drills through your soles to your scalp, and out pops a lamp-post covered with hair. I'm not going to London again for years; its intelligentsia is so hurried in the head that nothing stays there; its glamour smells of goat; there's no difference between good and bad.

The whole of civilization seems likewise bent on its own destruction; but the poet's job as a writer is to look at it squarely, to assert the 'difference between good and bad'.

The next two lines of the poem, like lines 3–4, which Thomas himself thought might be 'put in a pair of brackets' (*Letters*, p. 396/448), are another self-conscious comment on what he has just done poetically, which is to have made substantive use of the story of Lot's wife and Sodom:

The salt person and blasted place
I furnish with the meat of a fable.

With the word 'meat' Thomas is continuing the food imagery. That the preceding year should be 'food for thought' is the basic conceit of the poem and it could have developed along the lines of the radio talk, 'The Crumbs of One Man's Year', of 1946 (*Broadcasts*, p. 153):

> Slung as though in a hammock, or a lull, between one Christmas for ever over and a New Year nearing full of relentless surprises, waywardly and gladly I pry back at those wizening twelve months and see only a waltzing snippet of the tipsy-turvey times, flickers of vistas, flashes of queer fishes, patches and chequers of a bard's-eye view.

This later broadcast piece went on to review the year, as Thomas intended to do with the poem. In sending 'Because the pleasure-bird whistles' to Vernon Watkins, 4 February 1939, Thomas said (*Letters*, pp. 354–5/406):

> Tell me: is it too short? Do I end before the point? does it need more room to work to a meaning, any expansion? I intended it as a longer & more ambitious thing, but stopped it suddenly thinking it was complete. How do you feel about it?

Since the 'Crumbs of One Man's Year' broadcast extended itself only by means of whimsical snippets, we can perhaps be happy that the poem did not go on further.

A point *is* made in the last four lines, a highly serious point. The only reason for expanding it would be that, as it stands in its concise and oblique imagery, its seriousness can hardly be credited.

> If the dead starve, their stomachs turn to tumble
> An upright man in the antipodes
> Or the spray-based and rock-chested sea:
> Over the past table I repeat this present grace.

I paraphrase this as: if anyone anywhere is starving to death, that individual's suffering undermines the poise of any upright person, even on the opposite side of the world or anywhere on the seven seas; and this is what one should think of as one sits down to one's own meal. In short, this is an extremely humanitarian grace to be repeated as a mantra before the feast or famine of the years.

Because a poet with Thomas's later reputation for selfishness could not have written these lines of universal caring, it is necessary to make some effort to discover the poet who did. Caitlin, who had harsh words to say about Dylan's waywardness, is also able to say that 'Dylan's philosophy was really that of the man who sympathises with the poor and downtrodden and looks to the Left for an answer' (*Caitlin*, p. 71). In this she was echoing Augustus John: 'He was not a student of sociology, but, I think, like so many of his generation, discovered in himself a fellow-feeling for the underdog' (*Adam*, p. 10). Augustus John also asserted that Dylan told him that he had joined the Communist Party, but Bert Trick, Thomas's left-wing mentor in Swansea, assured Constantine FitzGibbon 'that Dylan was not a Communist during this Swansea period' (FitzGibbon, p. 78) and Randolph Swingler did the same for the London period (FitzGibbon, p. 80). Jack Lindsay also checked it out, on the grounds that Thomas's humanitarianism might very well have led him there:

> I have asked various persons who were in a position to know if Dylan ever joined the CP in London: A. L. Morton (who helped Neuberg on the *Sunday Referee* and recalled the arrival of Dylan's first poem), Randall Swingler, and Edgell Rickword. None of them had ever heard of Dylan as a Communist. Further, Dylan said to me more than once, around 1949–50, 'If all the party-members were like you and John Sommerfield, I'd join on the spot.' He never suggested that he had already joined and been driven out by sectarianism.

Lindsay continues in his detailed and feeling memoir, *Meetings with Poets* (Lindsay, pp. 29–30):

> The essential point, however, is that, despite his deepgoing anarchism, he was never hostile to any part of the Left and that he remained all his life, as John says, a champion of the underdog . . . Dylan signed the Stockholm Peace Petition, the Rosenberg Petition, and actively supported the Authors World Peace Appeal. Doubtless there were many other such expressions of his downright political position; for I never knew him hesitate a moment before giving his support to such movements. He was always ready to collaborate with us in Fore Publications, though we forbore to ask him for poems, since he was hard-up and we did not pay. However, when Paul Potts (whom I had introduced to Dylan and who did much to help the Thomases in the last part of their Chelsea period) got together a collection for *Our Time* in honour of Lorca, Dylan at once offered *Ceremony After a Fire Raid*.

I hope that this is sufficient testimony to enable us to add 'Because the pleasure-bird whistles' to those of Thomas's poems (notably 'The hand that signed the paper') which expressed sympathy with the politically oppressed. The year 1938 saw the continuation of the Spanish Civil War, with Franco's ascendancy very clear by December. Caitlin says that Dylan 'seriously thought of going off to fight' in Spain (*Caitlin*, p. 44), in spite of his pacifism. There was Hitler's occupation of Austria in March and Czechoslovakia in October, after the Munich appeasement. By the time Thomas wrote his year's end poem, England was mobilizing. He asks: shall I sing sweeter if I blind myself to these perilous events? Only a person in a drugged state could not look back and absorb the fearful message. The violence and suffering in the world does not allow us to ignore it; we remember it every day as a grace before food. The poem's affirmation comes through the gloom.

Before I knocked

(please turn to *Collected Poems*, p. 11)

'I care not a damn for Christ,' wrote Thomas to Pamela Hansford Johnson in a letter dated Christmas Day 1933, 'but only for his symbol, the symbol of death' (*Letters*, p. 82/99). If we see Christ as the 'I' narrator of 'Before I knocked', as I think we must – he called it 'the Jesus poem' (*Letters*, p. 22/40) in sending it to Miss Johnson on 15 September 1933 – we should be careful not to get trapped into thinking of the poem as a conventional dramatic monologue. Its plangency should not make us 'care a damn' for the narrator, only for the symbols.

> Before I knocked [at conception] and flesh [the womb] let [me] enter, [before I] with liquid hands tapped on the womb, I who was shapeless as the water that shaped the [river] Jordan near my [Galilee] home WAS brother to Mnetha's[1] daughter and [either sex possible] sister to the fathering worm [God/Death].

---

[1] Perhaps meant to be taken as an anagram: the Man. There is plenty of evidence that Thomas found anagrams interesting (take the short story 'The Holy Six' of May 1934, for example). Mnetha is actually a character in Blake's *Tiriel*, where her role has some relevance to the use of the name in 'Before I knocked'. Or at least Mnetha's daughter Heva does, being described by Blake as sharing kinship

I who was [still unconceived] deaf to spring and summer, who knew not sun nor moon by name, FELT THUD beneath my [future] flesh's armour, [which] was as yet in molten form [in the sperm], the [hail-like] leaden stars [seed], [and] the rainy [seed-pouring] hammer [thudding] swung by my father[2] [like a smithy] from his dome [sky].

I KNEW the message of the winter [mortality], the darted hail [hitting like darts], the childish [during childhood] snow, and the wind WAS my sister suitor [petitioning kin]; wind in me LEAPED, [also] the hellborn dew [bad blood]; my veins FLOWED with the Eastern [Holy Land] weather; ungotten [unbegotten] I KNEW [already] night and day [mortal time].

As yet ungotten, I DID SUFFER [anticipating the Cross]; the [torture] rack of dreams DID TWIST my lily [Easter] bones into a living cipher [zero], and flesh WAS SNIPPED [on an operating table] to cross [make a cross with] the lines of gallow [or gallows'] crosses [stigmata] on the liver and [of] brambles [like a crown of thorns] in the wringing [mourning] brains.

My throat KNEW thirst [like Christ on the cross] before the structure of skin and vein around the well [throat] where words and water make a mixture [talking and drinking] unfailing till the blood runs foul [old age]; my heart KNEW love, my belly hunger; I SMELT the maggot [of death] in my stool [faeces].

And time CAST FORTH [at birth] my mortal creature [living self] to drift or drown upon the seas [which are] acquainted with the salt adventure of tides that never touch the shores [being in the mind]. I who was rich [in pre-knowledge] WAS MADE the richer by [being made incarnate] sipping at the vine of days.

I, born of flesh [Mary] and [Holy] ghost, WAS neither a ghost nor man, but mortal ghost [incarnated deity]. And I WAS STRUCK DOWN by death's feather.[3]

with all things. See *Collected Poems*, p. 181, for a reproduction of a Blake etching of a hooded female sitting encircled by a huge worm. The caption reads: 'I have said to the Worm: thou art my mother and my sister.' Thomas would have seen it in the 1927 Everyman edition of Blake's works.

[2] When Thomas had this poem typed up to send to publishers he gave 'father' here a capital letter, also the 'his' a capital 'H', not present in the notebook version (see *Notebook Poems*, pp. 186 and 269). If this is phallic imagery it is also meteorological. 'I think in cells,' Thomas wrote in a letter of this time; 'one day I may think in rains' (*Letters*, p. 82/99).

[3] 'There is scarce anything that hath not killed some body; a hair, a feather hath done it', said John Donne in *Devotions*, which we know from letters Thomas had read. The phrase 'death's feather' is used half a dozen times in the poetry. Thomas may merely be thinking of the common phrase: 'you could have knocked me down with a feather'.

I WAS mortal to the last long breath that carried to my father [God] the
message of his dying christ.[4]

You [churchgoers] who bow down at cross and altar, REMEMBER me [human
Christ] and PITY Him [Son of God] who took my flesh and bone for armour
[during mortal life] and doublecrossed [cheated] my mother's womb.

Apparently Pamela Hansford Johnson objected to the word
'doublecrossed', for Thomas wrote to her on 15 October 1933: 'There
is always only the one right word: use it, despite its foul or merely
ludicrous associations; I used "double-crossed" because it was what I
meant' (*Letters*, p. 25/43). He does not elaborate. I take it that, rather
than allowing her a normal son, God gave the Virgin Mary two crosses
to bear, the pain of giving birth and the cruelty of Calvary. The 'Him'
of this last stanza will be the Son-of-God Christ, who appropriated the
mortal Christ's body for God's purposes. The Virgin Mary is further
double-crossed by a sort of deception involved in having to give birth
to this double, the mortal son and the Heavenly Son.

The whole poem has a tone of grievance. The mortal Christ seems
to want a life apart from his sacred mission, but is chained to the final
crucifixion-bound twin. There may be an undercurrent of anger, but in
the end he requests pity for the usurper. In this he is quite Christian.

In spite of many lines of conventional beauty and emotive force,
however, I cannot believe that the poet's purpose here is to engage us in
the feelings of a betrayed mortal Christ, a sort of poetic version of D.
H. Lawrence's *The Man Who Died*. We have to acknowledge the
dramatic monologue form, but surely the words Thomas puts into the
mouth of this mortal Christ are his own complaint at being given a
body that can be painfully hurt and a death that is calculated to nullify
all ambition. What is the point of beginning this Christian story with
womb imagery if it is not to establish this Christ as every mother's son.
He can then speak a general complaint: all mothers are double-
crossed, and all sons carry with their last long breath that message.

---

[4] In the British Library typescript, not only Christ is capitalized but also 'His' and
in the previous line 'Father'. Presumably the message Thomas had in mind was
Christ's 'Why has thou forsaken me?' This would be the mortal part of Christ
speaking to the spirit part, no doubt a heretical notion. T. S. Eliot, as editor of
Criterion, rejected the poem (*Letters*, p. 22/40).

Ceremony After a Fire Raid

(please turn to *Collected Poems*, p. 107)

Thomas is here writing a new Mass for the Dead. He had done a short elegy, 'Among those Killed in the Dawn Raid was a Man Aged a Hundred', early in the war (1941). Two years later he was moved to gird himself to do it over, and he wrote down on a sheet of paper: 'Among Those Burned To Death Was A Child Aged A Few Hours'. This mimicking of a newspaper headline was not something to do twice, and was dropped. But if it was not a news item that focused and pressured his horror of war into a major elegy, what was it? Clark Emery assumes that Thomas actually saw a burnt child and was shocked by the visual image into writing this poem (Emery, p. 168). There is no evidence for this. Thomas like everybody else did some fire-watching, which involved extingishing incendiary bombs that came one's way, but there is no record that any came Dylan's way.

I have always felt that 'Ceremony After a Fire Raid' was connected with his daughter Aeronwy, who was born 3 March 1943 during an air raid, a 'tremendous air raid', as Caitlin describes it (*Caitlin*, p. 83):

> I had gone into Mary Abbotts Hospital for the birth, and I can remember a frightful noise in the skies, which seemed to be just above the labour ward . . . Every time there was a vast explosion I felt the baby was going to explode out of me. I was really beyond fear.

Dylan – though he was not present at the birth – would not be beyond fear. His imagination might envisage 'the little skull' as 'a cinder' (part II, line 8). Out of such personal fear might come a universal anthem of the closeness of birth and death.

> Myselves [the general 'I'][,] the grievers[,] GRIEVE among the [people of the] street burned to tireless death [death is never tired] a child of a few hours with its kneading [working at the breast] mouth charred on the black [burnt] breast of the grave [that] the mother dug [by dying ahead of her child], and [with] its arms full of fires [holding the mother].

> BEGIN [the ceremony] with singing[,] SING [of] darkness kindled [burnt] back into beginning when the caught [aflame] tongue nodded blind, [and

when] a star [fire bomb] was broken into the centuries [hundreds of pieces] of the child [whom] myselves grieve now, and [for whose death] miracles cannot atone.

FORGIVE[,] us FORGIVE[,] GIVE[1] us your death [as a sacred relic] [in order] that myselves[,] the believers[,] may hold it till the blood shall spurt in a great flood [in the firmament], and the dust [ashes of the child] shall sing like a bird as the grains [immortal seeds] blow, as your death grows [in healing efficacy], through [the feeling substance of] our heart.

[We] crying your dying cry [as though it were ours], child beyond [the sound of] cockcrow, by the fire-dwarfed [burnt down] street we CHANT [of] the flying [freed into spirit] sea in the [child's] body bereft [of any new dawns]. Love IS the last light [or word of the ceremony] spoken. Oh seed of [future] sons left [as ashes] in the loin of the black husk [of the child].

To read this first part aright, let us think of it as a film about the civilian casualties in the Second World War, in which there is a funeral scene in St Paul's Cathedral, with a small coffin and a congregation of mourners in black. We have the organ music; and the poet is to supply the voice-over script. Thomas actually did filmwork of this kind; for example, the patriotic, 'Our Country', done in 1944 (*Filmscripts*, p. 68):

(St Paul's Cathedral)	There is peace under one roof.
	And then birds flying Suddenly easily as though from another country.
(Blitzed streets)	And all the stones remember and sing the cathedral of each blitzed dead body that lay or lies in the bomber-and-dove-flown-over cemeteries of the dumb heroic streets.
	And the eyes of St Paul's move over London.

This places 'Ceremony After a Fire Raid' in its genre.

As to the form of part II of the poem ('I know not whether . . .'): it is a respected literary trope that, by claiming ignorance of which of

---

[1] The 'Give' of the Ohio MS and the first periodical printing was somehow dropped when the poem was reprinted in *War Poets* (1945), which version seems to have been used for *Deaths and Entrances,* and thus *Collected Poems* (1952). It was one of the happy restorations in *Collected Poems* (1988).

several alternatives pertains, a poet is enabled to enrich his verse by mentioning them all. This device allows Thomas to incorporate the reverberations of 'bullock', 'lamb', 'virgin' – traditional victims of sacrifice – along with 'Adam and Eve', the first sacrificed humans, the skeletons of the Garden of Eden.

With the child's death 'the nurseries / Of the garden of wilderness' (part II, lines 27–8) are 'bare'. This is the kind of hyperbole Donne used in his *Anniversaries*, which suggest another genre for 'Ceremony After a Fire Raid': that of religious meditation. The child is given cosmic dimensions; the fate of the world is affected by her death. Satan would have been conquered by her securing 'the serpent's / Night fall'. Her fruit would have been like the sun, reversing the loss of the Garden of Eden. But the new beginning has now 'crumbled back to darkness' (lines 23–6).

Part III of 'Ceremony After a Fire Raid,' which, in sending a clipping of the poem to Watkins, 27 July 1944, Thomas called a musical 'voluntary' (*Letters*, p. 518/580), needs no explication once the syntax is clear. It is the sea which is now carrying the child ('infant-bearing sea' – line 14) and saying mass for it. Or rather 'masses', which form gives the feeling of massive movement when the speaking of the mass erupts, fountains, and enters with its 'Glory, glory, glory' into the organpipes and steeples, into the weathercocks' molten (because of the fire raid) mouths, and into the dead clock, which is burning time over the urn which the street has become; and finally, after all the elements of the death scene are provided with the mass from the sea, it enters the bread and wine transubstantiated into wheatfield and burning brandy for the sublime act of the ceremony.

The last line, 'The sundering ultimate kingdom of genesis' thunder', is to be taken as in apposition with 'Glory, glory, glory'. The mass celebrates the 'kingdom come' of the Lord's Prayer. The ultimate result of God's thundering at Adam and Eve in the Garden is this child's death. But the Gloria too is part of the mass.

Deaths and Entrances

(please turn to *Collected Poems*, p. 97)

Gwen Watkins places the inception of this poem in May 1940, while Caitlin and Thomas were staying in Bishopston and able to see a good deal of Vernon (*Portrait of a Friend*, p. 88):

> Vernon, Dylan and Caitlin went to a performance of *The Marriage of Figaro* in the Empire Theatre. Before the performance Dylan quoted to Vernon the first two lines of a new poem which he was going to call *Deaths and Entrances*:
>
> > On almost the incendiary eve
> > Of several near deaths
>
> and said that he was going to call his next book by the same title 'because that is all I ever write about or want to write about'.

Thomas is drawing on the language of John Donne's last sermon 'Death's Duell': 'Deliverance from that death, the death of the wombe is an entrance, a delivery over to another death.' It would seem that the womb-tomb theme is what Thomas meant as his past and future subject. Yet by this time, and with this poem in particular, Thomas is well removed from the elemental light/dark imagery of his earlier verse and its abstract notion of death. The deaths of 'Deaths and Entrances' are specifically the anticipated war deaths, and the 'entrances' are the expected German invasions.

In May 1940 Thomas had not personally experienced bombing raids, but by the time he had finished the poem he knew more of what he had been fearing. In a letter to Watkins in late August he wrote (*Letters*, p. 463/524):

> I had to go to London last week to see about a BBC job, & left at the beginning of the big Saturday raid. The Hyde Park guns were booming. Guns on the top of Selfridges. A 'plane brought down in Tottenham court Road. White-faced taxis still trembling through the streets, though, & buses going, & even people being shaved. Are you frightened these nights? When I wake up out of burning birdman dreams – they were frying aviators one night in a huge frying pan: it sounds whimsical now, it was appalling then – and hear the sound of bombs & gunfire only a little way away, I'm so relieved I could laugh or cry.

These nightmares get into 'Deaths and Entrances'. There is also the added fear of enemy occupation. The letter to Watkins continues (*Letters*, p. 463/524):

> What *is* so frightening, I think, is the idea of the greyclothed, grey-faced, blackarmletted troops marching one morning, without a sound up a village street. Boots on the cobbles, of course, but no Heil-shouting, grenading, goosestepping. Just silence. That's what Goebbels has done for me. I get nightmares like invasions, all successful.

He says in a letter that he has not been able to settle down to a poem for a long time; he will do so soon, 'but it mustn't be nightmarish' (*Letters*, p. 463/524). A vain hope. The war was a nightmare, and would have to be written about as such. In a letter a little later, in the middle of writing the poem, he called it his poem 'about invasion', and told Watkins not to stare at the sky too much: 'The wrong wings are up there' (*Letters*, p. 464/526). The war was getting to him.

The finished poem ended up being about three war deaths: a close friend, an unknown enemy invader, and finally, since the 'you' of the poem must be himself, his own death.

> On almost the incendiary [bomb] eve of several near [dear] deaths, when one [at least] at the great least of your best loved and always known [friends] must leave [say goodbye to] lions and fires [roaring and burning] of his flying breath,
>
> of your immortal [forever] friends who'd raise [even] the [pipe] organs of the [dead] counted dust to shoot [bring forth out of the earth] and sing your praise, one who called deepest down [into the poet's being] SHALL HOLD his peace[,] [a peace] that cannot sink or cease[,] [hold it] endlessly to his [fatal] wound in [the midst of] many married London's estranging [ending the marriages] grief.

He is expecting that one at least of his very best friends will have to die, perhaps a pilot with 'flying breath' (line 5). No specific candidate for this friend comes to mind. It is a personification of the best qualities of supportive friendship.

> On almost the incendiary eve when at your lips [mouth] and keys [door], locking [in combat], unlocking [invading the house], the [about to be] murdered strangers weave [as in air battle],

one who is most unknown [an enemy], your polestar [far off] neighbour, sun of another street, WILL DIVE [to his destruction] up to his tears [in pain].

[He] who strode for [attacked] your own dead he'll BATHE [shed] his raining [spilling] blood in the male sea [made male by his blood] and WIND [as he spins in the sea] his globe [body] out of [with] your water thread [sea currents] and LOAD [burden] the throats of [sea] shells with every cry [he has built up within him] since light flashed first [at birth] across his thunderclapping eyes.

This stranger's eyes are thunderclapping as he drops his bombs on London, but there is more sadness than hate in this stanza. The strangers are already as if murdered as they fly in to attack. Thomas did not, would not, contribute to anti-German 'flogged hate' (*Letters*, p. 415/469), 'fostering of hate against a bewildered, buggered people' (*Letters*, p. 417/471). Later in the war, commissioned to write the script for a propaganda film about the Nazis, 'These Are The Men' (1943), Thomas could go so far as to say (*Filmscripts*, p. 43):

> Young men like you have hacked and blasted
> The lands and the homes of strangers who did you no harm,
> Burned men and women alive
> And left a slug-trail behind you of terror and death.
> You obeyed your leader's word.
> You must suffer his reward.

But he also goes on to refer to (*Filmscripts*, p. 43):

> Some of the young men, not utterly scarred and poisoned,
> Who have grown into manhood out of a school of horror

– these 'may yet be our comrades and brothers, workers and makers, / After the agony of the world at war is over'. At the time of 'Deaths and Entrances' he was adamant in his neutrality; in a letter to Clement Davenport of 2 April 1941, he scorned the idea of war work in a factory, as it would be helping to 'kill another stranger' (*Letters*, p. 478/540).

Dylan Thomas was, I think, truly one of those souls who would rather be killed than kill. In the third and last stanza of this poem he envisages his own death, without defiance.

On almost the incendiary eve of [the war] deaths and entrances
[invasions], when near [friend] and strange [enemy] wounded on
London's waves [blitz] have sought your single grave [as the next to die],

one enemy, of many, who knows well your heart is luminous [a clear
target] in the [fire] watched dark, quivering [flickering its light fearfully]
through locks [keyholes] and [hidden] caves, WILL PULL the thunderbolts
[door bolts pulled thunderously] to shut [the door on] the sun, PLUNGE [as
a paratrooper or bomb], MOUNT your darkened keys[1] [as if a horse] and
SEAR [with explosion] just riders [rescuers] back, until that one loved least
[the bombarder] looms [as] the last [blind] Samson [self-destroyer] of
your zodiac [fate].

This is Samson at the end, when he has accepted his fate: this is the
figure Thomas brings in to be a talisman of his own possible death in
the war. His heart is luminous, he cannot really hide. But there is
more resignation here than self-pity. He stands in the final stanza not
as a special death to which others are leading, but more as a
resolution to the antithetic two, the friend and stranger. Their deaths
matter more, really.

A story told by Vernon Watkins adds confirmation to this notion.
The time is a little later (1943); the setting is a London air raid while
Vernon was staying with Dylan at the Manresa Road studio in
Chelsea. *Portrait of a Friend* recounts (p. 106) that they both
crouched under a big round table:

Dylan was trembling so violently that the table shook. Vernon, to calm
him, began talking of his belief in immortality, and Dylan, still trembling,
made a reply which Vernon never forgot:

> 'My immortality', he said,
> 'Now matters to my soul
> Less than the deaths of others . . .'

---

[1]   A strange image. How can one mount keys unless by climbing on a piano? 'I went
to see a smashed aerodrome,' Thomas told Watkins in a letter of summer 1940.
'Only one person had been killed. He was playing the piano in an entirely empty,
entirely dark canteen' (*Letters*, p. 463/525). The image may have originated there –
the poem also: it had been his one war experience to date.

Note on 'Deaths and Entrances'

Gwen Watkins's comments in *Portrait of a Friend* (p. 88) indicate that the early draft proposed a very different ending from what was finally come to:

> The last lines originally held a hyena image suggested by one of his favourite passages from *Nightwood*:
>
>> 'For the lover, it is the night into which his beloved goes',
>> he said, 'that destroys his heart; he wakes her suddenly,
>> only to look the hyena in the face that is her smile, as she
>> leaves that company . . . '

A draft worksheet, now at Texas, shows that the final enemy of the last stanza was at one time going to be a 'She' with a hyena face. If this was Caitlin or the poem was to end with the threat of another's invasion into their marriage, it is something we can glance at in passing, but not dwell on, for the poem has nothing of this in its completed form.

Do not go gentle into that good night

(please turn to *Collected Poems*, p. 148)

Speaking of the period from May 1949 when the Thomas family moved into the Boat House for good, Dylan's parents having taken a rented house called Pelican on the Laugharne main street, Constantine FitzGibbon has said: 'When Dylan was at home there was never a day that he did not go to see his father, to chat and do the crossword together and, so long as D.J. still could cross the street, to drink a pint at Brown's' (FitzGibbon, p. 337). Thomas was in a good position to see his father's slow decline in health and the psychological changes attending it. Out of this diurnal filial experience Thomas wrote one of his great short poems, 'Do not go gentle into that good night'.

In sending the finished poem to the editor of *Botteghe Oscure*, Marguerite Caetani, 28 May 1951, Thomas said: 'The only person I can't show the little enclosed poem to is, of course, my father, who doesn't know he's dying' (*Letters*, p. 800/892). Though D. J. Thomas did not die until 15 December 1952, eighteen months later, a man who had had a bout of cancer twenty years before, had had to retire from teaching early because of general ill health, and had been beset by various illnesses since (if Dylan's solicitations in letters are any guide), if such a man was such a clear thinker as D.J. was, then he should know something about his limits by the time he reaches the age of seventy-five. A brilliant poem addressed to him should not, other things being equal, be anything but a thing of pride. Was it really the scruple of not wanting to remind his father about his death that kept Dylan from showing this poem? If the message of the poem – to rage against the dying of the light – was genuinely meant, his father should have had it. The poet's hesitation in this regard makes us want to pry into the poem to see what prohibited it from being offered as a real conduit of feeling between son and father in these particular circumstances.

On reading the topic sentence that begins this poem, 'Old age should burn and rave at close of day', one's instincts say that this burning and raving must be a good thing. Yeats's later poems come to mind, at least those in which we find old age resisted with stoic gaiety. The first example Thomas gives, however, has 'wise men' burning and raving because 'their words had forked no lightning'. They know 'dark is right', that death is our inevitable end and therefore we must, if we are wise, be resigned to it. But they are aggravated by their failure to have put a spark into their philosophizing that might have changed the world in a lightning flash. Next, the 'good men', who know their actions must be considered 'frail' in the general scheme of things, at the end rage because they could have done better; their deeds 'might have danced'. Then the 'wild men', the poets, who captured some of the vitality of the natural world and 'sang the sun in flight', find that they have been serenading a passing scene and they cannot be happy when their total output is one big elegy. Finally, 'grave' men, who have prided themselves in their fitting solemnity and have limited their emotional life, near death see with sudden illumination that their 'blind eyes could blaze like meteors and be gay', and therefore rage that they cannot change. All these are examples of frustration. There is no gaiety here. The raging is real anger. This is not a Yeats poem.

If, then, Thomas is putting his father into the same category as these failures who have lost their way and are angry at not fulfilling themselves, the 'fierce tears' he is asking of him will be expressions of chagrin and laceration. If the truth be told, D. J. Thomas was most certainly in that category. The biographer Constantine FitzGibbon seems to have had sympathetic insight into Dylan's father's predicament (FitzGibbon, pp. 11–12):

> There was a tragedy, perhaps more than one, in D. J. Thomas's life. In the first place he would have liked to be a poet and was not – a frustration which was to find its echo in Dylan's own last years. He got a job at Swansea Grammar School as soon as he left university in 1899, and except for a brief interlude a couple of years later at a school in Pontypridd he remained at that school until his retirement in 1936. But he seems to have regarded the teaching of English to adolescent boys as a career not worthy of his talents. There is a rumor that when the University College of Swansea was founded in 1920, D. J. Thomas applied for the newly created chair of English and that he believed he had been shortlisted for the appointment. His lack of academic experience would make this appointment unlikely. In any event the chair was given to a man whom D.J. regarded, rightly I am told, as his inferior. He remained the provincial schoolmaster, nor did he attempt to write. Why did he acquiesce in this defeat of his ambitions?

'Acquiesce' is hardly the proper word. There is evidence of depression and drink. The latter had come close to 'ruining his life' (FitzGibbon, p. 12). The former exhibited itself in a retreat from all social life except for the quasi-anonymous pub evenings. He did not acquiesce; he became morose and bad tempered, even to the point of violence in the classroom (FitzGibbon, pp. 13–14): 'D.J. would address the boys of his class, collectively and singly, as guttersnipes or worse. Nor was his violence purely verbal. If a boy earned his displeasure he would cuff him or kick him right across, sometimes out of, the room.' When retirement deprived him of this captive audience, his unhappiness with the world apparently took the form of pure glaring resistance. 'My father is awfully ill these days', Thomas wrote to Watkins, 28 March 1945 (*Letters*, p. 548/610), 'with heart disease and uncharted pains, and the world that was once the colour of tar to him is now a darker place.' Thomas summed up his father's view of things in a letter of 12 November 1949 as 'This is the end of civilization' (*Letters*, p. 726/809).

It would not be out of line, therefore, to see D. J. Thomas as close kin of the wise, good, wild and grave men of 'Do not go gentle into that good night', with genuine anger his proper portion.

And you, my father, there on the sad height,
Curse, bless, me now with your fierce tears, I pray.
Do not go gentle into that good night.
Rage, rage against the dying of the light.

It is as though curses would be appropriate and expected, and fierce tears would be a proper blessing. In other words, Dylan wanted his father to die as he had lived. There was one occasion on which Thomas said this in public, when, at a University of Utah seminar, he

> began to talk in a soft voice about his father, who, he said, had been a militant atheist, whose atheism had nothing to do with whether there was a god or not, but was a violent and personal dislike for God. He would glare out of the window and growl: 'It's raining, blast Him!' or 'The sun is shining – Lord, what foolishness!' He went blind and was very ill before he died. He was in his eighties, and he grew soft and gentle at the last. Thomas hadn't wanted him to change . . .[1]

Given D. J. Thomas's atheism, it follows that what Dylan is asking for in the poem are the fierce tears of existential rage. This is the blessing his father should continue to give him. He is asking his father to be true to his vision of an unjust providence and to the anger which has become his essential nature. Consequently, if his father had, as Thomas, says above, grown 'soft and gentle' in his seventy-fifth year, there could only be a perverse cruelty in presenting to him a poetic request that he revert from the kind King Lear at the end of the play to the angry and hurt King Lear of Act 2.

In any case, one does not preach to one's father. This poem was never meant for D. J. Thomas. I am convinced that Thomas wrote the poem for himself. It is a lament that *his* words had forked no lightning, that *his* frail deeds had not danced, that *he* had learnt important things too late; and he is asking for the anger to go with it, the anger his father had convinced him was a true response to the world. Thomas is asking to live in the shared truth of things.

The anger is also the way out – or so it is hinted, especially in the fifth stanza; for, if it is lost opportunity that makes the 'grave men' rage in exasperation, there also seems to be a chance that the raging

---

[1] Marjorie Adix in Tedlock, p. 66. FitzGibbon, speaking of the influence of Wells and Shaw on D. J. Thomas, concluded that Dylan's father was an atheist (FitzGibbon, p. 13).

is a way to have their blind eyes blaze, as they know it could be, like meteors. Thomas is saying to himself that he still has his chance. The curse of despair is the blessing of 'blinding sight'. His glittering eyes may yet be gay, gaiety transfiguring all his dread.

Do you not father me

(please turn to *Collected Poems*, p. 42)

'**Y**ou are all these, said she . . . All these, he said': thus the third stanza of 'Do you not father me' comments on the first two stanzas and allows us to see the poem as falling into Thomas's pangenetic mode. He is not only fathered and mothered but brothered and sistered, and calls himself 'love's house' (penultimate line of the poem), a sort of turreted panabode. He feels his makeup is the result of a number of relationships. He wants us to feel these kinships as valid, not clichés. In his effort to state these common feelings with originality, he has written one of his more obscure poems.

Hear him first on a poem by Pamela Hansford Johnson in which she seems to have been competing with Thomas to outdo the pantheism of 'The force that through the green fuse', which had been published on 29 October 1933. Her letter and poem are not extant, but this is Thomas's rejoinder in his Christmas 1933 letter (*Letters*, p. 78/95):

> You started off with a very simple thought (I, for one, will never believe that the most valuable thoughts are, of necessity, simple); you confessed that you were one with the 'sparrow', and then, as a natural conclusion, went on to say that you were one with the 'arrow', too. If it comes to that, you can say you are one with the barrow as well. For you are, my dear, you certainly are. I'm not trying to be flippant; I'm merely trying to show you, by any method, how *essentially* false such writing is.

> > I am one with the wind and one with the breezes,
> > And one with the torrent that drowns the plain,
> > I am one with the streams and one with the seas-es,
> > And one with the maggot that snores in the grain . . .

> there's too much 'Uncle Tom Collie & all' about that. Primarily, you see, the reader refuses to believe that *you* believe you are one with all these

things; you have to prove it to him, and you most certainly won't by cataloguing a number of other things to which you *say* you are related. By the magic of words and images you must make it clear to him that the relationships are real.

Thus, we see why, in reapproaching this theme in 'Do you not father me', Thomas feels he has to go to extremes to make relationships 'real'. Instead of saying, 'You gave me your flesh and blood', he may have to say, 'Did you not, father, for my tall tower's sake cast the erected arm in her stone? Did you not lie suffering my stain, mother?'

Moreover, this will be a very abstract 'real'. I do not think we are to look for any personal attributes of Thomas's actual family coming through – clearly not in the case of the 'brothering', since he did not have a brother. The brothering aspect seems to be voyeuristic (lines 8 and 10–11), and the sister seems to be associated with sin and being saved (lines 6 and 12). But maybe in summarizing in this way we have not yet reached the abstraction that Thomas is imaging. He is saying: if I am a house on the beach, this is how I was built. Or in its most abstract form: these are me. 'You are all these . . . All these . . .' (line 17–18).

The trouble always is that we feel that the details of the images are important in telling us exactly what the poem means; but maybe they are not. Maybe the specifics are, in some sense, irrelevant to the job of expressing the idea of relationship, and that the stretch of the metaphysical image is valuable not in where it gets as much as the distance it is stretched, since any direction of stretch would make the same point. The real is in the abstraction that the stretched image snaps back to when it snaps.

For instance, with the third stanza, after the mother and father have made their comment, we have the curious line: 'Up rose the Abraham-man, mad for my sake'. 'Abraham-man' is in some dictionaries as a fraudulent lunatic beggar. But one can flow with the wording and see that whatever it is that has risen up must be something of a tower: 'rise, (ah, phallic)', as Thomas put it in a letter around this time (*Letters*, p. 171/196). And in Eric Partridge's *A Dictionary of Slang and Unconventional English*, p. 2, there we have it: 'Abraham – the penis'. The code, then, is cracked! The father is fathering him. Snap!

> I am, the tower told, felled by a timeless stroke,
> Who razed my wooden folly stands aghast,

> For man-begetters in the dry-as-paste,
> The ringed-sea ghost, rise grimly from the wrack. (stanza 3)

What was raised is now razed, by a stroke – or stroking, anyway.

How far can one go with this? There are no letters where the author has helped elucidate this poem; we are on our own, trying to imagine what the poet would be thinking. What can the 'ringed-sea ghost' possibly be? Could it be a puddle of sperm – a small round salty residue of what could have been live people but is now one ghost dump? Then 'dry-as-paste' would not be a totally unapt apposition, and 'man-begetters' would be the seed that miraculously are rising 'grimly' (another word for 'ghostly') from the wrack (a dictionary definition of 'wrack' is 'washed-up seaweed') or wreck of the wooden folly ('wood' is another slang word for erect penis; 'folly' is a flamboyant tower), the ruined detumescence of the tower of love's house. If these conjectures about Thomas's narrative of images have hit the mark, it means that something has happened to demolish the house. It would be true to Thomas's idiom that whoever was fathering, mothering, brothering and sistering might also be the forces of destruction.

'Do you not father me on the destroying sand?' begins stanza 4. Because of the word 'destroying' the question is ambiguous. Lines 2–4 are, unfortunately, too enigmatic to be helpful. How can anyone be his sister's sire? 'Seaweedy' is definitely a washed-up wrack. 'Proper gentleman and lady'? I doubt it. The best we can say is that there is created some sort of antithesis so that the poem can end with a synthesis:

> Shall I still be love's house on the widdershin earth,
> Woe to the windy masons at my shelter?
> Love's house, they answer, and the tower death
> Lie all unknowing of the grave sin-eater.

The question that motivates the poem, it seems, is: can the poet's heart revive after the fall of the tower? Can he still be love's house, can his sexuality survive the assault of the 'windy masons' and the 'proper gentleman and lady' as agents of entropy, who can debuild a house by blowing it in? His world has turned about, 'widdershin'. Can he keep at bay these threatening people and say woe to those who would make private sex into sin?

No, he seems stuck with his feelings of guilt after the tower of love's house has died. A sin-eater eats over a coffin and takes on himself any of the bad consequences others might otherwise have from handling the corpse. There will be no help for the 'I' of the poem with *his* sin. Those who did the fathering and mothering and sistering in the end turn out to have an overwhelming presence and inhibiting effect. If this were a different sort of poem, this voice of society and family might have been defied; he might have been 'a shouter like the cock, blowing the old dead back' ('Our eunuch dreams'). The feeling at the end of this poem, however, is heaviness, as though he will never erect his tower again.

Ears in the turrets hear

(please turn to *Collected Poems*, p. 49)

This poem is practically unchanged from its appearance in Thomas's notebook, 17 July 1933 (*Notebook Poems*, p. 173), and takes us back to a time when the young poet was trying out various styles. The adjacent poem in the notebook is a speech from a poetic drama, headed 'The Woman Speaks'; it is a mourning threnody for a slain soldier. 'Ears in the turrets hear' is likewise a monologue of a female, in this case a virgin captive in the tower of her own hesitancy in the face of the temptation from the ships and sailors anchored off the bay. In the second stanza Thomas could not resist making the tower the anatomy of her own body, but otherwise 'Ears in the turrets hear' reads like a conventional newspaper poem. 'Dare I?' was the title *John O'London's Weekly* used when printing it (minus the second stanza) in its issue of 5 May 1934. Thomas knew which of his poems to send to editor Frank Kendon: 'a mild (very mild) poem . . . a terribly weak, watery little thing', he admitted to Miss Johnson (*Letters*, p. 131/158). He passed over the poem when putting together *18 Poems*, but when he needed poems for *Twenty-five Poems* he included it. The second anatomical stanza is restored, but that does not disturb the poem's emotional soft centre.

It makes its point, however. It was the first poem that Thomas pulled out to read to Vernon Watkins when they met in February 1935. He had some inkling, we suppose, of its likelihood of hitting a nerve. Watkins was twenty-nine and still living at home with his parents in Pennard, a village just outside Swansea (*Portrait of a Friend*, pp. 3 and 25). But the best commentary on this pasteboard gem is Thomas's own ambivalence about leaving home. When, in April 1936, he had almost literally 'run to the ships', having gone to stay in a Cornwall fishing village, he wrote to Watkins that he was 'full of nostalgia': 'Now in a hundred ways I wish I hadn't come away' (*Letters*, p. 222/248);

> I stand for, if anything, the aspidistra, the provincial drive, the morning café, the evening pub . . . And living in your own private, four-walled world as exclusively as possible isn't escapism, I'm sure; it isn't the Ivory Tower, and, even if it were, you secluded in your Tower know and learn more of the world outside than the outside-man who is mixed up so personally and inextricably with the mud and the unlovely people.

In 'Ears in the turrets hear' the implied decision surely is to stay in the island of the self. It is as though the poet knew, this early, that poison and grapes were not alternatives but the same thing.

Elegy

(please turn to *Collected Poems*, p. 155)

One of the worksheets of this poem (now at Texas) is written on the back of a draft letter to Dent's dated 15 September 1953, which indicates that Thomas was working on the poem close to leaving for his final visit to America. It is a heartfelt elegy for his father: 'Until I die he will not leave my side' was the way he put it in one of the draft pages. As it turned out, there was less than a year between his father's death in December 1952 and his own in November 1953.

The poem is unfinished, but p. 2 of the Texas manuscripts is a fair copy of the stage the poem had reached at the time Thomas ceased work on it. The editors of the 1988 *Collected Poems* write (p. 264):

> We have kept strictly to this version, taking one liberty: we have retained the last two lines, though Thomas was apparently dissatisfied with them,

and struck them out. They are valuable lines; and there is reason to think that they would have been utilized in some similar form, if the poet had had a chance to return to the poem. We have concluded that there is no justification for extending the poem as Vernon Watkins did, as all the extant worksheets lead up to the version printed here.

Printings of the *Collected Poems* after 1956 had contained an 'Elegy' where the Texas p. 2 had been expanded by Watkins utilizing worksheet phrases the poet had really discarded in his mind in finalizing the Texas p. 2 version. Watkins was influenced by a prose note among the manuscripts indicating the way, at one point, the poet thought the elegy to his father might go:

(1) Although he was too proud to die, he *did* die, blind, in the most agonizing way but he did not flinch from death & was brave in his pride.
(2) In his innocence, & thinking he was God-hating, he never knew that what he was was: an old kind man in his burning pride.
(3) Now he will not leave my side, though he is dead.
(4) His mother sd that as a baby he never cried; nor did he, as an old man; he just cried to his secret wound & his blindness, never aloud.

Some of these ideas found a permanent place in the nineteen finished lines, but most of them did not, and they should not deflect our attention from the version printed in the 1988 *Collected Poems*.

The setting of the poem is the scene at the deathbed, which Thomas described briefly in a letter to Alfred Janes, 5 January 1953 (*Letters*, p. 860/959):

Thank you, very very much indeed, for writing on my father's death. Poor old boy, he was in awful pain at the end and nearly blind. The day before he died, he wanted to get out of bed & go into the kitchen where his mother was making onion soup for him. Then, a few hours afterwards, he suddenly remembered everything, & where he was, & he said, 'It's full circle now'.

Thomas's using the word 'brave' in line 3 of the poem and the phrase 'did not turn away' in line 2 can from the above comment be seen as a recognition of D. J. Thomas's clarity in the final minutes of his life. The line 'he longed all dark for his mother's breast' (line 9) also gains some re-evaluation. On first reading it causes something of a shock, which one immediately wants to defuse by saying that of course it is Mother Earth, but the longing for the mother – in the form of onion soup – was also, we see, part of the actual death.

There are a couple of surprises in these few lines. First, the wishing that his father might 'grow young, under the grass, in love' (line 6). Thomas's love for his father produces a yearning for immortality and rejuvenation. This elysian vision of things can coexist with the notion of the 'darkest justice of death' (line 11), which is a climb to a 'crucifixed hill' (line 18). Thomas is still allowing polarities to exist in the same space, carrying them forward with a strong, unifying emotion. 'I saw / Through his faded eyes to the roots of the sea' (lines 16–17): the blind father enables the son to see deep to the bottom of things.

What will chiefly be remarked upon with this 'Elegy' is the conspicuous contrast with 'Do not go gentle into that good night'. It is almost saying that one *can* go gentle:

> Go calm to your crucifixed hill, I told
> The air that drew away from him.

The earlier poem was a conspiracy with the father to blast the universe. This one is a record of love. Constantine FitzGibbon's memories of D. J. Thomas not only aid in our understanding of 'Do not go gentle' but also allow us to understand how Dylan can here use the word 'love' (FitzGibbon, p. 15):

> I only saw them together once, in London in 1945, and I was struck then by how much Dylan was on his best behaviour with his father, how anxious that his friends too should make a good impression. And the pride that the old man took in his famous son was quietly apparent. I believe that they were always close to one another but that it was by D.J.'s wish, a closeness that found only limited expression. It was love rather than friendship.

It is on record that Dylan did hold his father's hand as he died (*Portrait of a Friend*, p. 140).

Especially when the October wind

(please turn to *Collected Poems*, p. 18)

What is there about this poem that makes it possible to assert without fear of contradiction that it was written by a born poet? Probably something in the insistent rhythms, the engaging half-rhymes, the thudding monosyllables, the turns of phrase that are both familiar and unfamiliar at the same time, the pacing, the crescendo: perhaps this is the place to admit that I have not in these explications taken on the job of trying to say what makes Thomas's poems magical when they are, as this one certainly is. What is definitely in my purview to say which can be said about this poem is that it shows the young poet going all out: and that is the poem's subject as well. A poem about writing your heart out. And it happens before our eyes. Sometimes youth cannot go wrong.

> Especially when the October wind with frosty fingers punishes [lashes] my hair, [especially when] caught [constrained] by the crabbing [making him into a crab] sun I walk on fire [fevered] and cast a shadow crab [of inner deformity] upon the land, by the sea's side, hearing the noise of the birds, hearing the [ominous] raven cough [with sickness] in winter sticks [trees], my busy [with poetry] heart who shudders [with fever] as she talks SHEDS the syllabic blood [poetry] and DRAINS [like blood loss] her words.

The poetry comes out of a sort of heart sickness, caught from a raven's cough, or the chill in the air that the sun only intensifies into a fever. This poetry comes on him like fibrillation; every syllable is blood-bursting, and the end is exhaustion.

> Shut, too [like the trees], in a tower of words [his upstairs room], I MARK on the horizon [like writing on the sky] walking like the trees [silhouetted hieroglyphs] the wordy shapes of women, and the rows [like notes on a musical staff] of the star-gestured [akimbo] children in the park [opposite 5 Cwmdonkin Drive].

'When I experience anything', Thomas told Alistair Reid (Tedlock, p. 54), 'I experience it as a thing and a word at the same time, both equally amazing.' So in this poem we get, to our amazement, the 'wordy' shapes of woman and the 'vowelled' beeches (line 13), the water's 'speeches' (line 16), and the 'dark-vowelled' birds (last line). Thomas is repeating over and over the word/thing linkage in order to establish it as the essential nature of his universe, where experiencing the threatening winter produces a poetry that exhausts him as the year runs itself out.

> Some let me make you of the vowelled beeches,
> Some of the oaken voices, from the roots
> Of many a thorny shire tell you notes,
> Some let me make you of the water's speeches.

'Some let me make you of' is a strange construction. Even if you turn it around and say, 'Let me make you some of . . .', it still is not quite right. We have to add a word: 'Some *poetry* let me make you of the vowelled beeches.' Words are made of the thing. 'Of the vowelled beeches let me make you some poetry.'

It is known that there was a pot of ferns in the window of the Thomas house. If that weed of weeds did not tell him anything, the wagging-fingered clock did. Time flies with the weighted pendulum's swing; death travels the nerves with its message, attacks the morning and promulgates mortality with the wind in the turning weather-cock. The grass is the sign that covers everything with its news-break; it comes up through the eye of the dead to announce the winter, the worm, death. Stanza 3 ends with the ominous raven again.

In the last stanza the poet carries the notion of the identical nature of word and thing to a logical extreme, where prophecy of doom brings doom, where to spell a word is to cast a spell, and the 'autumnal' spell brings a Fall. He has been forecasting changes by means of the alchemy in his blood, which is now depleted. There is no more heart in his words. He leaves it now to the birds on the sea shore, whose vowelled cries are the sounds of death.

> The heart is drained that, spelling in the scurry
> Of chemic blood, warned of the coming fury.
> By the sea's side hear the dark-vowelled birds.

How many opened their copy of *18 Poems* when it was pristine and shuddered at this stanza in recognition of a poet? My own constraint to a task of decades began here.

Fern Hill

(please turn to *Collected Poems*, p. 134)

'War can't produce poetry' – these words from a Thomas letter to Oscar Williams of 30 July 1945 (*Letters*, p. 561/625), a maxim given some prominence when Williams included it in later editions of *A Little Treasury of Modern Poetry* (1948), are accurate enough when we consider the poet's own output. He wrote no poetry that we know of between 'Among Those Killed in the Dawn Raid' (15 July 1941) and 'Ceremony After a Fire Raid' (April 1944). Nothing that he finished, anyway. It was only after D-Day (6 June 1944), with the prospect of victory and peace, that Thomas began to revive. 'Fern Hill' is Thomas's great poem of peace, written soon after VJ Day (15 August 1945).

That 'Fern Hill' is the poem that Dylan Thomas was born to write is confirmed by its universal appeal and continued appearance in anthologies of all kinds. It puts the poet's ever-nagging death theme into a balance with life in a gallant way. Time *does* let one hail and climb, play and be golden. One *does* get a chance to run one's heedless ways.[1] In one's best moods, one cares nothing for the fact that we are allowed few such moments and that one is bound in the chains of time just as much as the sea is ruled by its tides. All this comes singing forth in the poem with great clarity of language.

There is only one crux where an image has caused trouble as regards meaning:

> Nothing I cared, in the lamb white days, that time would take me
> Up to the swallow thronged loft by the shadow of my hand,
>   In the moon that is always rising . . .

Time is taking the young boy by the hand up to the loft where the swallows are gathering to depart at the end of summer, symbolic of the end of an era. This takes place 'in the moon', not in the sun, though, like the sun, the moon also rises, in the Ecclesiastes sense of repetition. In his memory the moon always seemed to be rising in the early evening before he went to sleep, but there is also the sense of the

---

[1] Thomas came to dislike this phrase. After a reading of 'Fern Hill' he told John Malcolm Brinnin that there was one line that embarrassed him: '*ran* my *heed*less ways!' (Brinnin, p. 127). I think we can afford to be less critical than the poet here.

passing of years. For Time takes him by the *shadow* of his hand. I believe the sense here is to be found in the common idea that as the years go by we sometimes feel we are a mere *shadow* of our former selves.

Commentators have been wrong to think of Thomas Traherne as a precursor in connection with 'Fern Hill'. It is true that within a year of writing the poem Thomas did a BBC programme of poetry of his choice, calling it 'Poems of Wonder', and led off with Traherne's *Centuries of Meditation*, 'the wonder of a child looking for the first time at the world' (*Broadcasts*, p. 64):

> The corn was orient and immortal wheat, which never should be reaped, nor was ever sown. I thought it had stood from everlasting to everlasting. The dust and stones of the street were as precious as gold: the gates were at first the end of the world. The green trees when I saw them first through one of the gates transported and ravished me, their sweetness and unusual beauty made my heart to leap, and almost mad with ecstasy, they were such strange and wonderful things. The men! O what venerable and reverend creatures did the aged seem! Immortal cherubims! And young men glittering and sparkling angels, and maids strange seraphic pieces of life and beauty! Boys and girls tumbling in the street, and playing, were moving jewels. I knew not that they were born or should die; but all things abided eternally as they were in their proper places.

Although aware of it, Thomas is not in this tradition of visionary wonder where 'the Light of Day' is a manifestation of 'Eternity' (*Broadcasts*, p. 65). 'Fern Hill' celebrates the literal Fernhill farm of his childhood and Thomas does not confuse his nostalgia with supernatural claims. He uses Garden of Eden imagery, but he knows where he is, his parents' retirement cottage, Blaen Cwm.[2] Dylan and Caitlin and Aeronwy had taken refuge there after leaving New Quay. This was no heaven of things abiding eternally in their proper place. In the letter to Oscar Williams quoted above he called it 'this house too full of Thomases' (*Letters*, p. 558/622). Here, next to 'undeniably mad unpossessed peasantry of the inbred crooked county' (not at all 'immortal cherubims'), Thomas was writing his finest poem of earthly wonder.

---

[2] Long before the poem was written, his aunt Ann Jones had died (in 1933 – memorialized in 'After the funeral' of 1938); Fernhill farm was no longer in the family. When Thomas told Edith Sitwell on 31 March 1946 that 'Fern Hill' was written 'in September, in Carmarthenshire, near the farm where it happened' (*Letters*, p. 583/653), he was referring to Blaen Cwm.

The real precursor of this poem was D. H. Lawrence. The BBC had sent Thomas a collected edition of D. H. Lawrence's poems on 19 June 1945 from which he was to make a selection for broadcasting on 9 September 1945. He wrote to Williams that he was 'liking them more and more' (*Letters*, p. 558/622). He is moved to quote, in the letter, part of Lawrence's 'Ballad for Another Ophelia':

> O the green glimmer of apples in the orchard,
> Lamps in a wash of rain!
> O the wet walk of my brown hen through the stackyard!
> O tears on the window pane!
>
> Nothing now will ripen the bright green apples
> Full of disappointment and of rain;
> Blackish they will taste, of tears, when the yellow dapples
> Of autumn tell the withered tale again.
>
> All around the yard it is cluck! my brown hen.
> Cluck! and the rain-wet wings;
> Cluck! my marigold bird, and then
> Cluck! for your yellow darlings.

'Fern Hill' is Thomas's Lawrence poem, spun, like *Birds Beasts and Flowers* was, out of trouble and weariness in temporary quarters.

Besides this leg-up from Lawrence, where did Thomas get the energy and hope to put together this amazing poem in just a few weeks? Besides the general end-of-war euphoria, Thomas had the possibility of making a personal new start: by going to America. Hence, the long, detailed and witty letter to Oscar Williams, who had agreed to cooperate in getting the family over there with employment for Dylan. This was not to be a visit, but emigration: 'I do not want to return to this country for a long time' (*Letters*, p. 559/624). The swallows are thronging indeed. This will be a Thomas-less land. With determination he writes: 'Let's get out, let's get out.' This is the renewal with which all emigrants are to some extent imbued – the chance to be 'young and easy' again. It is this mood of freedom, I believe, that enhances 'Fern Hill'. He is saying goodbye to the farm of his youth once more, but there is undoubted buoyancy in the poem which comes from expectations of adventure in a far-off land.

Note on 'Fern Hill'

Thomas was referring to 'Fern Hill' when he wrote to David Tennant on 28 August 1945 that he had 'managed to write one new poem and will bring it up to show you when we meet, I think you will like it, it's a poem for evenings and tears' (*Letters*, p. 565/629). If, then, the poem was started at Blaen Cwm it could not have taken more than a couple of weeks to write. That Thomas did not work on 'Fern Hill' as hard as he did on some later long poems – the stanzas are not strictly symmetrical nor are the rhythms consistent – puts in perspective John Malcolm Brinnin's claim to have seen 200 worksheets of 'Fern Hill' still at the Boat House in July 1951 (Brinnin, p. 125). With some wariness I would like to propose that the worksheets around in July 1951 would be those for 'Poem on his Birthday', about 200 pages of which are now at Texas (with also about seventy pages at Harvard).

On 24 November 1949 Thomas wrote to Margaret Caetani:

> I am glad you like Fern Hill best of my poems to date. I also used to like it, and think it was among the, say, half dozen of mine which came nearest to what I had in heart and mind and muscle when first I wished to write them. (*Letters*, p. 733/816)

The 'used to like it' expresses a retrospective caution.

Find meat on the bones

(please turn to *Collected Poems*, p. 53)

In the first stanza of this poem we find a father urging *carpe diem* anthropophagy:

> 'FIND meat [for sex] on bones that soon [with death] have none, and DRINK IN [totally] the two milked crags [breasts], [and] the merriest [courtesan] marrow [elixir of life] and the dregs before the ladies' breasts are [like those of] hags and the limbs are torn [by the ravages of sex and time],

DISTURB no winding-sheets,[1] my son, but when ladies are cold as stone [dead] then HANG a ram rose[2] over the rags [residue of the flesh].[']

That women are to be consumed like meat and drink seems a wild extrapolation upon anything that D. J. Thomas might have offered as worldly advice to his son, though one could find a text for such a mad sermon in *King Lear* (4. 6. 112–4): 'The wren goes to't, and the small gilded fly / Does lecher in my sight. / Let copulation thrive.' That the voice of the poem's 'father' might have been suggested by tendencies in the actual father is something to examine, but not to maintain beyond the cursory. It would be in line with Thomas's methodology to prop up a scarecrow 'father' for a couple of paragraphs as one side of a dialectic 'argument', abstracting and imaging qualities that will be opposed subsequently. The 'father' of the poem continues:

[']REBEL against the binding [constraining] moon and the parliament [law-making] of the sky, [against] the kingcrafts [dictatorial methods] of the wicked sea, [against] autocracy [tyranny] of night and day, [against] dictatorship of sun. REBEL against the [natural confines of] flesh and bone, [against] the word [command] of the blood, [against] the wily [treacherous] skin, and the [natural scavenger] maggot no man can slay [it being an agent of death].'

This philosophy of rebellion also seems quite unlike – in its degree anyway – anything the schoolmaster disciplinarian would propose.

The quasi-dramatic dialogue continues with the son's reply in stanza 3. We gather he took the 'father's' advice about women; and now he has the appearance and feelings of a debaucher. This is followed by utmost contrition in the fourth stanza's 'I cannot murder, like a fool, / Season and sunshine, grace and girl' (lines 30–1).

---

[1] The 'father' draws the line at necrophilia, apparently. See *Letters*, p. 92/110: 'The most terrifying figure in history is, to me, the French abbé who became, through some sexual stringency or latitude, a connoiseur of the grave and a worshipper of his sister Worm. He would not lie with a woman unless she dressed herself in a shroud.'

[2] This would be presumably a symbol of rape. Desmond Hawkins asked about 'ram', and Thomas replied (*Letters*, p. 218/244): 'It's funny about ram. Once I looked up an old dictionary and found it meant red, but now I can't find it in any dictionary at all. I wanted ram in the poem to mean red *and* male *and* horny *and* driving *and* all its usual meanings. Blast it, why doesn't it mean red? Do look up and see for me.' Neither Hawkins nor anyone else has reported finding the meaning 'red' in any dictionary.

I think we can leave D. J. Thomas out of this altogether and see it as two sides to Thomas's adolescent character. Early letters to Trevor Hughes illustrate the point. The first can be dated some time in 1934 when Daniel Jones was visiting: 'last night and the night before we wasted our substances and distended our bellies with low company' (*Letters*, p. 160/144). They decided that sex for them was just 'an instrument to annoy women with' (*Letters*, p. 161/145):

> We started to remember old cruelties, the purposeful raising of desires in girls we knew & the purposeful unsatisfying of them, the tongue-cuts, the embarrassments, the ungrateful things we had done, the muck we'd uttered with our tongues in our cheeks.
> We're over-ripe, we night-walkers, cunt-stalkers, wall-chalkers. The women of the world, perpetually out of perspective, cry, Focus, Focus. Is it our fault that we misinterpret them?

This kind of callousness is the dominant feature of the first three stanzas of 'Find meat on bones' and is repudiated in the fourth in a way that is echoed in another letter to Trevor Hughes (*Letters*, pp. 92/110–11):

> Love is onesided, I admit, for it lies more in what you put into a woman – and for once I am not speaking anatomically – than in what you take out of her. The cynic would say that it is the other way about; but then the cynic is a dead man.

Perhaps this is a good time to reiterate that the poet recognized both a 'beast' and an 'angel' in himself (*Letters*, p. 297/343). We have these two sides of his character debating here. The one side is dissolute (or imagines debauchery) with Domdaniel[3] Jones; the other refuses, like Everyman, to listen to Vice.

Stanza 4 also contains a rebuttal of the cosmic nay-saying of stanza 2, where the protagonist had been told to rebel against the coerciveness of natural law. Now these forces 'rebel' back, but in imagery that is hard to fathom:

---

[3] The protagonist of the novel he was trying to write at this time, snatches of which survive, for example, in *Collected Stories* (pp. 109–10): 'No, not for nothing were these two intangible brandymaids neighboring Daniel who cried, syringe in hand, Open your coke-white legs, you ladies of needles, Dom thunder Daniel is the lightning drug and the doctor.'

> The maggot that no man can kill
> And the man no rope can hang
> Rebel against my father's dream
> That out of a bower of red swine
> Howls the foul fiend to heel.

'The man no rope can hang' is not Christ per se, but is equivalent to the immortal maggot. They stand, I believe, as symbols of the inviolate order to which the soul must attend. Their enemy is a soul-destroying rationality: the 'father' has a vain dream of being able to control the strong invisible forces of evil. It is a reversal of the Gadarene swine story of the New Testament: here, instead of the evil spirits entering the swine, the 'dream' has the 'foul fiend' howling out of them and coming to 'heel'. It is the discounting of these primal powers that the atheistic position asserts and by doing so 'cataracts the soul'.[4]

The refutation continues in the final stanza:[5] the comforting regularity of a hierarchical cosmos is proffered where 'light and dark are no enemies', but like Blakean 'contraries' are 'one companion'. Then we hear the mephistophelean father's voice in frenzy:

> 'War on the spider and the wren!
> War on the destiny of man!
> Doom on the sun!'

'Doom on the sun!'[6] – this is as bad as it gets. The poet comes back at this blackness with an emphatic last line: 'Before death takes you, O take back this' (that is, revoke your position).

I doubt that, at this time, Dylan was worried about his father's soul. More likely he was worried about his own, and brought a fictitious diabolical 'father' into the poem to represent one side of a

---

[4] This is a phrase from the early version of the poem, dated 15 July 1933 in a notebook (*Notebook Poems*, p. 172).

[5] The 1952 *Collected Poems* closed the quotation at the end of stanza 4; the 1988 edition followed the notebook poem in including the fifth stanza. This decision seems to make good sense, since the 'you' of the last line presumably is addressing the 'father'.

[6] *Doom on the Sun* was to have been the title of the novel Thomas was writing in May 1934: 'So far it is rather terrible, a kind of warped fable in which Lust, Greed, Cruelty, Spite etc., appear all the time as old gentlemen' (*Letters*, p. 134/160). The 'father' of the poem is drawn from that ambience.

life problem of some importance to any young man: shall he follow a
natural rebelliousness against restraints, indulging in sexual aggress-
iveness and general licentious thinking about the world, or shall he
listen to that inner voice of calm we call the soul?

Foster the light

(please turn to *Collected Poems*, p. 50)

Though Thomas revised the first draft of this poem (*Notebook
Poems*, p. 214) for publication in *Sunday Referee* on 11 February
1934 (*Notebook Poems*, p. 229), he left it out of the *18 Poems* (1934).[1]
This is strange, for 'Foster the light' expresses more directly than any
of his poems the concept that was driving his thinking and poetic
methodology in that formative period. That Thomas hesitated and
tinkered may have something to do with the poem's inception:
it was written with some deliberation as a rebuttal to his friend
Trevor Hughes. But he kept it heavily disguised. Hughes never knew
that, in appropriating his phrase 'foster the light', Thomas had
negated it.

The background is that Trevor Hughes was the model for
'Raymond Price' in the sad story of *Portrait*, 'Who Do You Wish Was
With Us?' It is a true-to-life representation of all of Hughes's
misfortunes (*Collected Stories*, p. 207):

> I used to hold my father down on the bed when he had fits. I had to
> change the sheets twice a day for my brother, there was blood on every-
> thing. I watched him getting thinner and thinner; in the end you could lift
> him up with one hand. And his wife wouldn't go to see him because he
> coughed in her face, Mother couldn't move, and I had to cook as well,
> cook and nurse and change the sheets and hold father down when he got
> mad. It's embittered my outlook.

---

[1] When Thomas felt he needed poems for his second volume (1936), he gave 'Foster
the light' a further revision. This is the version we have in *Collected Poems*.

Hughes left Swansea for London, and there was a moody exchange of letters, where Dylan tried to match Hughes's misery and, alternately, cheer him up. About 12 January 1934 he wrote of some bad news that had made him 'understand a little, but only a little, of the circumstance that has played so hard with you' (*Letters*, p. 89/108). Dylan's father has had to be operated on for cancer of the throat: 'today he went back to school, weak, uncured. And only a little while ago I learnt the truth of my own health' (*Letters*, p. 89/108). There is a typed memoir (now at Buffalo) in which Hughes quotes his own reply: 'Not the sympathy of words on news of your father's illness.' Then he continues: 'About our own health let us not be perturbed. We shall see no seventh stage, but we shall have our deserts, I doubt not.' There is a fatalistic formality about these sentences. Hughes is leading up to the phrase, 'Foster the light':

How shall a man die if he has never lived, or see the beauty of the stars through the lenses of his own darkness? For so many God has never lived, the faint glimmer within them the glimmer of their own mean ego. This dies upon them, and they must die in darkness; die in the night and move to the eternal fields of darkness. Foster the light, and God be with you.

I cannot think that Thomas enjoyed reading this. When six weeks later he went up to London he handed Hughes 'a sheet of paper, and muttered shyly, as usual, something about "a new poem"' (Buffalo TS). It was, in fact, 'Foster the light', the first version as copied into his notebook the day he left for London. It begins (*Notebook Poems*, p. 214):

> Foster the light, nor veil the bushy sun,
> Nor sister moons that go not in the bone,
> But strip and bless the marrow in the spheres;
> Master the night, nor spite thy starry spine,
> Nor muster worlds that spin not through the skin,
> But know the clays that burrow round the stars.

Shy he might well have been, for the poem used Hughes's phrase 'Foster the light', but surreptitiously applied a syntax which turned it into its opposite. Hughes had taken the Christian viewpoint that God is light and we must foster that light, otherwise darkness condemns us to complete ignominy. If he had read Thomas's letter without blinkers he would have seen that Thomas's view of the world was quite different (*Letters*, pp. 89–90/108):

I become a greater introvert day by day, though, day by day again, I am conscious of more external wonders in the world. It is my aim as an artist . . . to bring those wonders into myself, to prove beyond doubt to myself that the flesh that covers me is the flesh that covers the sun, that the blood in my lungs is the blood that goes up and down in a tree. It is the simplicity of religion.

Simple, maybe, but nothing that Hughes would be likely to recognize as religion. 'A process in the weather of the heart' is the poem Thomas was working on when he received Hughes's letter, suggesting he should 'foster the light', he who was trying his best to meet in verse the dialectical reality of nature.

No, he would not foster the light. But he was mischievous enough to appear to be acquiescing in beginning his poem 'Foster the light', while knowing full well that when you follow such an assertion with 'nor' it has the effect of negating it, since there is never a 'nor' without a 'neither'. According to H. W. Fowler's *Dictionary of Modern English Usage* (first published 1926), p. 382, the 'neither' must always be present in prose, but may be omitted in poetry. In this poem it is omitted, but should absolutely be understood as present: 'Neither foster the light, nor veil the bushy sun, / Nor sister moons that go not in the bone, / But . . .' The 'but' is the syntactical marker indicating that *all* that has been asserted before is to be countermanded, including the fostering of the light.

With the 'neither' in place, the first stanza of the notebook version is saying: neither foster the light nor veil the sun; do not be concerned with any light that does not go in the bone; but rather use the marrow-light that is in cosmic bodies. Neither master the night nor refuse the stars, which are your own spine; do not deal with worlds that are not within your skin; but rather learn about the mortal flesh that exists around the stars.

This may be mysticism, difficult to grasp as 'the simplicity of religion', but it is exactly what Thomas had expressed as his belief: 'the flesh that covers me is the flesh that covers the sun' (*Letters*, p. 90/108). 'Fostering' light is mysticism of a different order, and as expressed by Hughes amounts to a vague Christian optimism in the face of adversity. Thus, to read the phrase in the poem's first line as confirming Hughes's earnestness would be far from the mark. Neither the syntax nor Thomas's stated belief allows for that deduction.

The proper reading takes us immediately into the obscurity that Thomas wants us to inhabit. 'My own obscurity', he wrote less than three weeks after 'Foster the light', 'is quite an unfashionable one, based, as it is, on a preconceived symbolism derived . . . from the cosmic significance of the human anatomy' (*Letters*, p. 98/122). The poem went through a couple of revisions, but the basic human-cosmos symbolism is retained in the *Collected Poems* version.

[Neither] FOSTER the light nor VEIL [conceal] the manshaped [human anatomied] moon, nor WEATHER [endure] winds that blow not down the [human] bone, but [on the contrary] STRIP [take for use] the twelve-winded [year's] marrow from his [the moon's] circle; [neither] MASTER [bully] the night [and dreams] nor SERVE the snowman's [analytic] brain that shapes each [burning] bushy item of the air [cosmic bodies] into a polestar on an icicle [frozen thought].

[Neither] MURMER [sweetly] of spring nor CRUSH the cockerel's [crowed over] eggs, nor HAMMER back a season [reversing spring] in [into] the figs [fruit of the season], but GRAFT these four-fruited [all season] ridings [areas] on your country [body]; FARMER [foster] in time of frost the burning [opposite] leagues [miles], SOW the seeds of snow by [to cool] red-eyed orchards, [and sow] in your young years the vegetable [slow-growing] century.

And [neither] FATHER all nor FAIL the fly-lord's acre², nor SPROUT [feed] on owl-seed [night semen] like a goblin-sucker [incubus], but RAIL [provide rails for bringing] the heart-shaped planet [Venus] with your wizard's [rail-like] ribs; high lord esquire,³ SPEAK of mortal voices to the ninnies' choir up the singing cloud, and PLUCK a mandrake [manshaped] music from the marrowroot [of nature].

[Neither] ROLL unmanly over this turning tuft [earth], o ring of seas, nor SORROW as I shift from all my mortal lovers with a starboard [cosmic] smile; nor when my love lies in the cross-boned drift [dead sea] naked among the bow-and-arrow [deadly cupid] birds SHALL YOU TURN cockwise [as a cock] on a tufted axle.

---

² 'Fly-lord' is a translation of the name Beelzebub, but the line is not suggesting one should go to the devil. Rather, we have, with flies, an extreme example of prodigious paternity – breeding like flies. The line says we should not fail in this department entirely.

³ For reasons that can hardly be guessed at, Thomas injects this nonce figure to make his request to. It is, as we see elsewhere, an anonoymous alter ego, like 'sir,' but now 'esquire' (to rhyme with 'choir'?) It would be funny, as would the word 'ninnies' (which we take to be innocent angels, the opposite of mortals), if the lines did not somehow miraculously maintain a perverse solemnity.

The first stanza can be summed up more or less as Thomas did in his letter: 'the cosmic significance of the human anatomy' (*Letters*, p. 98/122). Neither nurture nor cut off light, but rather use the cosmic forces that are in the self. In the second stanza he uses the seasons to preach his doctrine of contraries. Third stanza: do not be overconcerned with breeding, but bring love into your heart as a planet. These are all recommendations for a sort of 'negative capability', endurance within complexities. In the fourth stanza, it is as though the ins and outs of his loves are equivalent in some way to the motions of the sea, so that when his love is dead the sea will not turn 'cock-wise on a tufted axle'. The image has the world turning on its axle: a weathervane with a cock on it. I think he is saying that nobody should crow about the downfall of love – nor shed a tear, for that matter.

For the last stanza, it is useful to go to the notebook version (*Notebook Poems*, p. 215):

> God gave the clouds their colours and their shapes;
> He gave me clay, and dyed the crowded sea
> With the green wings of fish and fairy men;
> Set thou thy clouds and daylights on my lips,
> Give me thy tempers and thy tides as I
> Have given flesh unto the sea and moon.

At least we can, from this, postulate that the 'Who' of the final version is God:

> [God] who gave these seas [of the previous stanza] their colour in a shape [their existence] SHAPED my clayfellow [mortal being], and the heaven's ark [the earth] in time of flood FILLED with his coloured doubles [all creatures].

Thomas, it seems clear, is willing to say that God created the world and its creatures. But then, I believe, the poem turns from that first creation to the poet's function in an ongoing creation. He is asking that he get from the world what he has put into creating the world out of himself:

> O who is glory in the shapeless maps,
> Now make the world of me as I have made
> A merry manshape of your walking circle.

Or, as he put it in the letter quoted above: the aim is to bring the wonders of the external world into himself. As a poet, he has used the images of the body to express the outside world; now he is asking for the world to supply images for his body: two ways of looking at the same process. He is, in short, seeking to be confirmed in his poetic methodology based on 'the cosmic significance of the human anatomy' (*Letters*, p. 98/122).

It should be emphasized that the role of the conventional Creator is limited to the first three lines of the last stanza – if, indeed, it has not been muted out altogether. I believe that the entity addressed in the line 'O who is glory in the shapeless maps' is, like the muse that poets invoke, whatever works to turn the 'shapeless' into poetry: which for Thomas at this point in time was nothing less than the sea and sky, the whole world itself.

We have come a long way from Trevor Hughes's 'foster the light' as a response to bad news. Despite Dylan's profession of friendship, there would seem to have been a divisive rivalry here. One party knows the gift of light and will foster it; the other's vision is that we are not separate from the light and therefore cannot foster it: our flesh clothes the sun.

From love's first fever

(please turn to *Collected Poems*, p. 21)

For this fairly simple poem Thomas allowed himself to follow the chronological stages of development from conception ('the soft second' of the parents' love-fever, which resulted in a child, the 'plague' – calamitous reproduction) on to weaning, walking and talking, 'the miracle of the first rounded word' (line 12).[1] The stages are registered numerically, babyhood with a 'one' (lines 8–9), the beginnings of self-awareness 'two' (line 16), puberty 'four' (line 20), and thence 'multiplying' (line 23) in a nice biological image of growth: 'Each golden grain spat life into its fellow' (line 24).

Since this is the development of a poet, sex and words go together: in section 4 he becomes 'wise to the crying thigh' and to the 'voice' of

---

[1] This line, which was present in the notebook version (*Notebook Poems*, p. 203) and in *18 Poems*, and was somehow dropped in the *Criterion* printing and the 1952 *Collected Poems*, is restored in the 1988 *Collected Poems*.

wind and sun, which in the next section becomes the voice of dead poets whose 'patch of words' he has to 'knit anew'. He learns his own secret 'code', his style, which is a 'code of night' because of his emphasis as a poet on nightmares, darkness, decay and death. The last section of the poem as published is a recapitulation: from one to two, to a score, and then 'a million minds' contributing to the poetic spark that 'forks' his poetic eyes.

So, we wonder, how is he going to end this poem? What does all this development lead up to in the present? The last three lines are:

> Youth did condense; the tears of spring
> Dissolved in summer and the hundred seasons;
> One sun, one manna, warmed and fed.

Sounds good. The youth consolidates himself. The tears from growing pains disappear with summer and the passing of time. One sun warmed, one manna (God's blessing to the Children of Israel in the wilderness) fed. Adolescence sounds just fine. But what about the 'code of night'? What about the 'root of tongues' ending in a 'spentout cancer, / That but a name, where maggots have their X' (lines 38–9).[2] The poem seemed to be heading in the direction of a protest against the world, but then turned suddenly: the tears dissolve, the sun shines, and the poet gets a good meal from his mother.

Should it not have ended quite differently? The fact is it did, in the notebook, with an additional eleven lines (*Notebook Poems*, p. 205):

> Now that drugged youth is waking from its stupor,
> The nervous hand rehearsing on the thigh
> Acts with a woman, one sum remains in cipher:
> Five senses and the frozen brain
> Are one with the wind, and itching in the sun.
> Stone is my mate? who shall brass be?
> What seed to me?
> The soldered world debates.

[2] Thomas was undoubtedly thinking of his father here; he had been treated for cancer of the mouth and was readmitted to hospital on 17 October 1934, the day this poem was finished and copied into the notebook. His father had wanted to be a poet. Is this what it all comes to? asks the son, who himself at this point has not had much acceptance as a poet.

> How are they seeded, all that move,
> With all that move not to the eye?
> What seed, what seed to me?

Pamela Hansford Johnson, we know, objected to these lines. For Thomas responded in a letter of 5 November 1933 (*Letters*, p. 38/56):

> Your remark about the end of my Feverish poem is entirely justified. I plead guilty to bathos, but offer in excuse the fact that I copied out the poem as soon as I had written it, wanting to get it off to you and too hurried to worry about its conclusion. In the ordinary way I would never have passed it.

So Thomas cut off the eleven lines, and in the course of this self-censorship not only the sexual bathos but the yearning at the end were taken out. What we lose is the truth of the poem as first written and sincerely felt, more accurate about adolescence, it would seem, than 'One sun, one manna, warmed and fed'. The soporific mood of summer was to have made way for discontent and bewilderment, the kind of ending that is hinted at by imagery earlier in the poem, one example of which we should look at because Thomas makes a comment on it.

The 'breaking' of the hair in line 11 was originally 'hatching' (*Notebook Poems*, p. 203). When Miss Johnson objected, Thomas pleaded (*Letters*, p. 38/56):

> Leave me my 'hatching of the hair'. It's verminous, I know, but isn't it lovely? And what is more refreshing than the smell of vermin? Hardy loved to sit beside a rotten sheep and see the flies make a banquet of it. A dark thought, but good and lively. One of the hardest and most beneficial kicks of life comes from the decaying foot of death.

But he remembered the objection and changed the word to 'breaking' for *18 Poems*, retaining the feeling of disease in the sense of 'breaking out' with a rash. In any case, this is the kind of imagery which prepares us for a different ending from the one the poem now has, an ending with which we can be comfortable only by amnesia about the way it originally ended.

Grief thief of time

(please turn to *Collected Poems*, p. 55)

G rief and pain bring on old age.

> Grief thief of time crawls off,
> The moon-drawn grave, with the seafaring years,
> The knave of pain steals off
> The sea-halved faith that blew time to his knees . . .

Time is a thief who crawls into one's life and steals the seafaring years of one's youth. 'Grief' is an adjective: the kind of thief we are talking about is one that produces grieving, thus a 'grief thief'. The thief is characterized, in an appositional phrase, as 'the moon-drawn grave', that is, a tidal wave that takes a sailor's life. Pain also is a thief; it steals one's faith in the future, a young person's faith which at its full can obliterate any sense of time coming to an end. One ends with not even half a hope ('sea-halved'). Life at sea has now become 'at sea'.

But, allied with the effects of grief and pain, the passing of the years induces a forgetting:

> The old FORGET the cries [of pain], [forget] lean time [bad times] on tide [at sea] and times the wind stood rough [adversity], they CALL back [recall] the castaways [shipwrecked] riding the sea light [moon on the water] on a sunken path, [and] the old FORGET the grief, hack of the cough, [and] the hanging [round the neck] albatross [of bad luck], [the old] CAST BACK [recast] the bone of youth and salt-eyed [in tears] STUMBLE bedward where [in memory] she lies who tossed the high tide [high living] in [once upon] a time of stories and [now] timelessly [without awareness of time] lies loving with the thief [in the bed of the grave].

The 'she' here is a flickering prevision of the long-dead Rosie Probert, to whom Captain Cat pleads (*Under Milk Wood*, p. 52). The 'castaways' on a 'sunken path' are like the 'dead dears', the drowned shipmates who speak to Captain Cat in his memory. This first part of 'Grief thief of time', then, strikes familiar chords. It is a reflective disquisition on the way old age looks back, remembers some things and forgets what is too painful. It exhibits a precocious maturity on the part of the eighteen-year-old poet, an ease with assumptions that have the air of experience. Alone, it would make quite a nice poem.

However, it is not alone. It *was* alone as copied into a notebook on 26 August 1933 (*Notebook Poems*, pp. 183–4), and it was revised into its present form on the opposing page of the notebook, with the note: 'Written and copied in later, August 1935, Glen Lough, Donegal.' It would therefore be some time after that that Thomas, leafing through the notebook again, had the idea to connect this revised poem to a later one, 'Jack my father, let the knaves.'[1] One cannot help but take into consideration this process of composition; it prepares one with a proper mind-set for the reading of the second half of the poem.

What did Thomas see in the 'Jack my father' notebook poem to make him want to link it up with 'Grief thief of time'? We would expect some kind of contrary, and that is what we get. In the first part 'the old forget the grief' (line 9); in the second part the 'twin-boxed grief' (doubly incarcerated) is released from its prison; and instead of partial memories which tend towards sentimentality, all will be remembered, including grief:

> All shall remain and on the graveward gulf
> Shape with my fathers' thieves.

Who are 'my fathers' thieves' who pull off this jail-break and through whose agency a total vision is 'shaped' at the end of life 'on the grave-ward gulf' in these last lines of the poem? Glancing through Robert Williams's *Concordance* to hand, I find, as I suspected, that Thomas uses this concept of 'thief' several times throughout his work, especially in the late 'In Country Sleep'; but it is not a counter that can pass from one poem to another at the same value. That's always something to be aware of, and especially here where the notebook 'thieves' seem to be engaged in sexual activity as the be all and end all of their existence (*Notebook Poems*, pp. 193, 197). What Thomas saw, I think, that enabled him to link this 'Jack my father' poem to the 'Grief thief of time' poem was that he could use the sexual as an *image* for recovery of grief. Thomas uses religion, sex, anything to make a point.

> Now [that] Jack my fathers[2] [has] let the time-faced [confronting time] crook, death flashing [like a knife or gun] from his sleeve, with a swag of

---

[1] Dated 26 September 1933 (*Notebook Poems*, p. 197). Thomas revised the first four lines of this early version, using the notebook page opposite. The rest of the revising was done in a manuscript not extant.

[2] Without commas, 'Jack my fathers' cannot be an addressee but must be the subject of a conditional clause: 'Now that someone has let something happen, something else can happen.'

bubbles [seed] in a seedy sack[,] sneak down the stallion [virile] grave [of dead memories], bull's-eye [shoot] the outlaw [banished from sight] through a eunuch [guarded] crack and free the twin-boxed [doubly suppressed] grief, [now that he has let] no silver [police] whistles chase him [the crook] down the weeks' dayed [made up of days] peaks [of strength] to [mere] day to death, [now that he has let] these stolen bubbles [which could burst] have [instead] the bites of snakes [that cannot let go] and the undead [revived grief] [have] [seeing] eye-teeth [to get their teeth into something], [now that he has let] no third [alien] eye probe [invasively] into a rainbow's [new hope] sex that bridges [youth and age] the human halves, [then] all SHALL REMAIN [in available memory] and on the graveward gulf [near death] [all shall] SHAPE [take shape] with [through the agency of] my fathers' thieves.

In this rephrasement I have downplayed the sexual side of the imagery; readers can rectify this omission if they wish. I have tried to bring out, though with some difficulty, the aspects of the images that support the main intention of the stanza in its linkage with the first stanza, that is, the release of grief so that it will remain available for a total vision in old age rather than the warped one of a 'Captain Cat' blinkered world. The phrase 'all shall remain' appeared in the notebook poem (*Notebook Poems*, p. 198) and must have been the pivot for the transformation (though in the early version it means one thing, in the later another). I am not sure the conversion was entirely successful. There were a 'brood of sneaks' in the draft version, but I count only one 'crook' in the final version, which makes the 'fathers' thieves' as a plural more difficult to rationalize. And what is the 'third eye'? The loose ends here are more annoying than usual, for they mar Thomas's worthy effort to counter rigorously what is a rather lazy first part.

Here in this spring

(please turn to *Collected Poems*, p. 41)

It is as though the poet were looking at an illustrated calendar or pointing to a book of seasons. For spring, stars are pictured floating in the universe; for winter, we see naked white snow (like down feathers). Summer is shown burying spring in the form of a bird. Someone has selected these symbols to represent the progress of the seasons. The autumn symbol of burning leaves and bonfires reminds us how the other seasons have gone up in smoke and the birds have sung their four seasons of notes in a dying fall.

The poem turns on a contrast between these decorative pictures and the reality of the world. 'I should tell summer from the trees', says the poet, mildly chiding himself for his previous attention only to the ornamental. The message sharpens when he considers worms as a *living* symbol of winter or the end of the sun and the world. When he looks at reality he sees the usurping cuckoo as the spring's harbinger, along with the slug that eats plants. A worm and slug communicate the eating away of time better than a clock or calendar. What is he told when a timeless insect (death that dissects) says the world wears away? The question is tautological, containing its own answer.

Needless to say, this is an early poem, revised with little expenditure of effort (*Notebook Poems*, p. 168).

Hold hard, these ancient minutes

(please turn to *Collected Poems*, p. 44)

Thomas wrote to Pamela Hansford Johnson early in March 1935: 'I've retired home, after a ragged life, for a few weeks' rest before I go to the country for the summer' (*Letters*, p. 187/214). He had led a riotous bohemian life since moving to London in November 1934. Now back home in Swansea he can write poetry. 'Conditions have more to do with writing than I realized', he told Bert Trick (*Letters*, p. 185/212). 'I do really need hills around me before I can do my best with either stories or poems.' So in 'Hold hard, these ancient minutes' Thomas can celebrate 'Glamorgan's hill' (line 2) from Cwmdonkin Drive, itself on a hill in Swansea, a town in Glamorgan.

But he is already thinking of Derbyshire, 'the country' to which he has been invited for the summer by Margaret Taylor and her husband A. J. P. Taylor, the historian, who was teaching then at Manchester University and living at Higher Disley. It is a time of possibilities. This is the mood that is reflected in the poem. He is telling himself to 'hold hard' as though he is about to ride horseback, with Time at the reins, as 'the horns of England' summon to the foxhunt.

It is not only the poet who has been on the move. All the old gang, practically, have left for England. 'It's very lonely here in Swansea', Dylan wrote to Glyn Jones (*Letters*, p. 186/213). All the birds had flown. Alfred Janes and Mervyn Levy had gone to London even before Dylan; Tom Warner was at Kneller Hall; Alan Stevens and P. E. Smart were in banking in the London area; Dan Jones was at the Royal Academy of Music, living in Harrow. These get into the poem as 'my men, my children' in 'the hanging south'. It is a poem about breaking up and dispersion, addressed to himself and the others who were young together.

> HOLD hard, [during] these ancient minutes in the cuckoo's month [April], under the lank fourth [April] folly [tower] of Glamorgan's hill, as the green blooms [of spring] ride [grow] upward, [hold hard] to the drive [riding] of time;

> Time, in [the form of] a folly's rider [riding around his folly], like a county man [or squire] over the vault [jump] of ridings [or counties] with his [fox] hound at heel, DRIVES FORTH my men, my children [childhood friends] from [their lairs in] the hanging south [of England] [where they hang out].

Daniel Jones and company would be quite surprised to find themselves referred to as 'my men, my children', and likewise the Taylors as foxhunters. We cannot claim that the poem is denotative in that exact way. But it is a reflection of the poet's current situation. He is running fast, as though to get as much into a short life as possible. He projects this race with time onto within-the-poem characters, his 'country darlings' (line 22), who seem to be in some kind of foxhunt where they are potential victims.

> Country, your sport [quarry] IS summer, and December's pools by crane [derrick] and water-tower by the seedy [dowdy] trees LIE [now] this fifth month [since December] unskated, and the birds HAVE FLOWN;

> HOLD hard, my country children in the world of [fox] tales, the greenwood dying as the deer fall in their tracks, [during] this first [spring] and steepled [follied/steeple-chased] season, [hold hard] to the summer's game [yourselves as victims].

And now the [hunting] horns of England, in [having] the sound of shape [creation], SUMMON your snowy [lagging in winter] horsemen, and the four-stringed [musical] hill, over the sea-gut [string/channel] loudening, SETS a rock alive [like Orpheus];

hurdles [fences] and [hunting] guns and railings, as the boulders heave, [and] crack like a spring [season] in a vice, [a clamp which is] bone breaking April, SPILL [trip up] the lank folly's hunter and the hard-held hope.

As the hunter's horse goes down, his hope spills out. April is the cruellest month; it breaks boulders in its grip. They open up and become alive. In this spring you can get blood out of a stone, because of the violence of the season.

Down FALL [spring's] four padding [like horses' hooves] weathers [changes] on the scarlet [hunt-liveried] lands, [which are] stalking [like game] my children's faces [ready to bloody them hunt-fashion] with a tail of blood, Time, in a rider rising, from the harnessed [constraining] valley;

HOLD hard, my county darlings, for a [preying] hawk descends, [while] golden [in sunlight] Glamorgan straightens [stands up in the spring weather], to [kill] the falling [when struck] birds.

Your sport is summer [ahead] as the spring runs angrily.

So spring 1935 was angry at Thomas. Time is threatening not only the poet but his 'children', those he cares for from his younger days. England calls, a summer vacation, but that too is unsettling. It is just a foxhunt there, and he will fall from his horse. The poem says to hold on to hope, hope that was generated in the balmy days of the Kardomah Café.

Constantine FitzGibbon referred to this as a 'patriotic poem' on p. 166 of his biography. If so, it is a very local patriotism. 'I'm surer of nothing than that that world' – Dylan is writing to Daniel Jones – 'was, and still is, the only one that has any claims to permanence . . . Didn't we work better, weren't poems and music better, weren't we happier . . . ?' (*Letters*, pp. 196/223–4). The above was written within three months of 'Hold hard, these ancient minutes'. I believe the 'ancient' minutes are old because of the passing of the old days, and the poem is trying to keep up hope that if they 'hold hard' to the old memories they can be maintained (*Letters*, p. 198/225):

We must, when our affairs are settled, when music and poetry are arranged so that we can still live, love, and drink beer, go back to Uplands or Sketty and found there, for good and for all, a permanent colony; living there until we are old gentlemen, with occasional visits to London and Paris, we shall lead the lives of small-town anti-society, and entertain any of the other members of the WARMDANDYLANLEY-WORLD . . .

'Warmley' was the name of Dan Jones's house; the word sums up everything. It is 'the hard-held hope' which 'bone breaking April', in 1935, was cracking open.

Holy Spring

(please turn to *Collected Poems*, p. 133)

After a night of London air raids and marital quarrelling, the poet walks out into the spring morning and surveys his condition. The 'ruin' that has brought 'an army' into their marriage is the dislocation that the war has caused in Dylan's and Caitlin's domestic life. Around the time of this poem, Thomas wrote to Vernon Watkins in great distress (*Letters*, p. 493/555): 'The place I'm staying in in London with Caitlin is closed after tomorrow or Friday and we haven't yet found anything new. We've been having an awful time, and I have felt like killing myself.' He speaks of 'hunger, anger, boredom hate and unhappiness' (*Letters*, p. 494/555). No wonder the marriage bed, 'that immortal hospital' of the opening lines, cannot soothe, even momentarily, this tension, the war so intrudes into their private lives.

Nor can Thomas rise to that other consolation, the patriotic glamour of war: 'I climb to greet the war in which I have no heart but only / That one dark I owe my light' (stanza 1). This is a fatalistic attitude like anti-flagwaving Falstaff's remark: 'we owe God a death' (*Henry IV pt. 2*, 3.2). Thomas is depressed by it all, but we know that he will use the rhyme-word 'blessed' in the second stanza.

O out of a bed of love [,] when that immortal [heavenly] hospital [lovebed as refuge] made one more move [through sex] to soothe the cureless [mortal] counted [doomed] body, and [when] ruin [war] and his causes [,] over the barbed [for defence] and shooting [for attack] sea[,] assumed [the equivalent of] an army and swept [invasively] into our [emotional] wounds and [private] houses,

I CLIMB to greet the war in which I have no heart but only that one dark [death] I owe my light [existence], CALL for confessor [to absolve him] and wiser mirror [than his own reflective self] but there IS none to glow [as a sign] after the god stoning night [with its bombs and blasphemous language] and I AM STRUCK as lonely as a holy maker [with a vow of silence] by the [morning] sun.

There is no God to appeal to; God has been stoned to death during the night. The sun's beauty makes the poet lonely and speechless. He might think to sing the praises of the spring morning, but he cannot.

No praise [can be sung] that the spring time is all Gabriel [divine annunciation] and radiant shrubbery [burning bush] as the morning grows joyful out of the woebegone pyre [ashes of the night before] and [as] the multitude's sultry [burning] tear turns cool on the weeping wall [of Jerusalem], my arising prodigal [out at night] sun the father [being present with] his quiver full of the infants of pure fire [sunbeams – Psalm 127],

but blessed BE hail [interrupting spring weather] and upheaval [because it is then] that[,] [being] uncalm still [always][,] it is sure [security for him] alone to stand and [to] sing alone in the husk [remnant] of man's home [the world] and [in] the mother [earth] and [in the] toppling [falling] house of the holy spring, if only for a last time.

The poignant and ominous last line sums up the uncertainty of war, and also of marriage, and indeed of life itself. In the midst of these conflicts the only surety is to be able to be alone. Yet, speaking of 'Holy Spring' in retrospect, Thomas called it 'a love poem' (*Letters*, p. 683/ 761). The word love, then, must be taken to include the hopeless longing of someone who feels himself lost, and expresses love chiefly in the act of singing in his aloneness, and blessing its causes, with full knowledge that he is not alone and there are wars he cannot avoid.

That Thomas titled his poem 'Holy Spring' seems to be a recognition that he *is* praising the season of renewal, for all its cruelty. This affirmation is universalized, if not before, then definitely in the last line of the poem. The blessing that the waning world receives from the poet is not really curtailed by any specific situation. The war might take him, so he may not have another chance to sing in this way. True enough. But what we all do, whatever our situation, is done as though it were the last time. Human life on earth has a limited span. Everything that is done is done within the certainty of that obliteration. Indeed, there is no essential difference between now and the end, five hundred million years from now. That ultimate limit is always, if one thinks about it, present in our acts. We do them, knowing everything will perish. Yet we do them, if only for a last time.

Note on 'Holy Spring'

'Here is a poem of mine,' Thomas wrote to Watkins, enclosing the poem on 15 November 1944, 'which I started a long time ago but finished very recently, after a lot of work' (*Letters*, p. 532/594). This is a recognition of its notebook origin (*Notebook Poems*, p. 133), and the wartime transformation of it, done in August 1941. We get this date from the fact that the poem was not listed as existing before July 1941 – a list of poems of that date in Thomas's hand is now at Buffalo – but the revision must have been begun before Thomas took his notebooks down to the bookseller Bertram Rota in August 1941. The first stanza of 'Holy Spring' is drawn directly from 'Out of a War of Wits', dated 22 February 1933 (*Notebook Poems*, p. 133).

How shall my animal

(please turn to *Collected Poems*, p. 75)

It was Henry Treece's article in the 28 October 1937 issue of *New English Weekly*, 'The poetry of Dylan Thomas: an assessment', that initiated a spate of introspection on Thomas's part. He was intrigued that Treece was contemplating a monograph on someone who had published only 'two small books of verse'. But he promised to help: 'I'd like to write at length. I could send you all the new work I have, and other sorts of material' (*Letters*, p. 273/316). He sent things only sporadically. One of them was 'How shall my animal', with a letter of 16 May 1938 in which he talked about his poetry in general and this new poem in particular (*Letters*, pp. 297/343–4):

Very much of my poetry is, I know an enquiry and a terror of fearful expectation, a discovery and facing of fear. I hold a beast, an angel, and a madman in me, and my enquiry is as to their working, and my problem is their subjugation and victory, downthrow & upheaval, and my effort is their self-expression. The new poem I enclose, 'How Shall My Animal', is a detailed enquiry; and the poem too is the result of the enquiry, and is the furthest I can, at present, reach or hope for.

Although Thomas later disavowed 'that remark of mine about "I have a beast and an angel in me" or whatever it was' (*Letters*, p. 373/430), it serves as a useful entry into 'How shall my animal'. At least we are permitted to understand that the animal is inside him.

How SHALL my animal[,] whose wizard [magic] shape I trace [discern] in the [my] cavernous skull, [which is both a] vessel of abscesses [like Job's] and [also its opposite] exultation's shell [amplifying seashell], ENDURE burial under the spelling wall [of written-down words], [under] the invoked [summoned by charms], shrouding [for burial] veil at the cap of the face [neocortex], who [my animal] should be furious, [should be] drunk as a vineyard snail, [should be] flailed like an octopus [with a drunk's movements], [should be] roaring, [and] crawling [drunk-like], [and should] quarrel with the outside weathers [defiant], [should] draw down to its weird [magic] eyes the natural circle of the discovered skies?

The poet's 'furious' animal is his poetic fervour: how can it survive being written down, spelled out, fixed in a poem? How shall it keep its power alive?

How SHALL it [with its animal magnetism] MAGNETIZE, towards the studded male [horse] in a bent [over], midnight blaze [fusion with explosion] that melts the lionhead's[1] heel and horseshoe of the heart, [how shall it magnetize] a brute [animal] land in the cool top [head] of the country days [in order] to trot with a loud mate the haybeds of a mile, [in order to] love and labour and kill in quick [alive], sweet, cruel light [of inspiration] till the locked [sterile] ground sprout out [in words], [till] the black [not blue], burst [killed] sea rejoice, [till] the bowels turn turtle [upside down], [and till the] claw of the crabbed veins squeeze from each red particle [of blood] the parched [with shouting] and raging voice [of poetry]?

[1] This word was discussed with Vernon Watkins: 'I'm as sure now as you are of the "lionhead"' (*Letters*, p. 287/336). But Thomas does not say why he is. It is a neologism, out of Revelation 9:17: 'The heads of the horses were like lion's heads.'

The poetic spirit, which appears to be female for the sake of the image, mates with a stud-horse, and then with the land itself to turn everything around, to get creativity out of cruelty. This really is a poem about being a poet and the pain of the creative act when it occurs on the extraordinary level that Thomas demands of himself.

There is a difference between poetries. 'How shall my animal' is trying to demonstrate something that Thomas spoke about in the letter to Watkins in which he enclosed a copy of the poem on 21 March 1938. Thomas is writing about a poem Watkins had sent him (*Letters*, pp. 278–9/325–6):

> All the words are lovely, but they seem so *chosen*, not struck out. I can see the sensitive picking of words, but none of the strong, inevitable pulling that makes a poem an event, a happening, an action perhaps, not a still-life or an experience *put down*, placed, regulated . . . I want a poem to do more than just to have the appearance of 'having been created'.

Here Thomas contrasts what he wants from a poem with what some other poets are content with. This is the contrast that begins the second stanza of 'How shall my animal', where, within a seascape, 'mermen' represent something 'having been created', something more charming than Thomas's 'animal'.

> Fishermen [poets] of mermen CREEP and HARP [play with the fingers] on the tide, sinking [with bathos] their charmed ['charmed, I'm sure'], bent pin with [using] bridebait of gold [glittering] bread,
>
> I [on the contrary] with a living skein [of blood vessels], [having] tongue and ear [as bait] in the thread, ANGLE the temple-bound[,] curl-locked and animal cavepools of [magic] spells and bone [the skull], [and] TRACE [draw] out a tentacle [organ of touch], [which is] nailed [hooked] with [through] an open eye, in the bowl [skull] of wounds and weed [brains] [in order] to clasp my fury [animal] on ground and clap [fling] its great blood [vitality] down . . .

In contrast with the nice way of writing poetry, the author's wrestling with the vital animal in his brain would be thought to produce a living poem.

But the poem twists at this point: though the level of activity is right, the result is a dead poem.

> Never shall beast be born to atlas the few seas
> Or poise the day on a horn.

The poet has nailed it and pinned it down. The animal (or inner poetic spirit) is caught, brought up from the depths of inspiration, or the sea of the unconscious, only to expire like a clobbered fish out of water.

In the final stanza the dying poem is addressed as it is being fixed in writing. There is a feeling of fatality:

> SIGH long, [you being] clay cold [in death], LIE shorn [cut], [you being] cast high, [and] stunned on gilled stone [the fish knocked into it]; sly [dexterous] scissors ground [sharpened] in frost CLACK [with sharp sound] through the thicket of strength [like Samson's hair]; lover [Venus] hewn in pillars [of words] DROPS [felled] [along] with carved bird, [stone] saint, and sun [at nightfall]; the wrackspiked maiden [guillotine] mouth LOPS [cuts] the rant [poetic words] of the fierce eye, as [though it were] a bush plumed with flames [the Celtic tree of poetry], [and] clips short the gesture of breath [the poem]. DIE in red [bloodied] feathers [as a shot bird] when the flying heaven [of poetry] is cut, and ROLL with the knocked [by the fall of the bird] earth: LIE dry [out of water], [and] REST robbed [of fury], my beast. You have kicked [like a colt] from a dark den [the womb], leaped up the whinnying[2] light [to consciousness], and dug your grave in my breast.

'How shall my animal' is a 'detailed enquiry' into how the angel-intellect wrestles with the beast of inchoate poetic stuff while the madman of words fixes the fight in imagery. The poem is 'the result of the enquiry', in that words have, in spite of the impossibility of the task and the terror of defeat, been found. The poem has been hooked out and grounded; that is the answer to the question of whether or not it can be done. Whether or not it can be done without the poem being bloodied is the other question that is answered.

Thomas said something else about 'How shall my animal' in the above-quoted letter to Treece (*Letters*, p. 297/344):

> The poem is, as all poems are, its own question and answer, its own contradiction, its own agreement . . . The aim of a poem is the mark that the poem itself makes; it's the bullet and the bullseye; the knife, the growth, and the patient. A poem moves only towards its own end, which is the last line.

---

[2] This adjective was apparently 'blowing' in the version sent to Vernon Watkins on 21 March 1938. Thomas asked (*Letters*, p. 280/327): 'About "blowing" light in the last verse. Can you think of anything better?' In his next letter he thanks Watkins for his suggested alternative: ' "whinnying" is certainly far better than my word and may – I am coming to think it is – be the best' (*Letters*, p. 287/336).

There is a nice ambiguity in the statement that the poem 'moves only to its own end'. Its end, as the poem emphatically states in the final stanza, answering the question of the first, is its death. By the last line, the passion of its making over, it has died into a complete shape.

How soon the servant sun

(please turn to *Collected Poems*, p. 48)

This is one of the two poems (the other being 'Now') that Vernon Watkins tried to persuade Thomas to leave out of *Twenty-five Poems* because they 'presented a face of unwarrantable obscurity' (*LVW*, p. 16). I do not think that this is the one of the two that Thomas said 'had no meaning at all'. In any case, he was firm about including both. 'When I said,' Watkins writes, 'that reviewers would be likely to pick these out rather than the fine poems in the book he smiled and said, "Give them a bone" ' (*LVW*, p. 16). So we have the bone, and we gnaw.

Grammatically, the poem consists of three sentences. The first two stanzas and the last two stanzas are each one sentence of similar form, and the middle stanza 3 constitutes one sentence, though with three main verbs. The first syntactical problem is the 'How soon . . .' construction that begins both stanzas 1 and 4. The 'how' does not lead off a question, nor is it, I think, an exclamation, expressing praise for the sun's promptness or whatever. It should be read as a concessive clause: 'however soon something is done, something else will follow'. The more common equivalent would be: 'As soon as . . .'

This is another poem which, in quick strides, takes the poet from conception up to the adolescent present.

How soon [as soon as] the servant [world supporting] sun can unriddle [order] time, and [can] unshelve [take from storage] the cupboard [wombed] stone [body-matter] [with the result] that all my gristles [skeletal matter] have a gown [exterior flesh] and the naked egg [of conception] stand straight [as a grown person],

Sir morrow [the future] at his sponge [soaking up time], [who is] the nurse of giants [the human race in aggregate] by the [caesarian] cut sea basin [of all oceans] TELLS [enumerates] you and you, my masters [everybody], as [while] his strange man morrow [time's agent] blows [blooms] through [because of] food.

We come into the world to be counted, with the sun as source of life. We are heliotropic and move at the sun's behest. We yearn towards the good in a 'rite of light', as the next stanza has it. But there is also the devil in the land, and mice have something to do with that.

All [my] nerves [ready] to serve the sun, [and] the rite of light, I QUESTION [confront] a claw from the mouse's bone, I TRAP the long-tailed [like a mouse] stone with coil [spring-trap] and sheet [shroud], LET the soil [stuff of creation] SQUEAL [that] I am the biting [cat] man and [that] the velvet [smooth as mice] dead inch out [of their mousehole].

In the story 'The Mouse and the Woman' we find *(Collected Stories,* p. 82): 'he had known at the ringing of the first syllable in his ears that nothing on earth could save him, and that the mouse would come out'. The mouse, 'working its destruction, inched into light' (p. 81). In the poem, by questioning 'the mouse's bone' and trapping the 'long-tailed stone' the narrator is serving the sun, and becomes a dentomaniac to do it. This poet bites.

In the final two stanzas he grows a soul, but it seems to end in hell.

How soon [as soon as] my level [of development], lord [sir morrow], shall raise a [spirit] lamp or spirit [raise] up a [spirit] cloud, [or shall] erect a walking centre [of life] in the shroud [of death], [or shall erect] a leg as long as trees invisible on the stump [of matter], this inward sir [spirit], mister and master, the womb-eyed, [who has] darkness for his eyes, CRIES, and all sweet hell, deaf as an hour's ear, BLASTS back the trumpet voice.

This 'inward sir' – can it be anyone other than the poet's essential being? – cries out; from darkness he is giving birth. But it seems to be hell he is going to give voice to; he's going to blast back at the trumpet that created him. 'Fog has a bone / He'll trumpet into meat', we heard in the first stanza in one of the parentheses. Now that the birth has happened, fog (who is Fog?) gets the trumpet blast back again. Anyway, this interpretation, which makes this a poem of adolescent protest, is one way of gnawing on the bone.

I dreamed my genesis

(please turn to *Collected Poems*, p. 25)

Victor Neuburg, who conducted the weekly *Sunday Referee* Poet's Corner and who had just awarded Thomas the 1934 Book Prize, wrote a puff in the issue of 13 May 1934. 'Vicky's article was nonsense', Thomas wrote to Pamela Hansford Johnson (*Letters*, p. 134/160). 'If you see him, tell him I am not modest, not experimental, do not write of the Present, and have very little command of rhythm.' Thomas is in a mood.

> Tell him I write of worms and corruption, because I like worms and corruption. Tell him I believe in the fundamental wickedness and worthlessness of man, & in the rot in life. Tell him I am all for cancers. And tell him, too, that I loathe poetry. I'd prefer to be an anatomist or the keeper of a morgue any day. Tell him I live exclusively on toenails and tumours. I sleep in a coffin too, and a wormy shroud is my summer suit.

> > 'I dreamed the genesis of mildew John
> > Who struggled from his spiders in the grave'

is the opening of my new poem. So there.

The spiders are dropped from the final version and the struggling into manhood is now a breakthrough like boring an iron eggshell with a drill. It is painful rebirth through metal.

Part of the problem is he feels he can no longer be carefree about his writing. 'I am getting more obscure day by day', he wrote in the same letter (*Letters*, p. 130/156): 'It gives me now a *physical* pain to write poetry. I feel all my muscles contract as I try to drag out, from the whirlpooling words around my everlasting ideas of the importance of death on the living, some connected words.' Poetry is like giving birth, a new genesis.

'The importance of death on the living': this phrase helps us to understand the simple world-view behind 'I dreamed my genesis'. Thomas is reifying the death pains of psychic rebirth.

> I DREAMED my genesis [birth] in [nightmare] sweat of sleep, breaking through the rotating [egg] shell, [being] strong as motor [drill] muscle [leaning] on the drill [to make an exit], driving through [by means of]

vision and the [steel] girdered nerve. From [my] limbs that had the measure of the worm [mortality], [I] SHUFFLED off from the [mortal coil of] creasing flesh, FILED [sawed] through all the [leg] irons in the grass [on his path], [which are made of] metal of suns [as in a smelter] in the man-melting night. Heir to [having received] the scaling [molten] veins that hold love's [refined] drop, [being] costly a ceature [created at great cost] in my bones[,] I ROUNDED my globe [world] of heritage, [which is a] journey in bottom gear [uphill] through [the lifespan of] night-geared man [driven toward death].

This is the first rising of the skeleton. But, 'the importance of death on the living' is such, it seems, that the dreamer has to die again in order to establish himself as a man. He has (in stanza 4) to become a war victim, 'Shrapnel / Rammed in the marching heart, hole / In the stitched wound and clotted wind, muzzled / Death on the mouth that ate the gas'.

Later, in writing a broadcast script on Wilfred Owen, Thomas was able to give vent to his opinions on the 1914–18 war. Owen's poems show 'the foolishness, unnaturalness, horror, inhumanity, and insupportability of War' and expose, 'so that all could suffer and see', the heroic lies, the willingness of the old to sacrifice the young (*Broadcasts*, p. 94). But, already, before 'I dreamed my genesis' there are expressions of this abhorrence, for instance (*Notebook Poems*, p. 132):

> Exsoldiers with horrors for a face,
> A pig's snout for a nose,
> The lost in doubt, the nearly mad, the young
> Who, undeserving, have suffered the earth's wrong,
> The living dead left over from the war,
> The living after, the filled with fear,
> The caught in the cage, the broken winged . . .

In a letter dated 'Armistice Day, 1933', he refers to himself and his contemporary, his correspondent Pamela Hansford Johnson, as 'children born out of blood into blood' (*Letters*, p. 54/71):

Genius is being strangled every day by the legion of old Buffers, by the last long line of the Edwardians, clinging, for God and capital, to an outgrown and decaying system. Light is being turned to darkness by the capitalists and industrialists. There is only one thing you and I, who are of this generation, must look forward to, must work for and pray for, and, because, as we fondly hope, we are poets and voicers not only of our personal selves but of our social selves, we must pray for it all the more vehemently. It is the Revolution.

That there is altruistic passion here cannot be denied, though it takes the language typical of its time. It is 'the Revolution' that is 'spat up from the resuffered pain'.

All that we ask for is that the present Dis-Order, this medieval machine which is grinding into powder the bones and guts of the postwar generation, shall be broken in two, and that all that is in us of godliness and strength, of happiness and genius, shall be allowed to exult in the sun.

These words were written exactly six months before 'I dreamed my genesis'. I do not think his opinions changed during that period. In the final lines of the poem, having described in metallic war imagery the struggle to manhood, Thomas, 'grown / Stale of Adam's brine', the sweat of the nightmare of rebirth, receives a vision of himself with new strength, and states simply: 'I seek the sun.' His letter indicates we would be wrong to take this as a personal vision only: 'we are', Thomas wrote, 'poets and voicers not only of our personal selves but of our social selves' (*Letters*, p. 55/72). To 'exult in the sun' was something he wished on behalf of the whole post-war generation. When in this poem he seeks the sun, I do not think he is being suddenly less inclusive.

I fellowed sleep

(please turn to *Collected Poems*, p. 24)

In one of his most definitive statements Thomas announced to Pamela Hansford Johnson in a letter of the middle of October 1933 (*Letters*, p. 25/43): 'I am in the path of Blake.' This was only a few days after he had copied into his notebook the poem that, when revised, gave us 'I fellowed sleep'. To quote in full a pertinent poem of Blake's, 'The Land of Dreams', might give some insight into what Thomas meant in relation to the poem just finished:

'Awake, awake, my little Boy!
Thou wast thy Mother's only joy;
Why dost thou weep in thy gentle sleep?
Awake! Thy Father does thee keep.'

'O what Land is the Land of Dreams?
What are its Mountains, & what are its Streams?
O Father! I saw my Mother there,
Among the Lillies by waters fair.'

'Among the Lambs, clothed in white,
She walk'd with her Thomas in sweet delight.
I wept for joy, like a dove I mourn;
O when shall I again return?'

'Dear Child, I also by pleasant Streams
Have wander'd all Night in the Land of Dreams;
But tho' calm & warm the waters wide,
I could not get to the other side.'

'Father, O father! What do we here
In this Land of unbelief & fear?
The Land of Dreams is better far,
Above the light of the Morning Star.'

It would not be inappropriate to propose this simple Blake lyric as a source for 'I fellowed sleep'. Thomas would have read it on pp. 328–9 in the Everyman's Library *Blake's Poems and Prophecies* published in 1927 and would have retained in the back of his mind the father–son dialogue about the dream of mother and the glow of the land above the Morning Star. In his own 'land of dreams' poem he put these elements to very different use, and one could say that he was more influenced in an enduring way by the acridity of 'The Mental Traveller', the poem adjacent to 'The Land of Dreams' in the Everyman volume.

In any case, where he felt his kinship with Blake, according to the letter quoted above, was in 'the idea of poetry as a thing entirely removed from such accomplishments as "word-painting", and the setting down of delicate but usual emotions in a few, wellchosen words' (*Letters*, p. 25/43). He was preparing Miss Johnson for the awkward, the absence of the suave.

I FELLOWED [made a bedfellow of] sleep who kissed me [anaesthetically] in the brain, [and who] let fall the [chloroform] tear of time; the [fellow] sleeper's eye, shifting to light [illuminating the dream world], TURNED on me like a moon. So, [air-]'planing-heeled [Hermes-like], I FLEW along my man [myself] and DROPPED on dreaming and the upward sky.

I FLED the earth and, naked, CLIMBED the weather [sky], reaching a second ground far from the stars; and there we WEPT, I and a ghostly other, my mothers-eyed, upon the tops of trees; I FLED that ground [for even further remove] as lightly as a feather.

The adjectival noun 'mothers-eyed' might be indicating a close kin as the poet's tree-top companion. Robert Williams has suggested this is an example of the 'Sibling Theme' in Thomas's works. There was an unnamed, stillborn, male child born to Thomas's parents ten years before Dylan (Ferris, p. 17).

But if we have in the poem merely a dream figure, we can accept it as a vaguely familiar 'ghostly other', without needing it to be specific or named. It is 'the black ghost' (*Notebook Poems*, p. 201) with whom the narrator engages in the strange dialogue of stanza 3:

> 'My fathers' globe knocks on its nave, and sings.'
> 'This that we tread was, too, thy fathers' land.'
> 'But this we tread bears the angelic gangs,
> Sweet are their fathered faces in their wings.'
> 'These are but dreaming men. Breathe, and they fade.'

Clearly Thomas considered this verbal exchange important to the poem, but it apparently mattered less – or not at all – who is speaking and who is replying. They are talking about whose land it is they are on. But where are they? How many moves has the dreamer of the poem made? Is he looking down on earth from heaven? Thomas referred to 'the nave of heaven' in another early poem (see *Collected Poems*, notes, p. 192). Is that where the 'fathers' globe' is, in heaven?

We should pause to establish that one of the things the young poet stood for was originality of spatial perspective. He gave a disquisition on point of view to Miss Johnson in his Christmas letter of 1933 (*Letters*, pp. 82–3/99–100):

Walking, as we do, at right angles with the earth, we are prevented from looking, as much as we should, at the legendary sky above us and the only-a-little-bit-more-possible ground under us. We can only (without effort) look in front of us and around us; we can look only at things that are between the earth and sky . . . what the insects under the earth see when they look upwards at the tree, & what the stars see when they look downwards at the tree, is left to our imagination. And perhaps the materialist can be called the man who believes only in the part of the tree he sees, & the spiritualist a man who believes in a lot more of the tree than is within his sight. Think how much wiser we would be if it were possible for us to change our angles of perspective as regularly as we change our vests: a certain period would be spent in propelling ourselves along on our backs, in order to see the sky properly and all the time; and another period in drifting belly-downwards through the air, in order to see the earth.

Strange viewpoints, then, are deliberately sought. Thomas is certainly belly-downward in 'I fellow sleep'.

Perhaps the time has come, too, considering the obscurity of such a line as 'My fathers' globe knocks on its nave and sings', to shift some of the responsibility for our difficulty in explication to the poet himself. In the following passage of a letter to Pamela Hansford Johnson of 9 May 1934, Thomas gives us every excuse not to blame ourselves (*Letters*, p. 130/156):

> when the words do come, I pick them so thoroughly of their *live* associations that only the *death* in the words remains. And I could scream, with real, physical pain, when a line of mine is seen naked on paper & seen to be as meaningless as a Sanskrit limerick. I shall never be understood. I think I shall send no more poetry away, but write stories alone. All day yesterday I was working, as hard as a navvy, on six lines of a poem. I finished them, but had, in the labour of them, picked and cleaned them so much that nothing but their barbaric sounds remained. Or if I did write a line, 'My dead upon the orbit of a rose', I saw that 'dead' did not mean 'dead', 'orbit' not 'orbit' & 'rose' most certainly not 'rose'. Even 'upon' was a syllable too many, lengthened for the inhibited reason of rhythm. My lines, *all* my lines, are of the tenth intensity. They are not the words that express what I want to express; they are the only words I can find that come near to expressing a half.

This is the occasion on which he called himself 'a freak user of words, not a poet' (*Letters*, p. 130/156). This mea culpa, a passing despair though it may be, is somewhat reassuring as we face a line like 'My fathers' globe knocks on its nave and sings', where we feel that quite probably 'globe' does not mean 'globe', 'knocks' does not mean 'knocks', 'nave' does not mean 'nave', 'sings' does not mean 'sings', and 'fathers' certainly has nothing to do with his dad or granddad. I am prepared to say, on the basis of the poet's confession, that it is indeed his fault that the reader does not really know where the 'I' of the poem has got to, except that he is in the clouds. Perhaps that is enough.

Or perhaps we should be very literal and take the poem at its word: that it is a dream. Dreams are bizarre. If Thomas is presenting actual dream stuff then the poem cannot be called to account in the usual way. Let us say that the dialogue of stanza 3 is a close representation of voices heard in dream. It then becomes most realistic. If a poet can get uncensored dream voices into a poem, then he has given us bedrock, not obduracy but the sibylline. Biblical scholars tell us that the most ancient parts of the text are ritual utterances that are entirely resistant to paraphrase. A creative writer of the present can only approximate such intensities of energy by opening up the deepest part of his psyche, which is sometimes available to the dreamer immediately upon waking. It is something of this order that we have, I think, in these lines of dialogue. Such are by their very nature 'black holes' for the explicator. I therefore propose to steer warily around stanza 3. It is a dream landscape, and there are angels.

He breathes on them and they fade. But I think we are still in the dream world, even when in stanza 4 he has put them back to bed in their graves and their oblivion. We are still in the dream world in stanza 5, when he climbs a pulpit of words supplied to him by all the matter of the living air, though the last two lines of the stanza, 'How light the sleeping on this soily star, / How deep the waking in the worldly clouds', seem less a vision than a commentary of a reflective voice, and the vision proper is contained in the next, final stanza.

> There grows the hours' ladders to the sun,
> Each rung a love or losing to the last,
> The inches monkeyed by the blood of man.
> An old, mad man still climbing in his ghost,
> My fathers' ghost is climbing in the rain.

Each rung of the ladder of life represents a victory or a defeat in love; each inch of the ladder is climbed ('monkeyed') by a man at the expense of lifeblood.

Then in the last two lines of the poem we get a final vision, 'an old mad man still climbing'. It is the ghost of 'my fathers', carrying all up the ladder in the rain. Are these the rains of life that one has to go through to reach the sun? The tone of the ending leaves some doubt as to whether or not he will ever reach the goal and in what state of mental health he will do it, but he is nevertheless climbing. There is the barest whiff of the inspirational here. Perhaps none was intended. More likely, this was in fact what came in a dream when the poet fellowed sleep, and what therefore had to be written down, in Blakean fashion, without 'word-painting'.

If I were tickled by the rub of love

(please turn to *Collected Poems*, p. 15)

This is the last poem in Thomas's extant notebooks (*Notebook Poems*, p. 221). It ends with no whimper but a flourish: 'Man be my metaphor.' It is dated 30 April 1934, and Thomas immediately sent off a copy to Pamela Hansford Johnson with the comment, 'The poem is, I think, the best I've written' (*Letters*, p. 126/152). This was a moment of high empowerment for the young poet. He had just returned from a visit to London where he had completely won over a beautiful and talented young woman, for whom he could write a poem of this magnitude and know that it would be read with enthralment when she opened the letter. Not only that, but this was the week when Victor Neuburg announced in the Poet's Corner of the *Sunday Referee* that Dylan Thomas had won the 'Book Prize' – that is, he would have a book of poems sponsored by the paper, just as Miss Johnson had had the year before. This is truly a high point. And the poem is a record of the inner struggle that got him there and of his success in finding a truth to declare before his fellow poets.

We do not know Miss Johnson's response. If she took the wording of the poem at its face value she could hardly have been flattered by lines such as 'Your mouth, my love, the thistle in the kiss' (last stanza). Earlier in the above letter he had done some 'sweethearting' (line 25) (*Letters*, p. 122/148): 'I believe with all my heart that we'll live together one day as happily as two lobsters in a saucepan, two bugs on a muscle, one smile, though never to vanish, on the Cheshire face.' But his poetic self had a different knowledge of the matter: he was 'daft with the drug that's smoking in a girl' (line 30). The poem is saying that neither the stimulus of love nor the fear of death is what counts now. Though he saves the expression of it until the last line, it is his poetic mission that the poem is about.

Meanwhile, the poem proceeds though a repeated syntactical construction: 'If I were tickled . . ., I would not fear . . .' The 'were' is a conditional subjunctive form that does not refer to past time but to an ongoing present condition of hypothetical circumstances.

If I were tickled by [happy with] the rub [act] of love, [by] a rooking [tricky] girl who stole me for her side [bedmate], [who] broke through her straws [leaving her nest], [myself] breaking [the protection of] my bandaged string [tying me to home],

if the red tickle [associated with blood of birth] as the [human] cattle calve [were] still set [as it once was] to scratch [tickle] a laughter [of derision] from my lung,

I WOULD NOT FEAR the apple [of Eden] nor [the punishment of] the flood nor the bad blood of spring [renewal of sinful lust].

If the 'I' of the poem were engaged by love-making or, alternatively, could laugh at the whole thing, he would not fear it. This has the appearance of some kind of psychological insight into his own, or human, nature; however, I believe that, if the statement is true, it is because it cannot be anything but true, being tautological, reducible to the form, 'If I were in a situation of the absence of fear, I would not fear.' Obviously, if he were tickled by love and life, fear of sex and death just would not enter in.

The logic of the second stanza gives us even greater pause, for similar reasons. It begins with a two-line vignette emblematic of Birth. This matches a similar two-line vignette at the beginning of the third stanza denoting Sex. The poet wants Birth and Sex fixed into the poem that firmly.

If I were tickled [pleased] by the hatching hair [at birth], [by] the winging [feather] bone that sprouted [in gestation] in the heels, [by] the [sexual] itch of man upon the baby's thigh,

I WOULD NOT FEAR the gallows nor the axe nor the crossed sticks [swords] of war.

Again this has the form of an 'If A, then B' sentence. Again, however, if the 'I' were 'tickled' then by definition he is not afraid.

The third stanza has further strange logic: if he were 'tickled by the urchin hungers / Rehearsing heat upon a raw-edged nerve', he would not fear the 'muscling-in of love'. Whatever the 'rehearsing' might be – and it usually is taken to be masturbation – it is certainly a rub of love; the 'muscling-in' sounds pretty much like a rub of love too. So, essentially, the sentence reads, 'If A pertained, I would not fear A.'

These sentences do not appear to have a normal declarative purpose. This phenomenon is what Donald Davie called 'pseudo-syntax'.[1] The syntax itself is very firm and is exactly what carries one along; Davie called it 'pseudo-syntax' because he saw that the sentences are put together without the intention of communicating what any reader might suppose was to be meant. But Thomas uses syntax in this way with such determination – and not just within this poem – that we should not dismiss it with the pejorative 'pseudo'. These are very strong sentences and do, with great intensity, communicate. The overall tone of the poem says: *of course* there is no way that I could be tickled, therefore I *do* fear. The statements are technically saying the opposite, but that is how irony works.

Stanza 4 is ironic almost to the point of sarcasm: the passing of time, and the 'crabs' (disease), and the 'sweathearting crib' (an ominous dependency in love) would leave him cold (without fear), but as cold as 'butter for the flies' (not a very comforting kind of fearlessness). The false note of bravado when he says the sea of scums could drown him and he would not care is entirely obvious. He has already in the first two lines of the stanza said that the lovers' rub does *not* wipe away sickness and death. So we have a sentence which, in effect, says 'If I were tickled by A, which does not actually affect B, then I would not fear B' – which is patently nonsense.

It all, however, makes sense as a cry of pain. The yearning involved in the 'If I were tickled' clauses may not have a logical relationship to the fear of 'the devil in the loin nor the outspoken grave' (stanza 3), but it increases the agony of the cry. It is not really conditional, but additive. The plaintive tone sweeps us along, so that we do get the message of his amalgamated pain. Seen in this light, then, the syntax is not 'pseudo' at all, but accomplishes exactly what it is meant to do.

In the first four stanzas – the poet drops it for the rest of the poem

---

[1] Donald Davie *Articulate Energy* (London: Routledge & Kegan Paul 1955), 196. See discussion in *Entrances*, pp. 46–9.

– this syntax establishes the concerns, chiefly death and sex, that he fears are dragging him down. With stanza 6, 'And that's the rub, the only rub that tickles', Thomas has switched to the serious meaning of 'rub': the obstacle or impediment that he really fears at this point in his life. Sexual involvement and moping about death arrest him rather than stimulate him into writing. He sits and watches the 'quick' of life (stanza 5) go by because he is 'daft' about a girl, and feels disabled by thoughts of his mortal corruption (the 'old man's shank' and the 'herrings smelling'). Ay, there's the rub: the delay, because of lethargy. The 'knobbly ape' aspect of himself cannot get a rise out of anything not even when he as a poet finds beauty in love or death. It just is not working for him any more.

In the last stanza he is building up to what should work for him, and it is not 'death's feather' or 'the thistle in the kiss' or (in a further, unexpected dimension) the 'thorny' cross. All of these might 'tickle' but they do not. His poetry of death has dried up. A person is addressed (presumably someone just parted from in London): 'your' hair has mortally wounded my words, he says (stanza 7). His wish is to be stimulated into poetry by reality, the 'rub that is'.

He has asked the question: what's the rub? He has answered in various oblique ways that sex and death have clamped his writing. He has got to get over these guilts and fears and write for humanity as a whole. The proper hurdle has been identified; this is now the fence to leap at with one's words. 'Man be my metaphor' is a one-line rallying cry against all the moaning that has gone before in the poem. It is still only a prayer, but he now has an inkling of what will motivate him in his future writing. He is giving himself the largest possible scope. 'Man himself is a work' (*Letters*, p. 111/136). This new perception is the tickle of the whip that will get him moving.

If my head hurt a hair's foot

(please turn to *Collected Poems*, p. 80)

Robert Graves quoted the first stanza of this poem in his 1954 lecture at Cambridge University entitled 'These Be Your Gods, O Israel!' and in an offhand way said he would give a pound note to anyone who could make sense of it. 'The ingenious Mr M. J. C. Hodgart of Pembroke', Graves wrote in a footnote to the published lecture (reprinted in *Casebook*, p. 165),

> has since come forward to claim the award. He suggests that the child about to be born is here addressing his mother. The child cries out that if he is to cause her any pain by his birth, let him not be born at all.

In spite of admitting there was a 'thin thread of sense', Graves withheld the prize. But Hodgart was quite right, and Graves's blustering merely covered his annoyance at having picked out an easy Thomas poem instead of a really obscure one.

'I refuse to believe', said Thomas introducing a reading of the poem on the BBC, 'that it is obscurer than pity, violence, or suffering' (*Broadcasts*, p. 215). 'But,' he added, 'being a poem, not a lifetime, it is more compressed.'

In the first three stanzas the about-to-be-born child[1] addresses the mother:

> 'If my head [is going to] hurt a [pubic] hair's foot [in coming out of the womb] PACK BACK [into the womb] the downed [haired/brought down] bone [skull]. If the unpricked ball of my breath [my yet unbreathing head] bump [hurtfully] on a spout [at the opening of the womb] LET the bubbles jump out [as I drown in the fluids]. Sooner [I would] DROP [as on the gallows] with the [umbilical] worm of the ropes round my throat than bully ill lóve [turn your love sour] in the [bandaged] clouted scene [the womb turned into a boxing ring].

> All game [blood sport] phrases FIT [can be metaphors for] your ring [womb] of a cockfight [both at conception and now]: I'll comb the snared woods [like a coxcombed poacher] with a glove on a lamp, peck [like a cock or a boxer], sprint, dance on fountains [bobbing] and duck [like a boxer] time [the bell] before I rush in a [boxer's] crouch [at] the ghost with a hammer,[2]

---

[1] Llewelyn Thomas was born 30 January 1939. 'If my head hurt a hair's foot' was described as 'just finished' in a letter to Vernon Watkins of 3 March 1939 (*Letters*, p. 359). It had been a while in the making, for undoubtedly it was begun in the period just prior to the birth which is its subject.

[2] 'The ghost with a hammer' was the nickname – well known at the time – of the south Wales coalminer Jimmy Wilde, who became the world champion fly-weight boxer. The name means that he was almost invisible, like a ghost, until his opponent got hit with the hammer of his fists. Hence, also, in line 7 the boxing glove on the miner's lamp.

[who is like thin] air, strike [hit/come into] light [outside the womb], and bloody [at birth or boxing match or hunt] a loud [with birth cries] room.

If my bunched, monkey [foetal] coming is cruel [to you] RAGE me back to the making house [the womb]. My hand UNRAVEL [for thread] when you sew [up] the deep door [blocking the womb exit]. The [birth] bed IS a cross [angry/antagonistic] place. BEND, if my journey [down the womb] ache [you], [reverse my] direction like an [electric] arc or make [me into] a limp and riderless shape [an un-thoroughbred] to leap [backwards through] nine thinning months [reversing gestation].'

Watkins had some doubts about this first part, but Thomas found himself unable to alter anything and felt he would have to 'leave it unsuccessful' (*Letters*, p. 366/420). The trouble is mainly in the second stanza where the unborn child gets very precocious about the metaphors it can find for the position it is in. That the birth process is like a boxing fight between mother and child: that would alone have made the point, without mentioning four or five other blood sports. There is also a foetal mannerism of clipt phrases.

But the concept is highly successful in its audacity. The offer to reverse the birth process and suffer extinction rather than hurt the mother is a tender emotion. I am sorry for Robert Graves that he could only see this selfless affection as a series of 'disgusting hyperboles' (*Casebook*, p. 165). Through the voice of the foetus the poet is saying that he feels terribly guilty to be bringing his wonderful wife to the threshold of so much pain.

In the second half of 'If my head hurt a hair's foot' the mother begins by answering the question in the form in which it was asked, by simply refusing the offer of terminating the pregnancy. For Christ's sake, no.

'No. Not for [the comfort of] Christ's dazzling [heavenly] bed or a nacreous [mother of pearl] sleep among soft particles and charms[,] my dear [child][,] WOULD I CHANGE my tears or your iron [tearing] head. Thrust [though you may], my daughter or son, to escape [birth], there IS none, none, none, nor [is there escape] when all ponderous [heavily premeditated] heaven's host [accompanying the saint about to fall] of [amniotic] waters breaks.

The mother now feels she has to reassure the child-to-be about being born at all; she intuits a hidden motivation in the child's offer not to be born, a secret unwillingness to leave the womb or, once born, to face life and the inevitable death, things she herself has known and must face again in sympathy.

'Now [we have] TO AWAKE[,] husked of gestures [the moving, gestating baby shelled from the husk of the womb] and my joy [after parturition] like a cave[,] to [experience] the anguish [a different tight constraint] and carrion [flesh immediately on its way to putrifaction], [to awake, that is] to the infant forever unfree [though free of the womb], O my lost [from the womb to mortality] love [child] bounced [by being born] from a good home;

the grain [the substance that will relive in you] that hurries [for the birth] this way from the rim of the grave [that will be yours] HAS a voice and a house [in your body], and there [ultimately in the grave] and here [as a newborn] you MUST couch [lie] and cry.

REST beyond [having no] choice in the dust-appointed grain [flesh furnished with mortality], at the [mother's] breast stored with seas [salt adventures]. [There is] no return through the waves of the fat streets [back into the womb] nor [through] the skeleton's thin ways [the escape through death]. The grave and my calm body ARE [both] SHUT to your coming [in] as [blocked by] stone, and the endless beginning of prodigies [the marvels of life][3] SUFFERS open [with birth].'

In introducing the poem on the air Thomas said (*Broadcasts*, p. 215): 'It is not a narrative, nor an argument, but a series of conflicting images which move through pity and violence to an unreconciled acceptance of suffering: the mother's *and* the child's.' I will add 'the poet's'. For the reality behind the fantastic dialogue of mother and child is the poet's feelings aroused by imminent fatherhood. He is bringing a life into the world: this is a deep challenge to his sense of the worthwhileness of living. Life has to be worth the pain of getting born. But is it? Up until the last line, the mother's voice expresses a fatalist attitude. The question at the back of it all seems to be, 'How can I escape?' Nothing has prepared us for that optimistic word, 'prodigies'. We were almost convinced to be content with being unreconciled to suffering, and then the poet hands us this gift: for a' that and a' that, life is prodigious still.

[3] The last line of the poem as sent to Watkins on 3 March 1939 was 'And the endless, tremendous beginning suffers open' (*LVW*, p. 59). The present line was 'worked from' Watkins's suggestion (*Letters*, p. 366/420).

I have longed to move away

(please turn to *Collected Poems*, p. 53)

'That early morning, in January 1933' – thus begins *Adventures in the Skin Trade,* the unfinished comic novel about a young 'Samuel Bennet' leaving home for London, meeting a used-furniture dealer in Paddington Station, and starting on a series of experiences which would see him shorn of seven layers of skin, as Thomas phrased it to Vernon Watkins, and leave him, in the end, 'stripped of all illusion' (*Portrait of a Friend,* pp. 93–4). The reason the story petered out was because – never capable of sustained fictionalizing – Thomas ran out of real memories very quickly. Thomas told Constantine FitzGibbon that 'on the occasion of his first visit to London he was so frightened that he never left the precincts of Paddington Station' (FitzGibbon, p. 90). This ignominious 'adventure' and turning of tail is the background for a poem about not being able to leave home, 'I have longed to move away', written into his notebook a few weeks later, on 1 March 1933 (*Notebook Poems,* p. 136).

The dual theme that motivates the poem is that of the lies of day and the lies of night: the first are the social lies, the 'repetition of salutes' (line 7), the 'parting of hat from hair' (line 16) – the conventional raising of the hat by the gentleman saying good morning – and 'pursed lips at the [telephone] receiver' (line 17): all are like leftover ghosts, but threatening like 'thunder' (line 10). The lies of the night are frightening nightmares and the general 'ancient fear' of the dark (line 15), 'the old terrors' continual cry / Growing more terrible as the day / Goes over the hill into the deep sea [of dreams]' (lines 3–5).

He images these two fears in the sustained metaphor of a firework cracker, representing what had been the vitality of Swansea and is now a spent squib of disappointment.[1] The stub of the firework is still 'hissing' on the ground (line 2), and it is naturally something he would want to move away from. But he is afraid that if he makes the slightest motion it might explode with unspent force and 'crackle' into the air, leaving him 'half-blind' (lines 12–4). The notebook

---

[1] As Thomas put it in a not unrelated notebook poem (*Notebook Poems,* p. 149): 'It was November there were whizzbangs hopping, / But now there are the butt-ends of spent squibs.'

version is even more emphatic than the published poem on this point (*Notebook Poems*, p. 136):

> I have longed to move but am afraid.
> Some life, yet unspent, might explode
> Out of the lie hissing on the ground
> Like some sulphurous reminder of November,
> And, cracking to the air, leave me half blind.
> This must be avoided at all costs.

That these 'last sparks' represent a great danger to the poet is a puzzle that needs some analysis. One can see quite well why Thomas would want to leave Swansea at this time. He had just lost his job on the local newspaper, perhaps by mutual agreement. He claimed to Trevor Hughes that they had offered him a five-year contract which he had refused, fearing he was already showing signs of 'a reporter's decadence' and feeling that in 'another two years I'd have been done for' (*Letters*, p. 10/28): 'No, what I feared was the slow but sure stamping out of individuality, the gradual contentment with life as it was, so much per week, so much for this, for that, so much left over for drink & cigarettes.' He had an abhorrence of settling into conformity. 'This bloody country's killing me', he wrote to Pamela Hansford Johnson (*Letters*, p. 30/48) – this was in October 1933 but the feelings were undoubtedly long-standing:

> It's impossible for me to tell you how much I want to get out of it all, out of narrowness and dirtiness, out of the eternal ugliness of the Welsh people, and all that belongs to them, out of the pettinesses of a mother I don't care for and the giggling batch of relatives.

So why can he not just leave? In the logic of the fire cracker image he would be in no danger at all from the 'old lie burning on the ground' (line 13) if he simply walked away from it. So why can he not move? He is standing there petrified as though the hissing thing were a snake that would strike at him if he moved a muscle.[2] What is this snake-like firework that will strike him if he moves? Is it not the same phobia that, on his first trip to London, kept Thomas paralysed in Paddington, the last symbolic link with Swansea? It is the

---

[2] The notebook version contained a snake image, 'the snake's head grinning in the soul' (*Notebook Poems*, p. 137).

vulnerability he feels in being about to betray old allegiances; they will strike back, will they not? The paralysis is irrational, of course, and the feared retribution imaginary.[3] The possibility of explosion is not real; this firework is a neurotic one, hissing in the poet's mind in that terrible hiatus before the leap, when he cannot move because of felt guilt. It is not fear of known consequences. The immobility is due to fear alone, inexplicable fear. The poem seems to me to be psychologically true.

[3] In *Adventures in the Skin Trade* Thomas gave it ominous actuality in Samuel Bennet's destruction, during the night before he left, of various things of value to his father, mother and sister. Thomas himself would not have done those cruel things; he is finding a way, in the story, to actualize the feeling that there will be inevitable retaliation at the treachery in his mind.

I, in my intricate image

(please turn to *Collected Poems*, p. 33)

When Thomas went up to live the bohemian life in London in the middle of November 1934 and *18 Poems* was issued a month later, there was the promise of a new stage in the career of the young poet. The move was inevitable, but it came near to being his downfall. The 'ragged life' (*Letters*, p. 187/214) was not conducive to the kind of poetic work that would lead to a second volume of poems. By the end of February 1935 Thomas has very sensibly cut his losses and retreated to Swansea, to his old room and daily poetry writing. He went back to the materials from which 'When, like a running grave' had come; there were still the makings there for the 'very long poem' that he had envisaged in October 1934 (*Letters*, p. 172/198) before he had left for London. From them he would do the big poem that would prove to the world that *18 Poems* was not just a flash in the pan.

We know something of Thomas's state of mind leading up to the writing of the poem because just at this time an old friend Charles Fisher asked him about his 'theory of poetry'. Thomas replied: 'I like things that are difficult to write and difficult to understand' (*Letters*, p. 181/208). Thomas deliberately made 'I, in my intricate image' difficult to write: his rigid stanza form and rhyme scheme meant that it has seventy-two line-endings which are variations on the letter *l* – as Thomas told Watkins, who had not noticed it, 'so subtle was the use of the variation and so powerful the poem's progress' (*LVW*, p. 15). Watkins did, however, confirm that the poem had achieved its purpose in being difficult to understand (*Portrait of a Friend*, p. 33): 'the lines were too packed with meaning . . . there were no "numb" words and lines to give [the poem] natural extension'. Watkins quoted lines of Yeats's in which at least half the words were 'numb'. But that was not Dylan's way. 'If my readers want a breather, they won't get one from me', he told Watkins. 'Let them go away and have a game of table tennis; then they can come back to my next line.' People who have followed Thomas's suggestion in the case of 'I, in my intricate image' have reported that their table tennis game improved significantly but the poem remained stubbornly opaque.

Glyn Jones, who knew Thomas well, has made a useful observation about the methodology in such poems as this (in *The Dragon has Two Tongues*, p. 194): 'I think that words or phrases which seemed to him potent and beautiful used to arise spontaneously in his mind and then, when he was writing a poem, these were unloaded, as it were, a glittering mass, on to the theme.' 'I, in my intricate image' does seem fishy in this sense. Thomas had had three or four months of hectic life during which he was netting many potent and beautiful phrases without having the stillness to sit down and make them into a poem. Now the catch was to be unloaded. As he said to Charles Fisher (*Letters*, p. 182/208):

> I like 'redeeming the contraries' with secretive images; I like contradicting my images, saying two things at once in one word, four in two words and one in six . . . Poetry, heavy in tare though nimble, should be as orgiastic and organic as copulation, dividing and unifying . . . I think it should work from words, from the substance of words and the rhythm of substantial words set together, not towards words.

Thomas is saying that, in his present methodology at least, he does not begin with a subject. He has his catch of words and he works them with the tool of his trade (*Letters*, p. 182/208):

> a poet's middle leg is his pencil. If his phallic pencil turns into an electric drill, breaking up the tar and the concrete of language worn thin by the tricycle tyres of nature poets and the heavy six wheels of the academic

sirs, so much the better; and it's work that counts, madam, genius so often being an infinite capacity for aching pains.

The images he had before him were, it seems, loaded with the metallic, from a life where he had, we deduce, been as hard as nails, having to put on a lot of armour to face the ambushes in 'death's corridor' (stanza 1). Or perhaps the iron images were the compensatory effect of a self-indulgent bohemian life. Be that as it may, here they are, on scraps of paper, and Thomas works them into a generalization (stanza 1):

> I, in my intricate image, stride on two levels,
> Forged in man's minerals, the brassy orator
> Laying my ghost in metal . . .

The images of iron are 'worked on a world of petals' (stanza 2). Spirit and body: there are myriad variations of this 'twin miracle' (stanza 3).

No doubt, if we worked on this poem as hard as Thomas did, we would discover how each image contributes to the one theme of duality. But somehow, with this poem, to know that we could do it makes us feel we do not have to; that, if we did, we would be walking out of the poem by the same door as the one we came in by. Is the effort, in this case, worth it? With a theme so broad, what have we achieved in discerning that an image fits under its umbrella, and the next image sort of does too, and the next image too? There are 108 lines in this poem saying the same thing. Thomas told Watkins he felt 'I, in my intricate image' was 'not entirely successful' (*Portrait of a Friend*, p. 33). It is not on record why he thought so, but in that concession he allows us to think it uniquely indefensible.

It is almost as though it *had* to be written as the culmination of the poet's 'early phase'. In commenting on Glyn Jones's review of *Twenty-five Poems* and his mention of 'rhythmic and thematic dead ends' (*Letters*, p. 243/272), Thomas admitted to carrying 'certain features to their logical conclusion'. He named in this connection the 'Altarwise by owl-light' sonnets, but I think he could more accurately have offered the poem we are here considering when he told Glyn Jones (*Letters*, p. 243/272): 'It had, I think, to be done; the result had to be, in many of the lines and verses anyway, mad parody.' Parody, we know, is the ultimate tribute to a writer whose style is utterly singular. But it is not a tribute a writer can pay to himself. The most judicious way of looking at it would be to suggest that Thomas was writing a blockbuster of a poem as the nineteenth poem of *18 Poems*, saying, 'This is the last time I'm going to write like this.' We can name this the genre of the final encore.[1]

---

[1] With greater fortitude than I, both Emery (pp. 312–17) and Korg (pp. 82–8) have attempted a full paraphrase of this poem.

I make this in a warring absence

(please turn to *Collected Poems*, p. 68)

This poem is unique in the amount of author's commentary available to us. After a reading at Goldsmith's College, London, Hermann Peschmann, the organizer of the occasion, asked Thomas for an explanation of this poem in particular. The reply came in a letter of 1 February 1938 (*Letters*, p. 269/313):

> I can give you a very rough idea of the 'plot'. But, of course, it's bound to be a most superficial, &, perhaps, misleading, idea, because the 'plot' is told in images, & the images *are* what they say, not what they stand for. Still, I hope this is of some assistance . . . The poem is, in the first place, supposed to be a document, or narrative, of all the emotional events between the coming and going, the creation and dissipation, of jealousy, jealousy born from pride and killed by pride, between the absence and the return of the crucial character (or heroine) of the narrative, between the war of her absence and the armistice of her presence.

Besides this summary of the poem, Thomas gave in the letter a stanza by stanza gloss, which I utilize in its entirety in the explication below.

Meanwhile, we should note that, since the title of the poem in its periodical printing was 'Poem (For Caitlin)', there is no doubt who the 'heroine' is. The first draft was finished in September 1937 and 'took two months to write' (*Letters*, p. 260/299); thus the poem was begun soon after the marriage of Dylan and Caitlin in 1937. The jealousies began that early.

Another questioner, Desmond Hawkins, who was preparing a review of *Map of Love* for the *Spectator*, asked about several poems in that volume, including 'I make this in a warring absence'. Thomas again responded fully, and gave the following as a general introduction to the poem (*Letters*, p. 397/449):

> The stanzas are a catalogue of the contraries, the warring loyalties, the psychological discrepancies, all expressed in physical and/or extra-narrative terms, that go towards making up the 'character' of the woman, or 'beloved' would be wider & better, in whose absence, and in the fear of whose future unfaithful absences, I jealously made the poem. I didn't just say in one line that she was cold as ice and in the next line that she was hot as hell; in each line I made as many contraries as possible fight* together, in an attempt to bring out a *positive* quality; I wanted a peace, admittedly only the armistice of a moment, to come out of the images of *her* warpath.
>
> * negate each other, if they could; keep their individualities & lose them in each other.

Thomas here found himself echoing a statement on his methodology which he had written in a letter to Henry Treece of 23 March 1938 (*Letters*, pp. 281/328–9), and which Treece was later to put into his book on Thomas (pp. 47–8); so he went ahead and quoted it for Hawkins (*Letters*, p. 397/449) and then applied it to the poem in hand:

> Excuse me, but this note I wrote for a my-eye essay by H. Treece may as well come in now: 'I make one image, though "make" is not the word; I let, perhaps, an image be made emotionally in me & then apply to it what intellectual and critical forces I possess; let it breed another; let that image contradict the first, make of the third image bred out of the other two together, a fourth contradictory image, and let them all, within my imposed formal limits, conflict'. A bit smug, and old stuff too, but it applies here. And the conflict is, of course, only to make peace. I want the lasting life of the poem to come out of the destroyers in each image. Old stuff again.

We should be prepared, then, for a hotchpotch? This might be so, if the images were merely obscurely descriptive of the situation, as at first sight they might surely seem. In the way Thomas goes on in his explanation to Hawkins, however, it seems that the conflicting and neutralized imagery has an intrinsic efficaciousness in solving the emotional problem that generated it.

Here, in this poem, the emotional question is: Can I see clearly, by cataloguing and instancing all I know of her, good and bad, black & white, kind & cruel, (in coloured images condensed to make, not a natural colour, but a militant peace and harmony of all colours), the emotional war caused by her absence, and thus decide for myself whether I fight, lie down and hope, forgive or kill?

In other words, the poem itself is a finding-out, a sort of self-therapy. With a certain amount of curiosity we can try to follow the poet's struggle with his own feelings and sense of movement towards outcome by means of the imagistic clues. 'The question', Thomas added, 'is naturally answered by the questions in the images and the images in the questions' (*Letters*, p. 397/449).

Stanzas 1 and 2, Thomas's summary for Peschmann:

The 'I', the hero, begins his narrative at the departure of the heroine, at the time he feels that her pride in him and in their proud, sexual world has been discarded. All that keen pride seems, to him, to have vanished, drawn back, perhaps, to the blind womb from which it came.

We can on this basis make a rephrasement of the stanzas:

I MAKE this [poem] in a warring [quarreling] absence [estrangement] when each ancient [slow-moving] stone [stiff]-necked minute of [their] love's [present] season harbours [constrains] my anchored [stopped] tongue, [and] slips the quaystone [dislodges the keystone of the mind], when, [parenthetically] praise is blessed, her [Caitlin's] pride in mast and fountain [sexuality] [which had been] sailed [set forth] and set dazzling by the handshaped ocean [of their hands], [her pride] in that proud sailing tree [mast] with branches driven through [penetrating] the last vault [furthest space] and vegetable groyne [the breakwater or groin of slow-growing love], and [through] this weak house [frail flesh] to marrow-columned heaven [strongly supported bliss] is corner-cast [thrown aside], [the pride having become] breath's rag [worn-out words], scrawled weed [worthless writing], a vain [empty] and opium [stupefied] head, crow stalk [scarecrow], puffed, cut, and blown, or [is] like the tide-looped breastknot [beating heart] reefed [shipwrecked or knotted] again or [is like] the roped [tied] sea-hymen [of a virgin] rent ancestrally [incestuously], and, [parenthetically] pride is last, [when her pride] is like a child alone by magnet winds to her blind mother drawn [by instinct], [the mother being] a bread and milk [soft food] mansion in a toothless town [not able to eat anything else].

The pride in the sustaining sexuality of their marriage has gone. The harshness of the loss is quite clear in the imagery, up to the nice-seeming mother image at the end. I do not think Thomas wanted this image to be as comforting as it sounds. Exactly like the rest, it is meant to communicate the idea that the pride has vanished. Perhaps if we think of the wife's threat to 'go home to mother', we are more on the right track.

Stanzas 3 and 4, Thomas's summary for Peschmann:

> He sees her as a woman made of contraries, innocent in guilt & guilty in innocence, ravaged in virginity, virgin in ravishment, and a woman who, out of a weak coldness, reduces to nothing the great sexual strengths, heats, & prides of the world.

> She MAKES [presents] for me a nettle's [deceptively stinging] innocence and a silk [deceptively inoffensive] pigeon's guilt in [the fact of] her proud absence, [she makes for me] in the molested [raped] rocks the [pearl] shell of virgins, [she makes for me] the frank [innocent], closed [hidden] pearl, [makes] the [virgin] sea-girls' lineaments glint [ominously] in the staved [beaten in] and siren-printed [deceptive] caverns, [she] IS maiden in the shameful oak [of satanic rites],[1] [and she] OMENS [makes herself an omen of] whalebed and bulldance [heavy sexuality], [and] the gold bush [pride] of lions [which are] proud as a sucked stone [marbles in the mouth denoting both posh accent and/or hunger] and huge as sandgrains [small, but large when a desert].

[1] Thomas explicated the third stanza for Hawkins up to this point as follows (*Letters*, pp. 397/449–50):

> SHE makes for me a nettle's innocence and a soft pigeon's guilt; she makes, in the fucked, hard rocks a frail virgin shell; she makes a frank (i.e. imprisoned, and candid and open) and closed (contradiction again here, meaning virgin-shut to diving man*) pearl; she makes shapes of sea-girls glint in the staved (diver-poised) & siren (certainly non-virgin) caverns; SHE IS a maiden in the shameful oak –: (here the shameful oak *is* obscure, a mixture of references, half known, half forgotten, nostalgic romantic undigested and emotionally packed, to a naughty oracle, a serpent's tree, an unconventional maypole for conventional satyrate figures).

> *This is adding to the image, of course, digging out what is accidentally there on purpose.

Responding to Hawkins's concern about the syntax, he added: 'The syntax *can* be allowed by a stretch or rack-stretches; the difficulty is the word Glint. Cut out "Glint" and it's obvious; I'm not, as you know too well, afraid of a little startling difficulty.' The sentence has to be understood as 'she makes something glint', as the poet makes clear in this gloss.

These ARE her [further] contraries [contradictions in her make-up]: the beast [in a man] who follows with priest's [devoted] grave foot and [a hunter's] hand of five assassins [for fingers] her molten[2] [red hot] flight up cinder-nesting [hot phoenix] columns, [and who] calls [in] the starved [hungry-flamed] fire herd, IS CAST [by her] in ice, [is] lost in a limp-treed [detumescent] and uneating [without kill] silence, [while on the other hand the beast] who scales a hailing [for prey] hill in her cold flintsteps FALLS on a ring of [hot] summers and locked [corralled] noons.

These are images of her contrary nature: if you seek warmth and sustenance from her you are left cold and starving; if you expect coldness, you fall into hot water. This is what is contained in the word 'warring'. Caitlin blows hot and cold, always contrary to expectation.

Stanza 5, Thomas's summary for Peschmann:

Crying his visions aloud, he makes war upon her absence, attacks and kills her absent heart, then falls, himself, into a ruin at the moment of that murder of love.

I MAKE a weapon [like Samson] of an ass's skeleton [his own body] and WALK the warring sands [the scene of their quarrels] by the dead town [of their love], CUDGEL great [empty] air, WRECK east [a mere direction], and TOPPLE sundown [which was already falling], STORM her sped heart [no longer there], HANG with beheaded [cut] veins its [the heart's own] wringing [writhing] [empty] shell, and LET her eyelids fasten [in death]. Destruction, picked by birds [vultures], BRAYS through the jawbone [of the ass he is], and, for that [love's] murder's sake, I SPRAWL to ruin [despair] dark with contagion [spreading disease] like an approaching wave.

Stanzas 6 and 7, Thomas's summary for Peschmann:

He falls into the grave; in his shroud he lies, empty of visions & legends; he feels undead love at his heart. The surrounding dead in the grave describe to him one manner of death and resurrection: the womb, the origin of love, forks its child down to the dark grave, dips it in dust, then forks it back into light again.

---

[2] Watkins apparently made specific suggestions about the wording here when consulted by Thomas, who wrote on 13 November 1937: 'I've used "molten", as you suggested, but kept "priest's grave foot", which is not, I'm sure, really ugly' (*Letters*, p. 263/304).

Ruin [suicidal despair], [which is] the room of errors,[3] [which has] dropped [the length of] one road down the stacked [against him] sea and water-pillared shade [weak support unable to keep the shade from falling on him], [ruin which has] weighed [down] in rock shroud [heavy as death], IS my proud [result of pride] pyramid [tomb of love];

where, wound [mummy-like] in emerald [cut stone] linen and sharp wind [like a knife], the hero's [his own] head lies scraped [by the rub of unlove] of every [living] legend, love's anatomist [pathologist] COMES with sun-gloved [oxyacetylene] hand who [ice-]picks the live heart [of the lover] on a diamond [the hardest of beds].

'His mother's womb had a tongue that lapped up mud,'[4] CRIED the topless [headless], inchtaped [measured for a shroud] lips from hank [curled wisp] and hood [of ghost] in that bright [phosphorescent] anchorground [sea bottom] where I lay linened [in a shroud], '[and] a lizard darting with black venom's thread [poison tongue] DOUBLED [itself], to fork [the mother's child] back, through the lockjaw [closed tight] bed [womb] and [through] the breath-white [cold], curtained mouth [womb] of seed.'

'See,' DRUMMED [exclaimed] the taut [drumskin] masks [of the dead], 'how the dead ascend [forked back]: in the [mother's] groin's endless coil [reincarnating spiral] a man [reborn] is tangled.'

Without Thomas's summary for Peschmann, it would be quite difficult to see these spoken words for what the poet intended: fellow suicides for love describing how one can escape that fate if the mother picks up the lost child out of the ashes and rebirths it as a new man.

---

[3] A letter to Desmond Hawkins of 30 October 1937 tells how Thomas was looking at a first draft of this section, 'which dealt with the faults and mistakes of death' and had what he hoped was a 'brilliant and moving description of a suicide's grave'. The original phrase was 'chamber of errors'; this was too close to 'chamber of horrors', and had to be changed (*Letters*, p. 262/304).

[4] With the letter to Vernon Watkins of 25 October 1937 (*Letters*, p. 260/302) Thomas enclosed what he called 'an epitaph' (British Library manuscript), which confirms the presence of suicide here:

He fed on the fattened terror of death, and died.
(And his mother's womb had a tongue that lapped up mud).
The terrible grave was lesson for the suicide:
He slit his throat in the coffin and shed dry blood.

Stanza 8, Thomas's summary for Peschmann:

And once in the light, the resurrected hero sees the world with penetrating, altered eyes; the world that was wild is now mild to him, revenge has changed into pardon.

> These [his] once-blind [with jealousy] eyes HAVE BREATHED [back from the dead into the air] a wind of visions [of a new life], the cauldron [of resurrection]'s root [growing] through this once-rindless [skeletal] hand FUMED [in anger] like a tree, and TOSSED [up now] a burning [phoenix] bird;

> with loud [shrieking from pain], torn tooth and tail [no longer a threat] and cobweb [now unbeaten] drum the crumpled [hornless] packs FLED past this ghost [himself formerly dead] in bloom, and, mild as pardon from a [previous] cloud of pride, the [past] terrible world [now] my brother [in feeling of kinship] BARES his skin [no longer threatening but vulnerable].

Stanza 9, Thomas's summary for Peschmann:

He sees his love walk in the world, bearing none of the murderous wounds he gave her. Forgiven by her, he ends his narrative in forgiveness: – but he sees and knows that all that has happened will happen again, tomorrow and tomorrow.

> Now in the cloud's big breast LIE quiet countries, my love WALKS [as though on] delivered [from harm] seas from her [previously] proud place with no wound, nor lightning [anger] in her face, [and] a calm wind BLOWS that [previously] raised the trees like hair [in fright] once where the soft snow's blood was turned to ice [with fear].

> And though my love [like a baby between tantrums] pulls the pale [quiet], nippled air, with [threatening] prides of tomorrow suckling [building up] in her eyes, yet this [poem] I MAKE in a forgiving presence.

We get a further view of this last stanza from a letter to Watkins of 13 November 1937 in which Thomas enclosed the poem (*Letters*, p. 263/305):

Once upon a time, before my death & resurrection, before the 'terrible' world had shown itself to me (however lyingly, as lines 6 & 7 of the last verse might indicate) as not so terrible after all, a wind had blown that had frightened everything & created the first ice & the first frost by frightening the falling snow so much that the blood of each flake froze.

Once we have caught on to the kind of literalism Thomas's images sometimes ask for, the opaqueness yields a simple beauty. Caitlin's bad temper and coldness froze Dylan's blood in fear, as though he were a falling snowflake. As the poem ends, things are all right; but it is intimated that there are snow warnings ahead.

Working out the duration of its composition, we practically have to think of 'I make this in a warring absence' as a honeymoon poem. In *Caitlin*, the autobiography which is subtitled 'A Warring Absence', we find a pertinent comment about the period during which the poem was written (p. 39):

> At that time, I think Dylan and I were faithful to each other; it was right at the beginning and anyway there weren't many practical opportunities to be anything other than faithful. I was half in love with one of Wyn Henderson's sons, Nigel, but nothing came of that. I used to get these regular infatuations, . . .

The 'prides of tomorrow', indeed. Paul Ferris in the Penguin *Dylan Thomas* (p. 161) passes on an anecdote of Oswell Blakeston's, who was around in Cornwall during this honeymoon time: the artist Max Chapman and Caitlin 'wandered off innocently during a pub-crawl in Penzance and Thomas had a fit of jealousy'. The poem raises to grandeur through its language these oversensitivities of a young husband of twenty-three who has taken on a woman with the froward nature of the archetypal Venus. *Caitlin* again (p. 29):

> In one sense Dylan and I were hardly made for each other. He needed someone with simple values to provide that sheltered, secure, deadly dull and warmly protective small-town Welsh home background in which his best work was always done, and I could only go so far.

Whether this is exactly true for Dylan or not, the threat that she cannot be dull is clear. Her waywardness, the poem tells us, brought the poet to suicidal impulses; and then came relief with her smiling face, even though he knows it will happen again. This pendulum of petty jealousies is nothing to be proud of and consequently we do not find in English literature many poems on the subject. When it is, this one time, written about, with this degree of accuracy and openness, there is perhaps something to be proud of.

Incarnate devil

(please turn to *Collected Poems*, p. 37)

'God was deposed years ago,' Thomas once wrote to Trevor Hughes (*Letters*, p. 162/145), 'before the loin-cloth in the garden. Now the Old Boy reigns.' The God of 'Incarnate devil' seems definitely to be playing second fiddle to Satan, who, embodied as the snake of Genesis 3, stung with his fangs the primordial zero into shapes of sin and pitchforked up the Big Apple (wearing a beard as a disguise). While God has heaven's hill, Satan has the plains of Asia in his garden. God fiddles while the world worms.

The problem Thomas is raising in his own ironic way is the dualist heresy, where God is not all-powerful but shares the stage of eternity with forces of evil that could triumph. The third stanza gives equal time to God and Satan. Three quite beautiful lines go to 'the secret guardian': while almost having to hide in his own Eden, God can be found in the sacred waters eternally temperate and in 'the mighty mornings of the earth'. Satan then brings in hell in a horn of plenty (with sulphur), showing his cloven hoof as symbolic of the cleavage he has made in heaven. His part is black as midnight; it is a gigantic 'fiddle'.

The intensity of the drama of this interlocking of good and evil signals inner spiritual cataclysm. I believe it is his apostasy from his inherited Calvinism that Thomas is concealing in the contest between the Guardians of Eden. But the poem is also a rationalization. One has to emphasize the 'we' in stanza 2: while *we* were still 'strangers to the guided sea', the 'cross' and the 'beast' were already fighting it out.[1] Thomas at the time this poem was first drafted was dedicating his poems to 'others caught / Between black and white' (*Notebook Poems*, p. 179). 'Incarnate devil' declares that 'black and

---

[1] The poem had a notebook version with the revealing title, 'Before We Sinned', and lines like 'Before we sinned was evil in the wind' (*Notebook Poems*, p. 158).

white' go back before the time humanity had any self-consciousness. It is not our fault. We inherited not original sin but the innate dualism in the universe, which is still being fought out over our heads. 'Now the Old Boy reigns', to continue the letter quoted above (*Letters*, p. 162/145), 'with a red-hot pincers for a penis. Here's to him . . . Like a devil, too, I wave my pincers at the stars.' If Thomas wanted to act the devil occasionally, he had, with this poem, found a way of saying, 'It's not my fault'. Or on a more philosophical level he could say that we are all victims of the forces of good and evil which have entwined us. They are bound to be fairly evenly matched in our behaviour as they are, and have been, in the world.

In Country Heaven

(please turn to *Collected Poems*, p. 155)

In these sixteen beautiful lines that the 1988 *Collected Poems* included in the definitive corpus of Thomas's work, we have a picture of God as an old Oedipus who has pierced his eyes in shame at the tragedy that he has allowed the earth to inflict on itself. Thomas started 'In Country Heaven' in March 1947 in the wake of the dropping of the atom bombs in 1945 and with the highly possible annihilation of the world in a Third World War.

> The godhead, the author, the first cause, architect, lamp-lighter, the beginning word, the anthropomorphic bawler-out and black-baller, the quintessence, scapegoat, martyr, maker – He, on top of a hill in Heaven, weeps whenever, outside that state of being called His country, one of His worlds drops dead, vanishes screaming, shrivels, explodes, murders itself. And when He weeps, Light and His tears glide down together, hand in hand. So, at the beginning of the poem-to-be, He weeps, and Country Heaven is suddenly dark.

This is how Thomas paraphrased, with some fidelity, the beginning we have of 'In Country Heaven'. He was explaining to the editor of *Botteghe Oscure* how 'In the White Giant's Thigh', which was to appear in the November 1950 issue, would take its place in a long poem, with the heavenly setting as a framework. He continued (see notes in *Collected Poems*, pp. 262–3):

> And the countrymen of heaven crouch all together under the hedges, and, among themselves, in the tear-salt darkness, surmise which world, which star, which of their late, turning homes in the skies has gone for ever. And this time, spreads the heavenly hedge-row rumour, it is the Earth. The Earth has killed itself. It is black, petrified, wizened, poisoned, burst; insanity has blown it rotten; and no creatures at all, joyful, despairing, cruel, kind, dumb, afire, loving, dull, shortly and brutishly hunt their days down like enemies on that corrupted face. And, one by one, these heavenly hedgerow men who once were of the Earth, tell one another, through the long night, Light and His tears falling, what they remember, what they sense in the submerged wilderness and on the exposed hairs-breadth of the mind, of that self-killed place. They remember places, fears, loves, exultation, misery, animal joy, ignorance and mysteries, all you and I know and do not know. The poem-to-be is made of these tellings.

This is Thomas's plan for what would be, in effect, Canterbury tales during a pilgrimage to save the world. As well as 'In the White Giant's Thigh', he had 'In Country Sleep' and 'Over Sir John's hill' ready. It was an expandable concept, and a magnificent one: to praise life through a vision of loss, to try to hold us, with the power of poetry, from the brink of the abyss.

> And the poem becomes, at last, an affirmation of the beautiful and terrible worth of the earth.
> It grows into a praise of what is and what could be on this lump in the skies.
> It is a poem about happiness.

It is easy to say that Thomas, had he lived, could not have pulled off such a grand scheme. Why could he not? In any case, the ambition is admirable. That anyone should have had it in him to try.

In Country Sleep

(please turn to *Collected Poems*, p. 139)

Who is it that we are to think of as addressed as 'my dear' in this poem? It is tempting to think of the poem as in the genre of Yeats's 'A Prayer for My Daughter'. William York Tindall thought it was, and asked Thomas about it (Tindall, p. 273): 'When I told Thomas that I thought the poem to be about how it feels to be a father, he cried, but whether from vexation, beer, or sentimental agreement I could not tell.' Aeronwy, who was four years old at the time the poem was written in the summer of 1947, has recalled in her *Christmas and Other Memories* (1978) that her father would often read to her: 'We both favoured *Grimm's Fairy Tales*. He would enact the main characters becoming the wolf or a child, giving creditable characteristics of evil and good. We both relished the thrill of horror and fear' (p. 14).

This agreeable picture is somewhat undermined by what we know of the specific circumstances of composition. 'In Country Sleep' was written during a three-month holiday in Florence, Italy. Edith Sitwell had got Thomas £150 from the Society of Authors, and he was under pressure to produce a poem for her. 'I am trying to write a poem,' he wrote to John Davenport from Villa del Beccaro, 'moping over it, every afternoon in the peasant's cottage: our little spankers [Caitlin's sister had also brought her two children] make so much noise I cannot work anywhere near them. God grenade them' (*Letters*, p. 633/705).

We do not have to take that last prayer for his daughter seriously! Our distrust of the father–daughter scenario has a firmer basis in the testimony of the reliable Helen Bevington in her *When Found, Make a Verse of* (1961), pp. 58–9:

So long as anyone would keep talking that night, Dylan Thomas talked, drank beer, chain-smoked, and refused to go to bed, though he had to be in New York next morning for a rehearsal of *Under Milk Wood*. Sometime after midnight I remember telling him that I knew his poem 'In Country Sleep' by heart and proceeding, with absurd temerity, to explain to him what it was about. It concerned, I said, a young child who is told at bedtime never to fear the fairytale witch or redridinghood wolf, for she lives in safe and holy country. The poet, her father, sits beside her bed and comforts her ('my dear, my dear') with the doubtful solace that she need fear nothing at all, only the Thief –

> My dear this night he comes and night without end my dear
>   Since you were born:

He comes slyly in the night like the fox and the wind, her father says, as he has come to her every night of her life. The child does not realize her danger. She yearns for him to come, because she cannot yet know, so young, of what to be afraid. Time is the thief, I said, who steals from her each night a little of her life and leaves her naked and forsaken.

One hastens to agree that this Aeronwy approach is backed up by many clues in the poem. But, unfortunately for our reasonable expectations, the poet vetoed this interpretation.

Dylan Thomas listened raptly, as if to some remarkable, breath-taking tale that he had never heard before. When I had finished, he sat for a while frowning in thought. He seemed reluctant to speak, and I began to wonder if perhaps I had offended him by unraveling his lovely poem. At last he spoke. 'No,' he said, gently, 'it isn't like that at all.'

'In Country Sleep' is not about a child at bedtime with her father, he said. It is a love poem, one he had written to his wife, addressed to someone who is much loved, extremely dear. The lover is in the bed beside his beloved, whispering the passionate words of solace and warning to her in the long night. He tells her of the Thief, who is the destroyer of love:

> He comes to leave her in the lawless sun awaking
> Naked and forsaken to grieve he will not come.

The Thief is the jealousy that steals and changes and destroys the purity of love.

'Something like that,' Dylan Thomas said, with an apologetic shrug of his shoulders. And we both laughed.

Caitlin's claim on the poem – and it is known she did claim it – is as its provoker. 'Dylan wasn't very nice to me out in Italy. He was probably a little jealous', she has suggested (*Caitlin*, p. 102); 'all the men were paying me attention, pinching my bottom as Italians do. I didn't have a proper affair, but I was followed constantly and I think he was jealous of the attention I was getting.' However, the poem transcends the ambience of the time and place of its writing. We might amalgamate both claimants and think of it as addressed to an imaginary Aeronwy inhering in a Caitlin who, as the poem hypnotically tells us, is safely sleeping like a child.

The first part of the poem tells the sleeper not to be afraid of traditional threats. There is nothing out there in the countryside but moonshine, nothing of the threatening wolves of fairy tales nor of the seductive prince charmings. Little Red Riding Hood or Briar Rose can sleep without fear of these characters. The next lines use a series of religious phrases, obvious enough even to the point of blatancy with *sanctum sanctorum* (holy of holies), leading up the 'The country is holy' (line 39) and beyond. But insinuating itself into the verse and into the countryside is a real threat: 'the Thief as meek as the dew' (line 38, stanza 6). 'Be you sure the Thief will seek a way sly and sure' (line 49, stanza 7) – 'Ever and ever he finds a way' (line 56, stanza 8).

With the religious imagery and the adjective 'meek' applied to the Thief, we might jump to the conclusion that it is 'Gentle Jesus, meek and mild'. 1 Thessalonians 5:2 has 'The day of the Lord so cometh as a Thief in the night.' Revelation 3:3 has the voice of the angel saying, 'I will come like a thief, and you will not know at what hour I will come upon you.' Thomas cannot have been unaware of these connections, and he does capitalize the word 'Thief' as someone to be in awe of, but by the end of part I all he has said is that the Thief finds a way each night to come amid falling snow, falling rain, falling dew, falling apple seed, as the world as a whole falls. The Thief is the companion of the falling, and of the sleeper whom the poet calls a 'falling star'.

Part II begins at full blast with wrap-around sound: 'Pastoral beat of blood through the laced leaves!' (line 8). Carmarthenshire fauna, plus a few exotics such as reindeer and the mythic roc, are clamouring, positively leaping, to tell about the Thief, 'who comes as red as the fox and sly as the heeled wind' (line 18). The Thief is well disguised if not invisible as he moves among the vibrant activities of the night.

He can come in close without hindrance or detection because, it seems, he is invited. The loved one lies so still that the watching poet feels she must be the unmoving pivot upon which the earth turns, and if her 'holy heart' was not so engaged in that night-time task the planets would collide, the stern deathknell would weep, and the night would gather her eyes rather than her eyes be heavy with the sand-man's sand. And also the Thief would fall like dew on the graveyard rather than come to her. But the Thief hears the world's wound inside her making its daily journey of pain, and he knows where he has to be. He is drawn there by something deeply fixed in the nature of the world and ourselves. Why is the world an imperfect place? Because something steals perfection which it is perfection's nature to attract. We begin to detect a feeling of inevitability. The Thief is not really breaking the rules; he is part of the design, and not malicious. See the outcome as the poet expressed it in the final lines. It is more positive than anyone could have expected:

> Ever and ever by all your vows believe and fear
> My dear this night he comes and night without end my dear
> Since you were born:
> And you shall wake, from country sleep, this dawn and each
> first dawn.
> Your faith as deathless as the outcry of the ruled sun.

The only indication that anything untoward might have happened is the word 'outcry', which is still ambiguous enough to include both joy and pain.

What has happened? It is not the loved one's physical glories that the Thief is after: not her 'kindled', flaming hair, not her eyes, not her riding high in her pride, not her 'tide raking [daily back and forth] wound' (which I surmise is sexual) – not any of the things that one might suppose the Thief would take if he were an agent of common mortality. It is something other than daily death going on here. It is to do with morale, affirmation, the attachment to life for which Thomas uses the word 'faith'. According to the poem, the Thief comes to steal (lines 39–43)

> her faith that each vast night and the saga of prayer
> He comes to take
> Her faith that this last night for his unsacred sake
> He comes to leave her in the lawless sun awaking
>
> Naked and forsaken to grieve he will not come.

Many of his readers will think that Thomas's cabalistic propensities have got the better of him at this point. I think that he is trying to reproduce that roundabout way the mind works when it is bolstering itself up. There are complicated circumstances to ensuring security, like a Chinese puzzle, a box within a box. The basic fear is to wake forsaken, to feel that the rules have been broken, that the sun is lawless. The Thief somehow is essential to the maintenance of confidence. As long as he keeps coming each night to try (and fail) to steal her faith then there is the presence of the shadow figure who is an essential element of the total landscape. Thomas presents this in a triple negative. She has this belief that each night he *will* come to eliminate her fear that this is the night he will come only to leave her forsaken, feeling he will not come: the threat is that this belief will be stolen from her. Each night his presence negates the fear that he will not come.

We can assert with some confidence this process of reasoning because a sheet of paper exists (at Texas) in which Thomas laid out for himself how this last stanza works:

> If you believe (and fear) that every night, night without end, the Thief comes to try to steal your faith that every night he comes to steal your faith that your faith is there – then you will wake with your faith steadfast and deathless.

> If you are innocent of the Thief, you are in danger. If you are innocent of the loss of faith, you cannot be faithful. If you do not know the Thief as well as you know God, then you do not know God well. Christian looked through a hole in the floor of heaven and saw hell. You must look through faith, and see disbelief.

In this way a poem of Experience emerges from the poem of Innocence that 'In Country Sleep' would have been if its theme had been simply the protection of the loved one. The Thief must come; he is part of the process of self-knowledge. This is not really a paradox but is, we feel, the result of Thomas's own life experience in the complexities of personal survival. He is praying that the loved one learn to know the uses of despair, to know that the positive always comes out of a struggling sea of negatives, and no other way is to be hoped for. The simple fairy-tale threats are nothing compared with the fear of the Thief who threatens one's faith in living. This is part I of the poem. Part II says he must come because we cannot do without him.

In the poem the exact nature of the Thief is left open as something to be created by each of us in our own image. The poet knew what it was for himself. Interviewed by Mary Ellis Barrett for *The Reporter* (27 April 1954) Thomas, when asked about it, said: 'Well, today for me the thief is this.' He was pointing to his empty glass. 'Alcohol is the thief today. But tomorrow he could be fame or success or exaggerated introspection or self-analysis. The thief is anything that robs you of your faith, of your reason for being.' Thomas knew what he was, each night, up against, and he persisted in knowing. This ended the luncheon interview in New York, as Mary Ellis Barrett records it. As they were getting up from the table Caitlin, who was also there – who, as we must now clearly see, was the recipient of the poem being discussed – turned to Dylan, saying: 'You should have eaten something solid.' To that extent, she knew too.

In my craft or sullen art

(please turn to *Collected Poems*, p. 106)

It would be gratuitous to propose to explain what this gem of clarity is saying. However, we definitely cannot accept it at its own evaluation. In the first place, Thomas, as far as anyone knows, never wrote at night. He was certainly ambitious as a poet and also wanted his pay, however meagre, for what poetry he wrote. He did not, of course, write his poems 'for the strut and trade of charms on the ivory stages', but he did, from earliest times, on the BBC and notably on his American tours, *read* his poems with a certain amount of 'strut' and in the way of 'trade'.

This is not to disparage the poem as hypocritical, but to acknowledge it as craft. It is a carved gem, and Thomas tooled the angles and surfaces with great artifice. Truth goes by the board for the sake of beauty. Indeed, the beauty of it is such that it could not possibly go unheeded by anyone. I am sure that many lovers abed have read it to each other, as I am sure Thomas knew they would. Beauty is Truth: romantics will see here portrayed the truest that a poet can be.

In the beginning

(please turn to *Collected Poems*, p. 22)

Two days before Thomas wrote the first version of 'In the beginning' into his notebook on 18 September 1933 (*Notebook Poems*, p. 193) he entered a poem which contained the lines (*Notebook Poems*, p. 191): 'We have no choice our choice was made / Before our blood.' 'In the beginning' takes us back to that time when our doom was sealed. In Thomas's case, his fate was that he should love words. Thus, stanza 4: 'In the beginning was the word.' This is a deliberate echo of the opening of the Gospel of St John 1:1, 'In the beginning was the Word, and the Word was with God, and the Word was God' – which is itself, of course, an echo of the first words of Genesis.

The poem obtains much of its power through repeated resonance of the biblical phrase, 'In the beginning', and through the audacity of rewriting Genesis in its own terms. The poem flirts with the orthodox story of creation. There is even an unmistakable allusion to Christ in lines 11–12: 'The blood that touched the crosstree and the grail / Touched the first cloud and left a sign.' There do not seem to be any others, which would be annoying if one wanted to read the poem as wholly a rerendering of the Bible. I am happy myself not to read it so, to accept that Thomas was referring to Christ in that one place only. For the poem is, I believe, a medley of origin images without progression. Each stanza has some quasi-subject (air, water, fire, word, brain) which pulls certain imagery towards it, but the poem would not be hurt if the stanzas were placed in a different order. Thus the significance is within each image, and common to all.

As far as Thomas himself could express it, we know what significance he meant this poem to have from general comments he made about the poetry he was producing at this time. 'They are, I admit, unpretty things, with their imagery almost totally anatomical,' he wrote to Trevor Hughes in January 1934 (*Letters*, p. 90/108):

> But I defend the diction, the perhaps wearisome succession of blood and bones, the neverending similes of the streams in the veins and the lights in the eyes, by saying that, for the time at least, I realise that it is impossible for me to raise myself to the altitude of the stars, and that I am forced, therefore, to bring down the stars to my own level and to incorporate them in my own physical universe.

In other words, the significance, for Thomas, resides in being able to view the history of the universe as something happening in his own body. That is what we find in this poem: the physical as metaphor for the cosmic. For instance, the first stanza has the beginning of the world be a 'three-pointed star', 'one smile of light across the empty face . . . One bough of bone', and the sun is 'marrowed'. This is using the imagery of the human body to talk about cosmic creation. (To be consistent the 'three-pointed star' would have to denote a part of the anatomy, presumably the part that the triangular fig leaf covers.) The rest of the stanzas follow suit in this repeated metaphoric act. It is a simple bending of an articulated muscle, each time lifting an image from human anatomy into a space denoting the beginning of things. 'Every idea, intuitive or intellectual', Thomas wrote to Pamela Hansford Johnson about this time (*Letters*, p. 39/57), 'can be imaged and translated in terms of the body, its flesh, skin, blood, sinews, veins, glands, organs, cells or senses.' And if the idea is a very inchoate one, as it is here, the work of the poem and its significance will be almost entirely in the terms to be found to express the body side of the equation. The metaphor, in effect, does not have two fixed points in the usual way, but only one: the notion of the beginning so vague that the significance is almost entirely in the image which images it as metaphor.

The feeling within the poem, however, suggests that more is going on than the above reductionist view would allow for. We have to think of the implications of such a flat statement as 'Everything began with the human body.' If we for one moment cease to think of it as metaphor and contemplate it as truth, the implications are tremendous. I think there is a specific source for this poem in the sense that Thomas is unlikely to have reached a position of such originality without having heeded the person who previously presented such ideas. In an early letter of May 1933 Thomas makes a passing reference to 'Lawrence's non-fiction prose' (*Letters*, p. 16/35). I wonder if he had read the foreword to *Fantasia of the Unconscious* (first published in 1923) where Lawrence is 'trying to stammer out the first terms of a forgotten knowledge . . . the real truth, the clue to the cosmos': 'Instead of life being drawn from the sun, it is the emanation from life itself, that is, from all the living plants and creatures which nourish the sun' (Penguin edition, p. 15). A few pages later (pp. 21–2) Lawrence expands this notion in a passage whose first words catch the eye:

> In the beginning – there never was any beginning, but let it pass. We've got to make a start somehow. In the very beginning of all things, time and

space and cosmos and being, in the beginning of all these was a little living creature. But I don't know even if it was little. In the beginning was a living creature, its plasm quivering and its life-pulse throbbing. This little creature died, as little creatures always do. But not before it had had young ones. When the daddy creature died, it fell to pieces. And that was the beginning of the cosmos. Its little body fell down to a speck of dust, which the young ones clung to because they must cling to something. Its little breath flew asunder, the hotness and brightness of the little beast – I beg your pardon, I mean the radiant energy from the corpse flew away to the right hand, and seemed to shine warm in the air, while the clammy energy from the body flew away to the left hand, and seemed dark and cold. And so, the first little master was dead and done for, and instead of his little living body there was a speck of dust in the middle, which became the earth, and on the right hand was a brightness which became the sun . . . Out of living creatures the material cosmos was made . . .

Much of Thomas's 'In the beginning' seems to indicate that he was stimulated by these ideas of Lawrence's. Line 4: 'The substance forked that marrowed the first sun', for example. Lines 16–18: 'Life . . . pumped from earth and rock / The secret oils that drive the grass.' Lines 11–12: 'The blood . . . touched the first cloud and left a sign' – Thomas makes it Christ's blood, but in keeping with this theme it could be anybody's, one of Lawrence's microchristus creatures. And the final lines of the poem: 'Blood shot and scattered to the winds of light / The ribbed original of love.' Not exactly the same as Lawrence, but if the poem is to be thought of as making a substantive statement, rather than being a medley of metaphors, it would be a statement similar to Lawrence's that out of living matter the cosmos began.

The fourth stanza – 'In the beginning was the word' – is perhaps no different in intent from the rest: the word flows up from the physical breath itself. If this stanza has a special feel to it, it is probably because we know how the poet lived by words, words in themselves. We learn from 'Poetic Manifesto' (*Early Prose*, p. 154) that in the beginning were words:

> I should say I wanted to write poetry in the beginning because I had fallen in love with words. The first poems I knew were nursery rhymes, and before I could read them for myself I had come to love just the words of them, the words alone.

In the White Giant's Thigh

(please turn to *Collected Poems*, p. 150)

Much of this poem is made up of descriptions of lusty farmhand sexual activity, where an explicator's help is entirely superfluous. It may appear to some that this sexuality is what chiefly motivates the poem, but I do not think so. There is no paean of praise for the libido here; these country matters all have a heaviness dragging them down. It is a world in which 'the vaulting does roister' ('roister' a lovely word with 'rustic' as its root), 'the horned bucks climb / Quick in the wood at love', and Rabelaisian 'butter fat goosegirls' are 'bounced in a gambo[1] bed'; but the more we get of it, the sadder it becomes, for this is activity without issue, and in the end only the yearning for unborn children is left.

But neither is this loss of children the mainspring of 'In the White Giant's Thigh'. I do not think Thomas would sit down and write a poem to gain our attention for women whose plight is that they have engaged in lots of the activity that should result in conception but did not; and just to make them all the more pathetic we are to suppose that they still want to do more of the same in death? This, if it were all, or even the main thrust of the poem, would be too sad altogether. I cannot imagine an argument that would persuade me that flaming 'like Fawkes fires still' is somehow glorious and that the poem was written to celebrate women of heightened and very persistent sexuality.

Rather, the women are – to coin a phrase – an 'objective correlative' for the narrator's predicament. The vitality of the language used for describing the women and their matings and subsequent longing puts the narrator in the background. But we lose the poem if we forget that these are the poet's emotions. It is he who is walking in the white giant's thigh (line 3); it is he who feels clasped 'to the grains' of the women (line 19), that is, to their dead dust or, in a dialect meaning, their groins; it is he to whom the women 'curlew cry' for him to kiss 'the mouths of their dust' (line 45); it is he who is held 'hard' (line 50). In short, we see him transfixed in reverie.

---

[1] 'Gambo', as a dialect dictionary will tell us, and Thomas told Oscar Williams in a letter, 'means a farmcart' (*Letters*, p. 798/890). Tindall (p. 295) adds that it is a 'kind of goose', but gives no authority for this.

It is the poet's lost opportunities and long-nagging bereavement that we have in this poem. He has worked so hard and produced so little. Indeed, to be specific, Thomas is writing 'In the White Giant's Thigh' in June–August 1950, and since 'Fern Hill' and the end of the war in 1945 he has written only 'In Country Sleep' in the summer holidays of 1947 and 'Over Sir John's hill' on taking up residence in Laugharne in May 1949. However great the two poems may be, it is only two poems in five years. It is not surprising that Thomas might feel himself almost posthumous as a poet, crying like a curlew over his own distributed ashes. For 'women', read 'me'.

The notes to *Collected Poems* (p. 257) present a photograph of the 'Mighty Giant of Cerne Abbas', wielding a club (which could have supplied Thomas with 'the cugelling, hacked hill') and an equally prominent male member. Tindall (p. 293) reports that Thomas told him he had never seen the White Giant 'and had no idea of its location, if any'. It is hard to believe that Tindall heard him right, for Cerne Abbas is a prominent hillside carving only about twenty-five miles from Blashford where he visited his in-laws many times and used to go on bicycle outings with Caitlin. Perhaps what Thomas meant to communicate was that we should not think of the white giant as being in a specific place, but rather as mental space that one seeks when one is in need. 'When the barren girls came hopefully to the Giant', Thomas also told Tindall (p. 293), 'they expected boys to jump from the bushes, where they had lain in wait, to serve the Giant's promise.' This again does not seem true of the women in the poem – they may be 'meridian' (line 59) in the imagined intensity of their unfulfilled desire, but they are buried there immobile. It is the poet who walks in that particular spot because of the 'Giant's promise'; he is placing himself there in hope of regaining vitality. The crucial line of the poem is eight lines from the end (line 53): 'Teach me the love that is evergreen'. He has conjured up these shades who are as forlorn as himself; he grants them in his imagination an enduring flame, and says, 'Teach me to be like you'.

To know how to ask is to have already received. It is my feeling that Thomas carries the torch high in this poem. When I stood in the amphitheatre at Epidavros, looking up at the circles of seats, what I found myself reciting as the only lines of verse I knew with the tensile strength and fullness of spirit to meet the demands of the occasion were the opening diatessaron of this prayer that Thomas was able to make in the white giant's thigh of his imagination.

Into her lying down head

(please turn to *Collected Poems*, p. 94)

In sending this poem to Vernon Watkins on 5 June 1940, Thomas summarized it as 'a poem about modern love' (*Letters*, p. 455/515). Since the poem is about betrayal, this would be a most cynical comment, as would also his proposed title, 'One Married Pair'. 'All over the world', he writes (*Letters*, p. 455/516), 'love is being betrayed as always, and a million years have not calmed the uncalculated ferocity of each betrayal or the terrible loneliness afterwards.' Can Thomas really mean *all* love is betrayal? I believe he does. He continues: 'Man is denying his partner man or woman or whores with the whole night.' It is not just Dylan and Caitlin; betrayal is the essence of love-making, everywhere and for all time. 'Into her lying down head' is 'a poem of wide implications', he concludes (*Letters*, p. 455/516).

Part III (if we can begin there) says that it is true of any two sand grains on a beach under the dome of the sky:

> Two sand grains together in bed, head to heaven-circling head, singly [each one] LIE [deceitfully, indiscriminately] with the whole wide shore, the covering sea their nightfall with no names [anonymous cover-up];
>
> and out of every domed and soil-based shell [on the beach] one voice in chains [all commonly guilty] DECLAIMS the female, deadly, and male libidinous betrayal, golden [sand] dissolving under the water veil [hiding the betrayals].

Then, continuing with part III, there are two images of the way lovers are with each other in betrayal.

> A she bird sleeping brittle [vulnerable] by her lover's wings that [en-]fold tomorrow's flight [in her womb], within the nested treefork [the groin] SINGS to the treading [mating] hawk [']Carrion, paradise, chirrup my bright yolk.[']

The female is enticing a rival predator to eat her egg, rather than have it fertilized by the husband.

The second image is simpler and more soulful: 'A blade of grass longs with the meadow.' And after betrayal: 'A stone lies lost and locked in the lark-high hill.'

Open as to the air to the naked shadow
O she lies alone and still,
Innocent between two wars . . .

'The naked shadow' – one might think of Jung's shadow, the archetype of the rival.

The problem is: how does the 'she' become 'innocent'? The situation is betrayal, but as usual Thomas cannot leave it without the polarity that he sees as basic reality. She is, perhaps not during the 'wars' of sex but in between, innocent. Whether or not a single word 'innocent' can establish this, the poet's intention seems to be that it should. If we can accept this, the word can be seen to connect with previous hints in the poem and thus provide an overall unexpected depth of feeling.

The end of the poem focuses on the husband: 'With the incestuous secret brother in the seconds to perpetuate the stars, / a man torn up mourns in the sole night.' At the moment of orgasm/conception the husband is replaced by an 'incestuous secret brother', the most mysterious and intimate of rivals, and he is rather cut up about it. But the mourning is soft, unvindictive. The betrayal is inevitable. The 'second comers, the severers, the enemies from the deep / Forgotten dark' are always present and 'rest their pulse' after sex and 'bury their dead' (pass on their seed); the wife's sleep is always 'faithless', unfaithful – without faith in the partner.

Thomas seems very knowing here – but not without precedent. Lust in action is essentially betrayal because one treats the partner merely as a thing-lusted-after. Both partners are not their true selves or even their ordinary identities, but are transformed by 'th'expense of spirit in a waste of shame' into callous strangers or even monsters. I do not know what Dr Kinsey has to say on this score, but it is not something that anyone would rush to deny, even though poetry has rarely dealt with it.

Having established the general condition of lust by looking at part III first, we need not fall into the trap of thinking the first two parts are a specific complaint of the poet's about his own life. At the same time, the general could not be intuited without the experience of the particular instance, where Caitlin must have told Dylan that she thought about others during sex and he therefore imagined them to be present in their bed.

Into her lying down head his enemies [rivals] ENTERED bed [as dreams], under the encumbered [heavy] eyelid, through the rippled [disturbed] drum of the hair-buried ear;

and Noah's rekindled now unkind dove [not at peace] FLEW man-bearing there [carrying rivals into her head].

The woman is like the long-legged bait will be in the 'Ballad' of the following year.

Last night in a raping wave whales unreined from the green grave [source of dreams] in fountains of origin [sperm/whale spouts] GAVE UP [released] their love,

along her innocence GLIDED [Don] Juan aflame and savagely young King Lear, Queen Catherine [of Russia] howling bare and Samson drowned in his hair [excessive sexuality], the colossal intimacies of silent once seen strangers or shades on a stair;

there [in her dreams] the dark blade [swashbuckling young man] and [also] wanton [after] sighing [with entreaties] her down to a haycock couch and the scythes of his arms RODE and WHISTLED [in reaping] a hundred times before the [cock-]crowing morning climbed;

Man WAS the burning [with ardour] England she was [randomly] sleep-walking [in her dreams], and the enamouring island MADE her limbs blind [in love] by luminous [movie star] charms,

sleep [then] STROKED and SANG to [comfort] a newborn [returned to innocence] sleep in a swaddling loin-[oak] leaf and [sleep] LAID his [the husband's] beloved childlike in the acorned [oak-seeded] sand.

In writing about the intimacies of strangers on a stair, Thomas must have had an inkling of what Caitlin later told Paul Ferris (in his *Caitlin*, pp. 78–9):

Sex in haste was not to be ruled out; after all it was no more than Augustus John had taught her to expect. Elaborate preliminaries (Caitlin said, when she was old) were disagreeable. Sex was 'something done in the dark and silently'. The sight of a naked man, she insisted, was unwelcome: 'I found men were very attractive *in* their clothes.' She pointed out that a man needed to take off only 'a tiny bit' of clothing in order to 'get that *thing* out'. By implication the act itself was low and contemptible.

One sees that, in detesting sex, Caitlin was somehow innocent.

When Dylan first met Caitlin she was being squired around by the famous painter Augustus John, a friend of her family, who had painted several portraits of her (*Caitlin*, pp. 26–8):

The first time I went to sit for him he didn't speak to me or say anything to put me at my ease: he just glared most ferociously, without the trace of a smile, with his long black hair and long black beard accentuating his fierceness. He usually offered his models £1, but he didn't pay me a penny, and then right at the end of the session he suddenly leapt on me, pulling up my dress and tearing off my pants, and made love to me, although you could hardly call it love. It was totally unexpected and I was still a virgin. He didn't ask for my consent or even try to woo me; he just pounced and I couldn't fight because he was an enormous, strong, bestial man. I was cowed and too frightened to resist. What drove me nearly crazy was that I had wanted Caspar and now I had his hairy animal of a father on top of me instead . . . .

I went and posed for Augustus again the next day – I had to, the painting wasn't finished – and the same thing happened.

Augustus did have a reputation for behaving like that, but nobody had warned me in advance. In the end I was more disgusted than frightened. Every time I did a sitting I knew what was coming at the end – the big leap. I just waited for it, thinking, 'Oh my God! If only I could escape' . . . I certainly had no pleasure myself – it was like being attacked by a goat. The saddest thing is that my whole sexual development happened the wrong way round. It was a catastrophe from which I have never quite recovered.

'Dylan was never aware that I had been to bed with Augustus,' Caitlin told George Tremlett on tape (*Caitlin*, p. 35). 'I didn't tell him and Augustus wouldn't.'

It seems strangely naive of Caitlin to think that Dylan would not know. She apparently never read the second part of 'Into her lying down head'.

There [in her lying down head] where a numberless tongue wound [encircled] their [bed] room with a male [the husband's] moan, [where] his faith [in her] around her flew undone and darkness hung the walls [of the bedroom] with baskets of snakes [symbols of revulsion, deceit and jealousy], a furnace-nostrilled [dragon-like] column-membered [priapistic] super-or-near man resembling to her dulled sense the [deflowering] thief of adolescence, early imaginary half remembered oceanic [overwhelming] lover [the one] alone [the husband's] jealousy cannot forget [even] for all her sakes, MADE his bad bed in her good night [dreams], and ENJOYED as he would.

Crying, white gowned, from the middle [of the night] moonlit stages out to the tiered and hearing tide, close and far she ANNOUNCED the theft of the [her] heart in the taken [raped] body at many ages, [even now in her dreams] trespasser [thief of adolescence] and broken [raped] bride celebrating at her side [in bed] all blood-signed [causing bleeding] assailings and vanished marriages in which he [the husband] had no lovely part nor could share, for [because of] his pride, to the least mutter and foul wingbeat of the [vulture-like] solemnizing nightpriest her holy unholy hours with the always anonymous beast.

The beast's name is never mentioned, but it is clear that Thomas knew there had been a 'thief of adolescence' for Caitlin, and he doubtless knew who it was. No wonder he thought of her as innocent.

This poem was begun in Caitlin's mother's house in Blashford, where the vestigial presence of Augustus John was always strong. Thomas announced 'an ambitious new poem' in a letter of 11 March 1940 (*Letters*, p. 445/504). It was completed after the move to Laugharne, and was enclosed to Watkins in the 5 June 1940 letter. It is not known that there were any infidelities in this period or even opportunities for such. The poem, it should be noted, is prior to Marshfield and Caitlin's farcical one-night-stand that became public knowledge. 'Into her lying down head' does not, therefore, commemorate, as far as we know, any overt act. It is, for the time being, all in the 'lying down' head.

As to that provocative phrase, 'lying' and 'down' joined together as an adjective would normally have a hyphen: 'lying-down head', indicating simply that the woman is sleeping. With two separate adjectives, we have a play on words: 'down' is a tender way of talking about the beloved's hair; 'lying head' is a brutal accusation. The poem swings between these two poles, betrayal and innocence, to try to get at the true nature of sex.

I see the boys of summer

(please turn to *Collected Poems*, p. 7)

It may help with this poem to know that it was written in two stages. The present part I was sent to Geoffrey Grigson, editor of *New Verse*, as 'a new poem, just completed' about 18 March 1934 (*Letters*, p. 105/129). The last of these four stanzas refers to 'men of nothing', whom the boys of summer, 'by seedy shifting', will grow up to be: it is doubtless this image to which A. E. Trick, Thomas's close friend at the time, was referring when he remarked in conversation that 'I see the boys of summer' had its origin when he and Dylan walking one day on the beach saw middle-aged men in Swansea Corporation bathing suits and the poet just came out with the phrase 'boys of summer in their ruin' as a response to the pathos of that scene.

But Thomas was not content to let the poem stay as a one-sided statement; he doubled it by means of a mirror image comprising four more stanzas, and then a 'coda'. The whole was entered into his notebook over the date 'April '34', and sent off to Grigson as 'the complete poem' (*Letters*, p. 120/143). In May 1934, discussing with Pamela Hansford Johnson the choice of poems for *18 Poems*, Thomas told her that ' "Boys of summer", though altered and double the length, is to open the book' (*Letters*, p. 125/151). It was a poem he now felt proud of. After *18 Poems* came out, he told Frederick Prokosch that it was one of the best two poems in the book (*Letters*, p. 208/235).

> I SEE the boys of summer in their ruin lay the gold tithings [wheat fields] barren, [I see them] setting no store by harvest, freeze the soils; there in their [summer] heat the winter floods of frozen loves they FETCH their girls, and DROWN the cargoed [harvested] apples in their tides.

There seems to be no further way of interpreting these images other than to note they represent the concept of opposition. In *Entrances* (pp. 20–1) I went so far as to diagram the oppositions of the second stanza with (+) for summer (positive poles) and (–) for ruin (negative poles):

> These boys of light (+) are curdlers in their folly (–),
> Sour (–) the boiling honey (+);
> The jacks of frost (–) they finger in the hives (+);
> There in the sun (+) the frigid threads
> Of doubt and dark (–) they feed their nerves;
> The signal moon (+) is zero in their voids (–).

Perhaps this is the optimum way of explicating this stanza and others like it; sheer opposition is what Thomas is getting at. Without such a graphic device the poet himself tried to put into words his methodology and came up with this (*Letters*, p. 281/328):

I make one image, – though 'make' is not the word, I let, perhaps, an image be 'made' emotionally in me and then apply to it what intellectual & critical forces I possess – let it breed another, let that image contradict the first, make, of the third image bred out of the other two together, a fourth contradictory image, and let them all, within my imposed formal limits, conflict. Each image holds within it the seed of its own destruction, and my dialectical method, as I understand it, is a constant building up and breaking down of the images that come out of the central seed, which is itself destructive and constructive at the same time.

Applying this to the above stanza we can see that 'curdlers' in the first line *bred* the 'sour' of the second, with a shift in its meaning, sour milk to unsweet honey. The 'boiling' suggested its opposite, 'freezing', and thus 'jacks of frost' (male member as icicle), while 'honey' gives them the 'hive' (a hot honey pot) to push into. Thus the 'dialectical' method moves through similarities and contradictions. The 'frost' produces 'frigid'; the boys feed into their nerves the frigid threads of doubt and dark. It is a different image from the preceding, 'contradictory' in the sense of thwarting our expectation of a continuing locale. The logic of this breeding and contradicting is simple association of ideas. The 'sun' suggests 'moon' two lines below it; 'nerves' makes the moon a 'signal' moon – though the signal is changed from electrical impulse to semaphore – the full moon, a harvest moon, signalling a change of weather, its roundness nullified by the boys of summer so that as a zero it ceases to be a signal. The adversarial nature of these wide-ranging images makes sure we do not rest anywhere but with the broad concept onto which the poet is hanging the poem. The 'jacks of frost' with their 'hives' could be taken on an entirely sexual plane, except that adding nerves and moon and zero and voids pushes the interpretation much further back into a very generalized notion, in this case, the idea of sheer opposition. In this surprising way, the disparateness of the images does the job of giving a strong core to the poem. Thomas's self-examination of his method concluded (*Letters*, p. 282/329):

Out of the inevitable conflict of images – inevitable, because of the creative, recreative, destructive, and contradictory nature of the motivating centre, the womb of war – I try to make that momentary peace which is a poem. I do not want a poem of mine to be, nor can it be, a circular piece of experience placed neatly outside the living stream of time from which it came; a poem of mine is, or should be, a watertight section of the stream that is flowing all ways; all warring images within it should be reconciled for that small stop of time.

The reconciliation lies in the unifying concept shared by all the images. We have a grip on the poem when, by retreating from specific to general, we find the basic premise upon which peace between the warring images is made.

The 'signal moon' has brought up the subject of the weather; in the third stanza the womb has 'weathers'. Weathers are the conditions through which time and the seasons work their changes on the world. Transposed, they become the atmospheric conditions within the human body, specifically here in stanza 3 within the 'brawned' or fattening womb. The unborn boys of summer are splitting up the weathers in the womb. They are agents of mutability. Gestation is the continual reduplication of cells. Pregnancy goes by the calendar. The first division is into night and day; two becomes four when the womb is 'quartered' with the seasons of the year. 'Dams' may be a harsh word for their mothers, but the boys have 'fairy thumbs'.

This Tinker Bell aspect adds a further dimension.[1] We cannot ultimately see the boys as cruel. Sunlight is present in the 'shelling', the making of the delicate egg-shell of their heads.

> I SEE that from these boys shall men of nothing [bankrupt] stature by seedy shifting [cell growth/unhealthy evasiveness] or [shall] lame the air [and themselves] with leaping from its [summer] heats; there from their hearts the dogdayed [soporific] pulse of love and life BURSTS in their throats [in bursts]. O see the pulse of summer in the ice.

'Bursts' could be negative, an explosion with a lot of blood. It does not much matter which way you take it, when the whole idea is to keep juggling positives and negatives in the air until it is clear that it is the process that counts, and then the poem can rest in its taut polarities. Thomas even substituted 'doubt and dark' for 'love and light' (line 23) in the *New Verse* printing.[2] It did not seem to matter to him that something could take the place of its exact opposite. Nor in this kind of polar poem does it matter, except at the end of this first part he

---

[1] 'A fairy is not supernatural', Thomas asserted in a letter of about this time (*Letters*, p. 91/109); 'she is the most natural thing in the world'.
[2] Editor Geoffrey Grigson said in conversation that these were Thomas's words as submitted; he would not himself make such changes.

does seem to want to lean toward the more positive. He could have written, 'O see the ice in the pulse of summer', but he did not.

But the point is the joust itself. That is what part II goes on to say. Without challenge one totters into 'a chiming quarter', moribund as an old bell-ringer in the dead of winter. We have to be deniers.[3] The poem then goes on in the whole of part II to show the boys denying: (1) summoning death from a 'summer' woman, (2) summoning life from lovers in their death throes, (3) summoning oil for the glow-worm flame of the miners' lamp (invented by Sir Humphrey Davy) from all the dead matter under the sea since geologic time in 'Davy Jones' locker' (as the saying goes), (4) summoning a man of straw disappointingly from a seeded womb. The boys uphold the sea-storm but drop the sea-birds; they drown the deserts with seawater; and they scour the country gardens only for a funeral wreath. In spring they make the mark of the cross on their foreheads with the holly of winter, opposing the seasons (as the birth and crucifixion of Christ also seem to do). Crucifying the 'merry squires' is an extreme form of the denying that is going on here.

In the last line of this part we are asked to see 'the poles of promise' in the boys. The two lines immediately preceding should be an expression of those poles of promise:

> Here love's damp muscle dries and dies,
> Here break a kiss in no love's quarry.

The first of these two lines is decidedly negative: 'damp' is one of Thomas's ways of saying that life is present; dryness is death, without equivocation. Whatever part of the anatomy 'love's muscle' might be, the line signifies the end of love. Does the breaking of a kiss in the next line mean the opposite, the beginning of love? 'Break' would normally mean that the kiss is destroyed, which would hardly supply a positive. But this, I believe, is essentially a stone-breaking image. Love is being sledgehammered into existence with this kiss in a feminine quarry which has been the quarry of no love. Interpreted in this way the two lines are polar, and meet the expectations set up by the poem.

Taking the first part (what he at one time thought a finished poem), we can see in it the poet's fear of the nullity that he might become if he stayed in Swansea until middle age, a man of nothing

---

[3] Correcting someone, Thomas made it clear (*Letters*, p. 322/371) that a 'denier' was not an ancient coin but a 'person who denies'.

but lost opportunities, the boy of summer come to ruin. This is
Thomas's mood as exhibited in a letter to Pamela Hansford Johnson
on a Sunday morning, 15 April 1934, the exact time he was redoing 'I
see the boys of summer' (*Letters*, p. 111/135):

> Life passes the windows, and I hate it more minute by minute. I see the
> rehearsed gestures, the correct smiles, the grey cells revolving around
> nothing under the godly bowlers. I see the unborn children struggling up
> the hill in their mothers, beating on the jailing slab of the womb, little
> realising what a snugger prison they wish to leap into.
>
> I wish I could see these passing men and women in the sun as the motes
> of virtues, this little fellow as a sunny Fidelity, this corsetted hank as
> Mother-Love, this abusing lout as the Spirit of Youth, & this eminently
> beatable child in what was once a party frock as the walking embodiment of
> Innocence. But I can't. The passers are dreadful. I see all their little horrors.

This ruin is to be resisted, and if adolescence is the time of resistance
then so be it. Nineteen at the time of writing this poem, Thomas
knew the awkwardness and surliness of youth from recent memory. A
precocious maturity with heightened self-awareness allowed him to
write coolly about matters so close to home. Things must be
challenged. Part II of the poem raises the 'ornariness' of adolescence
to a cosmic vision.

The six lines of part III are immensely difficult because of the
brevity of each one-line pronouncement and its apparent isolation
from any illuminating context except the poem as a whole.

> I see you boys of summer in your ruin.
> Man in his maggot's barren.
> And boys are full and foreign in the pouch.
> I am the man your father was.
> We are the sons of flint and pitch.
> O see the poles are kissing as they cross.

We can only take this as a coda encapsulating the previous ideas of
the poem, the first line obviously so. In the second line, the 'men of
nothing' are worse than nothing; their flesh is a maggot[4] whose
corruption is barren. On the other hand, the boys are 'full' with
harvest and, as a positive contrary, 'foreign in the pouch' like a
cuckoo: they have the range, for and against. The fourth line is a

---

[4] See the Blake illustration, *Collected Poems*, p. 179.

conundrum. It can hardly be taken as the dramatic revelation of hidden paternity. It sounds a bit like Hamlet's ghost wearing a Swansea Corporation bathing suit warning the boys that they might become the ruin he has become. But it is very much shorn of reference, perhaps only serving to set up a strange generation gap for the 'sons' of the next line, which gets us back firmly to the dialectical forces that have been operating throughout the poem. 'Flint' (hard) and 'pitch' (soft) produce a spark and flame; they are poles kissing as they cross, breaking a kiss, as it were, in no love's quarry. This is recapitulation, Thomas forcing upon us a recognition of 'I see the boys of summer' as a tightly formed poem, a 'watertight compartment' of words (*Letters*, p. 298/344). The last line of the poem is a climax prepared for by the last lines of the previous two parts:

(I)　　O see the pulse of summer in the ice.
(II)　　O see the poles of promise in the boys.
(III)　　O see the poles are kissing as they cross.

Mutability is the subject of part I until the end when the dual nature of destruction is hinted at. Part II stated and illustrated the superiority of challenge over stagnation. The boys denied everything and thus turned out to be partly creative. Part III is a tight balancing act; the poles kiss, reiterating the essential creativity available in the resistances of youth.

It is the sinners' dust-tongued bell

(please turn to *Collected Poems*, p. 71)

In a memorial broadcast of 5 March 1958 Vernon Watkins described Thomas coming to his house one day (this would have been late October 1936) and saying,

> I've been reading a thriller, a very bad thriller, but I came on the most wonderful line in the middle of a lot of trash, which was 'the shadow is dark directly under the candle' . . . Out of that line I'm going to make a new poem which is going to be my best, about churches. (BBC typescript)

Thomas was not telling Watkins the whole story. During that same Swansea visit, he signed a copy of *Twenty-five Poems* to his old school friend John Prichard with a mock-blurb about himself that included the sentence: 'His name has appeared on several case-lists which take venereal disease seriously' (copy in possession of Robert Williams). The churches in the poem have 'stained' glass (*Letters*, p. 398/450).

I think we have to take venereal disease seriously as the dark directly under the candle-flame of love in 'It is the sinners' dust-tongued bell'. The 'plagued' groom and bride of the next to last line were originally, in the first periodical printing of the poem, the 'clapped' groom and bride, which, along with the 'claps' of the first line, points to gonorrhoea as the subject. This is the 'urchin grief' that Dylan and Caitlin have produced. At the time of this poem they were not yet married and there was no pregnancy. 'I know that Dylan did have the disease', Caitlin told George Tremlett (*Caitlin*, p. 35), 'because he told me about it, and soon after I met him I had to go into hospital myself when I caught gonorrhoea.' She said she did not catch it from Dylan, but he perhaps did not know that (and how could she?). A letter written to Caitlin in hospital is full of great concern: 'Are you better, and please God you aren't too miserable in the horrible hospital?' (*Letters*, p. 241/271). This cry of a heart tinged, possibly, with guilt is undated, but Ferris places it in the *Collected Letters* at November 1936, exactly when 'It is the sinners' dust-tongued bell' was written.[1]

> It is the [fellow] sinners' dust-tongued [death-clappered] bell claps [tolls] me to churches [for a black mass] when, with his [smoking] torch and hourglass [sands of time], like a sulphur [devil's] priest, his beast heel cleft [like the devil's] in a sandal, Time marks [notes] a black [church] aisle kindle [catch fire] from the brand [torch] of [death's] ashes, [marks] Grief with dishevelled [wringing] hands tear out the altar [holy] ghost and [marks] a firewind [from hell] kill the [altar] candle.

The poet has been summoned to a black mass for his sins. The service seems to be taking place underwater.

---

[1] In a letter to Kenneth Patchen (in the new edition of *Letters*, p. 488) Thomas, recalling his first months in London, speaks of 'obtaining at considerable cost the clap'.

Over the [Time's] choir minute I HEAR the [Time's] hour chant [louder]:
Time's coral [underwater choir] saint and the [sea] salt grief DROWN a foul
sepulchre and a [treacherous] whirlpool DRIVES the prayerwheel; moonfall
[on the water] and sailing emperor [moth], pale [with fright] as their
tideprint [reflection on the water], HEAR by death's accident the clocked [by
Time] and dashed-down [by Grief] spire [of the church] strike [by falling]
the sea hour through bellmetal.

It is as though someone was expecting a marriage but it has all fallen
through, including the church spire. The next stanza points out that
things go by contraries, even extreme opposites of expectation.

There IS loud [noise] and dark directly under the dumb [speechless] flame,
[there is] storm, snow, and fountain in the weather of fireworks, [and
there is] cathedral calm in the [bell] pulled house;

Grief with drenched [wet] book and candle CHRISTENS [sprinkles with
tears] the cherub time from the emerald, still [still as a precious stone] bell
[underwater]; and from the pacing [going back and forth] weathercock
[of the sunken spire] the voice of bird [cock] on coral [saint] prays.

There is something quite sad going on: Time has produced a cherub
only to have it christened with a deluge of the tears of grief.

> Forever it is a white child in the dark-skinned summer
> Out of the font of bone and plants at that stone tocsin
> Scales the blue wall of spirits . . . .

A start on the fourth stanza is provided us by the poet's own
explanation in a letter to Desmond Hawkins (*Letters*, p. 398/450):

The blue wall of spirits is the sky full of ghosts: the curving crowded
world above the new child. It sounds as though it meant the side of a
chemist's bowl of methylated spirits, & I *saw* that too and a child
climbing up it.

'There's a pretty fancy', he added, and well he might. This is more
metaphysical than the Metaphysicals. All he is doing in this gloss is
explaining the image as image. He is not saying what it is an image
of. The 'child' is hidden from the tanning sun. It climbs out of the
birth font of (presumably sexual) 'bone and plants', at the call of the

'tocsin' alarm bell. It scales up the side of a 'chemist's bowl', in need of medication.

In the second three lines of stanza 4, the 'child' comes from a 'blank and leaking winter', in colour. I wonder what colour. In the next line it is wearing a crab-coloured shroud. Not auspicious. It wants to be heard, however. It shakes bell notes from the church turrets. One cannot ignore VD.

The 'child', then, is venereal disease, that unexpected darkness from the bright flame of love. The poet, this subject thrust upon him, chooses to talk about it in disguised language. He is not interested in the bathos of candidness. When, in stanza 5, he takes on the air of explanation, it is only the manner of such; the cover is still being maintained by the images.

I MEAN by time the [out] cast and curfew[outlaw] rascal [urchin grief] of our marriage, at nightbreak [broken night] born in the fat [pregnant] side, from an animal [sexual] bed in a holy [love] room in a wave [of passion];

and all love's [fellow] sinners in sweet [perfumed] cloth KNEEL to a hyleg[2] image; [and] nutmeg, civet, and sea-parsley SERVE the plagued [diseased] groom and bride who have bought forth the urchin grief.

Clearly the couple have come to the church of love only to come to grief. The urchin they have 'conceived' is a grief, a disease, and they need all kinds of spices and perfumes to sweeten them. Time is always the enemy, but here a good time has turned into a bad time. Writing to Desmond Hawkins from Swansea in the middle of 'It is the sinners' dust-tongued bell', Thomas said (*Letters*, p. 240/269): 'I've got some new poems and some new jokes and some new diseases.' The poem confirms that he was not joking.

---

[2] Thomas wrote (*Letters*, p. 398/451): 'Oh yes, *hyleg*. It's a freak word, I suppose, but one or two every now & then don't hurt: I think they help. It was what I wanted & happened to know the word well.' A dictionary definition is 'the ruling planet at a nativity.' Here it will be the image that governs the birth of the 'urchin grief', which would be a sort of degraded Venus.

Lament

(please turn to *Collected Poems*, p. 148)

This poem is a well-written caricature – of the poet's persona of course, though one likes to think Henry Miller may have had a share in it. Thomas met Miller with Lawrence Durrell in London in 1939 and renewed his acquaintance at Big Sur in April 1950 during his first American tour (*Letters*, p. 757/843):

> Last week I went to Big Sur, a mountainous region by the sea, and stayed the night with Henry Miller. Tell Ivy that; she who hid his books in the oven. He lives about 6,000 feet up in the hills, over the blinding blue Pacific, in a hut of his own making. He has married a pretty young Polish girl, & they have two small children. He is gentle and mellow and gay.

'Lament' may have had its inception with this glimpse of the twentieth century's greatest sex braggadocio in his late domesticity. Thomas made a point of sending him an autograph copy of the poem signed: 'for Henry Miller from Dylan Thomas, 1951' (MS at Texas).

Dylan did not really need a mentor in swaggering. The trip to America had resulted in a dangerous alliance with someone Brinnin in his book decided to call 'Sarah' (Ferris in his biography follows suit). When 'Sarah' decided to come over to England, demanding Thomas as an escort in London, his image among his Soho friends was amplified accordingly. To Caitlin, who found out about it, Thomas claimed 'Sarah' was 'a bloody nuisance, one of these mad American women who kept following him around' (*Caitlin*, p. 146). Though the marriage was never the same again, Caitlin confesses, 'our lives did settle back into some kind of normality' (p. 148). It was in this aftermath that 'Lament' was written. About this time (*Letters*, p. 788/859) Thomas wrote to his worldly friend John Davenport from Laugharne: 'Oh, how far, far away I feel, here in my *horribly* cosy little nest, surrounded by my detestable books, wearing my odious, warm slippers, observing the gay, reptilian play of my abominable brood, basking in the vituperation of my golden, loathing wife!' This same mood of exaggeration pervades 'Lament'.

At the same time, autobiographical elements are at a minimum in the poem. This is not the poet's own voice. One of the many worksheets (at Texas) has the title: 'The Miner's Lament'.[1] The 'black spit' and 'ram rod' sound like colliery terms; 'coal-black' appears in each stanza. This is a song in a working-class accent.

It is in keeping with the character of the British worker that the one who here laments would be adept at sexual double entendres. When in doubt, use a slang dictionary; 'ram-rod' is there, meaning 'penis'. Even the soul is imaged as a penis, in the penultimate stanza, when the 'hero' feels a diminution of powers and his soul starts to peek out of its 'foul mousehole' (given Thomas's long-standing phobia about mice, that is the worst place possible):

> And I gave my soul a blind, slashed eye,
> Gristle and rind, and a roarer's life,
> And I shoved it into the coal black sky
> To find a woman's soul for a wife.

In spite of having decked his soul out and rooted the sky, the narrator seems to be indicating that a new kind of search has entered into his sexual activities; his love-making has thus attracted a soul-mate. Just in time, I should think, but the poem pretends it's a catastrophe.

The Dylan Thomas–Henry Miller–Mr Waldo character cannot really be complaining about the unexpected turn of events. There is more than a bit of tongue-in-cheek in the last few lines. He is not really a tragic figure, just pretending to be:

> Chastity prays for me, piety sings,
> Innocence sweetens my last black breath,
> Modesty hides my thighs in her wings,
> And all the deadly virtues plague my death!

Deadly virtues instead of deadly sins: it's not a bad trade-off, and the tone indicates that he secretly knows it.

---

[1] One thinks of the close analogue that can be found in *Under Milk Wood* (p. 60): Mr Waldo's 'chimbley sweep' song, 'In Pembroke City when I was young'.

Lie still, sleep becalmed

(please turn to *Collected Poems*, p. 113)

Though his father's cancer was of the mouth (Ferris, p. 88) Thomas described it as 'cancer of the throat' twice in letters (*Letters*, pp. 63, 89/100, 108), so we take the 'sufferer with the wound in the throat' of this poem to be D. J. Thomas. Two days after his father went for treatment to a London hospital, Thomas wrote in his notebook 'Take the needles and the knives' dated 12 September 1933. The surgical imagery of this poem, which was left unpublished (*Notebook Poems*, p. 188), was no doubt suggested by the radium insertion procedures used. 'Lie still, sleep becalmed' very likely had an early version at this time, though we have no record of it.

D. J. Thomas survived the radium treatment and had permanent remission of the cancer, but as late as 27 October 1935 Thomas is writing to his married sister, 'Dad has a very painful throat' (*Letters*, p. 202/229). So some problem in that area was continuing. In 1943–4 when Dylan and Caitlin visited his parents, now retired to their Carmarthenshire cottage, the earlier feeling of concern may have revived and produced this poem (or a revision of the postulated earlier draft).[1]

The poem sustains a nautical imagery throughout. The 'salt sheet' is the bandage wrapping the wound, thought of as the sail of a sailing ship; and when a storm tears the 'sail' it is like a fatal flow of blood. The all night sound of the throat breathing in pain is then replaced by 'the voices of all the drowned'. The care-givers hear a request coming over the waves from the patient:

> Open a pathway through the slow sad sail,
> Throw wide to the wind the gates of the wandering boat
> For my voyage to begin to the end of my wound.

This plea for the ship of death to be prepared and the gates to be opened to allow passage is a very quiet expression of a wish for help in dying.

---

[1] The first version of which we are aware was sent to T. W. Earp in April 1944. It is now deposited with the Earp papers at Ohio State University, and differs mainly in the manner of the person addressed. 'Lie still, you must sleep' is used twice; it has more of a patient-caring tone to it. The revised 'Lie still, sleep becalmed' remains a caring poem, addressed to someone whose life was feared for by the 'we' of the poem.

There is plenty of reason to think that D. J. Thomas, with his stern view of life and death, would have had a 'living will', if such had been known at the time. There may have been discussions about 'heroic measures' to sustain life in hopeless medical situations. 'My father is awfully ill these days, with heart disease and uncharted pains', Thomas wrote to Vernon Watkins on 28 March 1945 (*Letters*, p. 548/610). This is a year after 'Lie still, sleep becalmed', but the same conditions had presumably existed for some time. In any case, the poem certainly seems to approach the question of assisted death:

> Lie still, sleep becalmed, hide the mouth in the throat,
> Or we shall obey, and ride with you through the drowned.

The watchers at the bedside are saying that, unless the patient finds rest in sleep and quietens the voice from the throat that has made the request to die, they will have to obey it, in which case they too will follow the departed kin into death. This may refer to retribution on the part of society for the deed of helping someone die, or it may be hyperbole for the grief they will feel. Both may have been in the poet's mind. This poem expresses filial devotion in an extreme form. That such feelings should exist in Thomas may surprise some readers; it should surprise no one who has read 'Do not go gentle into that good night' and 'Elegy'.

Light breaks where no sun shines

(please turn to *Collected Poems*, p. 23)

Light BREAKS [dawns] where no sun shines [where it is night]; where no sea runs [in the dead body], the [life-giving] waters of the heart PUSH IN their tides [blood transfusion]; and, broken ghosts [dead] with glow-worms [alight] in their heads, the things of light FILE through the flesh [bringing light] where no flesh decks the bones [skeleton].

These are all images of transformation with the coming of light to previously dark places, when dawn turns the dead night into the living day. This poem was written into a notebook on 29 November 1933 (*Notebook Poems*, p. 209); on about 21 December 1933 Thomas wrote to Pamela Hansford Johnson his current theory on the basis of which this poem seems to have been composed (*Letters*, pp. 72–3/89):

> For the time at least, I believe in the writing of poetry from the flesh, and, generally, from the dead flesh. So many modern poets take the *living* flesh as their object, and by their clever dissecting, turn it into a carcase. I prefer to take the *dead* flesh, and, by any positivity of faith and belief that is in me, build up a *living* flesh from it.

We take Thomas at his word: this is a poem where dead flesh is conceived of as being built up into living flesh by an act of faith. It would take an act of faith to assert that light can break where there is no sun. In the next stanza he raises the sexually dead.

> A candle in the thighs WARMS [inflames] youth and seed and BURNS [up] the [sexual] seeds of age [producing impotence]; [but] where no seed stirs [in old age], the [dried] fruit of man UNWRINKLES [enlarges] in the stars, bright [with starlight] as a [seedy fresh] fig; where no wax [flesh] is, the [sexual] candle SHOWS its [pubic] hairs.

The next stanza we get some help on from Thomas himself. The first three lines are simple enough as images of the coming of light and life. The remaining three lines of the stanza, pivoting on the word 'rod', were naturally taken by some readers to have gross sexuality as their subject. No, no, says Thomas (*Letters*, pp. 108/131–2):

> After my poem in the Listener ('Light Breaks Where No Sun Shines') the editor received a host of letters, all complaining of the disgusting obscenity in two of the verses. One of the bits they made a fuss about was:

> > 'Nor fenced, nor staked, the *gushers* of the sky
> > *Spout* to the *rod* divining in a smile
> > The *oil* of tears.'

> The little smut-hounds thought I was writing a copulatory anthem. In reality, of course, it was a metaphysical image of rain & grief.

'All my denials of obscenity were disregarded', he added. We do not know whether or not his correspondent Pamela Hansford Johnson believed these protestations, but she would, considering all the candles, seeds, hairs of the previous stanza, have every right not to.

But Thomas was right, of course. This is not a penis image, it is a divining-rod image. It is somewhat disingenuous of him to suggest that it would never occur to him or anyone else that the divining-rod might also contain the idea of a penis; but he knows what he is doing with these images: he is creating an abstract idea from quasi-particulars, saying repeatedly that something comes out of its opposite, usually life out of dead matter. Here he is supposing that behind a dead smile there are real tears, gushers of tears. Then, in the next stanza, the blind see.

> Night in the [eye] sockets ROUNDS [makes a circle], like some pitch [black] moon, the limits [circumference] of the [eye] globes; [but] day LIGHTS [up] the bone; where no cold is [felt], the skinning [blowing the skin off] gales UNPIN the winter's robes [sloughing off the cold]; the film [blocking out vision] of spring [new life] IS HANGING from the [eye] lids [ready to fall and restore sight].

And, finally, enlightenment in thought:

> Light BREAKS [dawns] on secret [burial] lots, [and] on [coal] tips of thought where thoughts smell in the rain [of spring]; when logics die, the [dark] secret of the soil GROWS [like a flower] through the eye, and blood JUMPS in the sun; above the waste allotments [the cemetery] the dawn halts [ready for light to break].

Logics must die in order that faith may flourish. The thoughts smelling in the rain are rotting thoughts belonging to the dead life; then, with the rain, they become shooting flowers that smell sweetly. The poet is building up the living from the dead 'by any positivity of faith' (*Letters*, p. 73/89, quoted above). Dead logics must get new secrets from the soil, and then things will dawn on us.

After such expression of faith, the final line cannot be one of foreboding. The dawn is not stopping, only halting, waiting. Light is ready to break on the wasteland (*Letters*, p. 141/168):

> Here there is still no light, only a new mile of suffering murk added to the horizon, and a fresh acre of wonder at this rotten state that might easily and sweetly be changed into the last long acre where the dead breathe for the first time.

✧

Love in the Asylum

(please turn to *Collected Poems*, p. 90)

I suspect that this poem had its inception in the early days of the love relationship between Dylan Thomas and Caitlin Macnamara, though it was prepared in its final form for publication several years later. As Caitlin describes that strange meeting of April 1936 there is a mesmeristic quality about it which is echoed somewhat in the poem. The scene is the Wheatsheaf pub in Fitzrovia, London (*Caitlin*, pp. 1–4):

> I was sitting on a stool, and I don't know how Dylan managed to get his head on my lap; I don't know how he did it, or how he was standing, but he seemed to fold up over me, and I immediately felt a great sense of closeness that I had never felt before with anyone. He was babbling away and there were three or four other people there at the time. He was telling stories and also muttering endearments to me. He seemed very close all the time. I couldn't follow what he was saying and didn't answer him, but it all seemed very soothing and pleasant. He told me that I was beautiful, that he loved me and that he was going to marry me, and he kept on repeating these phrases as though he had at last found the girl who was right for him . . . there was nothing very sensational about his love-making. He seemed timid, and this again emphasised his child-like quality to me. We just held each other very close, clinging to each other as we went to sleep, and we were still clinging to each other when I woke up again. We stayed at the Eiffel Tower for five or six nights.

> A stranger has come
> To share my room in the house not right in the head,[1]
> A girl mad as birds . . .

In the first draft of the poem (manuscript at Buffalo) the bed of line 5 was also given the adjective 'mad'. Madness is something Dylan associated with Caitlin and their relationship from the start. 'There is', he tells her in an early letter (*Letters*, p. 242/271 – dated by Ferris as late 1936),

---

[1] In his first letter letter to Caitlin, now come to light in the new edition of *Letters* (p. 262), Thomas speaks in similar imagery: 'You can have all the spaces between houses, and I can have a room with no windows; we'll make a halfway house; you can teach me to walk in the air.'

a sort of sweet madness about you and me, a sort of mad bewilderment and astonishment oblivious to the Nasties and the Meanies; you're the only person, of course you're the only person from here to Aldebaran and back, with whom I'm free entirely; and I think it's because you're as innocent as me. Oh I know we're not saints or virgins or lunatics; we know all the lust and lavatory jokes, and most of the dirty people; we can catch buses and count our change and cross the roads and talk real sentences. But our innocence goes awfully deep, and our discreditable secret is that we don't know anything at all, and our horrid *inner* secret is that we don't care that we don't. I've just read an Irish book called Rory and Bran, and it's a bad charming book: innocent Rory falls in love with innocent Oriana, and, though they're both whimsy and talk about the secret of the language of the hills and though Rory worships the moon and Oriana glides about in her garden listening to the legendary birds, they're not as mad as we are, nor as innocent. I love you so much I'll never be able to tell you; I'm frightened to tell you. I can always feel your heart.

A stranger [new lover] HAS COME to share my room in the house [asylum] not right in the head, a girl mad as birds bolting the night of the door [confining him] with her arm [which is] her plume [wing].

Strait [-jacketed] in the mazed [labyrinthine/amazed] bed she DELUDES [tricks] the heaven-proof house [formerly secured against happiness] with [by means of] entering clouds [disguised as depressed] [further] yet she DELUDES with [the ruse of] walking the nightmarish [asylum] room, at large [free] as the dead, or RIDES the imagined [expansive] oceans of the [forbidden] male wards.

She HAS COME possessed [enraptured/with gifts] who admits [allows in] the delusive [foiling] light [of sanity] through the bouncing [padded cell] wall, [and] possessed by the skies [diaphanous] she SLEEPS in the narrow trough [of the bed] yet she WALKS [elated over] the dust [dirtiness] [further] yet RAVES [freely] at her will on the madhouse boards [previously] worn thin by my walking tears [of self-pity].

And taken [possessed] by light in her arms at long and dear last I MAY without fail [failure] SUFFER [experience fully] the first vision that set fire to the stars [of hope].

The poem as a whole, and the last line especially, is a tribute to Caitlin as the poet's muse, the bringer of vision. The implication is that her 'madness' is an essential ingredient of his working life, no matter that it may seem from the outside to impede it. People might think she has taken him into a madhouse, but he knows she has opened up the madhouse that he was trapped in before he met her. Her impulsiveness has deluded the defenses with which he surrounded himself, deep in the 'male wards' (line 9).

She has given him a like freedom in his poetry: in the year before he married, Thomas had written very little; in the year after the marriage he wrote two new poems and revised six others. In his adolescent years Thomas had been very aware of the visually dominating new Swansea Asylum building going up not too far from his home: 'It leers down the valley like a fool' (*Letters*, p. 18/37). He often, in an exploratory way, flirted with insanity, madness being akin to genius in the romantic view. Caitlin changed that morbid preoccupation to another kind of madness, a mutually endearing madness, within which the poet felt secure and productive. Asylum is also where one finds protection.

My hero bares his nerves

(please turn to *Collected Poems*, p. 13)

This self-absorbed poem was written on 17 September 1933 in the complete isolation that Thomas sought in the family cottage of Blaen Cwm, Llangain, near Carmarthen (*Letters*, p. 29/47):

> I am staying, as you see, in a country cottage, eight miles from a town and a hundred miles from anyone to whom I can speak to on any subjects but the prospect of rain and the quickest way to snare rabbits. It is raining as I write, a thin, purposeless rain hiding the long miles of desolate fields and scattered farmhouses. I can smell the river, and hear the beastly little brook that goes gurgle-gurgle past this room. I am facing an uncomfortable fire, a row of china dogs, and a bureau bearing the photograph of myself aged seven – thick-lipped, Fauntleroy-haired, wide-eyed, and empty as the bureau itself.

In this description, and in the poem, he has only himself to face. 'My hero bares his nerves': how many people are actually present? One, of course; the poet solus. But, in order to have some kind of narrative to carry the images of this mirror watching, Thomas, as is his wont, creates a split personality, so that someone can do something to or for someone. Here is a 'hero' of no specific characteristics whose manipulation of the alter ego's body is a means of carrying the feeling forward on this 'lovelorn paper' (line 7).

We assume that there is no specific lost love in Thomas's life at this time; the poem bemoans a general dawdling. The mood is lifelorn. An undated letter of 1933 puts it thus (*Letters*, p. 8/26): 'In my more melancholy moods . . . I turn over, with a certain perverse pleasure, all my ill-fortunate experiences which amount as nearly to heartbreak as one, like myself, who has never felt the desire to fall in love, can realise.'

> My hero [alter ego] BARES his [or my] nerves along my [or his] wrist that rules [movement] from wrist to shoulder, UNPACKS [the contents of] the head that, like a sleepy [daydreaming] ghost, leans [nods] on my mortal ruler [the backbone measuring its own aging], the proud spine spurning [withstanding] turn and twist [with rectitude].

The poet is gearing himself to write, getting his writing arm ready and clearing his head. He sloughs off lethargy and begins to write a poem. Though Thomas's handwriting was extremely neat in actuality, he wants to characterize it here as his 'unruly scrawl' (line 8) to help portray a despairing mood.

In the third stanza the 'hero' strips the body, and looks through to his heart, which seems to be walking the flesh like Botticelli's Venus (illustrated on p. 184 of *Collected Poems*). This painting, *The Birth of Venus*, was well known to Thomas, who later had two reproductions of it on the wall of his writing shed at Laugharne. The long strands of reddish hair in the painting might have suggested the image of 'plaits' of veins from the heart. This 'naked Venus' rouses him, and promises 'a secret heat' in his loins.

Nothing could be clearer. After that we are certainly allowed a sexual interpretation of the fourth and final stanza:

> He [the hero] HOLDS the wire [like a light pull] from this [brain] box of nerves praising the mortal error of [the human condition] birth and death, [which are] the two sad knaves of thieves [of happiness], [praising too] the [love] hunger's emperor [appetite for life]; he [the hero-lover] PULLS the chain [of nerves], the cistern MOVES.

Research has not revealed whether Blaen Cwm cottage had an outhouse or a water closet. We do here seem on the face of it to have a lavatory image. Thomas may have been specifically defending this last line when he wrote to Pamela Hansford Johnson on 5 November 1933, having sent her 'My hero bares his nerves' on 15 October 1933 (*Letters*, p. 39/57): 'It is polite to be seen at one's dining table, and impolite to be seen in one's lavatory. It might well have been decided, when the tumour of civilisation was first fostered, that celebrations should be held in the w.c.'

However, though the word 'cistern' lays itself open to a sewage disposal interpretation, it is the same word as the anatomical term 'cisterna': any sac in the body holding fluids. 'To pull one's wire' is in Eric Partridge's *A Dictionary of Slang and Unconventional English* as '(Of the male) to masturbate; low; late C. 19–20.' In one of Thomas's stories, 'The Holy Six', we have a man who eschewed female flesh, 'and the male nerve was pulled alone' (*Collected Stories*, p. 97). Earlier than this poem Thomas had used the phrase 'cistern sex' (*Notebook Poems*, p. 154). We are drawn inevitably to the view that the 'love hunger' being 'uttered' in this poem, a forlorn response to the emptiness of life, involves the opening up to self-pleasure as the only release available. The hero-self makes love to the body-self. There is a sadness in these lines, but no recrimination. The word 'praising' (stanza 4) is a crucial indication of Thomas's attitude.

My world is pyramid

(please turn to *Collected Poems*, p. 27)

This poem in two parts was published first in *New Verse* (December 1934), and was, it seems, submitted to Geoffrey Grigson as two separate poems (*Letters*, p. 163/191). Perhaps it was at Grigson's suggestion that they became one.[1] In any case, I treat them seriatim as published.

---

[1] 'I hope in a few days to be able to send you two new poems', Thomas wrote to Grigson in an undated note of the middle of July 1934 (*Letters*, p. 153/179). Somewhat later, with another undated note, he sent 'the two poems I said I'd send you' (*Letters*, p. 163/191). The 'them' became the 'one' before 2 August 1934 when he sent 'My world is pyramid' as 'my new poem' to Pamela Hansford Johnson (*Letters*, p. 166/190). He thought it would be going into *New Verse* 'this month' (it did not get in until the December issue), and added: 'I took a long time over it, and, at the moment, anyway, I'm a little bit pleased with it. Not much – just a little bit.' There are no extant manuscripts; it is written after the last of the notebooks.

Half of the fellow [being of the] father as he [the father] doubles
[reproduces] his sea-sucked Adam [first born] in the hollow hulk
[wombed ship], half of the fellow [being of the] mother as she dabbles
[dips] tomorrow's diver [who will dive tomorrow] in her horny [bone-
making] milk,
 bisected shadows on the thunder's bone BOLT [together] for [to make]
the salt [sailor-boy] [as yet] unborn.

Back to gestation, as in so many of these early poems: the bisected
halves from the father and mother bolt together as a thunderbolt
enters the womb as bone, and begin to give single form to what are
still merely shadowings of the future.
 But things immediately go awry.

The [one] fellow half WAS FROZEN as it bubbled [as] corrosive spring [acid
sperm] out of the iceberg's crop [sac], the [other] fellow [of the primal
mixture of] seed and shadow as it babbled the swing [music] of [breast]
milk WAS TUFTED [cut off short] in the pap [baby-food stage], for half of
love[-seed] WAS PLANTED in the lost [soul], and [half in] the unplanted [as
yet unconceived] ghost [spirit].

I do not think we are to take these 'halves' as dramatis personae. I
believe the 'halves' are just a way of saying that we are born with
fractured personalities, so that contradictory things can be expected
of us. It might appear important in these first two stanzas that,
genetically, half of us comes from each parent; but these gender-
related differences do not lead to specific outcomes in the poem. The
halves 'bolt' together (line 6) and in stanza three are 'fellowed', and
any difference appears to be forgotten in seeing what they do
together. We have here another of Thomas's devices for making a
quasi-narrative of images which, in the end, are going to tender us a
rather static concept, such as incarnation or mortality or fear. In
stanza 3 we 'limp' into the nightmare world which haunted Thomas
during his often restless nights. This is fear.

The broken [corroded] halves ARE FELLOWED [joined] in a cripple,
[becoming] the [skeletal] crutch that marrow[-]taps upon their [the
halves's] sleep [disturbing them into nightmare], LIMP in the street of sea,
among the rabble of tide-tongued [not tongue-tied] heads and bladders in
the deep, and STAKE [tether] [themselves] the sleepers in the savage grave
[with the result] that the vampire laugh [at their availability].

The patchwork [roughly joined] halves WERE CLOVEN [split] as they scudded [skimmed] the wild [cloven-footed] pigs' wood, and [scudded] slime upon the trees, [they] sucking the dark, KISSED on the cyanide [slime], and LOOSED the braiding [interweaving] adders [poisonous snakes] from their hairs;

rotating [drilling] halves ARE HORNING [creating horns] as they drill [question] the arterial angel.

To drill the arterial angel is, I think, to ask pointed questions of what is closest to one's heart. In the next stanza the 'halves' tremble to ask, but do pointedly ask, certain questions, piercing the air with a pin's point. They prick at heaven, which becomes thumb-stained with blood even though wearing a thimble. The cloven ones register a palpable hit, and 'the ghost is dumb that stammered in the straw'; Christ is dumbfounded. On the other hand, 'the ghost that hatched his havoc as he flew' is doing well; he has blinded the 'cloud-tracking', heaven-questioning eye of the humble halves.

This second 'ghost' I take to be the Devil himself. We can then begin to see the relevance of previously puzzling references to cloven hooves, the tufted goatee beard, horns, wild pigs (of the Gadarene variety, then), the poisonous snakes, vampire, all of which can be thought of as associated with the satanic. It begins to dawn on us that the underlying metaphor in the concept of the 'halves' is that they are 'cloven' like the Devil. 'Everything we do drags up a devil', Thomas wrote to Trevor Hughes a few months before the present poem (*Letters*, p. 161/145), speaking of the seamy side of his bachelor life in Swansea with Dan Jones: 'Perhaps we've got to be superstitious, natural, supernatural, all one huge satanic process.' Thomas is styling himself 'a little devil', not only in the pub but in his writing. 'Our words', he added (*Letters*, p. 161/145) 'are spells to drag up the personified Domdaniel pleasure' – where Domdaniel refers to the anti-Christian hero of the *Pilgrim's Progress* novel he was currently trying to write.

In 'My world is pyramid' (part II, stanza 4) it as though the Devil was about to be bred in him as he ('the fellow halves') is being born:

The fellow halves that, cloven [like the devil] as they swivel [turn in the womb] on casting [forming/casting out] tides [of birth spasms], ARE TANGLED [by the umbilical cord] in the [sea] shells [on the shore of existence], [and] bearding [giving a beard to] the unborn devil [in them], [they] BLEED from [being pricked by] my [the devil's] burning [pitch-]fork and SMELL my [sulphur] heels.

The tongues of heaven gossip [about the birth] as I glide [down the womb] binding [securing] my [fallen] angel hood [cawl].

Though nothing is certain in this strange multi-person landscape, the 'I'-speaker will have to be the Devil with his traditional pitchfork and smell, and will therefore have to be the angel fallen from heaven.

The Devil gets around, as we shall see in looking at the first three stanzas of part II. Thomas had an early poem in this vein which he probably saw as he was glancing through his notebooks at this time[2] (*Notebook Poems*, pp. 112–13):

> Nearly summer, and the devil
> Still comes visiting his poor relations,
> If not in person sends his unending evil
> By messengers, the flight of birds
> Spelling across the sky his devil's news,
> The seasons' cries, full of his intimations.
> He has the whole field now, the gods departed . . .
>
> The welcome devil comes as guest,
> Steals what is best – the body's splendour –
> Rapes, leaves for lost (the amorist!),
> Counts on his fist
> All he has reaped in wonder.

This poem is two years before, and, though the Devil seems a fairly minor deity here, by June 1934 Thomas is writing (*Letters*, p. 144/170) that 'the beautiful world has been made foul by the men who have worked against men, by the devil in man which has worked against the God in man'. A month later, even more seriously, he is expounding his ideas on the true Christ and the false, the anti-Christ (*Letters*, p. 152/178), and sums up: 'Our symbol of faith must be a naked life, not a pale cross of death done up in a mummy blanket and surrounded by the Pyramid walls of an established stupidity.'

This gets us to the Devil's role in the Egyptian burial imagery of the first stanza of part II of 'My world is pyramid':

My [the devil's] world is pyramid [of death]. The padded [with mummy clothes] mummer [performer] WEEPS on the desert [yellow] ochre and the salt[-]incising [corrosive] summer.

---

[2] It is a poem dated April 1932 on a page of the notebook opposite a poem which contains the word 'parhelion' (line 6, part II).

My Egypt's armour [mummy case] buckling [warping] in its sheet [shroud], I SCRAPE through resin [mummy lacquer] to a starry [incised] bone and a blood parhelion [mock sun].

Our devil is at home in the death cult of Egypt.

The second stanza gives us the death cult of Europe, and a more recognizable evil, indeed a very current one. The 'Austrian volley' refers to the violent repression instituted by Engelbert Dollfuss when he decreed one party rule in Austria in February 1934. Stephen Spender had written an eye-witness account of the heroic socialist resistance in a book-length poem called *Vienna*, published by Faber. Geoffrey Grigson sent this volume to Thomas in mid-July 1934 (*Letters*, p. 153/179) and a review by him appeared in the December issue of *New Verse*. Spender's poem obviously riled him. According to Bert Trick (in conversation) Thomas in a competitive spirit sat down and wrote six stanzas of his own on the subject of the massacre of workers in Vienna. This effort does not now exist, but his review gives some indication of why he wanted to do it. 'There is more than poetry in poems', he asserts (*Early Prose*, p. 169), including 'the necessity for a social conscience': 'In a poem, however, the poetry must come first; what negates or acts against the poem must be subjugated to the poetry which is essentially indifferent to whatever philosophy, political passion, or gang-belief it embraces.' Thomas's six stanzas, in rivalry with Spender, would, then, have been heavy on 'social conscience' but within the demands of the poem as it developed. Certainly, in the second stanza of part II of our poem, where we have, I believe, the remains of what Thomas considered could be written about the Dollfuss brutality, the 'Austrian volley' could in the end, because of the requirements of the poem, become only a glimmer in a panorama of evil which includes, without further context, 'an English valley'!

The next stanza, 'My grave is watered . . .', stresses the widespread aspect of sin and death. There is nothing difficult about the stanza (except perhaps the word 'scut', which is in the dictionary). It is just that this stanza does not – nor do the previous two – help us to pin down with certainty who the 'I'-speaker is. I suppose, because of the phrasing of the last two stanzas, that it is the Devil in traditional garb. The Devil works his way in the world, but it seems 'the fellow halves' (part II, stanza 4) will find their chief role in asking questions, in being Devil's advocates. The questions of part I, stanza 5, pin-prick heaven: What is glory worth? Why is there death? In the poem as we have it, we have to wait until the last stanza of part II for some kind of an answer. 'Who blows death's feather?' The answer comes: 'I blow the stammel [blood red] feather in the vein.' It sounds like a devil's boast. 'What colour is glory?' is twisted to 'What glory is colour?' without changing the challenge at all. The Devil in the flesh replies: 'The loin is glory in a working pallor' – no colour at all. Death is the feather in the Devil's cap; glory is the pale working of sex.

Did Thomas really believe in the Devil? It seems so. Or these are devilish images for a more amorphous evil, whose first-person speaking voice can claim its world is pyramid but also many other things. When we come to the last three lines of the poem the speaker is quite muted:

> My clay unsuckled and my salt unborn,
> The secret child, I shift about the sea
> Dry in the half-tracked thigh.

Here we have the 'halves' again, the 'clay' and the 'salt' about to be born, as they were in the very first stanza; but now they are a 'secret child', who in the first person 'I' speaks of a sea journey. He is still dry even though he moves about in or on the sea; he stays safe in a thigh which is 'half-tracked', not completely explored. The words 'secret child', especially, are quite touching, and make us think of anything but the Devil. But Thomas once wrote (*Notebook Poems*, p. 189): 'a child might be my slayer'. So one can never be sure.

As of the present reading of 'My world is pyramid', I have to say that the protagonists of the action appear to fall quickly in and out of any discernible character. We have learnt to expect this.[3] The essence of Thomas's unique style is 'the conscious rapidity' with which he changes 'the angles of the images' (*Letters*, p. 77/94), but – and this is the saving grace – 'with one idea and one image, changed and transfigured as that image may be'. In other words, 'pyramid' is more important than 'my' in the title of the poem at hand. 'Pyramid', we can be sure, contains the central idea of death; the 'my' denotes merely one carrier of the idea in a multi-charactered narrative.

---

[3] Its beginning as two poems would be a further reason to expect this kind of difficulty. It is a safe conjecture that the first poem as submitted was made up of part I plus the last two stanzas of part II, and the second would be the remaining three stanzas of part II.

Not from this anger

(please turn to *Collected Poems*, p. 75)

Sending this poem to Vernon Watkins on 21 March 1938 Thomas called it a 'short simple' one (*Letters*, p. 279/326). Short, certainly. Simple? Perhaps that is what we will discover if we can break the code. Thomas intimated that there might be a problem in code-breaking. He further described it to Watkins as 'matter-of-fact' but illogically so: 'illogical naturally: except by a process it's too naturally obvious to misexplain' (*Letters*, p. 270/315). Thomas is advising Watkins that he will not state the obvious about the poem but he is implying his reader should discount the apparently illogical. The sentences may be disconcerting, may not be reasonable, but the illogicality should not prevent us from jumping to an obvious conclusion. There is an intuitive process by which one can turn aside the syntax, the statements given by the syntax, and leap to what he is really getting at.

It is true that on the face of it 'Not from this anger' is rather wacky. It says, twice, that because of 'this anger' something is *not* going to happen. One usually expects anger to have consequences. Here, the poem supposes things will happen after the 'refusal', but not because of the anger. Then why mention the anger at all? The answer must lie in the special nature of the anger: 'Not from *this* anger . . .' It is, I believe, an anger that is turned inward not outward, and therefore does not hurt the partner, only the person feeling it: which in this case will be Thomas himself.

One should know that 'Not from this anger', in the form we have it, was written in Blashford in January 1938 when Dylan and Caitlin were still newlyweds. Thomas called it his 'anticlimactic' poem (*Letters*, p. 287/336). The double meaning in that word is the key to opening its obscurity: besides the conventional meaning of disappointment, the word broken into its parts gives us 'against climax'. What is thwarting the climax here is the non-functioning of exactly what would produce the climax if it was functioning. It is refusing to work; it strikes the female partner's loin with the flaccidity of a 'lame flower' (line 2). The refusal strikes her like 'a bell under water' (line 12). In that viscosity a bell will have great difficulty getting its clapper to work. Poor Dylan. He is as agonized as a deep sea carilloneur. His head hangs in shame. He thinks of his member as a flower drooping for lack of water, or like a beast in a famined country bent down to lap the only puddle (lines 2–3). The result is that 'she' receives 'a bellyful of weeds' (line 5), that is, the opposite of fruitfulness, and has to bear the tender little shoots his hands seem to be as he extends them diffidently towards her across a chasm which seems as wide as two seas. This plaintiveness is what Thomas's anger at his failure, internalized, has turned into, and therefore the result is not from anger except in a circuitous way.

This poem represents a moment of forlornness in love-making. Lines 8–10 depict by a sun image the end of the honeymoon's bliss. Lovers smiled at each other as though exchanging a golden ball;[1] but now, for Dylan and Caitlin, the sky sags and the sun rolls down out of the heaven the lovers were in. After the 'refusal' her smile 'breeds' another behind the mirror so that when he looks in the mirror his embarrassed eyes burn, as no doubt do his cheeks (lines 12–14).

Statistics about such sexual failures should have reassured this young husband even if Caitlin did not. He apparently does not know any better than to be angry at himself. Certainly, his anger, the poem insists, will not be directed at her. Actually they might be better off if his anger were released, but he will not allow that. He is too courteous, too ashamed. This is, in the illogical way Thomas has warned us of, a love poem. The situation, the poem implies, is a result of the opposite of anger, a result of his overwhelming, disabling love.

---

[1] Thomas might have remembered this as an image of seduction in *The Greek Anthology*, ed. W. R. Paton, 5 vols (London, 1916), quite probably in his father's library.

Now

(please turn to *Collected Poems*, p. 45)

In his *A Personal History* (1983) A. J. P. Taylor presents a vignette of Dylan at work while visiting him at Higher Disley in Cheshire in April–May 1935 (p. 130):

He sat at the window looking over to Kinder Scout and writing his lines in pencil. His method of composition was curious. He wrote a straightforward line that I could understand. Then he crossed out the principal words and substituted others in the manner of a *Times* crossword puzzle. Then he did it again. I asked him why. He answered with a cruel giggle, 'He, he, it makes things more difficult for the readers.'

It is well known that A. J. P. Taylor had a jaded view of our poet.[1] We must also admit, however, that the poem 'Now' – which he very well could have been writing during that Cheshire visit – is one that makes even the most devoted explicator feel that maybe, in this case, Taylor was right. Vernon Watkins reports that when he challenged Thomas on this poem's 'unwarrantable obscurity' (*LVW*, p. 16), the reply was that 'so far as he knew it had no meaning at all'. This might totally absolve the explicator from further effort if it were not that Thomas resisted Watkins very firmly and included the poem in *Twenty-five Poems*. It was among the poems that Thomas defended when he submitted his new book to Richard Church of Dent's (*Letters*, p. 205/232): 'every line *is* meant to be understood; the reader *is* meant to understand every poem by thinking and feeling about it'. Glyn Jones also saw what A. J. P. Taylor saw but, in *The Dragon has Two Tongues* (p. 194), put it in a somewhat different light:

> What is it that makes a poet alter a word, or several words, in a poem? How does he know which words to alter and how does he know when he has got the right ones? What tells him when to stop altering? For Dylan the words had to be *right* (whatever that means), and in achieving this the meaning for the reader might recede further and further with each emendation.

It has been my assumption that there will always be something in Thomas's final choice of words that will enable us to get back to the original impulse with which the poem began, the concept that fuelled the poet's energy.

If we have the working assumption that Thomas's obscurity has something to do with what I called in *Entrances* (chapter 4) 'Distancing the Intimate', we might expect that the more there is to be disguised the more obscure the poem will be. With 'Now', then, we

---

[1] We also know that Thomas's manners at any time were usually a keen judgement about the kind of company he was in.

should be thinking of what in Thomas's life might have the greatest need to be disguised.

'Now say nay' – this is a poem of a big 'No'. Our job is to lever from the poem, if we can, what it is that Thomas would be saying no to so emphatically. I think we can immediately detect that Thomas is saying no to no. As Clark Emery has put it: 'Since in this poem every Nay opposes a negative or defeatist point of view, it states unqualifiedly though gaily Thomas's Everlasting Yea' (Emery, p. 288). Emery is undoubtedly correct to hear Hamlet's meditation on self-slaughter in the background. (Thomas lifted the word 'handsaw' (line 14) from *Hamlet*.) I would put the 'To be or not to be' soliloquy in the foreground of this poem. Not that we would expect the poem to fit neatly into that frame, but if we are looking for a forbidden topic, suicide would be it. Poets have often been half in love with easeful death. But how many have tried to find a poetic expression for a personal experience of the suicidal impulse?

There was a period in the second half of 1931, when Thomas was approaching his seventeenth birthday, that has the earmarks of a traumatic breakdown (*Notebook Poems*, pp. 74–100, with commentary on pp. xiii–xix). The tension of the morbidity sometimes breaks the poems of this period into incoherence, such as this from poem 'XL' dated 11 September 1931 (*Notebook Poems*, p. 93):

> Let's kill the young man he don't care
> For without any blood he don't wish to live,
> And who took his blood and who took his blood
> And you took his blood, and I took his blood,
> Wanting to die for we got no blood,
> No guts or no bones to catch on the stones.

Some are much more disastrously out of kilter than the above, but these lines in their babble warn of suicide: 'So are we tired of reality'. In the adjacent poem of the same date (*Notebook Poems*, p. 92): 'Love, sleep, and death the only plan'. And, for good measure, on the contemplation of suicide (*Notebook Poems*, p. 105):

> Knowing all's nothing,
> Worth nothing, ends nothing,
> We own negation.

Head in the oven, no nearer heaven,
Full-veined, we may be empty,
The good we get
In slowly for an empty end
Senselessly lifting food to mouth, and food to mouth,
To keep the senseless being going.

There are a few jocular references in letters to looking meaningfully at the gas oven, but no confession of serious thoughts of suicide.[2] Perhaps he was always ambitious enough as a poet that any thoughts of suicide were just one part of the spectrum of emotions available, always well within the range of 'what if?' The poem 'Now' is, of course, within the range of 'what if?' since it has far too many subjunctives to be a suicide note.

But it is true that the current 'downer' around the time 'Now' was forming in his mind was the worst of his life. He had tried living in London for an intense four months, and its rewards (apart from literary successes) had been tawdry. 'The trials of life have proved too much for me', Thomas wrote to Glyn Jones, having retreated to Swansea in March 1935 (*Letters*, p. 186/213), 'the courts have found me guilty, and, rather hollow eyed and with little real work to my credit, I've returned home.' What if this was the end of the line? What if *18 Poems* was just a flash in the pan? What if an addiction to pub company had sapped all his creative energy? What if he just did not stack up, in spite of all his boasts? These are the kind of 'what ifs' that I feel are hovering around 'Now', which I take to be an anti-suicide note.

Now SAY nay, man dry man [addressing his dried out self], [that the] dry lover [should] mine [dig] the deadrock base and blow [up] the flowered [exploding like petals] anchor [sanity], [even if] should he, for centre sake [to find the ultimate middle], hop in the dust [by suicide], [if he should] forsake, the fool, the hardiness of [living] anger.

This is the kind of reduplication we expect sometimes of Thomas. He is telling himself twice not to destroy himself, not to blow up his anchor and not to leave his anger at the world by seeking the central caves of death.

---

[2] Perhaps one: 'I have been so utterly and suicidally morbid' (*Letters*, p. 36/54 – early November 1933).

> Now
> Say nay,
> Sir no say,
> Death to the yes,
> The yes to death, the yesman and the answer,
> Should he who split his children with a cure
> Have brotherless his sister on the handsaw.

This is saying death to the yes which is the yes to death, the yesman's death and, reading between the lines, the suicide's yes. Whoever split his children with a cure did something rather indefinable, but if he then went on to 'have brotherless his sister', by whatever means, then he is killing himself.

> Now
> Say nay,
> No say sir
> Yea the dead stir,
> And this, nor this, is shade, the landed crow,
> He lying low with ruin in his ear,
> The cockerel's tide upcasting from the fire.

This third stanza seems to be saying no to the idea of resurrection. Dost think the dead stir, dost think the crow on the ground or the king with poison in his ear will rise at the crowing of the cockerel? No, there is no rub there. Nothing.

The next stanza postulates the result on the cosmic scale if one did really say nay: the star would fall, the world would fail, the sun would dissolve. The last stanza says that he does not care a fig for death, which seems to indicate he has got over his morbidity.

> Now
> Say nay
> A fig for
> The seal of fire,
> Death hairy-heeled, and the tapped ghost in wood,
> We make me mystic as the arm of air,
> The two-a-vein, the foreskin, and the cloud.

Goat-heeled devil and table-tapped ghost should cause no problems, but the last line has always raised eyebrows. William Empson said he had no theory about the line but added: 'I am sure there is a reason why it seems very good' (*Casebook*, p. 112). (He did not, however guess at the reason. So I take this merely as a vote of confidence in Thomas.) I think any theory about the line would involve the proposition that the three images are not there to distinguish three separate ideas but, on the contrary, amount to the same thing. There is a 'we' who makes a 'me' have a state described as 'mystic' (mysterious) or, indeed, invisible, like an 'arm of air'. Certainly the 'I' – who has not got much personality, having not appeared previously in the poem – wants to have even less, wants all the camouflage he can get. Luckily images that make him mysterious are myriad, any image will do,[3] the more outlandish the better: 'foreskin', yes; 'two-a-vein', yes. 'Cloud' is rather tepid and gives the whole game away, really.

So this poem in the end calls for cloud cover. Thomas is invoking the magic that will protect him. If he is very quiet, disguised or preferably invisible, death will pass him by. We have postulated that the death feared in this poem is not the conventional romantic tuberculosis. Thomas had that anyway, or so he thought. It is the fear most borne by the insomniac (which Thomas also was in his youth): that the only way to sleep is to choose the sleep of death. This poem is not a psychological study or a reflective debate: it is, I believe, a series of phrases/images that are Thomas's best attempt, for this time, at making a poem out of the shards of a fractured reality.

[3] 'Any image will do', said Thomas in another context (*Letters*, p. 81/98).

O make me a mask

(please turn to *Collected Poems*, p. 72)

Written in November 1937 during the honeymoon at Blashford (their hostess, Caitlin's mother, was generously away), 'O make me a mask' is a poem of great openness. It acknowledges that, in a relationship, the 'you' will have 'spies' out watching with a sharp eye for anything in the partner's behaviour that would affect the marriage. It acknowledges that the 'me' will have incipient resistances and even cruelties of tongue alternating with flatteries. The request for a mask or a gag, therefore, is deeply ironic when made to the loved one in such revealing terms that everything is, in its intention, unhidden and said. They are beyond masks and gags. He is acknowledging ahead of time that there is no way that he will be granted 'the countenance of a dunce' (line 7) as armour to protect his 'glistening' thoughts from being examined by her. And he knows it is in vain that he requests a deceptive callousness. This is love and commitment, and he can never expect to have dry eyes in that way again. In talking about 'others' pretending to have feelings when they do not, when they smile behind their hand or laugh up their sleeve, he is saying goodbye to a time when, with the amoral acquaintances of his youth, he could scoff at any eventuality. There will be no fake grief from now on, but the griefs of the ages that they as lovers will have in their arms.

On a Wedding Anniversary

(please turn to *Collected Poems*, p. 103)

'In this house Caitlin and I have our bedroom on the top floor', Thomas wrote to Vernon Watkins from John Davenport's Wiltshire 'Malting House' where they had found a retreat for the summer of 1940, 'and so far we haven't got up even when the German machines are over us like starlings' (*Letters*, p. 463/524). He had been to London and was to make enough such trips to know what the Blitz was like. So that when Thomas discovered that Caitlin had had (was having?) an affair with another member of the household, he framed his shock in the image of a marriage, which had seemed so secure even in its attic nearest the danger, as now bombed out.

Caitlin in the tapes done for George Tremlett confessed to her indiscretion with the 'beautiful' musician William Glock (*Caitlin*, pp. 74–5):

> Occasionally, we would meet in the garden and he would hold my hand and be very tender. There was a feeling between us when we were together like falling in love, and we conceived this idea of having one night of love in Cardiff: it was the first time I had ever calculated an infidelity . . .

I had told Dylan that I would spend three nights in Swansea, and this farce turned into a real drama when his wretched mother gave the game away by telling him I had only spent two nights there. The Welsh mind is like that, noticing everything, taking it all in. She wrote to Dylan, and he *realised*. He was very upset and started cursing me. I was never planning to leave Dylan: it was just intended to be one night of love, and I thought I was getting my revenge because Dylan was always going off to London and having affairs. It was all agonisingly painful. Dylan threw a knife[1] at me (which missed me by miles), and for a long time after that he wouldn't come near me. He just turned his back on me, and it was ages before we sorted ourselves out.

Telling Ferris about this later, Glock said that though the Cardiff night had been a failure, he and Caitlin 'didn't give up but tried again at Marshfield shortly afterwards'. This time they were successful (Ferris's *Caitlin*, p. 88). It was apparently several weeks before Thomas discovered this liaison and blew up, taking Caitlin away from the house immediately. 'I was very muddled and unhappy', he wrote to his host John Davenport, apologizing for 'the morning rush away' and subsequent silence. He 'didn't feel a bit like having any contact at all – until the muddles were straightened in my head – with anyone in the place where for months I had been so happy' (*Letters*, p. 472/534).

It seems that Thomas had had in mind to write a poem in celebration of his third wedding anniversary (11 July 1940). Perhaps he had already begun it; we do not know. In any case, 'On a Wedding Anniversary' was finished in the aftermath of the Glock affair. The skies have fallen. 'Love and his patients roar on a chain' is an extreme Marquis de Sade emblem for the emotion of loss. 'From every true or crater / Carrying cloud, Death strikes their house.' Clouds seem 'true', but all hide bombs.

> Too late in the wrong rain
> They come together whom their love parted:
> The windows pour into their heart
> And the doors burn in their brain.

The couple are back together again. It was 'their love' that parted them – not necessarily their love for each other! But, in a sense,

---

[1] This becomes a fork in other tellings. In discussing her infidelities with Ferris (his *Caitlin*, p. 82) Caitlin said that Dylan 'did make a few protests, but rather feeble ones. Once he threw a fork at me. Can you imagine anything feebler than a fork?'

parting in order to return is exactly what lovers do with their love sometimes. In any case, the poem says it is too late; some far too disabling wrong has happened. They will probably stay together (we know that Dylan and Caitlin did), but the rain of tears pours through the windows into their heart(s) (singular in the poem – a sign of togetherness in spite of everything?). 'And the doors burn in their brain' – these must be exit doors. The possibility of leaving is now branded into their minds.

Once below a time

(please turn to *Collected Poems*, p. 109)

The lighthearted volte-face of the first line – this story does not begin *upon* a time but *below* a time – alerts us to the poem's jocular attire. There is something low-life about it; it is a picaresque, mock-epic tale, a story of escape and capture, bluster and eventual quiescence. It was probably written in December 1939 and in its spiritedness anticipates Thomas's Christmas visit to Swansea. 'I want to see our beautiful drab town', he wrote to his Swansea friend Charles Fisher early in the month (*Letters*, p. 434/494).

> I want to have smuts in my eye in Wind Street, I want to hear the sweet town accent float into my ears like the noise of old brakes . . . reserve two seats (and one seat specially sawed down) in the Kardomah my Home Sweet Homah.

This is the mood captured beautifully later, in the broadcast 'Return Journey' (1947) where the poet imagines seeking out his former selves in Swansea; for instance, 'Young Thomas', the reporter on the local newspaper, who 'used to wear an overcoat sometimes with the check lining inside out . . . and a perched pork pie with a peacock feather' (*Broadcasts*, p. 183). As in 'Once below a time' (for it is sartorial poem), the clothes, in his memory, denote the man (*Broadcasts*, p. 180): 'a bit of a shower-off; plus-fours and no breakfast, you know . . . a bombastic adolescent provincial bohemian with a thick-knotted artist's tie made out of his sister's scarf . . . and a cricket-shirt dyed bottle-green; a gabbing, ambitious, mock-tough, pretentious young man'. This is the kind of person the poet wants to present himself as in the poem, yet at the same time seeing through his own pretentions. If he was once below a time, hopefully he will rise above it.

> Once below a time, when my pinned-around-the spirit [on a tailor's dummy] cut-to-measure flesh bit [like a tight suit], [the flesh being a] suit [bought] for a serial sum [regular payments] on the first of each hardship [month's hard labour], [the flesh being] my paid-for-slaved-for own too late in love torn [in the thickets of love] breeches and blistered jacket [singed and almost caught] on the snapping [dentata] rims of the ashpit [of love] . . .

He is being fitted into his flesh like a suit bought on the 'never never'; it is a jump suit made for love, but he does not seem to be able to jump quickly enough and his flesh becomes torn and burnt in the experience.

When we ask what experience he is getting into here, we are given the line: 'In grottoes I worked with birds'. This has got to be one of the worst lines in Thomas's whole collected poems, perhaps the only truly embarrassing line. It is the artist as a young bird-dog, I suppose, and working with birds he is a retriever or something. Does the line not have any guile at all? I suppose the point is that he is, in this ill-fitting suit, a clownish figure, wearing a spiked mastiff collar, also tasselled and decked out, both in a basement cutting room as well as on a cloud (not sword) swallower (high platform).

In the next section the hero bursts from the sea in 'common clay clothes' but disguised as a merman or a 'he-god'. In any case, he does whatever it takes to astound the tailors who made his flesh; they are taken aback by his precocity. The tailors are presumably the parents, or others in his young life who have helped to stitch him together and are now impressed with their handiwork.

> Then, bushily swanked [dressed pretentiously] in bear wig and tails, hopping hot [footed] leaved and feathered from the kangaroo foot[1] of the earth [antipodes], from the chill, silent centre [of the world] trailing the frost bitten cloth [of his explorer self], up through the lubber crust of

---

[1] 'Yes, the Lawrence calling-up-of-memory in the kangaroo lines was intentional' (*Letters*, p. 437/497). This comment, however, gives little clue to what the intention was.

Wales[2] I ROCKETED to astonish the flashing needle rock [sea-worn crust] of squatters [tailors], the criers [decrying] of Shabby and Shorten, the famous stitch droppers.

Thomas thought of this poem in his own mind as having the title 'Shabby and Shorten' (*Letters*, p. 818/914). It seems that here we have a chorus of detractors. He is all dolled up and they scoff with their tailor-like disparagements – or they would if he did not have it in him to astonish them.

There is reason to think that, on one level, Thomas gave a great deal of attention to dominating by conversation whatever company he was in, even while on another level he knew better. Very early he confessed to Trevor Hughes (*Letters*, p. 9/27):

> All I may, eventually, do is to
>
> > Astound the salons & cliques
> > Of half-wits, publicists & freaks.
>
> I was cut out for little else.

'Once below a time' describes him being 'cut out'. He is tailor-made for what kind of show he will put on for the world.

The second part of the poem goes on to relate how clothes can veil our motives and disguise our flaws.

My silly [innocent] suit [flesh], hardly yet suffered for, around some coffin carrying birdman [death-defying aviator] or told [story book] ghost I HUNG. And the [wise] owl hood, the [devil's] heel hider, claw [hiding] fold and hole [hiding place] for the rotten [evil] head, DECEIVED, I [hopefully] believed, my maker, the cloud [high] perched tailors' master [stitching] with nerves for [instead of] cotton.

If this is supposed to be God the Father – as some have said – then I'm a tailor's dummy, because I think it is Thomas's headmaster. No, not really – the headmaster at Swansea Grammar at the time was not that kind of imposing figure in the clouds (Ferris, pp. 43–4):

---

[2] The jocular echo would be the 'blubber crust of whales'. In the letter of 30 January 1940 in which Thomas thanks Vernon Watkins for typing the poem, he wrote: 'Actually, although I thought the pun out quite coldly, I wanted to make the lubber line a serious one' (*Letters*, p. 437/496).

The headmaster, Trevor Owen, was a big, genial man with a booming voice and a mild speech defect that boys would imitate, just below hearing-level . . . In one version of a school anecdote, he catches Dylan Thomas sneaking off the premises . . .

Headmaster: 'What are you doing?'
Thomas: 'Playing truant, sir.'
Headmaster: 'Well, don't let your father catch you.'

Ah, D. J. Thomas is a much better candidate for this God the Father whom the young Thomas thought he was deceiving, hiding from him the devilish traits he had assumed. This is the archetypal adolescent posture of resistance to fathers and teachers. If the 'idol tailor's eyes' of the next section are not his father's, then they must be the piercing eyes of someone of equal steeliness, who saw through Thomas's cover and punctured his pretensions in a most serious way.

On the old seas from [boys' adventure] stories, thrashing my [young seabird's] wings, combing [parrying waves] with antlers, [like the explorer] Columbus on fire [with zeal], I WAS PIERCED by the idol tailor's eyes, [was GLARED [down] through [the slits of a] shark mask and navigating [prow figure] head, [through] cold Nansen [the arctic explorer]'s beak on [at the front of] a boat full of [slave galley] gongs, [reduced by the glaring] to the boy of common thread, the bright pretender, the ridiculous sea dandy with [now revealed] dry flesh and earth [not sea adventure] for adorning and [down-to-earth] bed.

It WAS sweet [the effort of pretence over] to drown in the readymade [like a suit] handy water with my cherry capped dangler [dangling punctured in its pride, now discovered to be] green as seaweed summoning a child's voice from a webfoot [cuneiform memorial] stone, [']Never never oh never to regret the [boasting] bugle I wore on my cleaving [knifing the waves] arm as I blasted [my youth's song] in a wave[']

Now shown [up] and mostly bare [of flaunting clothing] I WOULD LIE DOWN, LIE DOWN, LIE DOWN and LIVE as quiet as a bone.

Thomas called the ending a 'pacific repetition' (*Letters*, p. 439/498). It was meant to balance the refusal to regret, which had been emphasized with the repetition of 'never' a few lines before. He has no intention of throwing out the past; the ball he threw in the schoolyard, when he had a throwing arm, will never, never, never reach the ground. His days of swagger are not repudiated. But something has brought them to an end. He has been stared down by life, cut down to size. He senses that he has reached the end of his rope as an *enfant terrible*. Shabby and Shorten, the tailors with their scissors, have snipped it. Fate.

There was one overwhelming, sobering fact that had come into the poet's life, everybody's life, at this time. 'Once below a time' was written a few months after the declaration of war. Fate was creeping towards Thomas in the form of call-up. In the same letter to Charles Fisher in which he was anticipating with some glee a Christmas in Swansea, he also has to mention the war: 'I'm not doing anything about the war; resigned to personal neutrality, I wait until I am called up' (*Letters*, p. 434/494). War is the ultimate Shabby and Shorten; it is the end of all personal pretensions and bohemian antics. He told Vernon Watkins at this time that what he wanted for Christmas was 'a lotion for invisibility' (*Letters*, p. 434/494). All he can do is to lie down, as quiet as a bone, lie down not even in conscientious objection, but solely in pacific repetition.

Once it was the colour of saying

(please turn to *Collected Poems*, p. 74)

Sending this poem to Vernon Watkins on 29 December 1938 Thomas called it a 'Cwmdonkin poem' (*Letters*, p. 347/396), and so it plainly is. He locates his writing desk on 'the uglier side of a hill' (line 2): his boyhood home, 5 Cwmdonkin Drive was on a hill, and opposite, on the less ugly side, was a grassy area and Cwmdonkin Park just beyond that. The girls' school referred to (in the field that from his window looked the size of a cap) was the private Clevedon College – it no longer exists according to James A. Davies's *Dylan Thomas's Places* (p. 31). At the time the poem was written, Cwmdonkin Drive itself no longer existed as a home, for his parents had moved to Bishopston, a small community in the environs of Swansea, soon after his father's retirement in December 1936. Thomas in this poem is deliberately taking us back to a blissful time when he was first writing poetry and his table was soaked with colour. The girls in their uniforms might have been a patch of black and white in his distant view, but the page on which he was writing was glowing with warmth and the words were gentle as though they were sliding on the shifting dunes of the seashore.

From his earliest notebooks (now at Buffalo) we know the kind of poetry Thomas is thinking of when he uses the phrase 'the colour of saying'. The extant notebooks open with a poem of 27 April 1930 (*Notebook Poems*, p. 17):

> He stands at the streaming river's edge
> With his soft arms in the air,
> And snares the sun among his tangled hair,
> And springs upon the wave's thick ledge,
> And curls his arms around his hips,
> Brushing the hot foam with his lips.
> Slowly the river covers him,
> The river of the webbed anemone,
> The sadr on its leaf-green stem . . .

And so on. These early poems are imagistic, in a range of languid moods, all laved with soft colouring – up to a certain point in time, about a year into the sequence, when the poems take on a detectable acridity. One can dip in almost anywhere after March 1931 and find the colours of death, for instance a poem of 3 July 1931 (*Notebook Poems*, pp. 82–3):

> I have a friend in death
> Daywise, the grave's inertia
> Mending my head that needs its hour's pain . . .
>
> Sober, he heaps his shadows on my aching mind,
> But, with the water on your hands,
> He plays his sun a time too loud,
> Deafens, and with his blood
> Drowns all the actions I have lied.

Or the next poem in the notebook, 28 July 1931, which begins (*Notebook Poems*, p. 83):

> It is the wrong, the hurt, the mineral,
> That makes its stroke
> Through wisdom, for my age,
> And sin, for my two-headed joy –
> The particles aren't more than dust,
> And whose affections aren't corrupt?

There is no equanimity now. Things have become jaded. He is taking it out on himself. I think this is what he means in 'Once it was the colour of saying' when he writes (line 12): 'Now my saying shall be my undoing'. A new period of self-consciousness has been inaugurated; he is taking himself apart in these poems; he is undone.

For the seven months from July 1932 to January 1933 there is no extant notebook. It is more than likely that our poem, in a first draft, was written during that period. We read (lines 5–6) that he intends to 'undo' his previous mode of composition and allow in the seamier side of life, 'that all the charmingly [magically] drowned [in his sleep world] arise to cockcrow [persist after waking] and kill [haunt him with the promise of death]'. With the opening of the next notebook that we have, begun in February 1933, we see this prescription for horror being carried out (*Notebook Poems*, p. 125):

> Companionship with night has turned
> Each ugly corpse into a friend,
> And there are more friends if you wish:
> The maggots feasting on dead flesh,
> The vulture with appraising beak,
> The redcheeked vampire at the neck,
> There is the skeleton and the naked ghost.
> Friend of the night, you are a friend of the night's friends.

Or the second poem (*Notebook Poems*, p. 126):

> It is death though I have died
> Many deaths, and have risen again
> With an unhealed wound and a cracked heart,
> It is death to sink again
> My breath and blood into another
> Who, too, has been wounded, has shown fight,
> Has been killed, raised with a cracked heart
> And is ready for the hundredth dying,
> Ready to perish again and be hurt, . . .

'Ready to perish again and be hurt' – he is winding off the thread of his life like a fisherman's reel as the sinker goes with the current; his life is so heavy that poems feel like stones ('Stone hard to lift', *Notebook Poems*, p. 60). When he says in the last line of 'Once it was the colour of saying' that he now winds off every stone like a reel it is, I believe, a comment on the arduousness of the new poetry of the 1932–3 period.

If this conjecture as to the early date of composition is correct, then in 1938, with a conjectured revision, we have a poem that is essentially a reminiscence, a looking back to that important juncture in his life and poetic development. I have examined Thomas's situation in late 1938 to see if this poem could stand as a declaration of intent, some kind of renewal, as of that time; but I conclude that 'Once it was the colour of saying' is a poem of remembered feeling rather than announcing any new resolution at the later date.

Indeed, I am convinced that it is the poem to which Thomas is referring in a letter to Vernon Watkins of 20 December 1938 (*Letters*, p. 343/393) where he says 'I'm enclosing a little new poem'.[1] He adds: 'been doing several little ones lately; send you them all soon'. This signals, to my mind, that 'Once it was the colour of saying' is in the category of what Watkins called 'opossums' to distinguish these shorter, less consequential poems from the 'opuses' which were claiming Thomas's best attention (*LVW*, p. 40; *Letters*, p. 287/336). If Thomas did not clearly identify it as such, that would not be unusual; the fact is he never did tell Watkins that the 'opossums' were early poems revised for quick publication.

Thomas responded to some suggestions of Watkins's (*Letters*, pp. 351/401–2):

> I'm glad you liked my last poem. I shan't alter anything in it except, perhaps but probably, the 'close & cuckoo' lovers. The 'dear close cuckoo' lovers is a good suggestion. I can't say the same for 'halo for the bruised knee & broken heel' which is esoterically *off* every mark in the poem. I see your argument about the error of shape, but the form was consistently emotional and I can't change it without a change of heart.

Without Watkins's letters it is difficult to evaluate these comments, except that it is clear Thomas does not intend there to be a 'halo' around the earlier times. There is no question that he feels the new poetry will be, though arduous, better.

---

[1] The fact is he did not enclose any poem then. 'Once it was the colour of saying' was sent in a letter nine days later (*Letters*, p. 347/396).

✧

On no work of words

(please turn to *Collected Poems*, p. 78)

When Thomas in the first line of this poem says he has not written anything for three months he is referring to June, July and August of 1938. Dylan and Caitlin were in Laugharne, and especially after they had settled in Sea View, a house with numerous guest rooms, there began a round of visitors: Augustus John, Norman Cameron and girl friend, Mervyn Levy, Keidrych Rhys, Caitlin's mother and her friend. Henry Treece, who was planning to write a book on Thomas, came with his fiancée Nelly for a week. 'Now they're all disappeared', Thomas wrote in a letter of 1 September 1938, 'and I'm forced to work' (*Letters*, p. 324/373).

He turned to his notebooks for inspiration and found a poem of a few lines which echoed his condition of self-reproach (*Notebook Poems*, p. 131):

> To take to give is all, return what given
> Is throwing manna back to heaven,
> Receive, not asking, and examine
> Is looking gift god in the mouth.
> To take to leave is pleasing death;
> Unpleasant death will take at last,
> Surrender at the very first
> Is paying twice the final cost.

To get himself started he wrote on the notebook page opposite this short poem three lines reflecting his current lethargy (*Notebook Poems*, p. 254):

> For three lean months now, no work done
> In summer Laugharne among the cockle boats
> And by the castle with the boatlike birds.

Dropping the specificity of locale he turned these lines into the first three lines of the poem as we now have it, and then set about recasting the notebook poem, crafting longer rhymed lines, but staying pretty well within the idea as he had it in February 1933.

To take [one's given talent] to give [to others] IS all [our whole duty], [on the other hand] [to] return [unused] what is hungrily given [leaving the giver hungry] [is] puffing [with exertion] the pounds of manna up through the dew to heaven [reversing Exodus 16: 14–16], [in a like manner] the lovely gift of the gab [talking with tongues – Acts 2: 4] BANGS back [like a bullet] on a blind shaft [of light, now put out in a reversal of Pentecost].

To lift [filch with one's talent] from the treasures of man [only] to leave [abandon it] IS PLEASING [ahead of time] death that will rake [like a croupier] at last [eventually] all currencies of the marked [like banknotes] breath and count the taken, [but then] forsaken [abandoned] mysteries [skills of a craft] in a bad dark [looking at the deed in a bad light].

To surrender [one's talent] now [ahead of time] IS to pay [the final debt to] the expensive ogre[1] [at great cost] twice.

Ancient woods of my blood [addressing his life], DASH [yourself] down to the nut[2] of the seas [return to pre-birth] if I take [only] to burn [wastefully] or return [unused] this world which is each man's work.

We can get some benefit from the explanation of the ending that Thomas gave in a letter to Desmond Hawkins (*Letters*, p. 396/448):

> The *sense* of the last two lines is: Well, to hell and to death with me, may my old blood go back to the bloody sea it came from if I accept this world only to bugger it up or return it. The oaktree came out of the acorn; the woods of my blood came out of the nut of the sea, the tide-concealing, blood-red kernel.

What Thomas said in a muted way in the notebook poem and what he says with some magnificence in the final version of 'On no work of words' is that he does not intend to mess up the job he has been given to do in life. In the face of the ogre Death the poet will be a Jack the Giant-Killer. For three months he has been letting the side down. 'The only things I've written', Thomas admitted in the letter

---

[1] Watkins apparently had difficulty with the word 'ogre' for death, but Thomas said he would 'listen to no criticism of it' (*Letters*, p. 329/377).

[2] '"Nut", yes, has many meanings, but here, in the same line as "woods", I can't really see that it can have any but a woody meaning. The actual line is a very extravagant one, an overgrand declamatory cry after, in my opinion, the reasoned and quite quiet argument of the preceding lines' (*Letters*, p. 396/448).

of 1 September 1938, 'have been letters to the Royal Literary Fund' (*Letters*, p. 325/373). He added: 'Poverty makes me lazy and crafty'. So in the poem he chides himself, taking to task his poverty and craft (guile). The luxury of summer Laugharne and the growing rotundity of his body mock his empty purse and the lean kine he is pasturing. But now, swearing on his own blood, he resolves to get down to his proper vocation. 'On no work of words' is not a bad start.

On the Marriage of a Virgin

(please turn to *Collected Poems*, p. 105)

The sun is a lover who comes to the young woman of the poem every night, and in the morning goes to his daily work, leaving her miraculously virginal. With her marriage, the sun is replaced with a human husband, made of a different mettle. This is the summary of a poem we find in Thomas's notebooks dated 22 March 1933. It certainly seems as though the young poet was preparing a prothalamion for his big sister's wedding, which finally came off in May 1933 and was definitely being talked about the previous March (*Notebook Poems*, pp. 137 and 255).

There does not seem to have been a wedding that prompted Thomas to turn to the notebook in January 1941 to work on the poem. The final version (it was further revised in July 1941) exists, then, because of the intrinsic attractiveness to the poet of the Zeus–Danae conceit ('the avalanche / Of the golden ghost' – line 11) that is the central motivating core of the poem.

> Waking alone [as she used to do] in a multitude of loves [doves and other morning beauties] when morning's light [the sun] surprised [caught still a-bed] in the [act of her] opening of her nightlong eyes his [the sun's] golden yesterday [still] asleep upon the [shining gold] iris [of her eyes] and [when] this day's sun leapt up to the sky [to his daily task] out of her thighs [his nightly couch] WAS [always] miraculous virginity old as [Christ's miracle of] loaves and fishes, though [indeed] the moment of a miracle is unending lightning and the shipyards of Galilee's [Christ's] footprints [on the water] hide a navy of doves [birds of love].

Not since Queen Elizabeth's time has virginity had such praise, and even then the poets restrained themselves from calling the royal virginity miraculous! Thomas is going out of his way to extol the special quality he feels exists in young maidenhood, which may dream of a multitude of loves, but wakes to sunshine, the purest of lovers, unscathed. He is the druid of her unbroken body, and is not content with anything but a magnified image. Once he has used the word 'miracle', the loaves and fishes are almost commonplace; 'unending lightning' might do as an inspired oxymoron. Or an image of more than typical Thomas complexity: 'the shipyards of Galilee's footprints hide a navy of doves' (line 7). Christ walks on the water of Lake Galilee (John 6:19). The prints of his feet become yards, shipyards, which in the thinking of wartime are camouflaged to hide a whole flotilla of ships. These are transformed by the miracle of Christ's feet into doves, the bird of the Annunciation and peace, as well as love in the courtly world. Thus the fecundity within the chastity of the premarital state.

But the lightning does end.

> No longer will the [light-wave] vibrations of the sun DESIRE [with its warmth] on her deepsea [drowned in sleep] pillow where once she [used to be] married alone [with her dreams], her heart all ears and eyes [with expectancy], [her] lips catching the [sunbeam] avalanche of the golden ghost [the sun] who ringed [as with a wedding ring] with his streams [of light] her mercury [quicksilver shining] bone, who under the lids of her windows [eyes] hoisted his golden luggage [moving in],

> for a man SLEEPS [in her bed] where a fire [from the sun] leapt down and she learns through his arm [around her] that other sun, the jealous coursing of the unrivalled blood.

One has the sinking feeling that the husband's 'jealous coursing' blood is 'unrivalled' because it brooks no rival. Apparently Mars has taken over from Apollo. If Thomas had wanted us to think well of this marriage he could have said more. About the premarital state he says too much: the young woman sounds a bit like a flying saucer abductee. Stern questions about how it relates to real life are probably out of order. What we are finally left with is the excitement of a change of guard through the act of marriage, tinged with some foreboding. We perhaps cannot ask more of this slender poem.

Our eunuch dreams

(please turn to *Collected Poems*, p. 17)

This is a poem of great simplicity of construction. Two threats to normal active life are exposed: dreams and films, in their darker modalities, are deceptive and misleading.

Part I is concerned with 'eunuch' dreams, incapable of issue, 'seedless' during the day hours. We might dream of light and love, 'the tempers of the heart'; but this sounds like 'tempters', and they 'whack [or wank] their boys' limbs'. These are sexual dreams. The seductive 'widows' in black winding-sheets are lifted into dreams as nightmare figures straight from the grave, parted from the worms and the bones of their men at sunset.

Part II likens films to dreaming. Both take place at night and are a false representation of love. The gunman and his moll[1] hide at dawn like vampires. Part III asks which of these two worlds or 'sleepings' is going to stay with us when the sick earth is cured and wakes up? The shapes of daylight acting stiffly in films, the sunny Hollywood leading men, the rich who welsh on their promises by offering us a vision of wealth in the movies that life cannot hope to provide, either these will be packed off or the nightmare shrouded figures will. But films are not true; dream figures are unreal, have no marrow. Neither of them should be honoured. Part IV, with a tone of fatalistic despair, declares that these two false things *are* our world.

Then there is a big leap with the words 'Have faith'. These two words are given the job of turning this whole discouraging poem around. As in so many of Thomas's poems, he is here trying to push himself into optimism in spite of all the odds he has stacked up against such a thing. Just prior to publication in *New Verse*, Thomas wrote to the editor Geoffrey Grigson that he himself felt the 'jarring optimism' (*Letters*, p. 106/130) and suggested the 'less false' alternative for line 6: 'Suffer this world to spin'. This would leave the false world to its own revolving. But, since the last six lines of the

---

[1] Apparently Pamela Hansford Johnson accused Thomas of being too much of a 'thirties' poet here. He expostulated with her in a letter of March 1934 (*Letters*, p. 108/132): 'There is no reason at all why I should not write of gunmen, cinemas & pylons if what I have to say necessitates it. Those words & images were essential . . . I wasn't conceding anything. I wanted gunmen, and . . . I bloody well had them.'

poem still strive for the same kind of optimism, such a change just delays slightly the shifting of gears. Grigson let the 'Have faith' stand, and Thomas did not amend it in later publications. It remains a deliberate lever to jack up the poem from despair to hope.

When Pamela Hansford Johnson taunted Dylan with being a 'pylon' poet she knew very well that, at this time of his life, he had quite a bit of earnest leftist radicalism in his make-up that would not be out of place in *New Verse*. She had heard him preach aplenty in letters; for instance, a section headed 'Hymn of Despair and Hope' in a letter of mid-November 1933 (*Letters*, p. 55/72):

> The hope of Revolution, even though all of us will not admit it, is uppermost in all our minds. If there were not that revolutionary spark within us, that faith in a new faith, and that belief in our power to squash the chaos surrounding us like a belt of weeds, we would turn on the tap of war and drown ourselves in its gases.

Now in 'Our eunuch dreams', written into the notebook in March 1934 (*Notebook Poems*, p. 215), he is willing to use the word 'faith' in an equally naked way: 'Have faith'.

> For we shall be a shouter like the cock,
> Blowing the old dead back; our shots shall smack
> The image from the plates;
> And we shall be fit fellows for a life,
> And who shall remain shall flower as they love,
> Praise to our faring hearts.

There *is* a new dawn. We shall greet it with fervour. We will blow with our lungs the 'old dead' of dreams back to their graves; we will shoot and crack the photographic plates and destroy fake gangsters. In the end we will win for ourselves an active, resourceful life. 'Praise to our faring hearts' – yes, Thomas here has joined Auden, Spender and C. Day Lewis: get rid of the old, and bring in the new. Clearly, the graveyard nightmare figures and the fake movie world stand for more than themselves; there is a general condemnation of society here. We have to take this poem as a commitment to total revolution. Writing a newspaper piece a few months later ('A Plea for Intellectual Revolution' in the *Swansea and West Wales Guardian* for 3 August 1934, p. 11), Thomas quoted Stephen Spender:

Oh, comrades, let not those who followed after
– The beautiful generations that shall spring from our sides –
Let them not wonder how after the failure of banks
The failure of cathedrals and the declared insanity of our rulers,
We lacked the spring-like resources of the tiger.

Thomas added: 'There must be intellectual revolution, or bloody revolution will beat us to it.'

Out of the sighs

(please turn to *Collected Poems*, p. 43)

In June 1932 when this poem was written, Thomas was living at home, unemployed, a frustrated bohemian, not remotely able to offer a local girl what she might have a right to expect from a relationship. As he says at the end of the poem, all he has in him to give he tenders, but it is little a girl could expect to relish: crumbs of emotion, barn as haybed, and halter for a servile role in the relationship. He has no prospects. The way he puts it makes clear he knows any advances, even if initially taken up, are doomed. Consequently, for his own part, he must steel himself, in anticipation, against hurt. At this time Thomas declared to Trevor Hughes that he had 'never felt the desire to fall in love' (*Letters*, p. 8/26). Such self-protection! Out of the sighs at a romance's end (stanza 1), a little feeling comes, but not of grief, for he has eliminated that before any agony can occur.

What, then, is the problem expressed in 'Out of the sighs' if it is not bitterness of loss? There is apparently worse torture than dying (stanza 2): it is the residual ache of having no regret for the ending, for 'leaving woman waiting'. In these verses Thomas is able to expose himself as more subtly sensitive than we would ever have expected. Aching over having no regret? That is a complaint that might require the rare dilutions of homeopathy.

In the same letter to Trevor Hughes (probably late 1932) Thomas gave the opinion that 'everyone nowadays is so terribly frightened of becoming maudlin' (*Letters*, p. 9/27). 'Out of the sighs' can stand as Thomas's declaration that he is not afraid. This poem was written by a seventeen-year-old who was acting his age: not forlorn at love's end, but forlorn at not being forlorn. That the poet chose this adolescent effort for *Twenty-five Poems* (1936) with hardly any changes from the early manuscript (*Notebook Poems*, pp. 110–11, 114) meant that he was inviting us to look at one of his earliest compositions. I have no problem in taking these verses as juvenilia.

Over Sir John's hill

(please turn to *Collected Poems*, p. 142)

The flow of feeling and the dignity of diction make this poem unimpeachable at every point. It is one of Thomas's diapason triumphs. Its poetic power, its specific description of the view from the poet's writing shed at Laugharne, and its universal message of mortality seem to me to be entirely open to any reader. The only thing I feel it is the duty of the explicator to take up is the question of God's place in the scene laid out before us. Two contrasting viewpoints can be cited. Aneirin Talfan Davies in his assessment of Thomas as a religious poet had this to say (*Druid*, pp. 54–5):

> This is a poem of 'judgment day', with the sun over Sir John Hill donning his 'black cap' of jackdaws to sit in judgment on the 'led-astray' birds. The whole of nature is involved, and the poet, casting himself once again in the role of nature's priest, with Saint heron, reads the water's psalms, and chants his litany of penitence.

> It is the heron and I, under judging Sir John's elmed
> Hill, tell-tale the knelled
> Guilt
> Of the led-astray birds . . .

> On behalf of the wayward birds, he confesses their guilt, and prays that God will have mercy upon them.

> . . . whom God, for their breast of whistles,
> Have mercy on,
> God in his whirlwind silence save, who marks the sparrows hail,
> For their soul's song.

This is the nearest we get to an open confession of 'guilt' in Thomas's poems. He is the 'led-astray' bird, who prays for mercy. He prays that God, for his 'breast of whistles', for his poems, his songs, will have mercy upon him.

Thomas is perhaps too reticent in his confession, but Aneirin Talfan Davies feels that orthodox Christianity is within the poet's grasp. We are given no sense by the critic, however, of what it is that constitutes the birds' 'guilt', or Thomas's. Why is God silent in his whirlwind? Even Job got some kind of an answer.

Does Thomas really expect mercy from God, or is it just a way of putting something else? It is perhaps more appropriate to be sceptical of religious claims for the poem, as Walford Davies is in his Open University monograph (Davies, p. 83) in discussing the poet's use of the words 'guilt' and 'souls' in relation to the slaughtered sparrows of the poem:

> In what sense are they 'guilty', or have souls? These are surely *human* considerations, all the more emphasized as such by being so deliberately and precariously foisted on non-human nature. Similarly, reading 'Over Sir John's hill' on its own, one might even deduce a specifically Christian belief on the poet's part. Yet it is possible to feel that the prayer to God in verse 4 is not as emphatically positioned as the simpler and more characteristic resignation with which the poet ends – engraving, 'before the lunge of night', the 'notes on this time-shaken / Stone' of the poem. As if the Christian consolation had been more entertained than actually believed in, the poet accepts that all he can really do is record and memorialize.

On the one or two occasions when Thomas felt called upon, outside of his poetry, to announce some kind of religious belief he did so with a degree of flippancy that implied there was no serious answer to a question better not asked. The most conspicuous example is the poet's prefatory note to the original *Collected Poems* (found on p. 174 of the 1988 *Collected Poems*), the pertinent part of which reads:

> I read somewhere of a shepherd who, when asked why he made, from within fairy rings, ritual observances to the moon to protect his flocks, replied: 'I'd be a damn fool if I didn't!' These poems, with all their crudities, doubts, and confusions, are written for the love of Man and in praise of God, and I'd be a damn fool if they weren't.

Our confidence in his statement that his poems are written 'in praise of God' is undermined by his likening himself to a shepherd making ritual observances to the moon, which is rather ridiculous. Surely Thomas does not expect us, on reflection, to consider the 'fairy rings' anything other than quaint superstition. He is putting his religious beliefs on the level of primitive habit. I think, however, he is being entirely accurate here in his estimation of his own inner workings. We would probably be wrong to understand him as trying, in a backhanded way, to express a deep Christian conviction.

Any temptation to do so would in any case be constrained by what Thomas said to John Malcolm Brinnin as his visitor was leaving Laugharne in July 1951: that he aimed to produce 'poems in praise of God's world by a man who doesn't believe in God' (Brinnin, p. 128). How can you believe in 'God's world' without believing in God? It does not seem logical, but there is a sense in which one can have an enormous feeling of gratitude for the world in its ordinary glories, and one's thanks may go to some vague source that habit of mind will call God.

'Over Sir John's hill' was written in gratitude for a world that had just been given him by God's plenty, through the agency of Margaret Taylor. His long-time patroness had bought the Boat House in Laugharne for the use of the Thomas family. In a letter of 11 May 1949 Thomas tells Margaret Taylor of the happiness in which he is beginning to write the poem (*Letters*, pp. 706–7/788–9):

> I can never thank you enough for making this fresh beginning possible by all the trust you have put in me, by all the gifts you have made me, by all your labour & anxiety in face of callous & ungrateful behaviour. I know that the only way to express my deep gratitude is to be happy & to write. Here I am happy and writing. All I shall write in this water and tree room on the cliff, every word, will be my thanks to you. I hope to God it will be good enough.

'I hope to God' – the phrase used casually in this happy letter bears some relationship to the 'God have mercy on them' and 'God save them' of the poem, which are certainly less casual but might equally come under the category of expressions of concern rather than of theological import. When we say, echoing the New Testament, that God takes note of every sparrow's fall, we are saying that the world is full of small events that *we* care about, that there is no disaster so small that we do not feel for it in sympathy. In the poem's assertion that God 'marks the sparrows hail' (line 45), it is the poet's caring that is registered.

Incidentally, the word 'hail' can denote two things: the sparrows are hailing in the sense of crying out in distress to attract attention or, with 'dilly-dilly' (lines 21 and 31), hailing death in greeting; and also we are watching the sparrows falling like hail, 'as the snapt feathers snow' (line 50). It is not merely incidental that 'Over Sir John's hill' is full of delightful puns, words whose multiple meanings do not annoy but work in context to contribute to a sense of the world's foison. One nice example is the word 'sedge' (line 21) where the heron is wading. It has the same meaning as 'siege', which the dictionary gives as 'The station of a heron on the watch for prey'. Another dictionary definition of 'sedge' is 'a flock of herons'. That Thomas knew of this is clear from a circled note he made in one of the poem's worksheets (now in Harvard library): 'Sedge is a lot of herons'. Nearby is the phrase 'a sedge of heron stilts'. He did not finally use that particular formulation, but the sense of it, we should allow, remains embedded in the phrase 'shallow and sedge' as an enrichment of diction. This song succeeds as its language is discovered to have the many-sidedness and liveliness of life itself.

This liveliness is what death takes away, which loss commands the elegiac strain in the poem. The place of death in life is what 'Over Sir John's hill' is asking us to puzzle about. It is the paramount question for which religion traditionally provides an answer in terms of life after death and the rewards of heaven. In returning time and time again to the poem I have never seen any hint of such orthodoxy. The third critic I would like to quote on this subject is myself as I put my conclusions in *Entrances*, pp. 109–10:

> Death is not just (or unjust), Sir John's hill is not judging, the birds are not guilty, the heron is not holy, and God is not, in any meaningful sense, merciful. What, then, are we to think of a poem in which such adjectives are applied to such individuals? Perhaps we should bear in mind, to begin with, that the common expression 'condemned to die' does not, when one thinks about it, really mean condemned, *punished* by death. It is just a way of saying 'shall or will die' – simple futurity. But there is a rightness about 'condemned'; it corresponds to the feeling of grievance against death. The word is not irresponsible; neither, I think, is Thomas. The poem may be expressing only the *fact* of death, and such words as 'guilt' may be empty of intellectual content; but a form of meaning is communicated to the emotions, the reader's compassion is guided. One usually frowns on poetry that has vague emotional wording without

precise denotation. Such a dismissal would not, I think, meet the case here. Thomas should be given credit for expressing truly the chief tenet of the non-religious: that the intellect cannot handle the fact of death, and that it is sternness, rebellion, hatred, self-pity, compassion – some naked emotion – with which we are left to face the situation. From among these emotions it is Thomas's inclination to choose compassion and to use the words, new or old, which will succeed in expressing it for him.

Paper and sticks

(please turn to *Collected Poems*, p. 97)

If this poem is to be taken as something more than a little ballad tossed off with the kind of celerity Thomas demonstrated many times in many pubs, it will be because the time and the situation in which it was written force us to look beneath appearances. Thomas had been a baby of the First World War and felt keenly its disastrous social consequences; at the time 'Paper and sticks' was written a European war was about to catch fire again, and the poem may be a response to this threat.

It is just too easy to explain Thomas's horror of the oncoming conflagration as fear for his own skin. The feverish poet thinking of himself is definitely available as a caricature, making it quite difficult to persuade anyone that Thomas had an honourable anti-war position. However, letters around October–November 1939 show his earnestness in marshalling his detestation of war into some kind of concerted protest. For instance, to Desmond Hawkins, 14 October 1939 (*Letters*, p. 421/476):

> I'm thinking of compiling for *Life & Letters* a thing called 'Objection to War'. Objections, not generalized but whole-heartedly practical, of various people, mostly writers. *Not* a Pacifist, pro-Russian, Mosleyite or literary peace-front, but the individual non-party non-political objections of people like you & me. I think, at this time, when many people who appeared trustworthy are turning out as penny heroes, guttersnipes, rattlesnakes, mass-minded fools or just lazy buggers, it would be valuable. Will you write your Objection – to war, to this war, to any war – briefly.

Will Barker write too? I'm getting in touch with him. *Life & Letters* will give the Objection a few pages. Write soon.

'Paper and sticks' is the only poem that Thomas wrote during this time of war anxiety. I think we should look at it closely to ascertain whether or not it could be the poetic equivalent of his anti-war effort.

On the face of it, we have here the kind of simple monologue of a housemaid that would fit quite well the character of Lily Smalls in *Under Milk Wood*, a mixture of dreaminess and realism. The speaker is trying to light a fire in a fireplace using newspaper, presumably the *News of the World*, full of all the stories of freaks, scams, fallen clergy and other disgraceful carryings-on that made it the most popular Sunday paper in Britain at the time. Her reminiscences while waiting for the fire to catch are of a liaison she had with a well-to-do young man, where money was clearly the chief motivation. When she addresses him in memory 'O my dear it's never too late / To take me away as you whispered and wrote'. We know that marriage was never a possibility. She is realist enough to call her words 'silly'. The dream is there in his remembered words: 'I'll share my money and we'll run for joy / With a bouncing and silver spooned kid . . .' But at the end, when the fire is catching at last, she has to admit, addressing herself: '*You* never did and *he* never did.' The young man did not catch fire, and so she could not catch him as her catch.

An immediate reaction to the poem might well be, 'Who cares?' I am going to propose that this apparently inconsequential poem is in fact an important statement by Thomas about his times, something along the lines of W. H. Auden's prior ballads 'Honeyman's NCP' and 'As I Walked Out One Evening'. Auden was using the ballad form and ordinary or tawdry people to communicate the tragedy of war. What if Thomas was doing the same, writing in an ironic mode about 'this low dishonest decade' (as Auden was just then putting it, in his poem 'September 3, 1939')? Thomas's knack for brilliant parody, along with a certain competitiveness, would make such a thing not unlikely. If this is really what is happening, he has certainly outdone Auden at his own game, making the irony so tight and cryptic that his contemporaries, as far we know, did not recognize it as such.

Let us lay out some possible clues to the poem's irony. A fire is being lighted, and why is the world about to go up in flames? The poem implies that it is because personal relations are governed by money: people cannot run for joy. Thomas's view of sexual morality was generally speaking Lawrentian. He believed that our society had perverted healthy sexuality. Take, for instance, this disquisition in a letter to Pamela Hansford Johnson (*Letters*, pp. 59–60/76–7):

The medieval laws of this corrupted hemisphere have dictated a more or less compulsory virginity during the period of life when virginity should be regarded as a crime against the dictates of the body. During the period of adolescence, when the blood and seed of the growing flesh need, for the first time and more than ever again, communion and contact with the blood and seed of another flesh, sexual relationships are looked upon as being un-necessary and unclean. The body must be kept intact for marriage, which is rarely possible before the age of twenty; the physical expression of sex must be caged up for six or more years until, for the price of a ring, a licence, and a few hampering words, opportunity is presented with all the ceremony of a phallic religion. But so often the opportunity comes too late; the seed has soured; love has turned to lust, and lust to sadism; the mind has become covered and choked by the weeds of inhibition; and the union of two starved creatures, suddenly allowed the latitude of their sexes, is doomed from the start. The woman carries her marriage licence about her as a bitch might carry the testimony of its liberated heat.

From the first months of puberty, girls & boys should be allowed to know their bodies (I am not trying to twist phrases, nor am I wishing to write down the bare words in all their ugliness). More than that, their sexual expression should be encouraged. It would be very nearly impossible for a young girl to live, permanently, with a young boy, especially if both were in school; they would not live together peaceably; they would have no money, and it would be difficult for them to earn. But the family of the girl should, for a certain time – the time of the mutual devotion of boy and girl – keep the boy in their house. And vice-versa. The lives of the boy and girl would continue individually – there would be schools and school associations for both of them – but their domestic closeness and their sleeping together would blend the two individual lives in one, & would keep both brains & bodies perpetually clean. And both would grow up physically and mentally uncontaminated and refreshened.

Don't think I'm regaling you with some crank-ridden, pornographic notion. I really believe in what I say, and no argument has ever shifted my belief. It is not a theory, but an adjustment of the present corrupted facts to uncorrupted ideals. The issues of such an adjustment are, of course, tremendous; they attack the basis of established morals and the foundations of society.

Sex as supplied and purchased for money – no matter that the aim as in 'Paper and sticks' is marriage – offends natural order.

Auden's great poem 'Spain' published around this time established the view that the Spanish Civil War was the result of all our greeds. Private vices, Auden maintains, had become public forces and produced international warfare. Thomas does not allow into his poem even a mite of such explanation, but, in keeping with Auden's ideology, the lovers in 'Paper and sticks' can be seen as representatives of the failure of personal relationships and the consequent imploding of peace and happiness on earth. I see here not a presaging of the human comedy of *Under Milk Wood* but rather a prelude to the tragic end of humanity as Thomas envisioned it in 'In Country Heaven' (*Collected Poems*, p. 262):

> The Earth has killed itself. It is black, petrified, wizened, poisoned, burst; insanity has blown it rotten; and no creatures at all, joyful, despairing, cruel, kind, dumb, afire, loving, dull, shortly and brutishly hunt their days down like enemies on that corrupted face.

This is news of the world indeed.

It may for most readers seem too far a stretch from 'The Maid's Poem' (Thomas's draft title in a manuscript list at Buffalo) to this apocalyptic vision; but we have one of two choices: (*a*) that Thomas wrote and immediately published (in *Seven* magazine, Autumn 1939 issue) a flat mean-spirited little ditty, irrelevant to the outbreak of a war that horrified him, or (*b*) that the poem he wrote and published at that crucial moment in time contained a momentous sadness, heavily disguised. Unless one wishes to see Thomas as some kind of scalliwag, the first choice is preposterous and the second recommends itself on the basis of the repulsiveness of the first.

One obstacle to taking 'Paper and sticks' seriously has been that, while including it in *Deaths and Entrances* (1946), Thomas asked for it to be dropped from the 1952 *Collected Poems* saying it was 'awful' and he had 'the horrors' of it (*Letters*, p. 839/936). The loss of the original wartime context had left the poem merely light verse: this could have been the cause (he gives no other) of his last-minute aversion. Hence, our effort here to supply that context, which makes the poem deserving of inclusion, as the editors of the 1988 *Collected Poems* decided (p. 160), in the corpus of Thomas's enduring works.

Poem in October

(please turn to *Collected Poems*, p. 86)

Readers unacquainted with how taut Thomas can stretch a syntactical construction without breaking it will need to be reassured that, in the first stanza, the poet woke on his thirtieth birthday to hear the morning itself calling him to come outside immediately. It takes him ten lines, the whole of the first stanza, to say that. It must be a record. Of course, he is also setting the scene in asides of some detail. We know at once where we are.

The journey the poet is to make is actual as well as visionary. The word 'border' (stanza 2), while intimating a changed psychological state, is literally Laugharne's old town line that one crosses at a certain point on the path up Sir John's Hill. George Tremlett has shown me the gateposts to which Thomas would be referring as the 'gates of the town'. Past that marker the poet manages to enter a world of his own before the town wakes to break the spell.

As he climbs, the October sun begins to feel almost summery: the wind is 'wringing' the rain in the harbour below him, but he has entered a benign clime. This is why critics have mentioned Henry Vaughan's 'Regeneration' – Vaughan in that poem walks out of rain up into 'new spring'. This is a parallel, but probably cannot count as a source. If the walk of Thomas's 'Poem in October' was an actual walk – as I think it was – then the walk is the source, not Vaughan. Besides, here we do not have a 'new spring' but a freak sort of balminess, such a 'marvel' (stanza 4) that Thomas has to acknowledge that the 'blooming' weather sounds like a 'tall tale'.

The poet was prepared to accept this warmth as an unexpected birthday present to bask in, but 'the weather turned around' (stanza 4). It becomes clear in stanzas 5 and 6 that this change of weather is in his perceptions. The new note which enters the 'blithe country' is induced by an overpowering nostalgia for his childhood. Why did this happen? I believe there is a reason other than mystical visitation. Thomas has reached an elevation from which he can see further to the east than is possible lower down. As anyone can who has made it to the top of Sir John's Hill, he has caught a glimpse in the far distance of the actual place, Fernhill farm, and the whole area around Llangain, where he played happily as a boy: 'These were the woods the river and sea / Where a boy / In the listening / Summertime of the dead whispered the truth of his joy' (stanza 6). Seeing this panorama has brought him into a new mood; the weather of the heart has been changed by the remembrances thus thrust upon him. I do not think it diminishes the poem to know that topography is the key factor in its motivation.

By the end of stanza 6 the poem has fully expressed the experience the poet wants to recall. There is, however, a final stanza 7, which seems to say that 'the weather turned around' a further time. I do not think we have to contemplate such a dizzying prospect. The weather does not turn around again; it is the same turning as before, repeated as a coda to the poem. 'And there could I marvel my birthday / Away': stanza 7 repeats exactly the wording of stanza 4 in recapitulation. It is not a new turn of events, merely lyrical reiteration of the main point of the poem: the past joy of childhood intruding with its 'heart's truth' into the birthday walk. And the poem ends with a simple wish that in a year's time he will again be attuned to the possibility of a similar experience of emotional connection with the purest joy he has known in his life.

Note on 'Poem in October'

If this is really a 'Laugharne poem', as Thomas told Vernon Watkins in August 1944 that it was (*Letters*, p. 518/580), and if it was at least three years in the making, as Watkins says (*LVW*, p. 115), then its inception must go back to October 1939 when the Thomas family was resident at Sea View, Laugharne. It was, all in all, a particularly happy time for the poet.

Poem on his Birthday

(please turn to *Collected Poems*, p. 144)

This poem 'celebrates and spurns' (line 7) the poet's thirty-fifth birthday. This would be 27 October 1949, but little was done on it at that time. Thomas was finishing 'In the White Giant's Thigh',[1] while preparing himself for his first visit to America. He could not concentrate on poetry writing. 'I'm having a tough time here at the moment', he wrote to James Laughlin in a letter of 23 November 1949 (*Letters*, p. 732/815):

> I want to write only poems, but that can't be. Never have I wanted to more. But debts are battering at me. I cannot sleep for them . . . I have only the scaffoldings of poems, never being unbadgered enough to put up roofs & walls. My table's heaped with odd lines, single words, nothing completed.

And the same thing to Marguerita Caetani the next day (*Letters*, p. 734/817): 'Nowadays, I can never spare the time to begin, work through, and complete a poem *regardless* of time; because my room is littered with beginnings, each staring me accusingly in the eyes.' No doubt these were the fragmented beginnings of 'Poem on his Birthday'.

Work on the poem covered the next two years and many worksheets (seventy-two sheets now at Harvard and about 200 at Texas). One of the Harvard worksheets was done a year later, headed 'Poem in October (1950)' and contains a reference to his thirty-sixth birthday:

> In this estuary room
> With Whitman over my head
> I, who am spat from the womb
> For 36 boiling years . . .

Thomas later reverted to thirty-five because, as he told Bill Read, who visited Laugharne in the summer of 1951 when Thomas was working on the poem daily, it is about a poet who realizes he has arrived at 'half his bible span'. In his book *The Days of Dylan*

---

[1] Contrary to the footnote on p. 727 of the *Letters*, the 'finished' poem of a hundred lines mentioned in the letter of 12 November 1949 is not 'Poem on his Birthday' but 'In the White Giant's Thigh'. Similarly *Letters*, p. 735. See the corrective footnotes in the second edition of *Letters*, pp. 810, 818.

Thomas, p. 149, Read presents a summary of the poem as supplied by Thomas himself:[2]

> He means both to celebrate and spurn his birthday in a house high among trees, overlooking the sea. Birds and fishes move under and around him on their dying ways,[3] and he, a craftsman in words, toils 'towards his own wounds which are waiting in ambush for him.' The poet 'sings in the direction of his pain.' Birds fly after the hawks that will kill them. Fishes swim toward the otters that will eat them. He sees herons walking in their shrouds, which is the water they fish in; and he, who is progressing, afraid, to his own fiery end in the cloud of an atomic explosion knows that, out at sea, animals who attack and eat other sea animals are tasting the flesh of their own death. Now exactly half of his three score and ten years has gone. He looks back at his times – his loves, his hates, all he has seen – and sees the logical progress of death in everything he has been and done. His death lurks for him, and for all, in the next lunatic war. And, still singing, still praising the radiant earth, still loving, though remotely, the animal creation also gladly pursuing their inevitable and grievous ends, he goes toward his. Why should he praise God and the beauty of the world, as he moves to horrible death? He does not like the deep zero dark, and the nearer he gets to it, the louder he sings, the higher the salmon leaps, the shriller the birds carol.

The references in this prose summary to 'the next lunatic war' and 'his own fiery end in the cloud of an atomic explosion' make clear the paranoid atmosphere in which 'Poem on his Birthday' was written. The threat of a Third World War appears in the poem with stanzas 4–6 where he describes himself as one

> Who slaves to his crouched, eternal end
> Under a serpent cloud, . . .
>
> And tomorrow weeps in a blind cage
> Terror will rage apart

---

[2] Read was told by Thomas that 'before he began the poem at all, he had the plan all worked out' (*The Days of Dylan Thomas*, p. 149). There was an actual written page given to Read, but he was not given permission to quote it in full. Hence, we have a paraphrase with occasional quotations.

[3] 'Doing what they are told' (line 12). John Malcolm Brinnin was also visiting Laugharne in July 1951 and drew Dylan's attention to a cormorant holding itself in a tortuous manner. 'He thinks that's what a cormorant *should* do', said Thomas. 'Nobody ever told him otherwise' (Brinnin, p. 104).

> Before chains break to a hammer flame
> And love unbolts the dark
>
> And freely he goes lost
> In the unknown, famous light of great
> And fabulous, dear God.

So, contrary to first impressions, perhaps 'Poem on his Birthday' is not entirely a poem of self-pity but in large part an elegy on the coming collective death and an inevitable questioning of God's role in it.

Like 'Over Sir John's hill' before it, this poem forces us to spend some time on the enigma of Thomas's concept of God. In the prose piece, he calls death 'the deep zero dark'. Does he believe in salvation or not? What is 'always true' is a 'heaven that never was / Nor will be ever' (stanza 6). It is a 'brambled void', yet in that void the dead grow like blackberries 'for His joy'. Thomas deeply wants it both ways. As he wrote in one of the Harvard worksheets: 'O God who is nowhere, let me be / Least of your believers'. So in the final lines quoted above, he is freed by death to go to God, but he goes 'lost / In the unknown, famous light', which is suspiciously gloomy; and God is 'fabulous' – colloquially, terrific, but in the end, it seems, only a dear fable: 'blessed unborn God and His Ghost' (stanza 7). Heaven is that 'cloud quaking' (the opposite of earth-quaking) peace that is much to be longed for, but which does not seem real except in the longing for it. He prays unto a Him, but faithlessly (stanza 8). Thomas seems to want a God, but cannot find it possible to depend on Him.

When we look at the formal prayer itself (from mid-stanza 9 to the end of the poem) we note that God does not appear at all.

> Oh, let me midlife mourn by the shrined
> And druid herons' vows
> The voyage to ruin I must run . . .

This is God's world without God. We remember Thomas told Brinnin during that July 1951 visit that his aim was now to produce 'poems in praise of God's world by a man who doesn't believe in God' (Brinnin, p. 128). By my reading of 'Poem on his Birthday' this is exactly what Thomas has done. When he starts counting his blessings (stanza 10) he puts God aside. The blessings are entirely of this world: first, the four elements of air, fire, earth and water; then the five senses that define the human being, plus the spirit which makes us capable of love even though life is a tangle on this spinning dunghill of a world. And where is our destination?

> To his nimbus bell cool kingdom come
> And the lost, moonshine domes,
> And the sea that hides his secret selves
> Deep in its black, base bones.

Though the 'nimbus' would give 'kingdom come' a halo, I do not see much heaven in these lines from stanza 10. He knows his body is like an old ship used as a prison ('hulks' – stanza 11), but, as he tackles each wave on the way to death, the world sings louder. I suppose one could claim that the 'triumphant faith' and 'praise' are in and for God, but I do not feel it. It is the world having faith in itself and singing its own praises. The 'bouncing hills' do not have a reason for growing 'larked and greener' (stanza 12). It is just that Thomas has managed to rise to the surface once more instead of sinking forever.

I am thinking of the image of himself as Houdini that appears in a searing letter drafted to Marguerita Caetani some time towards the end of his life (*Letters*, p. 915/1021):

Deep dark down there, where I chuck the sad sack of myself, in the slimy squid-rows of the sea there's such a weed-drift and clamour of old plankton drinkers, such a mockturtle gabble of wrecked convivial hydrographers tangled with polyps and blind prawns, such a riffraff of seabums in the spongy dives, so many jellyfish soakers jolly & joking in the smoke-blue basements, so many salty sea-damaged daughters stuffing their wounds with fishes, so many lightning midnight makers in the luminous noon of the abysmal sea, and such fond despair there, always there, that time and time again I cry to myself as I kick clear of the cling of my stuntman's sacking, 'Oh, one time the last time will come and I'll never struggle, I'll sway down here forever handcuffed and blindfold, sliding my woundaround music, my sack trailed in the slime, with all the rest of the self-destroyed escapologists in their cages, drowned in the sorrows they drown and in my piercing own, alone and one with the coarse and cosy damned seahorsey dead, weeping my tons.'

This despairing cry Thomas can write one day, and, on the next, he rises from the abyss, feeling that he does not have to be alone, and writes his equivalent of 'No man is an island':

                how
More spanned with angels ride
The mansouled fiery islands! Oh,
   Holier then their eyes,
And my shining men no more alone
   As I sail out to die.

It is the Blake in Thomas that etches this vision, but a Blake living in an existentialist era. The holiness comes from caring about one's fellow creatures not from religious ecstasy. The rainbow of angels is what we can see when we realize we are all in the same boat in this sailing out.

Prologue

(please turn to *Collected Poems*, p. 1)

Its origin as epistolary verse is discernible in this introductory poem to the *Collected Poems* of 1952, the last poem Thomas finished before his death. One of the 166 pages of the worksheets (now at Harvard) is headed 'Letter, To A Friend, On Returning To Wales from the U.S.A. 1952' and begins:

At home, sweet Christ, at last
Wet Wales and the nightjars,
Memory at half mast
In the barlights of the stars . . .[1]

These colloquial short lines provided a ready-made pattern when Thomas saw that he could switch from a personal communication to a more formal 'prologue' addressed to the readers of the proposed *Collected Poems*. He had been asked by Dent's for a prose preface

---

[1] There are other such beginnings, one to Thomas's hostess in San Francisco, Ruth Witt-Diamant (see notes to *Collected Poems*, p. 176). After the twenty-third worksheet the title 'Prologue' begins to appear. 'Author's Prologue', as it was in the 1952 volume, was a title supplied by the publisher, Dent's.

but, as he wrote to David Higham on 28 June 1952, he 'had no interest whatsoever in it' (*Letters*, pp. 830–1/927):

> What I *am* doing, and doing quickly, is writing a Prologue in verse: not dense, elliptical verse, but (fairly) straightforward and colloquial, addressed to the (maybe) readers of the Collected Poems, & full (I hope) of references to my methods of work, my aims, & the kind of poetry I want to write.

This resolve to be discursive about methodology soon waned, and Thomas retreated to his abiding subject, the condition of his 'sea-shaken house' (line 4). His long reading tour across the North American continent is glanced at in the phrase 'the cities of nine / Day's night' (lines 19–20). These are the places where he was a nine day's wonder, but where his drinking and torments were such (he was with Caitlin on this tour) that they now seem like something out of James Thomson's *The City of Dreadful Night*, doomed to conflagration in the 'religious wind' of the Day of Judgment. Now he is 'at poor peace' (line 23), with emphasis on the word 'poor'. 'Here,' he told Oscar Williams, 'we are not as we are in the States, where we don't think or care about what we spend. Here, we have nothing to spend, and think and care about it all the time' (*Letters*, p. 841/939).

As he works through the summer in his Laugharne writing shed, however, Thomas builds up morale and energy. He hammers his ark of a poem through 'a burning and crested act' of creative will that almost matches the great farewell of 'Poem on his Birthday'. The threat of atomic war hovers over this poem too, with its 'fountain-head / Of fear, rage red' (lines 47–8); the flood of hate flows almost to his beloved Wales in his arms (line 52). He has to be like a Noah to try to save his world, and in the second part of the poem he addresses the animals and hails God's 'beasthood' (line 76) as the 'barnroofs cockcrow war' (line 81):

> O kingdom of neighbours, finned
> Felled and quilled, flash to my patch
> Work ark and the moonshine
> Drinking Noah of the bay . . .

Thomas is very disarming: the poem is a mere patchwork ark, and this Noah has had a sip or two of whisky like the first Noah (Genesis 9: 21). He does not expect much: he and his crew will 'ride out alone' under the starlit sky of Wales. And then comes the miracle, the same epiphany as in 'Poem on his Birthday'. They are suddenly not alone. They cry out to see how much company there is in this effort to save the world (lines 93–5):

> Multitudes of arks! Across
> The water lidded lands,
> Manned with their loves they'll move.

'Loves' man the fleet that will combat the flood of anger, and the poem ends very positively.

> My ark sings in the sun
> At God speeded summer's end
> And the flood flowers now.

When the poet says that 'the flood flowers', he is affirming the success of the forces of good in the world. The hateful flood is compelled to change its nature and to flower benignly in the sun. The summer's end is 'God-speeded', which the dictionary gives simply as 'well-wishing'. The success of summer's end is harvest. All is safely gathered in.

In sending the finished poem to E. F. Bozman of Dent's on 10 September 1952, Thomas wrote (*Letters*, p. 838/935): 'I hope the Prologue *does* read as a prologue, & not just as another poem'. In spite of Thomas's wish, I do not think we can look to this 'Prologue' as giving retrospective insight into his life's work; but it does do what he says in this letter he set out to do: it 'addresses the readers, the "strangers", with a flourish, and fanfare, and makes clear, or tries to make clear, the position of one writer in a world "at poor peace" '. If it were not that the time ahead was so short, one could almost think of this last poem as prospective.

Shall gods be said

(please turn to *Collected Poems*, p. 40)

'The universe is wild and full of marvels', Thomas wrote to Pamela Hansford Johnson in a New Year letter for 1934 (*Letters*, p. 82/99). 'In the shape of a boy, and a funny boy at that, I have only a very short time to learn how mad and marvellous it is.' A few days later he was saying to Trevor Hughes (*Letters*, p. 91/109) that

> this new year has brought back to my mind the sense of magic that was lost – irretrievably, I thought – so long ago . . . a man who believes in the supernatural is a man who takes things literally. It is the aim of the church – that embodiment of a medieval moral – to do away with men's sense of the literal. How much better to say that God is big than that he is 'all-pervading'.

On the basis of these remarks I shall take seriously the questions posed in 'Shall gods be said', a poem Thomas wrote into his notebook the previous August (*Notebook Poems*, p. 177). I shall take them seriously by presuming the answer to each of them is yes. Do gods thump the clouds to produce thunder? Yes. Are rainbows the tunics of the gods? Yes. Does rain come with love from the breasts of old goddesses when the night scolds us like a wet nurse? Yes. A dropped stone drums on the ground, and flung gravel chimes? Yes.

I am responding here to a literal pantheism that gave security to Thomas in his childhood and which at age nineteen he is stating in a mildly provocative manner with questions that only someone imbued with a new wonder at the supernatural would be able to answer in the affirmative. The questions may provoke, but the final hortatory wish confirms that there is no irony here. 'Let the stones speak / With tongues that talk all tongues.' As he put it in his new year's letter (*Letters*, p. 81/98):

> A chunk of stone is as interesting as a cathedral, or even more interesting, for it is the cathedral in essence; it gave substance to the building of the cathedral and meaning to the meaning of the cathedral, for stones are sermons, as are all things.

These comments, echoed in the poem, indicate that the young

Thomas could be, or was trying to be, as earnest as we all have been to find value in the immediate world.

Should lanterns shine

(please turn to *Collected Poems*, p. 52)

I take it that the mood here is one of self-reproach. The poet feels he has not yet matured. He is still a young schoolboy whose life has been arrested in mid air like a ball without gravity. The advice he had been given over and over (lines 16–17) should have made a difference, but it has not. He is still not spontaneous and fluid in his personality. He has been told (by whom? by D. H. Lawrence perhaps?) to 'reason by the heart' or the pulse (line 11), but he does not have enough faith in himself, even though he can vividly imagine it empowering him to move faster and make better use of his time.

The above summarizes the discursive second half of the poem. The first part is a sustained image of his self-arrestment.

> Should lanterns shine, the holy face,
> Caught in an octagon of unaccustomed light,
> Would wither up, and any boy of love
> Look twice before he fell from grace.
> The features in their private dark
> Are formed of flesh, but let the false day come
> And from her lips the faded pigments fall,
> The mummy cloths expose an ancient breast.

Along with the Egyptian 'gentleman' (line 14) this picture of opening a pyramid tomb (nineteenth-century investigators using an octagonal lantern) is something the young Thomas may very well have seen in Arthur Mee's *Children's Encyclopaedia*.[1] How the image works in

---

[1] Or in the old silent film *The Mummy's Claw*, which Thomas had seen in the Uplands Cinema in his youth. According to Gwen Watkins (*Portrait of a Friend*, p. 136), in a later get-together Dylan re-enacted a scene from the film with Daniel Jones and Vernon Watkins:

> Dan was a Pharaoh, looking noble and aloof in a mummy-case (an old zinc bath stood upright on its large end). Dylan was an Egyptologist searching in tombs, and Vernon was co-opted as a rather sheepish grave-robber, whereupon the Pharaoh's mummy emerged majestic and sinister from his case.

the poem is that the poet himself as 'any boy of love' is adoring a 'holy face' in muted light. He does not allow his heart to take him closer in his devotion to the beauty of the loved one. He instead imagines the beauty to be false. If light shone piercingly on her, he thinks to himself, the face would wither up and he would be revolted by her as though she were a mummy being uncovered. That day would be 'false' because revealing her falseness. The possibility of falling from grace (line 4) is a young man's fear of getting attached to an unworthy person. He fears that present beauty is only an appearance and will curdle under closer investigation, and that there is always true beauty elsewhere in the future.

One finds this adolescent concern in notebook poems around March 1933, for instance (*Notebook Poems*, p. 141):

> each pretty miss who passing
> Smiles back confessing a treacherous heart.
> Unlicensed promise under a cheap skirt,
> Bee's sting under her mask of paint.

There is no manuscript version of 'Should lanterns shine' but I conjecture it could have been the missing poem 'Fifteen' torn out of the February 1933 notebook (*Notebook Poems*, p. 137). It seems to belong to the time when Thomas was writing to Trevor Hughes in February 1933 about the artist's 'consciousness of beauty': 'what that elusive thing is I haven't the remotest idea; woman isn't, because she dies. Nothing that dies is truly beautiful' (*Letters*, p. 11/29). The heart as much as the head leads helplessly at this time. The poem could have been written any time up to its publication in *New Verse* December 1935, but someone who has had the experience of going up to London in 1934 and squiring a stylish young woman like Pamela Hansford Johnson would not write like this. We have here the self-entanglements of an earlier Thomas.

The conversation of prayers

(please turn to *Collected Poems*, p. 85)

This is a companion poem to 'This side of the truth (for Lleweyn)'. They were sent together to Vernon Watkins on 28 March 1945 (*Letters*, p. 548/611), and grew out of the concerns Thomas had for his son. Circumstances kept Llewelyn with his grandmother at Blashford (a safe country location) for much of the war. Thomas wrote to him sometimes – an example is on, p. 903/1006 of the *Letters*. It is endearingly whimsical. After the address, 'My dear Llewelyn', the text reads: 'What are you doing, always catching colds? You are the coldest boy in England! You should be an Eskimo [drawing] living in a [drawing of an igloo] and fishing in a [drawing of a kayak].'[1] That is all very well, but there was no doubt a great deal of frustration and guilt because of the long months of separation. A child of six has nightmares and needs to be comforted. I believe 'The conversation of prayers' is in lieu of the consolation that Thomas could not offer his son in a day-to-day parental situation.

The child in the poem is praying for a secure sleep as he kneels by his bed; the man on the stairs prays for his love whom he thinks may be dying in her attic room. It seems that only one of the prayers can be answered, and which one depends on the conversation that the prayers themselves are imagined to be about to have. The outcome this time is that the man gets his wish and the loved one does not die, while the boy has a nightmare about being dragged up the stairs to see a corpse.

The idea for this rather unexpected pass probably came to Thomas with the discovery that 'converse' and 'conversation' are etymologically related. Converse-ation, the turning of a thing into its opposite, is what a conversation might be about. There is the other play on words: we speak of a conversation 'turning' on a subject, meaning that the subject is a fulcrum by which the conversation is given the direction that produces an outcome. Thomas invented a

---

[1] The letter is not dated, being merely a draft, never sent. Ferris places it towards the end of Thomas's life, but it seems to me more suitable for a six-year-old, Llewelyn's age at the time this poem was written. No other letters to Llewelyn from his father are known to exist.

situation where the interplay of these various implications of the word 'conversation' could be used to good effect.

The decision 'turns on the quick and the dead' (line 14); that is, it is a matter of life and death. There is no hint, however, of any moral considerations. Both parties seem to be equally potential victims of converse/perverse fate. The 'answering skies' (line 7) give their answer, but the heavens are capricious. This is obviously not conventional consolation, but it is essentially the same as Thomas was trying to tell Llewelyn in 'This side of the truth':

> . . . all is undone
> Under the unminding skies,
> Of innocence and guilt
> Before you move . . .

This is the point of view of someone who has come to believe that prayers are not answered. There are no promises. Thomas guessed that Llewelyn probably knew it already. That is how these poems could come to be written as consolation.

The force that through the green fuse

(please turn to *Collected Poems*, p. 13)

There is a lovely intricacy of imagery and theme in this justly famous poem.

The [natural] force that through the green fuse [the flower's stem as conduit for explosive force] drives [pushes] the flower [the exploding petals] DRIVES my green [youthful] age; [the force] that blasts [blights] the roots of trees IS my destroyer.

And I AM dumb to tell the crooked [misshapen] rose [that] my youth is bent [like an old person] by the same wintry fever [blasts of sickness].

The poet participates in both metabolic processes, the building up and the tearing down, a universal condition. But the refrain laments the destructive aspect to the exclusion of the positive. This pattern is repeated, with some variations, in the next two stanzas. The natural force that produces the gushing of streams is the same as that which circulates the bloodstream; the force that dries up the water flow dries up his blood in death. The estuary mouth of the river of time sucks at the mountain spring drawing it to its end in the sea; the same mouth sucks at his veins like the leech of time. The hand or force in nature that creates a whirlpool also creates the quicksand where one sinks; the hand that governs the sail of a leaping boat is also making it a barge of death.

In the third stanza the message is complicated by a dialectical subvoice. The imagery seems to work both ways. The whirling action, which is positive and vigorous, produces a whirlpool action which is destructive; the quicksand is associated with the 'quick' of life as well as death. To rope the blowing wind is to constrain it, whereas the word 'haul' is very active even when associated with the funereal. These subversive images, which build up the feeling that negative and positive contain each other, prepare us for the notion of the identity of life and death forces. This is the pathos of the poem: that one cannot have life without death. What oft was thought but never before expressed with such intense conjunctiveness.

> And I am dumb to tell the hanging man
> How of my clay is made the hangman's lime.

We note again a fulfilling double edge in the word 'lime', which, like 'quicksand' above, will give the connotations both of death in the quicklime used in the burial of corpses and of life in the element 'quick'. When we also know that from the decomposition of dead flesh the loam of the earth receives nutrient vitality, we have here a rich image, made all the more complex by the poet's assertion that the hangman's lime is made of his own body. There could hardly be anything more appalling than to imagine one's flesh used to hasten the disintegration of a hanged criminal in a lime pit. One is dumbfounded before such a prospect. Yet there is the positive side in the expressed brotherhood: all flesh fuses together in the end and renews itself in the catabolic process which creates further life.

The next stanza confirms that renewal is where the poem is heading, though again the imagery is coldly dialectical beneath its emotive power.

> The lips of time [personified] LEECH [sucking blood] to the fountain head [source of life]; love [lifeblood] DRIPS and GATHERS [like a boil], but the fallen blood [as in medicinal leeching] SHALL CALM her [love's] sores.

And I AM dumb to tell a weather's wind [of mortality] how time has ticked a heaven round of the stars.

Time, usually considered destructive (ticking like a time bomb perhaps), here in the end gives us the security of a heaven around the stars, in mutability's despite. It is another case of Thomas forcing a positive into his poem against expectation.[1]

But the lament of the final two lines restores the 'plangency':

> And I am dumb to tell the lover's tomb
> How at my sheet goes the same crooked worm.

When this final couplet is linked with the couplet that ends the first stanza of the poem it is clear that Thomas had in mind William Blake's 'O rose, thou art sick', a small poem where an 'invisible worm' destroys a rose. There is the same lament for life's corruptibility.

More than this specific echo, 'The force that through the green fuse' seems predicated on Blake's idea of 'contraries'. 'A Negation is not a Contrary', Blake wrote on the title page of the second book of his *Milton*. 'Contraries are Positives'. Thomas acknowledged around this time that he was 'in the path of Blake' (*Letters*, p. 25/43), and he would have seen the quotation on, p. 146 of the Everyman's edition of Blake (1927). Opposites as complementarities in the general positive scheme of life and death is something we see Thomas trying to express time and time again. In December 1933 he tried to explain himself to Pamela Hansford Johnson in criticizing a poem of hers (*Letters*, p. 79/96):

> Though you talk all through of the relationship of yourself to other things, there is no relationship at all in the poem between the things you example. If you are one with the swallow & one with the rose, then the rose is one with the swallow. Link together these things you talk of; show, in your words & images, how *your* flesh covers the tree & the tree's flesh covers you. I see what you have done, of course – 'I am one with the opposites', you say. You are, I know, but you must prove it to me by linking yourself to the opposites and by linking the opposites together.

---

[1] In the notebook version (*Notebook Poems*, p. 274) the lines were: 'And I am dumb to tell the timeless sun / How time is all.' This proposes that the sun is not really timeless, and that time will take everything away in the end. If this pessimistic meaning comes over into the revised version, the 'heaven' cannot be a religious consolation at all but only what time allows in its turning. A positive thrust must be present in the word 'heaven', but none, Thomas knows, do there embrace.

He refrained from mentioning that he had done all this very efficiently in 'The force that through the green fuse', but he could have: it was written two months earlier on 12 October 1933 and published on 29 October 1933 in the *Sunday Referee*. To feel the bursting of life in nature as his own youth, to feel death of every mortal substance as something in which his own flesh participates, and to have all life and death as equivalent: yes, he could have cited this poem as epitomizing his pantheistic philosophy of process.

Indeed, one might say that, like 'A process in the weather of the heart' and other 'process' poems of *18 Poems*, this too is a poem whose imagery is there to be cut down to the core to produce the abstract assertion of process. One could say this, except for one thing: 'The force that through the green fuse' inculcates the absolute conviction that the poet is grief-stricken, that we have here a voice of true feeling. Just before he wrote this poem Thomas had had a shock about his health. 'A misanthropic doctor', he wrote to Pamela Hansford Johnson (*Letters*, p. 43/61), 'has given me four years to live.' He was counting the time: 'Four years, my sweet, 1340 days and nights' (*Letters*, p. 50/67). Presumably he had been diagnosed with TB, for he speaks of 'consumption'. He claims it is not having 'very much effect on what I write' (*Letters*, p. 50/67) – but how can he claim such a thing, having written of 'the lover's tomb' and 'how at my sheet goes the crooked worm'? He says he is dumb to speak of these things, and it is a beautiful poetic convention. Actually, this is the poem in which Thomas is least dumb to tell.

Note on 'The force that through the green fuse'

An interesting fact has come to light which relates to the line 'How time has ticked a heaven round the stars' (line 20). In the *Sunday Referee* printing this line was simply: 'How time is all'. Thomas expanded this in an amazing way, looking up the word for 'time' in *Spurrell's Welsh–English Dictionary*, which was *amser*, and then splitting this word into *am* and *ser*, which gave him the Welsh words for 'round the stars'. We know that etymological punning in Welsh was Thomas's route, on the evidence of a single worksheet in the possession of Robert Williams. Thomas there makes a note: 'am/sêr np 339,' which refers to page 339 in the two-volume 1925 edition of Spurrell, where we find 'sêr np stars' ('np' being the abbreviation used for 'noun plural'). The means by which Thomas got to 'time' ticking a heaven 'round the stars' does not really affect the meaning of the line but it does tell us a rather astounding fact about the mind that put the meaning there.

The hand that signed the paper

(please turn to *Collected Poems*, p. 51)

When Thomas joined Auden, Spender, MacNeice and others in the BBC Manchester studios on 18 October 1938 to read poems on the air under the title 'The Modern Muse', the poem chosen was 'The hand that signed the paper'. It was the one poem of Thomas's that fitted into the 'thirties' political aura of that company.

In the notebook, dated 17 August 1933, the poem was dedicated to 'A.E.T.' This was 'comrade' Bert Trick, who had presided over the young Thomas's socialist education (*Notebook Poems*, p. 181). Looking back on the old Swansea days from Blashford in March 1939 he wrote to Trick (*Letters*, p. 364/417): 'I long for my old, but never properly mounted, soapbox of bright colours, and my grand, destructive arguments learned so industriously and vehemently from you on winter evenings . . . you gave my rebelliousness a direction.' There are numerous evidences that Thomas learned his left-wing lessons well – none more striking than 'A Plea for Intellectual Revolution' which appeared in the *Swansea and West Wales Guardian* for 3 August 1934 (not yet reprinted). Thomas opens with the proposition that 'this system of society' is 'fundamentally evil': 'the society that feeds one member and starves another, that increases its murderous air-fleet rather than its dole, is a society with its roots in filth and injustice'. War can only be described, he says, in a word he cannot print. 'Let it be realized for once and for all that war is a capitalist machine utilized for the benefit of the few by the blood and bone of the many.' He uses his invective against 'the militarist who explains to a school of boys that man is naturally a fighting animal, that war is a glorious adventure, and that the great men of history are always the great butchers'. It is to counter this kind of jingoistic

Speech Day visitor that this prose piece, and 'The hand that signed the paper' of a year earlier, were written.[1]

As he put it in a letter to Pamela Hansford Johnson of January 1934 (*Letters*, p. 88/105), getting close to the essential point of the poem:

> you know as well as I do that patriotism is a publicity ramp organised by holders of excess armament shares; you know that the Union Jack is only a national loin-cloth to hide the decaying organs of a diseased social system; you know that the Great War was purposely protracted in order for financiers to make more money; that had it not been for the shares in the armament firms the War would have ended in *three weeks*; that at one period of the War French and German were shelling each other with ammunition provided by the same firm, a firm in which English clergymen and politicians, French ambassadors and German business men, all had a great deal of money invested.

From this we see that it is not just the signatures on a declaration of war or an evil treaty that are Thomas's concern. We are permitted to see 'the paper that felled a city' (line 1) as an armaments deal or a callous economic decision. It could equally be a communist czar as a fascist: 'the Marxian pseudo-scientists', Thomas wrote in the same newspaper piece, 'solving all economic problems with a frozen impersonality and a gold nib, caring more for the intellectual solidification of an argument than for the welfare of the workers'. The 'gold nib' becomes a 'goose's quill' in the poem (line 7). One can without difficulty see Stalin putting 'an end to murder / That put an end to talk', that is, signing the death warrant of the murderer he used to silence an opponent.

These are not wild ideas for the time. Raised eyebrows come only with the penultimate line: 'A hand rules pity as a hand rules heaven'. Is Thomas saying that God 'has no tears to flow'? Any reader of the Old Testament might come to that conclusion, but Thomas would rather (or also) be thinking of the state churches that on both sides support the war effort, that have 'clothed Christ in khaki and will clothe him so again whenever the Government or powers decide to transform the starving belly of Europe into a womb of dynamite' – this from the newspaper article again –

---

[1] A letter of 8 August 1934 is included in the new edition of *Letters* (p. 192), written jointly by Thomas and Trick asking to join the 'No More War' movement.

where the teachings of Christ are of far less importance than the inculca-
tion of an emotional fear of the fire-spouting Jehovah who is, according
to the corrupted interpretations of His priests, naturally biased in our
favour in the event of the outbreak of any and every profiteering war.

The poem ends in great sadness: 'Hands have no tears to flow.' With
the mention of 'pity' we are reminded of Wilfred Owen's statement
(which the young Thomas well knew): 'My subject is War, and the
pity of War. The Poetry is in the pity.' Thomas wrote of Owen in the
Swansea Grammar School Magazine in December 1929 (*Early Prose*,
p. 85), including him among the heroes of the Great War 'who built
towers of beauty upon the ashes of their lives'. When Thomas in this
poem came to make his small contribution to memorializing those
who died in the war, he gave a nod to the pity of it, but reserved his
main attention for those warmongers who would do it over again for
profit. These he would have no pity for. The Poetry is in the bitterness.

The hunchback in the park

(please turn to *Collected Poems*, p. 93)

'Cwmdonkin Park was a favourite haunt of truants from Swansea
Grammar School', Daniel Jones tells us in his notes to his
edition of Thomas's poems (*The Poems*, p. 271), 'because it was
bordered on one side by a road that led directly to the school, but
sometimes didn't. Thomas and I often met there.' And he adds:
'There was, indeed, a hunchback who seemed to have nowhere else to
go, who stayed from the moment the park opened until it closed.'
Thomas himself confirmed that 'The hunchback in the park' came
directly out of actual experience when he said, introducing a reading
of it:

the park itself was a world within the world of the sea-town; quite near
where I lived, so near that on summer evenings I could listen, in my bed,
to the voices of other children playing ball on the sloping, paper-littered
bank; the Park was full of terrors and treasures. The face of one old man

who sat, summer and winter, on the same bench looking over the swanned reservoir, I can see more clearly, I think, than the city-street faces I saw an *hour* ago.

He also in the same 'Reminiscences of Childhood' (*Broadcasts*, p. 5) mentions the park keeper who appears in the fourth stanza of the poem:

In that small, iron-railed universe of rockery, gravel-path, playbank, bowling-green, bandstand, reservoir, chrysanthemum garden, where an ancient keeper known as Smokey was the tyrannous and whiskered snake in the Grass one must Keep Off, I endured, with pleasure, the first agonies of unrequited love, the first slow boiling in the belly of a bad poem, the strutting and raven-locked self-dramatization of what, at the time, seemed *incurable* adolescence.

After this confession that it was in the park that he himself had fantasies of a loved one, we know a little better how to interpret his later remark (*Broadcasts*, p. 6) about the hunchback sitting alone with 'images of perfection in his head' and the poem's lines in the same vein, where the hunchback

> Made all day until bell time
> A woman's figure without fault
> Straight as a young elm
> Straight and tall from his crooked bones
> That she might stand in the night . . .

If the poem does not cry out to us 'The poet is the hunchback!' then all we have is bathos, Wordsworth's leech-gatherer. No, the poet is the maker. It is he who creates the perfection that will 'stand in the night'. The notebook version leaves us with no doubts on this score (*Notebook Poems*, p. 110). With reference to the 'figure without fault', it says, without batting an eye, 'It is a poem.'

Then was my neophyte

(please turn to *Collected Poems*, p. 57)

Thomas chided Glyn Jones for not mentioning 'Then was my neophyte' in his *Adelphi* review of *Twenty-five Poems*. He himself considered it the best in the book (*Letters*, pp. 243/272–3): 'Nobody's mentioned it; perhaps it's bad; I only know that, to me, it is clearer and more definite, and that it holds more possibilities of progress, than anything else I've done.' We have, then, to view this poem not only as trimmed and scoured with much effort to produce regularity of rhyme and syllable line length, but also as revealing its meaning in a 'clearer and more definite' way. Of course these are relative terms. 'Then was my neophyte' is still vexatiously obscure, 'clearer' only in comparison with the 'Altarwise by owl-light' sonnets at the tail end of which it came.

It was a moment of change. Thomas was conscious that he had to change. In announcing this poem to Vernon Watkins in a letter of 20 April 1936, he said (*Letters*, p. 223/249):

> Perhaps, as you said once, I should stop writing altogether for some time; now I'm almost afraid of all the once-necessary artifices and obscurities, and can't, for the life or the death of me, get any real liberation, any diffusion or dilution or anything, into the churning bulk of the words; I seem, more than ever, to be tightly packing away everything I have and know into a mad-doctor's bag, and then locking it up: all you can see is the bag, all you can know is that it's full to the clasp, all you have to trust is that the invisible and intangible things packed away are – if they *could* only be seen and touched – worth quite a lot.

We infer that Thomas was taking a final look at the sonnets before he sent them off, and seeing them, as we outsiders have tended to, as a 'churning bulk of words . . . a mad-doctor's bag'. He was aware he had to liberate himself; and the poem on which he was working, 'Then was my neophyte', will, he intended, be more diffuse for the sake of clarity.

One great contribution to clarity, if we can only take it to its ultimate conclusion, is that there is conspicuously a male person in charge of the action. The 'He' is capitalized several times in the poem; I do not think that device can signal anyone other than God.

God is in charge. God, indeed, is here a film-maker and with his prescience has filmed our lives ahead of time. In the poem he is showing the poet his future life while still in the womb. This much we gather from what Thomas apparently told Vernon Watkins. As reported in *Portrait of a Friend* (p. 33) the poem is 'a prophecy of his own melodramatic death, shown to him on a film which he as a child, whose character has not been formed, sees unwinding and projected on a screen . . . under water'. This moving-picture image is specifically present in stanza 3 ('He films my vanity'), but it helps us to grasp what is going on in the poem from the start if we imagine the poet looking up at a screen on which various stages of his life are seen retrospectively beforehand.

The first snapshot is of the boy who is praying for his life in the foetal position.

> Then WAS my neophyte [newly admitted into the order of life], child in white [surplice] blood [incarnate] bent on its knees [a foetus in prayer] under the [sea church] bell of rocks, DUCKED [in baptism] in the twelve, disciple seas [in tutelage to life] [that] the winder of the water-clocks [God in charge of time] calls a green [growing] day and night.

This is baptism by amniotic waters. The stanza goes on to baptism by fire.

> My sea hermaphrodite [as yet undifferentiated sexually], snail [hermaphroditic] of man in His [God's] ship of fires [passions] that burn the [worm-]bitten decks, KNEW all His horrible desires [prepared for him by God] [that] the climber of the water sex [into puberty] calls the green [youthful] rock of light [for guidance].

The boy stood on the burning deck – but in this case it is all the God-given sexual desires that are burning into play. This is getting to be a 'blue' movie, if not a horror one.

He is a lost boy in the never-never land.

> Who [of us] in these labyrinths [of life], this tidethread [Ariadne's life-line] and the [life-]lane of scales [which one climbs], [which is] twine [of fate] in a moon-blown [weather-beaten] shell [of the body], ESCAPES to the flat [laid out] cities' [port] sails furled on the fishes' house [the sea] and hell, nor FALLS to His green myths?

How do we get home to land (or out of the labyrinth) to furl our sails and safely escape hell? Who does not fall into hell or another of God's 'green myths', things that are not real but seem so at the time? By 'myths' I do not think Thomas means organized religion, though he has much to say on that subject. The myths will be the illusions of youth (hence 'green') that the world will reward him with something other than death or that his desires will be anything but horrible.

> STRETCH [like canvas] the salt [undersea] photographs [stills of his life], [which show] the landscape [as] grief [existentialist despair], [and] love [which is also grief] in His oils [as God has painted] MIRROR [expanding for observation] from man to whale [maximum enlargement] [in order] that the green child see like a grail [vision][,] through veil and fin and fire and coil[,] Time [approaching] on the canvas [portrayed] paths.

The scene is similar to that in sonnet V, a contemporaneous poem, where stills were 'snapped by night' in the womb, except that here the photographs are an alarmingly enlarged preview, acquainting the foetus with the threat of Time.

This sense of predestination is furthered in the next stanza, where God, 'the winder of the clockwise scene', is a projectionist of the film he has made of the individual's life, showing that all is vanity.

> He FILMS my vanity [empty life]. Shot [filmed] in the wind [of time], by tilted [askew] arcs [lamps], over the water COME children from homes [orphanages] and children's parks who [deaf and dumb] speak on a finger and thumb, and [with them] the masked [as yet unfeatured] headless [incomplete] boy. His [the boy's] reels [dances and staggerings] and mystery [secret life] the winder [cinematographer] of the clockwise [mortal] scene WOUND like a ball of lakes [water-laminated] then THREW on that tide-hoisted [movie] screen [of the womb] love's image [of future romantic disasters] till my heartbone breaks by a [melo-]dramatic sea.

Melodramatic? Who cannot look back on adolescence and not consider it overwrought? Everybody's story is melodramatic: one's heartbone breaks with an anguished snap. A poet who uses the dictionary as Thomas did will also know *melos* as song. This is a foetal elegy of future adolescence signifying, as we shall see in the final stanza, nothing, a 'green nought' (stanza 4, line 9).

Who kills my history, my life's story? asks the neophyte. The last stanza answers the question fairly unequivocally. Job is again challenging God. Thomas asks the question before he is ever born, still a 'tomorrow-treading shade' looking at his future with an 'oracle' eye. God asks, 'Who could snap off the shapeless print?' Like Job, Thomas understands who it is that could, and says, 'Time kills me terribly'. 'Time shall not murder you,' God replies. This is the prayed-to Father who will protect us from time and mortality. 'Who could hack out your heart?' He asks. But the question is not rhetorical. It does have an answer. 'I saw time murder me.' God does not seem to be able to keep his promise.

Insofar as Time is God's agent, the accusation of murder extends to the divine 'winder of the water clocks'. Thomas gives himself no escape-hatch in this poem. Like his father's, the atheism Thomas approaches here has 'nothing to do with whether there was a god or not, but was a violent and personal dislike for God' (quoted, in Tedlock, p. 66). God teaches his neophyte a lesson: trust nothing but death. He is the abbot conducting the novitiate into the order of life with its traps, griefs, horrible desires, all leading to death. It is as though God already had our lives on film and is projecting everything on a screen as we live – with a preview in the womb. He cuts the film as He wishes, and lies to us, offering hope only in order to maintain suspense.

There was a saviour

(please turn to *Collected Poems*, p. 104)

On Christmas Day 1939 Thomas, who had brought his wife and son with him to spend the holidays with his parents at Bishopston (near Swansea), pulled from the shelves his father's copy of Milton and gave a reading of 'On the Morning of Christ's Nativity'. This is conjecture; but likely, seeing that in the following days and weeks he set himself the task of writing a poem based closely on the stanzaic form of Milton's hymn, which he on one occasion told Kathleen Raine was his favourite poem. In a letter to his father of 29 August 1939, five days before the declaration of war, Thomas wrote: 'If I could pray, I'd pray for peace' (*Letters*, p. 402/455). Now that war has come he begins an attempt at a prayer for peace through the discipline provided by one of the greatest poems of peace ever written:

> No war, or battle's sound,
> Was heard the world around;
>   The idle spear and shield were high uphung;
> The hookèd chariot stood,
> Unstained with hostile blood;
>   The trumpet spake not to the armèd throng;
> And kings sat still with awful eye,
> As if they surely knew their sovran Lord was by.

The very methodicalness of his effort to imitate Milton's stanzaic grandeur released Thomas's voice. 'Now I'm working on a new poem,' he wrote to Vernon Watkins on 30 January 1940, 'a poem which is giving me more pleasure than I've got out of any work for months, or even years' (*Letters*, pp. 437/496–7).

'There was a saviour' is certainly an anti-war poem; it should also be taken at its face value as a poem with a Christian attitude to war and peace. When Thomas was thinking he might have to face a tribunal as a conscientious objector to war, he wrote to a like-minded friend Desmond Hawkins on 14 October 1939 (*Letters*, p. 421/475): 'I'm afraid I couldn't honestly *plead* as a Christian, although I think I am one.' The poem contains this distinction. Thomas cannot officially plead as a Christian because that would require a denominational affiliation and, as the first part of the poem shows, Thomas had a loathing for the confined thinking that organized Christianity appears to him to be. However, the later stanzas of the poem portray the kind of Christianity that Thomas, can, in good faith, plead.

The first stanza is a rather difficult test case for this theory of the design of the poem, for it appears to begin with a shining Jesus. But we are soon forced to temper that first impression.

> There was a saviour
> Rarer than radium,
> Commoner than water, crueller than truth;
>   Children kept from the sun
>   Assembled at his tongue
> To hear the golden note turn in a groove,
> Prisoners of wishes locked their eyes
> In the jails and studies of his keyless smiles.

The solemnity of these lines makes them seem devotional, but the 'children kept from the sun' must be in Sunday School, 'assembled' to hear what in the original might have been 'golden' but, in the sermons which interpret and reiterate Christ's message, is like a cracked record turning 'in a groove'. Christ's smiles, as these 'prisoners' see them, are 'keyless', cannot be opened, and the children's eyes are locked into them as though in classrooms or jails. So that when we read of the saviour 'rarer than radium', it sounds nice but we know that radium is not really – and X-rays see through one, 'crueller than truth'. One cannot escape scrutiny: Jesus is everywhere, 'commoner than water'. This, anyway, is what children are told when religion is being used for discipline. The epithets used for Jesus in this first stanza must be tilted in the way these children would view things from their 'lost wilderness'.

The next two stanzas have the children speaking, with one voice, of the false use that has been made of the Saviour. They speak with wisdom beyond their years, with the authority of victims.

> There was calm to be done in his safe unrest,
>   When hindering man hurt
>   Man, animal, or bird
> We hid our fears in that murdering breath,
> Silence, silence to do, when earth grew loud,
> In lairs and asylums of the tremendous shout.

What have been the uses of religion? We could, the poem says, find calm in the promise of being personally safe or 'saved', though the world may go to rack and ruin; we could hide within the consolation of Jesus's sayings, which Thomas calls 'that murdering breath'. What an indictment! State religion is complicit in war-mongering and its consequences. With the inclusion of 'animal, or bird', the offence of 'hindering man' is broadened to cruelties against all living things. Religion condones or rationalizes these things; hence, 'murdering'.[1]

---

[1] That this unforgiving word 'murdering' was meant by the poet to apply to the 'Saviour' figure in the poem is a conclusion we cannot escape from. Apparently in the version sent to Vernon Watkins (not now extant) the phrase was 'his murdering breath'. 'I've turned "his" in line 6 of verse 2 into "that" ', Thomas told Watkins in a follow-up letter of 6 March 1940 (*Letters*, p. 443/503). 'To avoid ambiguity.' There would be no ambiguity if 'his' was referring to the nearest possible antecedent, that is, 'hindering man'. That is not Thomas's intention; so to avoid that connection he substitutes 'that', which allows us to seek the referent in the main subject of the poem, the Saviour.

Or, rephrasing it, when 'earth grew loud' as the war geared up to pitch, one could find silence in hiding in the 'lairs' or religious 'asylums' provided for by 'the tremendous shout', which could be a Joshua's battle cry, self-righteous indignation of the religious fanatic outdoing the clashing of the armies themselves.

Thomas's scorn for what he called the 'false' Christ is on record in a letter written to the editor of the *Swansea and West Wales Guardian* in the 6 July 1934 edition (*Letters*, pp. 150–2/176–8). The piece was entitled 'The Real Christ – and the False', probably by the editor; but he got the point. Thomas had been listening to an open-air preacher with dismay and mounting anger that the preacher's God could allow Hitler, 'a megalomaniac drunk on words and blood', to thrive:

> Can this timid emblem of suffering stare around at our contemporary world, and, sickened of the waste and murder, the obscene hypocrisy of those war-mongers and slave-drivers who venerate His name and void their contagious rheum upon the first principle of His gospel, afford no more proof of His living energy and His Messiahdom than the mere offer of a heavenly accommodation (h. and c., cherubs, every godly convenience) at the end of this giddy life?

The emotions that produced this invective against Christian war-mongers infused 'There was a saviour', written five-and-a-half years later.

At the same time, the newspaper letter refers to a Christ of 'living energy' and earlier to Christ as 'a reawakened, revolutionary force' (*Letters*, p. 150/177). In 'There was a saviour', even while talking about the false Christ of the preachers, there are reminders of a true Christ in words like 'radium' in its shining aspect, 'golden note', 'smiles', 'tremendous shout', which latter is so overwhelmingly positive in itself that it is hard to see the negative until one realizes that it is probably meant to be part of the loudness of the 'earth', or at least in conjunction with it, and thus part of the din of war. Likewise, one can hear 'glory' in his churches while the church itself kills in Christ's name:

> There was glory to hear
> In the churches of his tears,
> Under his downy arm you sighed as he struck,
> O you who could not cry

On to the ground when a man died
Put a tear for joy in the unearthly flood
And laid your cheek against a cloud-formed shell:

William T. Moynihan, quoting this stanza, says that Thomas's point is that

> the believers were comfortable, complacent, and sentimental in their religion. But there was no real brotherhood, no real humanity there . . . the churchgoer was unmindful of real suffering and wept self-indulgently about 'unearthly' sorrows, taking comfort in an empty shell of belief with no more substance than a cloud. (Moynihan, pp. 178–9)

I concur. The poem goes on to tell 'how the war has changed this indifference' (Moynihan, p. 179). The 'Now' in the pivotal last line of stanza 3 refers to the war and the present time, January 1940:

> Now in the dark there is only yourself and myself.

We are now in the dark, say the lost children, all of us, and we must do without the religion that removed us from the reality of suffering. The effort to hide from the humanness of existence is at an end. It is as though the coldness of the winter (Robert Williams has done the research to find out that it was the coldest winter in forty-five years) has shorn everyone of their protection, the comforts that kept them apart. We are now all vulnerable, to the freezing weather, and the war.

The war comes to the fore with the adjective 'blacked'. Responding to Vernon Watkins's suggestions about the poem, Thomas refused to change that word (*Letters*, p. 442/502):

> I like the word 'blacked', by the way, in spite of its, in the context, jarring dissonance with 'locked'. I had, quite apart (that is absurd, I mean secondarily to) from the poem, the blackout in mind, another little hindrance on the scene, & the word seemed, to me, to come rightly.

The image is of two brothers sitting side by side for minimal comfort in an air-raid shelter surrounded by the hindrances of war, small and large, and re-evaluating their previous complacency. Like the children of stanzas 2 and 3, these brothers speak, in unison, the final two stanzas of the poem.

O we who could not stir one lean [small] sigh [of sympathy] when we heard greed on man [opposite of peace on earth] beating near and fire [far arson] neighbour but [instead] wailed [at the wailing wall] and nested [comfortably] in the sky-blue wall [of heaven] now BREAK a giant tear [of pity] for the little known fall [the unknown soldier], for the drooping [collapse] of homes that did not nurse our [rather, a stranger's] bones, [for] brave deaths[2] of only ones [or sons] but never found [lost at sea], [we] now SEE, alone [as we are] in us [ourselves], our own true [corresponding] strangers' dust [of death] ride[3] through the doors of our [previously] unentered [guarded] house [consciousness].

Love thy neighbour (Luke 10:27): this is the 'Real Christ' of Thomas's previously quoted newspaper piece (*Letters*, p. 150/177):

> The orator, and his bannered boy, forget that the boulders at the gate of the tomb were thrown aside, and that the raised and living Christ came out like a man from anaesthetic, a symbol of life, a reawakened, revolutionary force, not a walking corpse with the words of a dead message stale and yellow on his mouth.

So the message here is brotherhood, and the war has forced it on us in a way that nothing else could. The previously proud brothers, tarred with the same brush, the same greed that stained the 'blackening church' of Blake's London, now have to sit side by side in the cold black-out.

But who are these brothers? To answer this question we should take a look at Thomas's reaction to the declaration of war in his letters from 3 September 1939 until 6 May 1940 (when he was classified grade III because of his lungs and no longer had to face the moral issue of combat). Thomas's immediate thought was to declare himself 'a neutral state' (*Letters*, p. 407/461): 'the Germans are not my enemies' (*Letters*, p. 449/510). He wrote to Desmond Hawkins on 24 September 1939 that he 'can't kill . . . I feel sick. All this flogged hate again' (*Letters*, pp. 414–15/469). A few days later he asks Bert Trick's advice about the war: 'I've only my feelings to guide me, & they are my own, and nothing will turn them savage against people with whom I have no quarrel' (*Letters*, p. 417/471). He will have

---

[2] Watkins remembers the line as first sent to him (*LVW*, p. 81) as 'Deaths of the only ones, our never found.' Thomas agreed (*Letters*, p. 442/502) that the line needed to be changed. He added the emotive word 'brave'; it guides our emotions.

[3] The verb 'ride' was originally 'fly'. While writing his 6 March 1940 letter to Watkins (*Letters*, p. 443/503) Thomas decided on 'ride': 'I'm sure of that: it's mysteriously militant, which is what I wanted.'

nothing to do with 'fostering of hate against a bewildered, buggered people'. In spite of xenophobic, hate-mongering state religions we must, says Thomas, persist in the Christian belief that no one is really our enemy. God's winter spreads over all of Europe and locks enemies together as brothers. Both the poet and his German counterpart are exiled in themselves from the hatred their respective states are trying to impose on them.

> Exiled in us we arouse the soft,
> Unclenched, armless, silk and rough love that breaks all rocks.

The two brothers are being told to have stony hearts and hate each other. Thomas pits his poem against that. He is proud to be soft, or 'silk and rough', in his love, which is so far from being a clenched fist as to have no arms at all.

The seed-at-zero

(please turn to *Collected Poems*, p. 39)

'The seed-at-zero' is nobody's favourite poem, and there is a danger of selling it short unless we look at its origins as a notebook poem dated 29 August 1933 (*Notebook Poems*, pp. 184–5), which is clearly a poem taking up serious religious questions. This notebook version begins with a reference to Genesis 49:10: 'The sceptre shall not depart from Judah, nor a lawgiver from between his feet, until Shiloh come.' Where can we look for salvation? Where will Shiloh's seed be sown? The starting point is Johanna Southcott's claim that she was to give birth to the promised Shiloh. This was in 1814; she was sixty-four and had dropsy. It was one of the most notable false pregnancies of history. Her presence in the poem is confirmed because Thomas himself in the notebook put an asterisk at the end of line 3 with the footnote '*Southcott?' – where the only disconcerting thing is the question mark. There seems to be no question really.

> Shiloh's seed shall not be sown
> In the garden of the womb
> By a salty dropsy sipping,
> No Redeemer shall be born
> In the belly of a lamb

> Dumbly and divinely leaping
> Over the godbearing green.

With the 'fanatic womb' of the last stanza of the notebook poem we are back with Johanna Southcott again:

> Shiloh's seed shall not be sown
> In the pastures of the worm;
> Not in the fanatic womb
> Shall the jelly mix and form
> That shall be the three in One,
> God and Ghost, Anointed Son.

The blip in pleromatic history that Southcott represents could hardly be of deep concern for Thomas. For this far-ranging poem she is a small stepping stone in and out. In her own dramatic way, however, she raised the biggest question of them all: is there a God who is interested enough to intrude Himself into the world in some identifiable form? Or is His 'seed' embedded in all natural processes of the earth's decay and renewal?

While the 'Shiloh's seed' notebook poem tended toward pantheism (expressed in a sexual profligacy: 'Now is sun and summer phallic', etc.), the 'seed-at-zero' revision involved a thoroughgoing change in imagery. The pastoral was abandoned for the military, the imagery of sexual conquest. This changed the tone completely, so that one might, if not forewarned, think that the resulting poem is about seduction or rape. Hence, our attention to the ur-poem as anchor. I think the religious dimension of the poem survived its restructuring.

> The seed-at-zero [hour] SHALL NOT STORM [assault] that town of ghosts [spirits in waiting], the [sexually] trodden womb with her rampart [part to be ramped] [presented] to his tapping [for an opening for the ghosts as at a séance], no god-in-hero [shall] TUMBLE DOWN like a [phallic] tower [attacking] on the town [womb] dumbly [as an infant] and divinely [as a god] stumbling over the manwaging line [of defense].

The second stanza is an almost exact repeat of the first. The idea must be to highlight those few words that are different. The womb is now 'manwaged' (line 9), a coined word which communicates the idea of waging war with a man. Conversely, the 'line' (line 14) is now 'warbearing', bearing war where one would expect bearing a child.

This exactly sums up what these stanzas seem to be saying: that no child will come in this violent fashion. Frontal attack is not the way the divine child will be produced. Both stanzas are saying this, so that the repetition must be for an incantatory effect. It is a chant in a ritual of aversion.

The next two stanzas retain the fortified castle image, but the seed does not attempt to storm in. It falls gently from heaven, though strained.

> Through the rampart of the sky SHALL the star-flanked [protected by the stars] seed BE RIDDLED [sifted], [providing] manna [nightly growth] for the rumbling [hungry] ground, [and providing] quickening [new life] for the riddled [shot with holes] sea; settled [like star dust] on a virgin stronghold [womb] he SHALL GRAPPLE with the guard [of her virginity] and the keeper of the key [to the entrance and revitalization].

The 'god-in-hero', it seems, has still to do some grappling, but in the last line of the repeated stanza the keeper loses the key to him. There is here, if you like, some increment to the repetition. Entry is achieved.

There seems to be a certain hit or miss quality about how the panspermia finds a home (stanzas 5 and 6). A humble village may labour to accept him and a continent deny access; alternatively, he may find no welcome on the village green, while taken in by high society. At least, stanzas 5 and 6 are saying, let him find some kind of shelter, even if it is only some Saundersfoot sort of place, a manger where the drunken sailors are the shepherds. We might look anywhere.

The last two stanzas represent a new move: there is repetition with a real difference. The imagery is similar to what we have seen already in the poem, but the 'town' is not the womb this time. There is a town that the 'man-in-seed' does not thunder on and then another town in the last stanza that he does thunder on. The first town has a 'star-flanked garrison' and is called a 'sky-scraping place' (stanza 7). I would suggest that this town is heaven, and no cannons are going to be ranged on it as a target. Zooming in from 'the star-flanked fields of space', or heaven, the man-in-seed finally gets to bomb the 'foreign' town which has a 'sand-bagged garrison' (stanza 8). The association with sand gives us this as the town of death; it is 'the grave-groping place' that the 'hero-in-tomorrow' will conquer. Let us borrow a word from the notebook poem and call this hero the Redeemer.

The only question finally is: is Thomas serious? Can we grant 'The seed-at-zero' the dignity of religious statement? My own feeling is that Thomas wanted a religious poem, and got it; but his heart fell out of the words as he put them into their battering-ram formation with an assertiveness that seems heartless.

The spire cranes

(please turn to *Collected Poems*, p. 72)

On 13 November 1937 Thomas sent to Vernon Watkins for typing his 'sixty-line-year's work', the poem 'I make this in a warring absence', an 'exhauster', as he called it. As a *jeu* to celebrate, he wrote out and enclosed 'The spire cranes', with a PS (*Letters*, p. 264/305): 'I've done another little poem: nothing at all important, or even (probably,) much good: just a curious thought said quickly. I think it will be good for me to write some short poems, not bothering about them too much, between my long exhausters.' Though he did not tell Watkins it was a *revised* poem (he never did for any of the revisions he sent him), Thomas had gone back to an early notebook used during his last year at Swansea Grammar School and a poem dated 27 January 1931 (*Notebook Poems*, pp. 68–9). The revision recast twenty-two lines of free verse into eleven rhymed longer lines (approximately hexameters).

It was no doubt revised quickly, but it was, and is, more than a 'curious thought'. Long before any of the poems of *18 Poems*, it is a statement of the poetic purpose that produced that singular achievement.

The [belfry] spire[1] CRANES [lifts the birds to its height]. Its statue [in the tower] IS an aviary [birds carved in stone]. From the stone nest it DOES NOT LET the feathery carved birds blunt [silence] their striking [as they fall]

---

[1] 'According to Thomas's friend Ralph Wishart', writes James A. Davies (in *Places*, p. 60), it was St Thomas's Church on Delhi Street, Swansea, that 'was the inspiration of' this poem. Rather, the poem seems to require a clocktower chiming the hours over the seashore. Robert Williams has suggested Llansteffan as a more likely location.

throats on the salt [sand] gravel, [or] pierce the spilt [bird-dropping] sky with [their] diving wing [crashed] in weed and [their] heel [colliding with shallow water] an inch in froth.

Chimes [from the belfry] CHEAT [escape] the prison spire, [and] PELTER in [metrical] time like outlaw [irregular] rains on that priest, water, [beating] time for the swimmers' hands, [making] music [in a certain key] for the silver [like the sea] lock and mouth [of swimmer and estuary]. Both note and plume PLUNGE from the spire's [crane] hook.

Those craning [stone] birds ARE choice for you [poet addressing himself], songs that jump back [up] to the built voice [belfry], or fly with winter [coldly] to the bells, but do not travel down dumb wind [profusely] like prodigals [spendthrifts].

The poet presents himself the choice between two kinds of poetry. One is associated with the words 'pelter', 'outlaw', 'down dumb wind', and 'prodigal'; the second is represented by the birds that also plunge but can return to their source and do not dissipate themselves. The spire has a crane's hook with which it holds to itself the best kind of poetry, which is hewn like a tower.

Thomas had an opportunity, writing to Henry Treece a few months after the revision of 'The spire cranes', to rephrase in prose this distinction (*Letters*, pp. 297–8/344). Stephen Spender had said in a review that his poetry was 'turned on like a tap; it is just poetic stuff with no beginning nor end, shape, or intelligent and intelligible control':

> Spender's remark is really the exact opposite of what is true. My poems *are* formed; they are not turned on like a tap at all, they are 'watertight compartments'. Much of the obscurity is due to rigorous compression; the last thing they do is to flow; they are much rather hewn.

The tombstone told

(please turn to *Collected Poems*, p. 77)

For the detective story plot – how did the subject die? – we have to go back to the notebook poem of July 1933 (*Notebook Poems*, p. 162):

> She wed on a wild March morning;
> Before she lay on her wedding bed
> She died, was death's bride.
> The tombstone tells how she died.
> She married on a mad Welsh morning,
> With March flowers over her head,
> A farmer up valley who needed a girl
> To sleep with and talk with, milk and clean sheds.
> She died in her white wedding dress,
> With a garland of roses, a Catholic cross,
> A cake, and a ring, and a mirror inside
> That showed death coming in.
> The tombstone tells how she died.

No Dylan Thomas sleuths have unearthed this tombstone, though it should not be impractical to survey all the Catholic plots in the vicinity of Carmarthen. Meanwhile, we are left to assume that Thomas is constructing this 'Hardy-like'[1] poem (*Letters*, p. 327/376) on the basis of the gist of a rum peasant tragedy carved on a gravestone that he had himself recently seen.

When Thomas turned to this poem in the notebook five years later and wrote up a revision on the opposite page (*Notebook Poems*, p. 262) he could add, among other things, some countryside gossip (lines 16–20):

> Among men later I heard it said
> She cried her white-dressed limbs were bare
> And her red lips were kissed black,
> She wept in her pain and made mouths,
> Talked and tore though her eyes smiled.

The bride is portrayed as undergoing extreme physical and mental stress, some kind of fit with hallucinations, from which she did not recover. Before she was her husband's bride she became, as the early version put it, 'death's bride'. Thomas imagines the deathbed to be like a bridal bed, and her last moments to be as though death were violently making love to her. He has her describe, in her derangement, how death's embrace felt (lines 26–30):

---

[1] Thomas may have been thinking of Thomas Hardy's 'Satires of Circumstance', perhaps 'Rain on a Grave' – its title anyway.

> I died before bedtime came
> But my womb was bellowing
> And I felt with my bare fall
> A blazing red harsh head tear up
> And the dear floods of his hair.

This is the rape of death. But what about the strange last line? Thomas was worried about it: 'In the ballad-like poem I'm not *quite* sure of several words, mostly of "great" floods of his hair. I think it's right though; I didn't want a surprisingly strong word there.' He thought about it and changed 'great' to 'dear', explaining in his next letter (*Letters*, p. 328/376):

> In the last line you'll see I've been daring, & have tried to make the point of the poem softer & subtler by the use of the dangerous 'dear'. The word 'dear' fits in, I think, with 'though her eyes smiled', which comes earlier. I wanted the girl's *terrible* reaction to orgiastic death to be suddenly altered into a kind of despairing love. As I see it now, it strikes me as very moving, but it may be too much of a shock, a bathetic shock perhaps.

The often reported calmness before death, the embracing of death with equanimity or even desire, this is what Thomas must be getting at. In 'The tombstone told', the actual dying is felt in sexual terms and the moment of death is a kind of despairing orgasm: 'her eyes smiled' (line 20). This is what the poet has added to what the tombstone told.

There is more still in the poem: the author adds himself as observer. I am not sure that the convolutions involved in giving us such an obtrusive narrator are not detrimental to what otherwise would have been an attractive 'ballad-like' achievement. The poet says he is seeing the death of the bride as though he were viewing a 'hurried film' projected on the 'mortal wall' (lines 21–3) of his mother's womb when a foetus. This strange point of view (though not very strange to Thomas, who uses it several times in his poetry) is what the poem uses to establish a weird sense of fate – not logical but emotive. If the poet saw it all happening before he was born (lines 6–9), to see the inscription on the tombstone would be a déjà vu. Maybe that is what Thomas felt it was, as he stood there in the rain in front of the tombstone. He says he struck the place 'one day by luck'. How could it possibly be felt by him to be lucky to be there? Perhaps it completed for him something that seemed to have been etched in his mind long before? Was there a connection between the poet and this woman? He saw the 'two surnames' (line 2) and they 'stopped' him 'still'. Rewriting this poem, Thomas has turned the detective story into a ghost story (lines 13–15):

> . . . that rainy tongue beat back
> Through the devilish years and innocent deaths
> To the room of a secret child . . .

The stone bird on the tombstone seems to know something but is speaking in a disguised way. Who is the 'secret child', the dead virgin or the poet in his mother's womb? It is eerie.

However, we should not allow the mystery of the child in this part of the poem to coax us into suggesting, as some have done, that the bride died giving birth in the church. That would be too much of a satire of circumstance. The 'red harsh head' and the 'floods of his hair' might seem to suggest birth, but Thomas's own statements contradict that interpretation. The head has to be penile, the hair pubic, both belonging to Death.

This bread I break

(please turn to *Collected Poems*, p. 36)

Positioned in the poet's notebook between 'Light breaks where no sun shines' and 'A process in the weather of the heart', this we take to be a process poem, left out of *18 Poems* only because it is lighter and more accessible than those Thomas chose for his first volume. It reiterates, nevertheless, what many of those poems assert: that the forces at work in nature are at work in a person's own bodily being, one force fulfilling the impulse of the organism to grow, the other 'making desolation in the veins' (line 12).

But there is here a familiarity factor: Thomas could not be unaware that 'This bread I break' would make his readers think of the Last Supper and the eucharist. This is a deceptive allusiveness, in my opinion. I agree with Clark Emery that, though 'nothing in the poem stops the Christian reader from taking the next step if he desires', Thomas would 'not choose to take it with him' (Emery, p. 209).[1]

Around this same time, for example, Thomas used similar imagery in a non-religious way in the short story 'The Mouse and the Woman' (*Collected Stories*, p. 76): 'He saw her flesh in the cut bread; her blood, still flowing through the channels of her mysterious body, in the spring water.' Thomas can be that secular with the sacraments.

So we can paraphrase the poem as follows: Just as man threshed the 'flesh' of the merry oat and extracted the 'blood' of the grape to make the bread and wine that the poet has before him (symbolic of the substance of his own body), so you, Death, when you break my flesh and let out my blood from my desolate veins, are taking the oat and grape and the wine and the bread (all the sustenance of this world) as well as the sensual body I have, in my growing, made out of them. We have, then, another poem of the interconnectedness of all the processes of mortality. If it is Jesus Christ speaking in this poem, he sounds just like Dylan Thomas.

[1] The notebook poem (*Notebook Poems*, pp. 212, 276) was given a title by the poet: 'Breakfast Before Execution'. Again the Last Supper is available to us, but there is a more general meaning: that the executioner for us all is death.

This side of the truth

(please turn to *Collected Poems*, p. 88)

In New Quay on the mid-Wales coast Thomas spent most of the afternoon of 26 February 1945 writing at length to his son Llewelyn, who was with his grandmother in Ringwood, in southern England, where he had been for most of the war. It had been reported that Llewelyn had fallen from a tree and split his tongue (*Letters*, p. 545/607). We do not have Thomas's consoling letter from which to gain a sense of his fatherliness. We do, however, have 'This side of the truth', which was written soon after and sent to Vernon Watkins with a letter of 28 March 1945 (*Letters*, p. 548/610). Subtitled 'for Llewelyn', it is a poem of profound consolation. The poet addresses his six-year-old son as still being 'this side of the truth', too young, of course, to have the self-awareness that a reading of the poem requires. Part of the touching quality of the poem is the faith that it will be there for Llewelyn to read when he moves to the other side of innocence.

Thomas, who once put the assertion 'Boys is nasty' into the mouth of a character in 'A Story' (*Collected Stories*, p. 35), is under no illusions. He early saw in eight-month-old Llewelyn his own kind of 'innocence' (in quotation marks): he had 'the familiar Thomas puffed innocence about him, lollypop eyes, and nose that looks to heaven' (*Letters*, p. 417/471). A few weeks after 'This side of the truth' was written, in a particularly happy moment at the end of the war, when Llewelyn was able to join the family, Thomas gives us this picture (*Letters*, p. 557/621):

> My son, in the nonstop probably frog-filled rain, is performing what seems, from this distance, to be an unnatural act with a beaver. Looking closer, I see he is only destroying his sister's doll – the little pixie.

'Destroying his sister's doll' – well, the 'wicked wish' (line 29) can be present within an innocence that does not know how wicked it is nor how inevitable it is, as the poem says, both in its fatal coming on and in its ultimate dissolution. 'Good and bad' – both are intertwined in the way we move about our deaths 'by the grinding sea' (line 15), the sea of mortality with its slow tidal abrasion of everything to sand or dust.

But in the end 'it all means nothing at all' – to quote a phrase from *Under Milk Wood* as a gloss on this poem. The boy who would not kiss Gwennie 'because my mother said I mustn't' (*UMW*, p. 45) is racked by the issue of good or bad, and is scapegoated (pp. 45–6):

> He blubbers away downhill with his patched pants falling, and his tear-splashed blush burns all the way as the triumphant bird-like sisters scream . . . It all means nothing at all, and, howling for his milky mum, for her cawl and buttermilk and cowbreath and welshcakes and the fat birth-smelling bed and moonlit kitchen of her arms, he'll never forget as he paddles blind home through the weeping end of the world.

It all means nothing at all. Good and bad (lines 17–24)

> Blow away like breath,
> Go crying through you and me
> And the souls of all men
> Into the innocent
> Dark, and the guilty dark, and good

Death, and bad death, and then
In the last element
Fly like the stars' blood . . .

The stars' blood (unlike Christ's blood of Christopher Marlowe's *Faustus*, which streams in the firmament of a condemning God) flows in 'unminding skies' (line 6). Others' nastinesses and our nastinesses, inevitable as they are ('cast' before we move – line 33), are wound in by the 'winding dark' (line 11) like a cold fisherman who catches everything. This is the indifferent universe of the existentialists, and I do believe that Thomas should be viewed as within that tradition.

But Thomas will not leave it quite there. There may be no Judge, but there is something that feels like unjudging Love (lines 34–6):

And all your deeds and words,
Each truth, each lie,
Die in unjudging love.

I have heard the phrase 'agnostical absolution' applied to the ending of this poem. Though I have forgotten who said it, I have remembered the phrase for its aptness, and would not want to avoid using it. It sums up the feeling of relief that everything is over: none record and none recover. It is a feeling that, when one anticipates it in speculation, seems akin to love. It is a fondness for the dark that we give ourselves as it becomes dark.

Thomas supplies another phrase for it in the same letter to Vernon Watkins in which he mentions Llewelyn's fall from a tree (*Letters*, pp. 545/607–8). He is increasingly finding, he says, 'that the problems of physical life, of social contact, of daily posture' plunge him into little hells, at which he rebels with 'truculent acceptance'. He can, he says, 'despair and, at rare moments, exult with the big last', that is, the major spiritual questions; but these 'ordinary moments' just leave him trembling or, at best, truculent in his acceptance of them. When he turns from writing to Watkins and faces a poem for his son, he calms down. It being addressed to an innocent loved one, the poem strains out the truculence: the residue is pure acceptance.

✧

Today, this insect

(please turn to *Collected Poems*, p. 38)

This is one of the poems on which Thomas worked, using a note-book original, when he needed ballast to float his second volume of poems. We do not quite know when the revision was done, but it is likely that it was in Ireland in the summer of 1935. It seems part of the same crisis of faith as the 'Altarwise by owl-light' sonnets.

The notebook poem that caught his eye was an early one, dated 18 December 1930, which begins (*Notebook Poems*, p. 63):

> Today, this hour I breathe
> In symbols, be they so light, of tongue and air,
> The now I have space
> And time that is already half
> More than that I tell you in,
> I have divided
> Sense into sight and trust.
> The certain is a fable.

In other words, there is no certainty. The notebook poem goes on to talk about an airplane, for instance, being deceptive, it being an 'iron bird'; the theme leads up to a complaint about the unpredictability of girlfriends. But as Thomas glanced over the poem there was enough in those first lines to strike a chord with the religious scepticism he was feeling in 1935.

He gave the idea a major rewrite, adding to the flat phrase 'I have divided sense' several images of division, notably the insect, which has the root meaning of 'segmented creature'. He put 'insect' in apposition to 'today', characterizing it as the day of division; the world he breathes is cut in two as of that moment. His thinking has brought him to cut himself off from his previous faith. It is a quick cut too, once he has made time for it.

Today, this insect [bisected], and the world I breathe [my life], now that my [poetic] symbols have outelbowed [made sufficient] space, [have outelbowed] time at the [London] city [time-consuming] spectacles [distractions], and [taking only] half the dear, daft [foolishly undeft] time I take to nudge the [this] sentence [to its meandering completion], in

[into] trust and tale [fact and fiction] HAVE I DIVIDED sense [meaning of life], [have] SLAPPED DOWN the [bisecting] guillotine, the blood-red [butchered] double [dichotomy] of head and tail [fact and fiction] made [thereby] witnesses [attesting] to this murder [by dissection] of Eden and green genesis.

Analysis of the Bible stories kills them. The gospel is supposed to be the certain truth, but 'the insect certain is the plague of fables'. This line will signify the same idea as the notebook poem's 'The certain is a fable'. The supposed certainty that has been *insected* reveals itself as one of the plagues of Egypt or anywhere, 'the plague of fables', as devastating to belief as locusts to crops.

Thomas has picked out Eden and the Genesis story (he capitalized 'Genesis' in the manuscript first sent to his publishers) as good examples of what is presented as fact and what his guillotine mind has cut down to fable.

This story's [Genesis's] monster [abnormal foetus] HAS a [Garden] serpent caul [appendage at birth], blind in the [serpent's] coil [it] SCRAMS [scrambles] round the blazing outline [of the story up in smoke], MEASURES his [the monster's] own length [knocked flat] on the garden [of Eden] wall and BREAKS his shell [coherence] in the last shocked beginning [awakening].

Imaging the Eden story as a 'monster' (and subsequently as a crocodile) these lines represent the violence of the hatching of the poet's disbelief. 'In the beginning' breaks its egg for the last time. This 'children's piece', as the poem goes on to say (lines 15–16), is now 'uncredited'. It is doomed to a horrible extinction like an insect scurrying around within a narrowing circle of fire. The story just will not fly. It is a crocodile before the chrysalis stage. This caterpillar will never be airborne. If it was once a 'flying heartbone' (line 15), its flight was wishful thinking and now there is the 'fall from love'. The Bible story has no more capability of flight than a 'sabbath ass' brought to Sunday school with wings on. Eden gets a destroying shout like that at Jericho, in this case a blast of disbelief.

At this dire point of utter scepticism the poem turns: 'The insect fable is the certain promise' (line 18). It turns, however, to an even more intense depression, for out of the dissected fable comes the one certainty, death. The loss of religious faith leaves death with its sting.

It is Death that speaks in the last lines of the poem. The universality of the speech is prepared for by a deliberate series of allusions to drama, novel and the Bible, 'fibs of vision' (line 21) where death has exercised his prerogative. Hamlet is named, and Macbeth's dagger is 'air-drawn'. The windmill on a wooden horse (line 20) makes one think of Don Quixote, though some people also think of the *Odyssey* as well. For 'John's beast' (line 21) we are probably meant to see the visionary red dragon of Revelation 12, though there are other possible animals there. But that is the point: add 'Job's patience' and you have a hotchpotch of madmen that death has dealt with in its indiscriminating and ageless *crucifictions* (to borrow a neat word from Tindall, p. 92).

When Death speaks of his love in the last four lines, we have, of course, a bitter irony. His embrace loves us to death. Adam and all humankind he loves; his love for madmen (and mad women, and even all of us who are not so mad) is endless. No deceiving lover offers an end more certain than Death does. He knows where all fibs and sweet-talking end up.

> All legends' sweethearts on a tree of stories,
> My cross of tales behind the fabulous curtain.

We are suckers for consoling legends, but all the stories end up crucified on Death's cross, which Death draws his own curtain of fables across. This ageless voice is the theme of Greek tragedy now speaking to Thomas in the Irish sea, on one shore of which is Wales.

It is perfectly obvious that Thomas did not need the notebook poem in order to achieve this expression of his most stolid scepticism. One can speak in general and say that he was quite inventive enough not to need the notebooks at all. But with approximately thirty poems published between 1936 and 1946 coming with varying degrees of indebtedness from the early notebooks, one has to ask the question why. Laziness can only be the answer in a few cases, not with a poem like 'Today, this insect', anyway. I believe the answer lies in one of the most salient qualities that has been noted in Thomas's poetry, his ability to express the feelings of youth (in such poems as 'Fern Hill'). It was not only to recall the wonder of things that he turned to his own early poems, but to keep faith with his own first awoken self in a whole range of feelings, scepticism along with the rest.

To Others than You

(please turn to *Collected Poems*, p. 89)

This poem in which Thomas impeaches all his friends – with a snide title releasing whoever is reading it from the accusations – was written around the end of May 1939 at a time when, with the new baby and no income, Thomas most needed his friends. He had written with some hopefulness on 11 May 1939 to John Davenport about a subscription idea (*Letters*, p. 378/427):

> I'm so penniless – the stamp on this letter's stolen – that I'm thinking of trying to work out a small income for myself on these lines: to get as many people as possible, people, that is, of assured incomes and some little interest in whether I do or not avoid the debtors' jug, to promise to send me five shillings (5/-) a week each; if I could get ten people, we'd flourish. I've thought of a possible few, including yourself and Norman, and what do you think of the idea?

Since he cannot make money by what he writes he had better concentrate, he says, on 'getting my living-money from *people* and not from poems' (*Letters*, p. 378/428).

It would have been safer to bet on the poems. Although 'To Others than You' was done before the 'Thomas Floatation' fund (as he was still referring to it in a letter to Davenport in July – *Letters*, p. 386/438) sank ignominiously, the poet had some inkling of the resounding silence with which the proposal was being greeted. Or maybe he was saying to himself, 'Why should *I* have to be doing this organizing? Where are my friends?'

Having to throw himself on the charity of his friends must have provided some of the annoyance at the back of the poem, but, if it were only that, we would have to put the poem down as overreactive. As far as we know there were never any grounds for Thomas to feel that his friends were positively treacherous over this business, especially in May when the poem was finished. No, there is much more going on in the poem than this. Besides, although Thomas casts his net wide in the last lines of the poem,

My friends were enemies on stilts
With their heads in a cunning cloud[1]

and the first line, 'Friend by enemy I call you out', seems as though he
is going to take them all on, one by one, the sixteen lines of the body
of the poem seem very much to refer to one particular former friend
and confidant whom Thomas now feels he was deceived by: the
friend 'displaced a truth' with a lie (line 17).

> You with a bad [counterfeit] coin in your [eye] socket, you my friend there
> with a [game] winning air who palmed [like a card-sharp or conjurer] the
> lie [false card] on me when you looked [over my shoulder] brassily [with
> brazen cupidity] at my shyest secret [hand of cards], [who] enticed with
> twinkling bits [coins] of the eye till the sweet [seeking] tooth of my love bit
> dry [on nothing sweet], [the tooth] rasped [ground down] at last, and I
> stumbled [like an old man] and sucked [without teeth or love], [you] whom
> now I conjure [summon with spells] to stand [exposed] as thief in the
> memory [previously] worked by mirrors [as in an illusionist's act],
> [enticed] with unforgettably smiling [performer's] act, quickness of
> [conjurer's] hand in the velvet glove and my whole heart under your
> hammer [ready to be smashed as part of the trick], WERE once such a
> creature, so gay and frank a desireless [undemanding] familiar [buddy] . . .

Thus the poem records a time when there was not only trust between
Thomas and this friend but also an effortless caring.

It has to be Geoffrey Grigson. In his 'Recollections of Dylan
Thomas', Grigson included himself along with Norman Cameron,
Bernard Spencer and Ruthven Todd as Thomas's real friends when he
first came up to London (*Casebook*, p. 261):

> He could enjoy with us verbal jokes and myths and inventions which
> committed him to no decision, no ideal of mental or spiritual conduct. He
> could trust himself to clown, to swear, to talk of women, or sex; he could
> borrow our beds, our underclothes and our cash, be washed, be on
> occasion mended and dry-cleaned by our wives . . .

---

[1] The friend/enemy is 'striding so high above the common earth . . . you cannot see
his eyes or know his faults' – as the notebook poem explains (*Notebook Poems*, p.
145). Thomas picked up only this one image from this notebook poem of April
1933, which has an unrelated theme. He borrowed 'desireless familiar' (line 15)
from another early source, in this case the published story 'The Orchards'
(*Collected Stories*, p. 48). Again the contexts are different, but his comment to
Watkins (*Letters*, p. 383/435) that seeing the phrase had caused him to write the
poem enables us to give the precise date of 25 May 1939 to the beginning of
composition, since Thomas was on that date checking the text of that story
(*Letters*, p. 381/432).

Grigson was like family. But he was more: he published Thomas's poems in the influential *New Verse* and, as literary editor of the *Morning Post*, handed him detective thrillers to review for regular pocket money. And more still: in the summer of 1935 Grigson organized a trip for the two of them to Ireland (*Casebook*, p. 261):

> There was a valley above the Atlantic entered by no road, not even a well-defined path, over a ridge of rock, peat and heather. In this valley of Glen Lough between Ardara and Killybegs, I knew a solitary farmer and his wife. A year or two before, the place had been discovered by the American artist Rockwell Kent, who liked its wilderness and loneliness between mountains, or mountains and lakes, and the sea. He had concreted a donkey-shed into a sleeping-room and studio, and had abandoned it. It was in that shed, on the edge of a small stream from the lakes, that Dylan and I lived for a while, building turf fires to dry ourselves out . . .

Grigson states casually what must have been an amazing experience of isolation with a chosen companion. When after a couple of weeks Thomas was left there to fend for himself (with the neighbour farmer's help with basic food and drink) he was, as letters testify (for example, *Letters*, p. 191/217), very lonely indeed after all that physical, if not homoerotic, intimacy. In later years, Grigson started spreading the story that, when Thomas finally left Glen Lough, he did so without paying the farmer what was owed. The story is told with unusual venom (not only in the essay in *Casebook*, p. 262, but also in an anonymous review in the *Times Literary Supplement*, 2 March 1967). Patently Grigson had a need to show Thomas as unworthy, beyond the pale. However, Robert Williams, asking around Glen Lough later, found no memories of any such misdemeanour on Thomas's part. Indeed, the record shows that Grigson did not break off his relationship with Dylan for over a year, and for a very different reason.

Thomas was back on the roster of *Morning Post* reviewers right up to 11 September 1936. That date is significant as the day after *Twenty-five Poems* was published. Here is when the break occurred. In 'A Letter from England' in *Poetry* (Chicago) of November 1936, Grigson wrote: 'My opinion of Mr Dylan Thomas' new *Twenty-five Poems*, for example, must be honest – that twenty-four twenty-fifths of them are psychopathological nonsense put down with a remarkable ineptitude in technique' (p. 103). This from the editor of *New Verse*, who had published one of them, the good one we presume. Of course this is not fair criticism; it is motivated by personal spite. The story behind it is one about which Paul Ferris must undoubtedly be right when he speaks of 'a new friend in high places, Edith Sitwell' (Ferris, p. 137): 'The fact that Thomas was willing to be flattered and approved of by her may have been a significant reason for Grigson's disenchantment with him.' Of course. Edith Sitwell was Grigson's Aunt Sally, at whom he was continually taking pot shots in *New Verse*. Thomas was not unaware of what was at stake. Writing to Rayner Heppenstall on 31 December 1935 in the interregnum, he said of Grigson (*Letters*, p. 207/234): 'I like him as a chap, but he's a mean little, cheap little, ostentatiously vulgar little, thumb-to-my-nose little runt when he tries to be funny at the back of New Verse.' This time it was 'ten nasty lines' about Heppenstall, but it was more often and fixedly Edith Sitwell. Thomas's accepting her patronage was bound to be the end of favours from Grigson.

We should look particularly for any clues to Thomas's attitude to Grigson in letters around May 1939 when 'To Others than You' was written. Thomas had been asked to contribute a statement for the Auden tribute in *New Verse* (November 1937); enclosing a short paragraph to Grigson (*Letters*, p. 259/298), he added: 'I'll give you a ring, if you like, when we're in town at the end of the month and we can meet and make a noise. If you like.' Apparently Grigson did not like. There are no more letters. A few months later in a letter of July 1938 to Henry Treece, Thomas disparages Grigson as 'leaning over his rackets to look at his balls' (*Letters*, p. 311/359); and in a similar vein to Tambimuttu in a letter of 9 June 1941 (*Letters*, p. 489/550): 'I don't think it's a bad thing to be a climber, as long as you make sufficiently entertaining noises as you slime your way up. Grigson did make some sort of simian show.' In mentioning 'To Others than You' to Charles Fisher on 14 June 1939 (*Letters*, p. 381/436) Thomas characterized himself there as being 'at his most secretive'. That definitely implies that he is hiding some specific person's identity. As the one important friend who had turned against the poet, this person must be Geoffrey Grigson.

Grigson had quite a 'winning air' when I met him in 1959 in Wiltshire, mowing the grass in front of the farm house in which he had settled with a new wife and child. He scoffed at my devotion to Thomas. No reasons he gave were sensible or sufficient.

Twenty-four years

(please turn to *Collected Poems*, p. 81)

Thomas sent this poem to Vernon Watkins on a postcard dated 24 October 1938 (*Letters*, p. 334/382) 'for my birthday just arriving'. It was entitled 'Birthday Poem' when first published in *Life and Letters Today* (December 1938), and is appropriately retrospective. Though Thomas sees himself as 'dressed to die', there is, with the phrases 'sensual strut' and 'red veins full of money', a defiance in the poem. He could not have written it if he had not been in good spirits. A specific reason was no doubt the trip to Manchester on 18 October 1938 to read on the BBC programme 'The Modern Muse' along with W. H. Auden, Stephen Spender, C. Day Lewis, Louis MacNeice, Kenneth Allott, Kathleen Raine, Charles Madge, John Short and Bernard Spencer, this first-team line-up introduced by Michael Roberts. Thomas read 'The hand that signed the paper' for a fee of 3 guineas. A setting of 'This bread I break' was sung by Frederick Seddon, 2 guineas to Thomas for the use of the poem. A travel voucher was paid in advance. His veins were full of money! In this company he had, at twenty-four, arrived.

In the poem he looks back at his birth, when he 'crouched' as a foetus, preparing for his life's journey by sewing, in a tailor's crouched posture, a shroud which he would wear as his mortal flesh. His body is meat which the sun will eat a little of each day until it is all gone at his death. In looking forward from his twenty-fourth birthday, he aims to endure his allotted 'forever', however long that may be. He is uncertain how soon he must join the elements or dust of the universe, but he will strut his stuff along the way.

Vernon Watkins was apparently mystified by the second line of the poem: '(Bury the dead for fear they walk to the grave in labour.)'. 'I do realise your objections to my line', Thomas wrote to him on 20 December 1938 (*Letters*, p. 344/393); 'I feel myself the too selfconscious flourish, recognize the Shakespeare echo (though echo's not the word).' I suppose he means that the line is faintly like something a character in the tragedies might say, extending an arm, as he leaves carnage on the stage. The line's actual role in the poem is an exhortation to himself, to counteract any possible maudlin element of the first line, 'Twenty-four years remind the tears of my eyes', with its possible echo of Milton's sonnet on his own twenty-fourth birthday. Time is the 'subtle thief of youth' which has stolen up on him, so that his birthday is a reminder that brings tears to his eyes. Thomas then, in parenthesis, urges himself to banish this melancholy by burying the dead years of the past in order that they will not burden him all the way to the grave and will not hold him back from at least a little more strutting. He had, as time unfolded, another fifteen years.

Unluckily for a death

(please turn to *Collected Poems*, p. 91)

The first version of this poem, as sent to Vernon Watkins in May 1939 and published in *Life and Letters Today* in October 1939, was entitled 'Poem (to Caitlin)'. It was a thoroughgoing love poem to his wife, though still hedged with ifs and buts. The revision in September 1945 heightened the expression of open love.

The poem is organized around the dire alternatives that would lie in wait for the poet if it were not for Caitlin's love. What is lucky for him is unlucky for a death that would be his otherwise. This death, waiting in the wings, as it were, is imaged as a phoenix bird and also a woman 'in shades'. The phoenix is self-destructive fiery passion, but what about this dark female figure – who or what is she? She is of the femme fatale tradition, but also, threateningly, a nun.

Unluckily for a death [cheated of its expectations] waiting with [myth bird] phoenix under the pyre yet to be lighted [by love's dying] of my sins and days, and [unluckily] for the woman in shades [hades] saint [-] carved [demure] and sensual among the scudding dead and gone ['in the burial holes of enticement'[1]], [the woman] dedicate [matched] forever to my self though the brawl of the kiss has not occurred, on the clay cold mouth, on the fire [-] branded forehead [with his brand of ownership], that could

---

[1] Occasionally the wording of the first version of the poem (see *LVW*, p. 64) is illuminating, as here, and will be presented in quotes. Mainly it is rather more obscure in its imagery than the revised poem and thus of limited use. In replacing it at a late stage of proof-reading of *Deaths and Entrances*, Thomas told Dent's he had 'completely rewritten' it (*Letters*, p. 569/633), but gave no hint of why.

bind her constant [in thrall to him], nor [have] the winds of love broken wide to the wind [releasing] the choir and cloister of the wintry nunnery of the order of lust [waiting] beneath my life [for love's death], [the nunnery] that sighs for the seducer's coming [to melt winter] in the sun strokes of summer, [unluckily for the woman] loving on this sea [-] banged guilt [sinful world] my holy [sanctified by love] lucky body under the cloud [storming] against love IS CAUGHT and HELD and KISSED [by his wife] in the [grinding] mill of the midst of the descending [after the fall] day, the dark [being] our folly [or 'pity'], [is] CUT to the [quick] still star [centre] in the order of the quick [life] but BLESSED by such heroic hosts [welcomings of bread and water] in your [his wife's] every inch and glance ['soothed of fever by your kind health'] that the wound [of love] is certain god, and the ceremony of souls is celebrated there [in the wound of love], and [also] communion between suns [galactic love].

Never SHALL my self CHANT about the saint [woman] in shades while [so long as] the endless breviary [prayer-wheel] turns of your [his wife's] prayed [to] flesh, nor SHALL I SHOO [into motion] the [phoenix] bird below me: the death biding two [woman and bird] lie lonely.

The poet imagines what it would be like to be without his beloved. It would be death, and he would have to conflagrate himself like the phoenix, or mate with a Lilith of the underworld, the alter ego of his wife. No, these shades will have to wait. He is lucky enough to have the flower and flesh of his living wife, whose mortal love is all the blessing he wants. All else in monstrous – like a minotaur or a 'tigron', the latter a made-up word from 'tiger' and 'lion'.

I SEE the tigron [monster] in tears [of frustrated longing] in the androgynous [freakish] dark, his [tiger] striped and noon [blazing lion] maned tribe striding to holocaust [destruction by the fire of desire], [I see] the she mules [sterile] bear their minotaurs [man-bulls], [and] the duck-billed platypus broody [sitting on eggs] in a milk of birds ['in the sterile bush'].

I SEE the wanting [lusting] nun saint [woman] carved in a garb of shades, symbol of desire beyond my [living] hours and guilts, ['all loaded events of her flesh'] great crotch and giant continence [waiting].

I SEE the unfired [waiting] phoenix, herald [of death] and heaven crier [immortality], [pointing] arrow now of aspiring and the renouncing of islands [of this world].

There are two kinds of artificiality, the bower of bliss and out-of-this world bliss. The woman and her tribe represent the 'monstrous' and the phoenix the 'immortal' alternatives to 'the full assemblage in flower of the living flesh' (lines 41–2). All other love than the love he knows with his wife is death, 'the grave its daughters' (line 42).

The poem imagines the possibility of such death if his wife left him. But he feels he has the luck to avoid losing her.

> Love, my fate [which I] got luckily, TEACHES with no telling [uninstructed] that the phoenix' bid for heaven and [alternatively] the desire after death in the carved [artificial] nunnery both shall fail . . .

Yes, but there is a condition. The poet must earn the love of the 'living flesh' (line 41). 'Both shall fail', but only if he refuses to do two things which are deceptively attractive: if he refuses to bow to his wife's blessing, and if he refuses to walk 'with immortality' at his side. Without these refusals, the woman in shades and the phoenix will succeed; they will succeed because they will then have entered the relationship and the vital love will have died.

The woman, who is called a carved nun or saint, must represent a certain kind of desire in the wife herself, the part that wants to give a blessing to the husband to make the relationship sacrosanct. This misguided aim will succeed if the husband bows to this aspect of the wife. The other threat to the relationship is to devalue the living mortal flesh in order foolishly to try to gain life hereafter: 'to walk . . . with immortality at my side like Christ the sky' (line 49). Christ 'the sky' is here to be contrasted with Christ 'the child' three lines later. The 'sky' represents a false promise; the 'cool of your mortal garden' is good enough without it. The 'herald' phoenix bird is barking up the wrong tree.

The husband's spirit may die, and these two fates may take over. But meanwhile they are out of luck. 'Lucklessly' (line 53) the nun/ saint aspect 'must lie patient' (hopefully forever), and the 'vaulting', heaven-bound phoenix must 'be still'. These two strange symbolic entities represent, in Thomas's exposition, real pitfalls of the marriage. They do not have to wait the literal death of the man; they are waiting in the wings if he weakens in relation to the wife's dangerous strengths.

At the same time, the poem indicates that in good part the man gets his knowingness and fortitude from the wife herself. What he knows about the threat to their marriage he knows 'from the native /

Tongue of your translating eyes' (lines 50–1). It was 'the young stars' in her eyes that told him, stars that seemed to have the power of a miraculous birth. The poem ends with an expression of thanks to the loved one, an outpouring of love without any ifs or buts: 'O my true love, hold me. / In your every inch and glance is the globe of genesis spun, / And the living earth [is spun in] your sons.'

Vision and Prayer

(please turn to *Collected Poems*, p. 114)

In the opening lines of the poem Thomas asks the questions that we as readers must also ask.

> Who
> Are you
> In the next room
> So loud to my own
> That I can hear the womb
> Opening and the dark run
> Over the ghost and the dropped son
> Behind the wall thin as a wren's bone?

On a mundane level one might immediately think of the birth of the poet's own son, his firstborn. The crisis of having fatherhood thrust upon him may have precipitated the poet into a terror of inadequacy such as is recorded in 'Vision and Prayer'. It is possible that the inception of the poem went back to January 1939 when Llewelyn was born, but the poem was not, so far as we know, composed until five years later – it was sent to Vernon Watkins on 26 August 1944 (*Letters*, p. 518/580). It soon becomes clear that the self-doubt in the poem is on a more spiritual level than the paranoia of paternity.

In spite of the eye-witness tone of 'birth bloody room' of line 10, we have it on good authority that 'Dylan wasn't present at the birth of any of his children' (*Caitlin*, p. 61). Actually, the image has a literary source. 'Dylan told me', reports Vernon Watkins (*Portrait of a Friend*, p. 119) 'that he had read a most wonderful statement of

Rilke about God being born in the next room.' Watkins recognized
this as a reference to Rilke's poem 'Du, Nachbar Gott' from *Das
Stunden-Buch*. Rilke there is saying that the wall between the poet
and God could be removed if either one spoke as neighbours are
supposed to. Inglinde Padberg has told me that the adjective used to
describe this wall, 'schmall', would be translated best with the word
Thomas uses, 'thin'. The idea of God actually being born in the next
room is a Thomas addition, as is the image of a wren's bone.

There is already in the first stanza a heavy hint that this birth is
extraordinary: the birth room (or womb, we could say) is 'unknown /
To the burn and turn of time / And the heart print of man'. It is
positively immaculate. In the second stanza, 'midwives of miracle'
attend and the 'head of pain' (later in the stanza 'his torrid crown') is
associated with the word 'thorn'. As the poem's diction takes us closer
and closer to a Christian interpretation, the striking adjective 'turbulent' suggests further confirmation might be found in another literary
allusion. Christ's birth is described in Yeats's 'Two Songs from a Play':

> In pity for man's darkening thought
> He walked that room and issued thence
> In Galilean turbulence.

Yeats is talking of historical epochs and keeps a lofty distance from
this Christian turbulence. Thomas is more like the Catholic poet
Francis Thompson, whose poem 'The Hound of Heaven' begins

> I fled Him, down the nights and down the days;
> I fled Him, down the arches of the years;
> I fled Him, down the labyrinthine ways
>   Of my own mind . . .

Thomas calls the new-born Christ 'turbulent' and other words like
'furied' (stanza 3) as a measure of what it is that causes him to flee:

> I shall run lost in sudden
> Terror and shining from
> The once hooded room
>   Crying in vain
>   In the caldron
>   Of his
>   Kiss

The room was 'once hooded' in that the babe is born into the shade, into the valley of the shadow of death. The dark overwhelmed the ghost or spirit (in stanza 1) and 'dark alone' (not baptism) bowed a blessing on the child. The birth head is 'shadowed' in stanza 2, but by the end of the stanza the dark (or hood) is thrown off, and in the next stanza there is 'the first dawn'. At the end of stanza 4 the 'lightnings' have come to a 'high noon' that blinds the supplicant poet. This is a progressive epiphany.

I cannot think that there is a secret agenda in this poem. Thomas is not saying one thing and meaning another. He says he was lost but is now saved, caught up in the flood which sweeps him to the 'man drenched throne' (stanza 4). The word 'adoration' places him at the manger in Bethlehem. He was lost but he has come to the 'finding one', whom we must take to be the Shepherd of mankind. He is dumbfounded, found again as an infant. These signs cannot be mistaken or argued away. 'Vision and Prayer' is as much a poem of religious exposure as T. S. Eliot's 'Ash Wednesday'. The 'who' born in the 'next room' is most assuredly Christ. The 'wren's bone' wall is no partition at all: when Aneirin Talfan Davies once asked Thomas about the 'wren's bone' (*Druid*, p. 42) he 'explained that all he meant by the image was that the wall dividing him from the birth room was so thin as to be non-existent'. Christ is being born in the terrified poet's psyche. He runs, but of course cannot escape his own thoughts and needs, which anxieties reduce him to a baby in the breast of Christ (stanza 5).

Stanza 5 indicates, however, that the protagonist of the poem does not *feel* safe in Christ's 'blazing breast'. In no time, it seems, he will be awoken to the Day of Judgment, to 'the judge blown bedlam / Of the uncaged sea bottom / The cloud climb of the exhaling tomb / And the bidden dust upsailing / With his flame in every grain'. Christ's flame empowers every grain of dust to ascend. All the waiting dead, from the Garden of Eden to the present, rise from all the graves of the world, the world's 'urn', which has been 'vultured' in the process of the shedding off of the mortal flesh. The sea 'uncages' its victims (stanza 5). The young from ancient times fly 'woundward' to Christ of the Cross (stanza 6). The dead soldiers stride to the sky. Saints enter the bosom of Christ as they always thought they would. The whole world is on its way home to heaven's shrine, which is the blazing breast of Christ, where the poet is crouched, seeing the 'judge blown bedlam' coming towards him. It is as though he has to accept all the ascending rabble. He is in Christ's breast; he cannot refuse them any more than Christ on the Cross could. All the sinners, all the innocent dead: the thought is too painful. He blacks out.

> And the whole pain
> Flows open
> And I
> Die.

This is the end of part I. The death is rather unexpected, and yet as a stage of the dark night of the soul – or any shamanistic initiation – the loss of self is essential to gaining a new self. To die, in the Christian vision of this poem, is to be overwhelmed by the Judgment Day, which is Christ's major promise, ascension to heaven for the saved. Many, assuming themselves worthy, have found joy in this promise, but Thomas as an unpractised novice is completely bowled over and experiences a death from overexposure to the world's pain.

He wakes in part II from his swoon in a posture of prayer. His thinking is lucid, but the form of the prayer is strangely perverse or wrong-headed. He is, it seems, praying in the name of the wrong people for the opposite of what he wants. This double-negative idea was offered in my *Entrances* (pp. 85–6) as the only logical solution to the mystifying praying that is going on here. I still believe that part II can only make sense if it is understood as proceeding – until the very last stanza – by the rhetorical trope of devious de-affirmation. He prays in the name of the lost that Christ will *return* to the 'birth bloody room' (stanza 8); he prays in the name of 'the wanton lost on the unchristened mountain' that Christ will *not* bring about the resurrection (stanza 9); and prays in the name of no one that Christ's martyrdom be nullified (stanza 11). He should be praying in the name of the Father, Son and Holy Ghost if he wants something to come about. But he does not so pray because he does not want these things mentioned to come about. He is not (as he makes clear in stanza 7) totally lost: 'I belong / Not Wholly to that lamenting / Brethren for joy has moved within / The inmost marrow of my breast bone'. On the basis of this joy, he can pray, but not yet, it seems, forthrightly.

Thomas is declaring himself new to the invasion of religious feeling. He knows the other, the fallen state, so well (stanzas 10–11):

Forever falling night [of despair] is a known star and country [familiar terrain] to the legion of sleepers [waiting for awakening] whose [collective] tongue I toll [like a church bell] to mourn [incapable of welcoming] his [God's] deluging [flood] light through sea and soil and we HAVE COME TO KNOW all places [and] ways [and] mazes [and] passages [and] quarters and graves of the endless fall [life without grace]. Now common lazarus [the beggar, not the one risen from the dead] of the charting [mapping the above-mentioned places] sleepers PRAYS never to awake and arise[;] for the country of death [which they inhabit] is the heart's size [where they want to be] and the star of the lost [is] the shape of the [resigned] eyes.

In the name of the fatherless [Godless] in the name of the unborn [unsaved] and the undesirers of midwiving morning's [Christ's] hands or instruments [forceps for rebirth] O in the name of no one now or no one to be I PRAY may the crimson [full-blooded] sun spin [in its diurnal movement] a grave grey [of death] and [may] the colour of clay [unlike Christ's blood] stream upon his martyrdom [negating it] in the interpreted [fully explained] evening and [in] the known dark of the earth amen.

The 'amen' here is a most daring use of bitter sarcasm. We only use 'amen' in affirmation, but this one comes at the end of prayers that are the opposite of what he would want. Christ's martyrdom becoming clay: this is not what he wants. It is reversed by praying for it in the name of no one. But, since this double negative is too intellectual by far and does not succeed in stemming the flow of despair, the 'amen' comes with a jolt, as undoubtedly it was meant to.

In terms of the narrative of the poem, it also jolts the protagonist. He immediately, in the final stanza, turns the corner, and the 'known dark of the earth' is banished by 'the sudden sun'. With a prayer in the name of the damned on his lips he is still capable of choosing the darkness, except he is not allowed to:

> The loud sun
> Christens down
> The sky.
> I
> Am found
> O let him
> Scald me and drown
> Me in his world's wound.

This, finally, is the genuine prayer of the novice caught in religious ecstasy. Robert Southwell's 'The Burning Babe' – a parallel if not a source – has Christ's 'newly born in fiery heats' with his breast a furnace where Love is the fire and 'the metal in this furnace wrought are men's defiled souls', which will be washed in His blood. The felt need is to fuse with Christ for cleansing. In the last lines of 'Vision and Prayer', this is achieved.

> His lightening answers my
> Cry. My voice burns in his hand.
> Now I am lost in the blinding
> One. The sun roars at the prayer's end.

Here is the Christian paradox: that to be lost in Christ is to be found.

Thomas left no doubt that 'Vision and Prayer' represents a Christian conversion when he acknowledged Francis Thompson as a literary analogue. 'Yes', he told Vernon Watkins in a letter of 15 November 1944 (*Letters*, p. 532/594), 'the Hound of Heaven is baying there in the last verse'. Here, as in Francis Thompson's 'The Hound of Heaven', it is Christ who is hounding the poet. Thompson's poem ends:

> Now of that long pursuit
> Comes on at hand the bruit;
> That Voice is round me like a bursting sea.

With its similar ending, 'Vision and Prayer' likewise represents the condition of conversion, a poem squarely in the tradition of religious fear and trembling. There is no other Thomas poem like it. If there was a particular wartime experience which brought Thomas to this pitch, we do not know of it. The poem is our only record of how extremely devout – on an apparently unique occasion – Thomas could admit to being.

Note on 'Vision and Prayer'

In regard to the stanza shapes, Aneirin Talfan Davies avers that Thomas did not have the diamond, tear drop, chalice or womb consciously in mind: 'at least, so he told me once. He was merely interested, he said, in the syllabic pattern' (*Druid*, p. 41). I have not discovered any correlation between theme and shape which would lead me to dispute Thomas's statement.

Was there a time

(please turn to *Collected Poems*, p. 44)

Thomas remembers a time when simple things banished troubles, when he could innocently shed a tear in reading a book. Feelings of mortality have undermined this security. He now knows too much. Only those without hands are clean; only those without a heart are unhurt. Best not look upon the world at all.

These lines of mild stoical resignation were lifted out of a notebook poem of 8 February 1933 (*Notebook Poems*, p. 129) and handed to Richard Church of Dent's to encourage him, by giving him something he could understand, to accept Thomas's second book of poems, which became *Twenty-five Poems*. As of 26 November 1935 Church had liked only three of the poems Thomas had sent him. 'I have quite a number of poems simple as the three you liked', Thomas wrote to him on 9 December 1935 (*Letters*, p. 205/232). He was thinking of his notebook store and immediately got down to rewriting 'Was there a time'. Thomas was accommodating, but also honest. He told Church that these would be poems 'to my mind, not half as good as the ones you cannot stand'.

Fair enough. But, the succinctness of the poem in its revised form, I think, pushes it from adolescent world-weariness into a tough irony. 'The blind man sees best': this is the exaggeration of satire. It is really exhorting us to see clearer. We must try to keep our hands clean, and try to retain some of the early innocence to make us better adults. These are not bad points to be making.

We lying by seasand

(please turn to *Collected Poems*, p. 70)

'Who Do You Wish Was With Us?', one of the stories of *Portrait of the Artist*, tells of an outing Thomas made with his Swansea friend Trevor Hughes in the summer of 1931 along the Gower peninsula to the furthest tip, Worm's Head (*Collected Stories*, pp. 205–6).

> Laughing on the cliff above the very long golden beach, we pointed out to each other, as though the other were blind, the great rock of the Worm's Head. The sea was out. We crossed over on slipping stones and stood, at last, triumphantly on the windy top. There was monstrous, thick grass there that made us spring-heeled, and we laughed and bounced on it, scaring the sheep who ran up and down the battered sides like goats. Even on this calmest day a wind blew along the Worm. At the end of the humped and serpentine body, more gulls than I had ever seen before cried over their new dead and the droppings of ages. On the point, the sound of my quiet voice was scooped and magnified into a hollow shout, as though the wind around me had made a shell or cave, with blue, intangible roof and sides, as tall and wide as all the arched sky, and the flapping gulls were made thunderous.

'We lying by seasand' likely recalls this 1931 occasion, which, as the story proves, was fixed in Thomas's memory in every detail. If this is so, the 'we' does not involve a girlfriend, but Trevor Hughes.

> We lying by seasand, watching yellow [sand] and the grave [sober and tomblike] sea, MOCK [those] who deride [those] who follow the red [sanguine] rivers [of life], [and we] HOLLOW [an] alcove [secluded spot] of words out of cicada shade.

The two young men in the story certainly did plenty of talking while they were on Worm's Head. Their aim was for that day at least to leave the 'town grey' (*Collected Stories*, p. 202) and unclench the 'cramped town' in the 'colours of our walk' (*Collected Stories*, p. 204). Within the logic of the colour imagery of the poem, they could be thought of as seeking the 'red', the excitement that they miss in their daily lives. Therefore they would be mocking, in their momentary euphoria, those who would deride their efforts in 'calling for colour' (line 6).

Unfortunately, this plan of escape was doomed. The place is too desolate. A letter to Pamela Hansford Johnson, written a few months after the first draft of the poem, emphasizes the disagreeable aspects of the place (*Letters*, p. 62/79):

> The bay is the wildest, bleakest, and barrennest I know – four or five miles of yellow coldness going away into the distance of the sea. And the Worm, a seaworm of rock pointing into the channel, is the very promontory of depression. Nothing live on it but gulls and rats, the millionth generation of the winged and tailed families that screamed in the air and ran through the grass when the first sea thudded on the Rhossilli beach. There is one table of rock on the Worm's back that is covered with long yellow grass, and, walking on it, one [feels] like something out of the Tales of Mystery & Imagination treading, for a terrible eternity, on the long hairs of rats.

This is why Thomas can call the scene a 'yellow grave' (line 5) and think of it as a moonscape or dried-out Mars (lines 9–11). The 'dry tide-master / Ribbed between desert and water storm' is an image where the physical landscape is referred to as a man in charge of the tide, which is now out, showing his naked ribs in the serriform sand. 'Cold came up, spraying out of the sea', Thomas writes in 'Who Do You Wish Was With Us?' (*Collected Stories*, p. 210), 'and I could make a body for it'. And he describes the 'body', in this case an animal, that he might make to represent the concept or feeling of coldness: 'icy antlers, a dripping tail, a rippling face with fishes passing across it'. This passage injected into the short story is an instructive revelation of how the poet's imagination works. In the poem Thomas creates a 'body' to represent the feeling of calm that exists at Worm's Head when the tide is out; the master of the tides is then dry and his ribs are showing (lines 10–11).

Is the storm forgotten? The calm should cure them of their ills with its undisturbing monotone; but the poem indicates that it does not. The trouble is the two young men bring their morbidity with them, especially the Trevor Hughes of the story, who is haunted by the months he has spent nursing his dying brother.

The Dylan of the story tries to counter this depression (*Collected Stories*, p. 208): 'but you loved the walk, you enjoyed yourself on the common. It's a wonderful day, Ray. I'm sorry about your brother. Let's explore. Let's climb down to the sea.' But 'the heavenly music over the sand' (line 14) is joined by the sound of the grains of sand (as dust of the dead) as they speed towards darkness, covering up the 'golden mountains and mansions' (line 16). The sandcastles of innocent childhood raised to mansions of ambition and mountains to climb are obliterated. The seaside land had the potentiality for gaiety, but they have brought to it an overpowering elegaic threnody, and the place becomes a grave (line 17).

> Bound [encircled] by a sovereign [golden] strip [of sand], we LIE, WATCH yellow [sand], WISH for wind [vitality] to blow away the strata [layers] of the shore and drown red rock;[1] but wishes BREED not [solutions to problems], neither CAN we fend off rock arrival [death], [so we] LIE watching yellow [sand] until the golden [sunny] weather breaks [into bad weather], O my heart's blood, like a heart [breaks] and hill [breaks].

The poet addresses his own heart, commiserating with himself, knowing that his heart will be broken on the hard rock of death, which will then be red with his blood.

'Who Do You Wish Was With Us?' ends with a symbolic death, as the sea rushes in to cover the one pathway of rocks to the mainland (*Collected Stories*, p. 210): 'A wind, cornering the Head, chilled through our summer shirts, and the sea began to cover our rock quickly, our rock already covered with friends, with living and dead, racing against the darkness.' Since 'rock arrival' certainly seems to mean death in the poem, there is a similarity of situation in the sea arrival of the story.

We are right to think of Trevor Hughes associated with the poem as well as with the story. The original version of the poem was copied into the current notebook on 16 May 1933, following on the poet's having written to Hughes about five days earlier (*Letters*, p. 15/34) and having received a reply which he called 'a vast wind of pessimism' (*Letters*, p. 18/37). 'I think you bleed more than I do, God help you', he told Hughes. 'Remember the Worm, read a meaning into its symbol – a serpent's head rising out of the clean sea.' Thomas has changed the symbology, as he was wont to do, but it shows that the Hughes connection was on his mind.

---

[1]   This must be a different 'red' from that in line 3, for the rock has to be considered a death symbol in line 22, equal to the 'sandy smother' of the notebook poem, 'the last smother of death' (*Notebook Poems*, p. 157). Inglinde Padberg after visiting Worm's Head informs us that Rhossili Bay is actually cut out of the red rock of the mainland (Padberg, p. 188). So the colour here may simply have been given by the landscape, or it may be a premonition of the broken heart's blood of the last line. To 'drown' the rock by covering it in blown sand would be to avert death.

When all my five and country senses

(please turn to *Collected Poems*, p. 70)

When asked in 1938 about influences, Thomas included 'the verse extracts from the "Plumed Serpent"' in the list (*Letters*, p. 297/343). The ritualistic hymns to Quetzalcoatl that Lawrence intersperses throughout *The Plumed Serpent* are intended as a replacement for the Christian vision. 'I will lift up mine eyes unto the hills': no, says Lawrence, we have had enough of Light; it is now the time of the Dark God, who enters not through the eyes but through the sensual centres of the body. 'Let me close my prying, *seeing* eyes, and sit in the dark stillness', says Kate, the protagonist of the novel (chapter 12).

> The itching, prurient, *knowing*, imagining eye, I am cursed with it, I am hampered up in it. It is my curse of curses, the curse of Eve. The curse of Eve is upon me, my eyes are like hooks, my knowledge is like a fish-hook through my gills, pulling me in spasmodic desire. Oh, who will free me from the grappling of my eyes, from the impurity of sharp sight!

The protagonist of Lawrence's short story 'The Blind Man' has no such problems and gains easy ascendancy over his cerebral rival.

When we narrow in on the possibly specific Lawrentian source for 'When all my five and country senses', our focus rests on the chapter of *Fantasia of the Unconscious* entitled 'The Five Senses'. In the scale of sensuality Lawrence puts all the other four senses ahead of sight (Penguin edition, p. 65):

> Sight is the least sensual of all the senses. And we strain ourselves to see, see, see – everything, everything through the eye, in one mode of objective curiosity. There is nothing inside us, we stare endlessly at the outside. So our eyes begin to fail; to retaliate on us.

Thus, in the poem, when all the senses are converted to sight, it is a *nullification* of the sensual. Love withers because it has become all a matter of seeing, which is the wrong kind of loving, tending to pruriency.

The word-playfulness of the poem rather obscures this deeper point. That is the trouble with 'a conventional sonnet' (*Letters*, p.

279/326). Expectations are set up by the engaging first-person voice; there is a witty twist near the end. Thomas admitted to his publishers that he was not sure about it: 'it seems mechanical' (*Letters*, p. 363/ 415). The fourteen-line regularly rhymed poem seems as though it is using a mere 'conceit', a hook on which to hang a pretty thought. It seems as though the aim is to out-artifice the artificial. We have to keep D. H. Lawrence in mind to counteract these false impressions.

When all my five and country[1] senses see, the fingers WILL FORGET green thumbs [fertility] and MARK how, through the halfmoon's [finger-nail's] vegetable [potato] eye, [heavenly love] [discarded] husk of young stars and [of] handfull [boisterous] zodiac, Love [chilled] in the frost [of all the cold eyes] is pared [skinned] and wintered by [in cold storage],

the whispering ears [reduced to a whisper] WILL WATCH love drummed [in a military funeral] away down breeze and [sea-sounding] shell to a discordant [loveless] beach,

and, [eye-]lashed to syllables [broken parts of speech], the lynx[-eyed] tongue [will] CRY that her [love's] fond [unwisely loving] wounds are mended bitterly [unlovingly].

My nostrils SEE her [love's] breath burn like a bush [expiring].

The final quatrain simply says that when the 'spying' voyeuristic senses (which touch, hearing, taste and smell have become) are blinded in sleep or broken, put out of action, then the lower sensual regions of the body will 'grope' blindly awake, and confirm love in all her countries.

In a letter to Trevor Hughes during the summer of 1934 Thomas said he wished he could 'shout, like Lawrence, of the red sea of the living flesh' (*Letters*, p. 162/145). 'When all my five and country senses' is not a shout; it is as much a witness to the power of love in the heart's blood as Thomas could make in a clever sonnet.

---

[1] The poem's subject is sensual love, what Hamlet referred to as 'country matters' (*Hamlet*, 3.2.123). The word sustains for a while in the poem a vegetable imagery, à la Andrew Marvell's 'vegetable love' in 'To his Coy Mistress'.

Note on 'When all my five and country senses'

There is no notebook version of this poem, but it was grouped with the 'opossums', the revised poems Thomas sent to Watkins on 1 April 1938 (*Letters*, p. 287/336) and published in *Poetry* (Chicago) in August 1938. The Lawrence connection would date its inception back to 1933.

When I woke

(please turn to *Collected Poems*, p. 111)

At the time this poem was written, during the summer of 1939, rumours of war were at a crescendo. Thomas wrote to Vernon Watkins on 25 August 1939 (*Letters*, p. 401/453): 'This war, trembling even on the edge of Laugharne, fills me with such horror and terror and lassitude.' Four days later he wrote to his father (*Letters*, p. 402/455): 'It is terrible to have built, out of nothing, a complete happiness – from no money, no possessions, no material hopes – and a way of living, and then to see the immediate possibility of its being exploded and ruined.' Thomas and Caitlin were now two years married, with their first child born at the beginning of the year. They have finally got a possibly permanent residence, Sea View, a substantial house in Laugharne. And then – war is about to be declared. In 'When I woke' Thomas imagines that this is the morning when his new world explodes.

It begins as an apparently normal day. But there are premonitions. He has been having disturbed sleep. The wake-up noises of birds, clocks and church bells are a din which drives away dream figures that have coiled around him; the nearby sea dispels, with its ordinary sound, nightmare creatures, including a succubus ('woman-luck'); while someone mowing the grass outside with a small scythe, a human 'double' of Father Time, bearded as this story-book person is usually pictured, cuts the morning off from the night by slashing, in the poet's imagination, the 'last snake' of his fretful dreams.

I particularly like, of all Thomas's images, the phrase 'up to his head in his blood' used to describe a full-bodied man thoroughly at work so that his blood is pounding at all points. On the other hand, I am not sure yet how the snake's tongue (line 15) can be 'peeled in the wrap of a leaf'. The leaf must look like a peeled snake's tongue? At least it connects the snake to a tree (in Eden?) as well as to Aaron's rod and the golden bough? In any case, foreboding has been established in the poem as a prelude to the psychosis of war.

The second part concerns the new thing that is different this day; but first we have the poet's waking as it usually is.

> Every morning I make,
> God in bed, good and bad,
> After a water-face walk,
> The death-stagged scatter-breath
> Mammoth and sparrowfall
> Everybody's earth.

This seems like the Carmarthenshire version of the astronomer in Dr Johnson's *History of Rasselas*, who claimed that he had had for five years the regulation of the weather and distribution of the seasons. Every morning the poet wakes like God in bed and makes the whole earth good and bad. Some critics have taken these lines seriously as expressing the creativity of the poet, the poet who notes everything, from the fall of the sparrow to the fall of a 'death-stagged scatter-breath mammoth'.

But the poet is 'God in bed'? This is where the men in white coats come and take him away – if he is serious. But surely there has to be a high degree of self-mockery here? He gets up and, like the spirit of God in Genesis 1: 2, moves upon 'the face of the waters'. Who? Thomas? He is just going to the bathroom to perform his ablutions.

Anyway, something has come to shatter all self-importance.

> I heard, this morning, waking,
> Crossly out of the town noises
> A voice in the erected air,
> No prophet-progeny of mine,
> Cry my sea town was breaking.

He wakes to hear a voice in the 'erected air', that is, from on high, quite outside his control, no 'prophet-progeny' of his, an uncooptable voice, saying that his seaside town was breaking apart, his world as he has known it coming to an end.

The version printed in *Seven* magazine (Autumn 1939) had a rather more earth-shattering ending. The voice was announcing not just the destruction of Thomas's village but 'humanity's houses'. So, in the final version, we can be sure that, when the clocks say 'no Time' and the bells ring 'no God', they are addressing humanity as a whole. The 'islands' (line 29) are 'the ruins of man' (as the early version had it). He is, in effect, covering everything as he draws the sheet in fear over his own corpse.

There is a casual reference in *Under Milk Wood* (p. 33) to 'Mrs Twenty Three, important, the sun gets up and goes down in her dewlap, when she shuts her eyes, it's night.' In 'When I woke', the poet wakes up to the fact that all who live at Number Twenty Three are finished; the coming war will do away with all 'playing God'. It is the end of egotistical poetry-making, the pretence that poets make the world. The world is falling in on the poets. The protagonist of the poem hears this prophecy through the coins on his dead-this-morning eyes. The sea-shell sound so beloved of Thomas is, in the summer of 1939, sounding ominously and imminently like the shell that explodes.

When, like a running grave

(please turn to *Collected Poems*, p. 19)

'I find, after reading them through again, that the poems in Vicky's confounded possession are a poor lot, on the whole', Thomas wrote to Pamela Hansford Johnson in late October 1934 referring to Victor Neuburg, who was in charge of producing Thomas's first book of poems; 'many thin lines, many oafish sentiments, several pieces of twopenny Christ, several unintentional comicalities, and much highfalutin nonsense expressed in a soft, a truly soft language' (*Letters*, p. 169/195). It is an author's privilege to speak so, as part of the process of moving himself forward: 'I've got to get nearer to the bones of words, & to a Matthew Arnold's hell with the convention of meaning & sense. Not that it matters, anyway. Life is only waves, wireless waves, & electric vibrations.'

Thus, in a nutshell, we get the method and the message of 'When, like a running grave', finished soon afterwards. When he called it 'by far the best thing I've done' (*Letters*, p. 172/198), he was probably praising it for what most readers find distressing: its impatience with the need for signposts and a cocky form of address.

> When, like a running [hounding] grave, time tracks you down, [when] your calm and cuddled [baby] is a scythe of hairs [like Father Time with beard], [when] love in her gear [armour] is slowly through the house, up naked [she is stripped of everything] stairs, [who was a young turtle dove and now] a turtle in a hearse, hauled to the dome [of heaven], [when] comes, like a scissors stalking, tailor age,[1] DELIVER [release] me who, timid in my tribe [of young men], of love am barer [shorn] than Cadaver's[2] trap [mouth] robbed of [the use of] the foxy [sly] tongue, his [Cadaver's] footed tape [measuring him from head to foot] [robbed] of the bone inch [skeleton-less], DELIVER me, my masters, [who are] head and heart, [when] heart of Cadaver's candle [phallus] waxes thin [worn out], when blood [heart], spade-handed [like a grave-digger], and the logic time [the head] drive children up [to maturity] like [with the violence of] bruises to the thumb, [deliver me] from maid [heart] and head . . .

The verbal pun, of course, is 'maidenhead'. It looks as though the poet wants to have nothing to do with that sort of thing, and can hardly wait to get old and be out of it. At the end of this opening five-stanza sentence, he 'halts among eunuchs', where apparently he wants to be. Love is only 'electric vibrations' (*Letters*, p. 169/195), after all:

> for, sunday faced [pretending], with [not knuckle-]dusters in my glove [codpiece], chaste and [pretending to be] the chaser [of women], man with the cockshut [impotent, not cocksure] eye, I, that [whom] time's [straight-]jacket or the coat of ice [death] may fail to fasten [entirely inexperienced] with a virgin o[3]

---

[1] See the *Strewwelpeter* 'scissor-man' pictured in *Collected Poems*, p. 188.

[2] Thomas had recently quoted in a letter Richard Aldington's line from 'A Fool i' the Forest' where the world is described as 'a cadaver factory' (*Letters*, p. 151/177). As the poem progresses, Cadaver as a personified entity is referred to six times, and becomes rather more than your normal dead body.

[3] This has nothing to do with 'raggletaggle gypsies o', Thomas wanted to make clear (*Letters*, p. 322/371): 'I meant a circle, a round complete o.' He told Henry Treece in conversation that it was not intended as a rhetorical exclamation but as a symbol of nothingness (Treece, p. 79).

in the straight [rigor mortis] grave, STRIDE through Cadaver's country [mortal world] in my force, [you] my pickbrain [nagging] masters [head and heart] morsing [tapping in code] on the [head-]stone [the message of] despair of blood [sex], [and] faith in the maiden's slime [repulsiveness of sex], [thus I] HALT among eunuchs [sexless], and the [embalming] nitric [acid] stain on fork [crotch] and face.

This would seem to be not so much loss of love as repudiation of the possibility of love. Thomas is earlier on record as admitting he is someone who 'has never felt the desire to fall in love' (*Letters*, p. 8/ 26). 'When, like a running grave' bears this out – so far, at any rate. What the poem later bears out is rather difficult to tell. This is where Thomas says, with a vengeance, to hell with the convention of meaning.

There are, however, along the way, some strikingly clear views. There is no point in pretending that the path is well signposted, but nothing could be flatter than 'Everything ends' (line 41) nor more embracing of the Freudian cliché than 'the tower ending' (line 41), especially coming after line 36: 'I damp the waxlights in your tower dome', and the aeronautical image: 'Cadaver in the hanger / Tells the stick "fail"' (lines 29–30). Thomas seems to be resigned that his sex life is over before it is fairly begun. 'Give, summer, over', he says (line 44), anticipating failure: the contagion of death is everywhere and the world is proof against his kissing.

Other than this, the poem does not welcome explication, no more than does 'I, in my intricate image', which I take to be the continuation of this poem that Thomas promised (*Letters*, p. 172/198). Other than this . . . but this is truth enough to give one pause. As Thomas was preparing in October 1934 to take up the bohemian life in permissive quarters near Fulham Road, London, it seems, on the evidence of this poem, that he knew, in one part of himself, it was all for naught.

When once the twilight locks

(please turn to *Collected Poems*, p. 9)

This is a poem in which the poet exhorts himself to fulfill the promise that is the birthright of every bright child. Time drags us from the womb, weans us, and presents the world to us as growing adolescents. But indolence can take over. Dreaming is a threat to action. We must keep awake.

When once [finally] the twilight [pre-birth] locks [gates of the womb] no longer locked in [confined] the long worm [as the foetus views it] of my finger nor dammed[1] [with lock-gates] the [amniotic] sea that sped [it seemed] about my fist, the mouth of time [as a baby] SUCKED, like a sponge, the milky acid on each hinge [nipple], and swallowed dry the [milky] waters of the breast [at weaning].

When the galactic [mother's milk] sea was sucked and all the dry seabed [outside the womb] unlocked [opened to him], I SENT my creature [conscious self] scouting on the globe [world of his own body], that globe itself of hair and bone that, sewn to me by nerve and brain, had stringed my flask [container] of matter to his rib.

My [green] fuses timed [like a bomb] to charge his [creature's] heart, he BLEW [up] like [gun-]powder to the light and HELD a little sabbath [holy innocent time] with the [nurturing] sun,

but when the stars, assuming [zodiacal] shape, drew in his eyes the straws of sleep, he DROWNED [destroyed] his father's magics [inherited powers] in a dream.

All issue [offspring from the grave] ARMOURED [put on armour], of the grave, the redhaired cancer[2] still alive, the cataracted [filmed] eyes that

---

[1] The 'damned' of *Collected Poems* (1952) was a misprint carried over from the Fortune Press resetting of *18 Poems*. *Collected Poems* (1988) corrected it, while acknowledging that 'damned' (which was in the notebook version though not in *18 Poems*) might be heard as a pun (pp. 179–80).

[2] 'But, honestly,' Thomas protested to Pamela Hansford Johnson (*Letters*, p. 57/74), 'the one "cancer" mentioned *is* necessary.' Not strictly so; he could have retained the notebook version line (*Notebook Poems*, p. 208): 'The issue armoured, of the grave / Of violet fungus still alive . . .' The notebook wording, incidentally, confirms that Thomas thought of 'issue' as a noun, not a verb.

filmed [made a haze of] their cloth [ghostly shroud]; some dead UNDID their bushy [bearded] jaws [to speak], and bags of blood LET OUT their flies; he [the dreamer] HAD by heart [close knowledge of] the Christ-cross-row [ABC] of death.

Sleep NAVIGATES the tides [and flotsam] of time; the dry Sargasso [seaweed choked sea] of the tomb GIVES UP it dead to such a working [dreaming] sea; and sleep ROLLS mute [dead] above the [sea-]beds where fishes' food [the drowned] is fed the shades [ghosts] who periscope[3] [rise to see] through flowers to the sky.

The hanged [corpses] who lever [wrench] from the limes [trees] ghostly propellers for their limbs [in order to fly], the [funeral] cypress lads who wither [disappear] with the cock [at daybreak], these, and the others in sleep's acres, MAKE moony suckers [gullible lunatics] [out] of dreaming men, and SNIPE the fools of vision [dreamers] in the back.

When once the twilight [pre-birth] screws were turned [opening the lock-gates of the womb], and mother milk was stiff as sand [at the end of breast-feeding], I SENT my own ambassador to [meet with] [day-]light; by trick or chance he FELL ASLEEP and CONJURED UP [in dreaming] a carcase shape [incubus] to rob me of my fluids [by nocturnal emission] in his heart.

This incubus or alter ego met in a world of dreams is called 'a poppied pickthank' in the final stanza. He is the drug-pusher ('pickthank' means 'flatterer') that the youth must shake off:

> Awake, my sleeper, to the sun,
> A worker in the morning town,
> And leave the poppied pickthank where he lies;
> The fences of the light are down,
> All but the briskest riders thrown,
> And worlds hang on the trees.

The daylight of the working world has broken through the confining fences. Other riders into life have been thrown from their horses in trying to stay the course, but the poet exhorts himself not to allow himself to be thrown or sidetracked. Worlds hang on the trees, ready for plucking by the active and worthy.

---

[3] In a letter of January 1934, not long before he wrote these lines, Thomas remarked (*Letters*, p. 92/110), presumably thinking of Walt Whitman: 'there is a delightful image somewhere which pictures each blade of grass as the periscope of a dead man'.

If this hortatory ending seems somewhat forced, it should be explained that it was not the original ending to the poem. The notebook version was (*Notebook Poems*, p. 209):

> There is no sweetness in the dead
> I feel not in my sleeping blood;
> Then sleep and dream, sleeps dreams and dies;
> When once the twilight locks no longer
> Locked in the long worm of my finger
> I did unlock the Sleeper's eyes.

Thomas was at that time (early November 1933) 'utterly and suicidally morbid' as he put it in a contemporaneous letter (*Letters*, p. 36/54). By the time of the revision five months later, he was able to say (*Letters*, p. 92/110) that viewing the living 'through the lenses of the dead' was 'an unpardonable fault'. He had amended his outlook, and changed his poem accordingly.

Where once the waters of your face

(please turn to *Collected Poems*, p. 14)

After about sixteen exchanges of letters in about as many weeks Thomas finally phoned Pamela Hansford Johnson on 20 February 1934. PHJ records in her diary (now at Buffalo) that he had 'such a rich fruity, old Port wine of '07 voice'. He would be coming up to London in three days; Pamela invited him to stay at Battersea Rise with her and her mother. First impression: 'Charming, very young looking with the most enchanting voice.' The next day (diary entry for 24 February 1934):

> Spent delicious afternoon with D – how I shall miss him when he goes! We went for short walk in afternoon. Teddy so took to D that he stayed to supper. We three went down and had a drink and D was very ridiculous and funny. T. went about 12 and D and I talked until about 1.

Sunday 25 February 1934: 'D and I fooling around in morning. My interview and photo in Referee. Sat around all afternoon. Runia, Victor, and Reuben in in evening. D arguing most glorious hokum. I sat up till 2.45 talking to D – quite dearest thing.' He was only supposed to be there for the weekend, but he stayed on in London, probably at his sister's, through the following week. Pamela saw him the next weekend. Diary entry for Sunday 4 March 1934: 'Sweet D in to dinner after interminable long week. Dear all day – perfect ass – insisted on gargling with me [she had a sore throat] . . . very happy day.' The next day he finally did leave: 'Saw him after work – he'd sold 3 poems and 2 stories but had no job offers that suited him so after ½ an hour of supreme depression, I saw him off to Wales on the 5.55.' It is not surprising, then, that Dylan wrote immediately on his return, though Pamela affected to be surprised at the contents of the letter. Diary Thursday 8 March 1934:

> I received letter this morning from darling Dylan telling me he loved me. Oh it *is* so difficult to reply! I don't know how I feel or what to do. Managed some sort of an answer. Felt bitter all day. Rehearsed in evening. Phoned Reuben. Letter from Tom.

Dylan's letter of protestation of love was mercifully mislaid by Miss Johnson (or Lady Snow, as she was when she presented the letters and diaries to the University of Buffalo). Likewise, a second letter, which presumably apologized for the first. The next letter after these two, dated by Thomas 'Round about March 21, '34', says he will 'endeavour to keep clear of the emotional element' (*Letters*, p. 101/125).

It is precisely during the days of outpouring from Swansea and rebuffs from Battersea Rise that 'Where once the waters of your face' was written, copied into the notebook on 18 March 1934 (*Notebook Poems*, p. 217). It thus reveals itself, in context, as a love poem, though heavily protected – as his two letters had not apparently been – by a completely caulked seascape imagery. The face, we cannot doubt, is that of Miss Johnson. He had in that week of seeing her been able to make her laugh, look depressed and sad. He had seen his effect on her, as if he had ridden a motor boat across a bay. Now she has stopped all that with a stern look.

> Where once the waters of your face spun [were churned] by my screws [boat propeller], your dry ghost [of a now dead self] BLOWS [in the wind],

the dead [which she now is] TURNS UP its eye [and nose]; where once the mermen [his selves] through your ice [cold manner] pushed up their hair, the dry wind [instead of his boat] STEERS through [dried out] salt and [exposed] root and roe [abandoned fish eggs].

Where once your green [lively] knots [on a log line measuring a ship's speed] sank their splice [joinings] into the tided [tied with tides] cord, there GOES the green unraveller [untying green things], [with] his [tailor's] scissors oiled [for easy snipping], [and with] his knife hung loose [from its sheath] [ready] to cut the channels [of love's spring] at their source and lay the wet fruits [love's harvest] low.

Invisible [having disappeared], your [regular] clocking tides BREAK [down] on the lovebeds of the weeds; the weed of love's LEFT dry; there round about your [hard and cold] stones the shades [unborn souls] of children GO who, from their voids [non-existence], CRY to the dolphined [fertile] sea.

Even if the last stanza is to be taken as representing only a barren period in a love relationship, the fact that the image of progeny (and denial thereof) should come to Thomas's mind at all reveals a seriousness that one would not expect of him at that particular time and condition of life. The idea of the loved one's hard-heartedness denying the possibility of issue is certainly present.

The first three stanzas have made quite an indictment: the free-flowing waters of the relationship have dried up. But the fourth and last stanza turns it all around:

> Dry as a tomb, your coloured lids
> Shall not be latched while magic glides
> Sage on the earth and sky;
> There shall be corals in your beds,
> There shall be serpents in your tides,
> Till all our sea-faiths die.

No, she is not dead to him really. Her eyes are not latched shut. There is the magic of love and it produces wonderful coral growth. One must have faith, such as faith in sea-serpents.

So we see that Thomas was saying in a poem, disguised, what he had embarrassed himself by writing straight out in letters. Whether the poem was effective in any practical way we have reason to doubt. There is no evidence in the diaries that it, in itself, was.

✧

Why east wind chills

(please turn to *Collected Poems*, p. 46)

Robert Williams has pointed out to me that Arthur Mee's *Children's Encyclopaedia* during Thomas's time used to have a serial feature called 'The Child's Book of Wonder', which addressed such questions as 'Why do things smell differently?' or 'Why do trees grow upwards?' The form of the questions in this poem are similar to these, and should really be answerable on that level. Why east wind chills and south wind cools have explanations in meteorological terms, as do the additional specific questions asked in the poem, for example, the origin of frost.[1] The equivalent on an adult level might be 'What happened before the Big Bang?' or 'How could a Big Bang produce, say, potassium?' To questions like these, says the poet, we will, during this life, have only a 'black' reply (line 9). The 'white' answer (line 15) will come when we die and all is revealed. All things are known, there in 'the towers of the skies' (line 19). The stars hint at answers and ask us to be content with hints and the knowledge that the full answer awaits us at the end of the world. The author-itarian cry 'Be content', as Thomas seems to hear it from the school corridors of his childhood, has an unsatisfying air to it; the phrase 'Know no answer' even more so. We should hope for better, but he himself cannot help with the question. The poem ends with his forlorn admission and the image of the children's fists raised in hopeless protest.

Along with a large dose of his father's scepticism about the world, however, Thomas injected into the poem a little of the faith he

---

[1] The notebook version, which was reduced on revision by half, has other such questions, such as 'Why grass is green and thistles prick' (*Notebook Poems*, p. 163). It is known that behind this poem was a specific question asked by a four-year-old in Thomas's presence. Once visiting Bert Trick's house in Swansea he heard Pamela Trick ask, 'What colour is glory?' This is included among the questions asked by the children in the notebook version of 1 July 1933 and was no doubt what prompted the poem at that time. Thomas could not use this specific question when he came to revise the poem (the revision copied into the notebook, 21 January 1936) because he had already plucked out the memorable phrase for use in the poem 'My world is pyramid'. The rest of the notebook poem was still available, and its point seemed to have validity even with the passing of five years.

received from his mother's milk that all will be answered one day, though the positive view seems to be not much more than a half line of hope in a poem of general despair.